# DATE DUE

# A North American Common Market

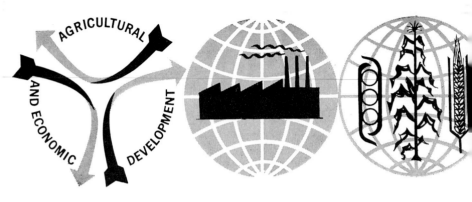

The Iowa State University Press,
Ames, Iowa, U.S.A.

Iowa State University
Center for Agricultural
and Economic
Development

# A North American
# Common Market

*Other publications of the Center for Agricultural and Economic Development are available as follows (work of the Center is supported in part by a grant from the W. K. Kellogg Foundation):*

**Books From the Iowa State University Press (hard-bound)**
Alternatives for Balancing World Food Production Needs, 1967
Roots of the Farm Problem, 1965
Economic Development of Agriculture, 1965
Family Mobility in Our Dynamic Society, 1965
Farmers in the Market Economy, 1964
Our Changing Rural Society: Perspectives and Trends (developed by the Rural Sociological Society under editorship of James H. Copp), 1964
Farm Goals in Conflict: Family Farm, Income, Freedom, Security, 1963
Resource Demand and Structure of the Agricultural Industry (Earl O. Heady and Luther G. Tweeten), 1963
Food—One Tool in International Economic Development, 1962
Labor Mobility and Population in Agriculture, 1961
Dynamics of Land Use—Needed Adjustment, 1961
Adjustments in Agriculture—A National Basebook, 1961

**Reports From the Center for Agricultural and Economic Development**
CAED 32    Farm Programs for the 1970's
CAED 31    Abundance and Uncertainty . . . Farm Policy Problems
CAED 30T  Capacity and Trends in Use of Land Resources
CAED 29    Implications of Changes (Structural and Market) on Farm Management and Marketing Research
CAED 28    A Recipe for Meeting the World Food Crisis
CAED 27    U.S. Agriculture in 1980
CAED 26    Weather Variability and the Need for a Food Reserve
CAED 25    International Home Economics
CAED 19    Fundamentals for Area Progress
CAED 10    New Areas of Land-Grant Extension Education

# Foreword

ONE OF THE major future problems posed for the world is that of an adequate food supply. Current growth rates in population clearly indicate a need for policies relating to those variables that concern economic development and human welfare. While the threat of population and food demand pressing against food supplies is as old as man, it has taken on added perspective in recent decades. Urgency in planning or policy for agricultural production, population, and food demand arises from several causes. The world no longer has large land masses which can be cultivated to provide food for settling populations and new economies. While technological improvements on existing agricultural land have been the main source of food supply increments for some time, there is some possibility that increases from this source cannot keep up with growth in food requirements resulting from world population growth and increases in per capita incomes. Impetus to population growth has come from widespread medical services and improvements which have greatly lowered mortality rates for the masses. Too, even in recent times, population growth has continued to follow its historic pattern of increases at geometric rates.

Recent advances on attitudes toward and technologies for birth control have great promise in reducing population growth rates to levels more consistent with food production potentials. But added emphasis needs to be given to altering these demand variables more nearly in line with the supply variables of world food conditions. However, even with these potential successes on the demand side, the process is still slow and the possibility of a critical shortage of food relative to supply is a prospect until sometime two to four decades in the future.

Until more rapid development of agriculture in the many less developed countries of the world is attained, a growing portion of the world's food supplies will have to come from devel-

v

oped countries where agriculture can produce in surplus over domestic needs. North America is a large region where this condition prevails and the tendency of Canadian and United States agricultures has been toward surpluses. With this prospect in view for the next few years, North American agriculture may eventually be called upon to intensify its food production as a means of meeting needs generated by world population growth. There are several ways this intensification might be attained.

One method would be creation of a "North American Common Market" wherein the patterns of resource allocation, production location, and market floors would be allowed to spread over the entire continent in the most efficient manner. The conference reported in this volume was organized accordingly. In view of the eventual pressure of world population, food needs, and food supplies, the authors examine the future potential of food production in Canada, the United States, and Mexico. Problems and possibilities of increasing this source of food supply are examined under conditions where (a) only commodities could flow into a common market without trade barriers, and (b) both commodities and resources could flow among agricultural regions and countries under these conditions. Finally, the many economic, institutional, and policy implications of these international arrangements and possibilities are examined.

The papers presented in the conference and published as chapters of this monograph provide some stimulating possibilities and represent original analyses of complex phenomena. They provided foundation for spirited discussion and debate among the several hundred participants from Mexico, Canada, and the United States who attended the conference.

This conference and the publication of papers were cooperative activities of the University of Manitoba Faculty of Agriculture and the Center for Agricultural and Economic Development of Iowa State University. In addition, numerous other institutions of both Canada and the United States contributed directly and indirectly in financing travel, providing data, and aiding participation. Dr. Gordon Ball, representing the Center, and Dr. Clay Gilson, representing the University of Manitoba, served as co-chairmen in planning and implementing the conference.

EARL O. HEADY
Executive Director
Center for Agricultural
and Economic Development

# Contents

# PART ONE

# Background of
# World Food Needs

# CHAPTER ONE

# Population Growth and Food Needs

RAYMOND P. CHRISTENSEN

THE UPSURGE in world population growth is a most important, if not the most important, social phenomenon of our time. It causes concern about the ability of the world to produce enough food to provide nutritionally adequate diets for all. It affects how rapidly economic development and rising incomes per capita can take place. It also has implications with respect to political organization of the world in which we live.

Hunger and malnutrition have been present in the world for many years. World economic development was held in check for many centuries by man's inability to control the hazards of nature and expand his food supply. Historical records show that it took hundreds of thousands of years for world population to reach 250 million at the time of Christ. It took 16 centuries more for that figure to double to 500 million. Population growth was held to a small fraction of 1 percent a year by starvation, disease, and violence.

Beginning in the 1700's new scientific discoveries vastly increased man's knowledge of agriculture. The land area under cultivation was increased. Higher crop yields resulted from the use of crop rotations, improved varieties of crops, and better soil management practices. Growth in food supplies resulting from

RAYMOND P. CHRISTENSEN, Foreign Development and Trade Division, United States Department of Agriculture.

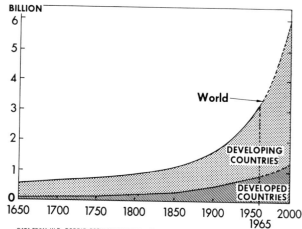

DATA FROM  W.D.  BORRIE, POPULATION GROWTH, INTERNATIONAL JOURNAL OF AGRARIAN AFFAIRS, MAY 1967,
OXFORD UNIVERSITY PRESS, UNITED NATIONS MEDIUM PROJECTIONS TO 2000.

U.S. DEPARTMENT OF AGRICULTURE

NEG. ERS 5363-67(9) ECONOMIC RESEARCH SERVICE

*Fig. 1.1—World population growth.*

these improvements made it possible for world population to increase six times from the beginning of the seventeenth century
to the middle of the twentieth century (Fig. 1.1). Moreover the
quality of diets was greatly improved. More nutritious and better
quality food led to longer life and healthier people.

Population growth data illustrate the wonders of compound
interest. It took 200 years for world population to double between 1650 and 1850 when population increased about .4 percent
a year. However it took only about 100 years for world population to double again between 1850 and 1950 when population
increased about .8 percent a year. The world population growth
rate now has accelerated to a little over 2 percent a year. If this
rate of growth continues, world population will double in the
next 35 years or by the year 2000.

It should be remembered that food shortages have limited
population growth in many areas of the world in the last 300
years. Famines, starvation, and malnutrition have been common.
For example, Ireland lost about a third of its population between
1845 and 1860 as a result of the potato famine. About a million
people died from starvation and malnutrition and another million and a half migrated to other lands. In India large-scale
famines have occurred as recently as 1943. At least a million and
a half people in Bengal died from famine and from the diseases
connected with it.

Countries can be grouped in two categories based on present population growth rates. Countries with population growth rates of 2 percent or more a year include all of the countries commonly classified as low income or developing countries. This group accounted for 70 percent of world population in 1965 and had a population growth rate of 2.3 percent a year in the 1960–65 period. Countries with population growth rates of less than 2 percent a year include the high income or developed countries. This group accounted for 30 percent of world population and had a population growth rate of 1.2 percent a year in 1960–65.

Population growth rates have gone up rapidly in the developing countries since 1900. For example, population increased at an annual rate of 2.3 percent a year in these countries in the 1960–65 period, compared with 1.6 percent a year in the 1930–60 period and only. 7 percent a year in the 1900–1930 period.

The current high population growth rates in developing countries have resulted from dramatic reductions in death rates accompanying improved health and disease control measures and continued high birth rates. On the other hand, the now developed countries experienced high death rates as well as high birth rates during early stages of their economic development. In these countries birth rates declined together with death rates, and population growth for this group of countries never has been more than 1.2 percent a year over an extended period.

Population and food supplies will be balanced at some level in the future. But how they can be brought into balance at improved levels of nutrition is the question that must be faced. Disease, pestilence, famine, and starvation no longer can be tolerated as a means of bringing population into balance with food supplies.

## FOOD CONSUMPTION AND PRODUCTION TRENDS

Thus far world agricultural production has kept pace with increasing population. Food consumption levels have improved in most less developed countries as well as in the developed countries in the last 30 years. Since 1954 the less developed countries have increased total agricultural production about as rapidly as the developed countries (Fig. 1.2.). However acceleration in population growth rates in the last decade has caused food requirements to increase much more rapidly in the less developed countries than in the developed countries.

Food production in the developing countries has not in-

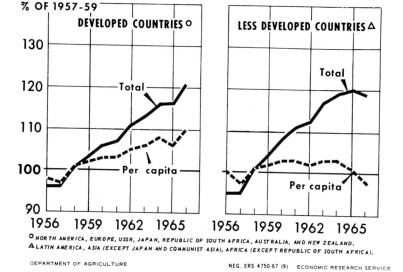

% OF 1957-59

DEVELOPED COUNTRIES ○    LESS DEVELOPED COUNTRIES △

130

120    Total    Total

110

100    Per capita    Per capita

90

1956  1959  1962  1965    1956  1959  1962  1965

○ NORTH AMERICA, EUROPE, USSR, JAPAN, REPUBLIC OF SOUTH AFRICA, AUSTRALIA, AND NEW ZEALAND.
△ LATIN AMERICA, ASIA (EXCEPT JAPAN AND COMMUNIST ASIA), AFRICA (EXCEPT REPUBLIC OF SOUTH AFRICA).

DEPARTMENT OF AGRICULTURE    NEG. ERS 4750-67 (9)    ECONOMIC RESEARCH SERVICE

*Fig. 1.2—World agricultural production.*

creased rapidly enough to keep pace with rising economic demands for food resulting from rising per capita incomes and population growth. Moreover crop failure caused by unfavorable weather has reduced food production in some countries and made necessary large food imports in some years. The outstanding example is India where low rainfall in 1965–67 reduced agricultural production and made necessary large imports of food grains to avoid famine and starvation.

Failure of food production to keep pace with increased demand for food in the less developed countries in the last 30 years has caused these countries as a group to shift from net exporters of grains to net importers. In the 1934–38 period the less developed countries had annual net exports of 14 million tons of grain. However they had net imports of 3 million tons a year in the 1948–52 period and 11 million tons in 1963, 1964, and 1965 (Fig. 1.3).

It should be noted that the less developed countries have achieved large increases in grain production. For example, the compound growth rate in grain production was 2.7 percent a year during the 1950–65 period, compared with a population growth rate of about 2 percent. Also it should be noted that net imports have been small compared with total grain production. For example, net imports amounted to less than 4 percent of

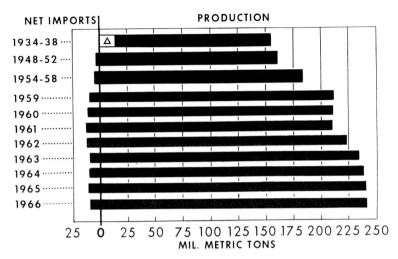

U. S. DEPARTMENT OF AGRICULTURE                    NEG. ERS 4749-67 (9)   ECONOMIC RESEARCH SERVICE

*Fig. 1.3—Production and net trade in grain, less developed countries—Latin America, Africa (except Republic of South Africa), and Asia (except Japan and Communist Asia). Year beginning July 1.*

total grain consumption in these countries in 1963, 1964, and 1965. Of course the less developed countries include net exporters of grain as well as net importers and some countries in this group have relatively large imports.

The less developed countries of the free world have relied heavily upon expansion in harvested area to increase grain production (Fig. 1.4). During the years from 1951–55 to 1961–65 harvested area in these countries went up about 15 percent and yields about 10 percent. This is in sharp contrast to the situation in the United States and other developed countries where yields went up 20 percent or more. In the future the densely populated developing countries will need to rely mainly upon higher yields per acre as a means of increasing food production. The outcome of the race between population growth and food production in the developing countries depends heavily upon technological advances which increase crop yields.

## FUTURE POPULATION GROWTH

Food requirements in the years ahead will depend upon population growth. The United Nations has made three projections

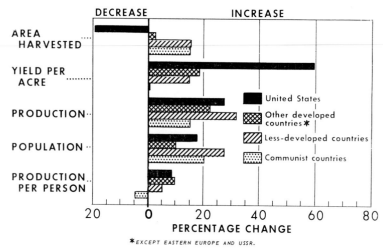

DEPARTMENT OF AGRICULTURE                    NEG. ERS 4751-67 (9)   ECONOMIC RESEARCH SERVICE

*Fig. 1.4—Changes in world grain production and population, 1951–55 to 1961–65.*

of population growth by regions of the world to the year 2000 based on different assumptions with respect to birth rates and death rates (Fig. 1.5).

The high projection, also referred to as continued trends, indicates continued acceleration in world population growth rates from 2 percent a year in 1960–65 to 3 percent a year in the last decade of this century. Birth rates would continue high and death rates would decline. World population would more than double between 1965 and 2000.

The medium projection indicates a gradual decline in world population growth to 1.8 percent a year in 1990–2000. It assumes gradual decreases in birth rates and death rates. World population would increase 80 percent between 1965 and 2000.

The low projection indicates a marked decline in population growth to 1.4 percent a year in the last decade of this century. It assumes sharp reductions in birth rates. World population would increase 60 percent between 1965 and 2000.

Donald J. Bogue has put forth the thesis that world population growth may be much less than indicated by the United Nations' projections. He points out that population growth rates can be expected to decline[1] because of the following: widespread

---

[1] Donald J. Bogue, "The Prospects for World Population Control," Paper presented at Conference on Alternatives for Balancing Future World Food and Production Needs, Iowa State Univ., Nov. 8–10, 1966.

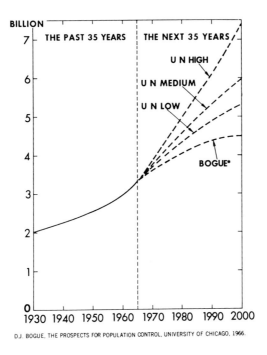

DJ. BOGUE, THE PROSPECTS FOR POPULATION CONTROL, UNIVERSITY OF CHICAGO, 1966.

U.S. DEPARTMENT OF AGRICULTURE                NEG. ERS 5362-67 (9)   ECONOMIC REARCH SERVICE

*Fig. 1.5—World population projections.*

grass roots approval of family planning, technological advances in the means of birth control, aroused political leadership to support fertility control programs, accelerated professional and research activity on improved family planning methods, a slackening of progress in death control, and a variety of sociological and psychological phenomena promoting rapid adoption of family planning. Bogue does not underestimate the crisis nature of the food problems faced by many countries, but he is optimistic about the potentials for slowing down population growth. His projections indicate that world population growth rates will decline to 1.7 percent a year by 1970, 1.3 percent by 1980, 0.8 percent by 1990, and 0.3 percent by 2000.

How rapidly population increases in the future will depend upon what happens to birth and death rates. How changes in birth and death rates affect natural increase in population is illustrated by data for Taiwan where historical data on population are as accurate as for any place in the world (Fig. 1.6). During the years from 1905 to 1955 the crude birth rate per 1000

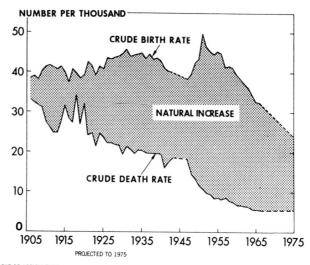

NUMBER PER THOUSAND

U.S. DEPARTMENT OF AGRICULTURE          NEG. ERS 5365-67 (9)   ECONOMIC RESEARCH SERVICE

*Fig. 1.6—Natural population increase in Taiwan.*

people averaged above 40. The crude death rate averaged around 30 until about 1920. The natural increase in population was only about 1 percent a year from 1905 to 1920. However death rates declined to around 20 in the late 1920's and 1930's and natural increase in population went up to over 2 percent a year. A further drop in death rates to below 10 in the early 1950's combined with birth rates over 40 caused natural increase rates to rise to over 3.3 percent a year. However the birth rate declined to 32 in 1966 and the death rate to 6, giving a natural increase of 2.6 percent. Reductions in birth rates that have occurred with the introduction of family planning programs are impressive. It is anticipated the natural increase in population will decrease to 1.7 percent a year by 1975.

Birth rates as well as death rates still average high in most developing countries. For example, birth rates in South Asia and Latin America averaged around 40 per 1000 people in 1960–65 which, together with death rates of about 11 per 1000, gave natural increase rates close to 3 percent a year (Table 1.1). Further reductions in death rates can be expected with additional improvements in health and sanitation measures. The big unknown is how rapidly birth rates will decline. Future population growth obviously will be influenced by the effectiveness of family planning programs now being initiated in many countries.

Population growth undoubtedly will be much more rapid in

TABLE 1.1

BIRTH RATES, DEATH RATES, AND RATES OF NATURAL INCREASE IN POPULATION
PER 1000 OF ESTIMATED POPULATION BY REGIONS, 1960–65

| Regions | Birth Rates | Death Rates | Natural Increase |
|---|---|---|---|
|  | (number) | (number) | (number) |
| East Asia | 32.5 | 18.9 | 13.6 |
| South Asia | 40.4 | 11.2 | 29.2 |
| Africa | 45.5 | 22.5 | 23.0 |
| Latin America | 39.3 | 11.1 | 28.2 |
| North America | 22.6 | 9.2 | 13.4 |
| Europe | 17.8 | 10.0 | 7.8 |
| U.S.S.R. | 22.1 | 7.2 | 14.9 |
| Oceania | 25.0 | 10.8 | 14.2 |
| World | 33.6 | 15.7 | 17.9 |

Source: Irene B. Taeuber, "The Dynamics of the World Population Situation," *Proceedings of Great Plains Agricultural Council*, Bozeman, Mont., July 28–29, 1966, p. 21.

the developing countries than in the developed countries in the next few decades. If the United Nations' continued trends or high projections take place, the developing regions would account for over 80 percent of the world's population in the year 2000 (Fig. 1.7). Asia alone would account for nearly 60 percent of the world's population. However it should be remembered that these projections assume continued acceleration in population growth rates.

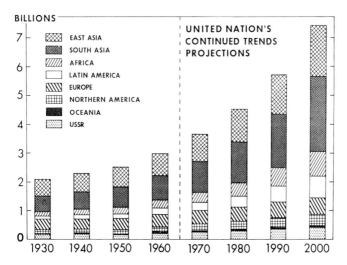

*Fig. 1.7—World population projections by regions.*

Some further acceleration in population growth rates in the developing countries in the next 20 years probably can be expected. There still are large potentials for reducing death rates in these countries. Moreover it probably will take several years before family planning programs can be carried out on a scale large enough to reduce birth rates very significantly in large countries like India and Pakistan. Perhaps it is most realistic to expect total population of the developing countries to increase 2.5 percent a year for the next 20 years, compared with 2.3 percent a year in 1960–65.

## FOOD CONSUMPTION LEVELS

Growth in population, together with changes in per capita levels of food consumption, will determine food requirements in the years ahead. But it is important to distinguish between requirements to provide nutritionally adequate diets and requirements to meet economic demands resulting from rising incomes.

Nutritional deficits in the diets of the less developed countries are well known. It has been estimated, for example, that two-thirds of the world's population live in countries with national average diets that are nutritionally inadequate with respect to calories, protein, or fat.[2] The diet-deficit areas include all of Asia except Japan, Israel, Taiwan, and the Asian part of the U.S.S.R., all but the southern tip of Africa, parts of South America, and almost all of Central America and the Caribbean.

In 1959–61, diets in the deficit areas averaged 750 calories per day below the level of countries with adequate national average diets. The diet was 170 calories below the minimum nutritional standard of 2400 calories required for normal activity and health. The daily consumption of protein in the less developed countries was only two-thirds the level of the diet-adequate countries.

The total additional grain which would have been required to meet the calorie deficit of the less developed countries, excluding Communist Asia, in 1959–61 was about 25 million tons, compared with actual consumption of about 215 million tons. A little over half of this deficit was in India and Pakistan. India had a deficit of 240 calories per person per day. It would have been necessary to add 27 kilograms of grain per person to the 159 kilograms available per person annually to overcome the

---

[2] *World Food Budget, 1970*, FAER-19, ERS, USDA, 1964.

calorie deficit. The increase required for Pakistan would have been 19 kilograms and the average for all less developed countries 18 kilograms or about 10 percent.

Protein was deficient in national average diets of most less developed countries. If consumption of grain were increased sufficiently to meet the calorie deficit, there would be adequate quantities of protein in the average diet of most countries. However protein would still be of low quality in most countries and diets would need to be supplemented by additional high quality protein foods to provide minimum nutritional requirements.

The report of the President's Science and Advisory Committee on the World Food Problem indicates that per capita consumption of food ought to increase at least 1 percent a year in the less developed countries during the next 20 years to correct nutritional deficits.[3] This, together with population growth of 2.5 percent a year, means that food supplies would need to increase about 4 percent a year or 120 percent between 1965 and 1985.

It should not be concluded that effective economic demand for food in the less developed countries will automatically increase 4 percent a year. If it is assumed that the income elasticity of demand for food (the percentage increase in quantity of food demanded for each percentage rise in per capita income) is 0.6 percent, per capita income would need to increase 2.2 percent a year to achieve a 1 percent increase in food consumption. Gross national product would need to increase about 5 percent a year to generate sufficient growth in demand for food to bring about a 2.2 percent growth in per capita income, assuming a population growth rate of 2.5 percent a year.

Food requirements will increase much slower in the developed countries than in the less developed. Population growth for the developed countries probably will average only a little over 1 percent a year. This, together with the relatively low income elasticity of demand for food, will mean that expansion in food supplies of around 1.5 percent a year will be sufficient to meet growing demand for food. Food production capacity in the developed countries likely will increase at annual rates in excess of 1.5 percent a year. The developed countries will be in position to export food to help meet rapidly expanding requirements in the less developed countries.

---

[3] *The World Food Problem,* a Report of the President's Science and Advisory Committee, The White House, May 1967.

## THE FOOD GAP IN DEVELOPING COUNTRIES

The size of the food gap in the developing countries in the years ahead will depend upon rates of increase in food production in these countries as well as upon rates of increase in population and per capita consumption. Projections of grain production, net imports, and disappearance for the less developed free world for 1985 from the report of the President's Committee illustrate what would happen under alternative assumptions (Fig. 1.8). All projections assume that population will increase 2.5 percent a year. Argentina, Uruguay, Paraguay, Mexico, and the Republic of South Africa, all grain exporting countries, are not included in the less developed countries in these comparisons.

These projections indicate that net import requirements for grain of the less developed countries could be as high as 95 million metric tons or as low as 15 million tons. Continuation of the recent growth rate in grain production of 2.7 percent a year, together with an annual increase of 1 percent in per capita consumption, would result in net import requirements of 95 million tons. On the other hand, if grain production increases 4 percent a year, net import requirements would decrease to 15 million tons, about the same as in 1959–61 and much less than in 1964–65.

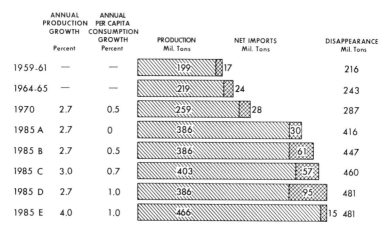

| | ANNUAL PRODUCTION GROWTH Percent | ANNUAL PER CAPITA CONSUMPTION GROWTH Percent | PRODUCTION Mil. Tons | NET IMPORTS Mil. Tons | DISAPPEARANCE Mil. Tons |
|---|---|---|---|---|---|
| 1959-61 | — | — | 199 | 17 | 216 |
| 1964-65 | — | — | 219 | 24 | 243 |
| 1970 | 2.7 | 0.5 | 259 | 28 | 287 |
| 1985 A | 2.7 | 0 | 386 | 30 | 416 |
| 1985 B | 2.7 | 0.5 | 386 | 61 | 447 |
| 1985 C | 3.0 | 0.7 | 403 | 57 | 460 |
| 1985 D | 2.7 | 1.0 | 386 | 95 | 481 |
| 1985 E | 4.0 | 1.0 | 466 | 15 | 481 |

ESTIMATES FROM REPORT OF PRESIDENT'S SCIENCE ADVISORY COMMITTEE, THE WORLD FOOD PROBLEM, VOL. II, PAGE 655
POPULATION GROWTH 2.5 PERCENT A YEAR

U.S. DEPARTMENT OF AGRICULTURE                                    NEG. ERS 5364-67(9)  ECONOMIC RESEARCH SERVICE

*Fig. 1.8—Projections for grain production, net imports, and disappearance—less developed free world, 1985.*

TABLE 1.2

PROJECTED ESTIMATES OF PRODUCTION, NET IMPORTS, AND DISAPPEARANCE OF
GRAIN UNDER ALTERNATIVE ASSUMPTIONS, LESS DEVELOPED COUNTRIES

| | Assumptions* | | | | |
| Years | Production growth rate | Per capita consumption | Pro- duction | Net Imports | Disap- pearance |
|---|---|---|---|---|---|
| | *(percent)* | *(kilograms)* | *(million metric tons)* | | |
| 1959–61 | . . . | 170 | 221.9 | 11.3 | 233.2 |
| 1964–65 | . . . | 176 | 254.3 | 13.7 | 268.0 |
| 1970 I | 2.7 | 179 | 289.7 | 19.6 | 309.3 |
| 1970 II | 3.1 | 179 | 295.8 | 15.8 | 311.6 |
| 1980 I | 2.6 | 184 | 374.0 | 38.5 | 412.5 |
| 1980 II | 2.7 | 185 | 381.5 | 34.3 | 415.8 |
| 1980 III | 3.1 | 191 | 399.3 | 29.7 | 428.0 |
| 1980 IV | 3.6 | 195 | 430.8 | 5.8 | 436.6 |

Source: Estimates from Martin E. Abel and Anthony S. Rojko, *The World Food
Situation, Prospects for World Grain Production, Consumption and Trade*, FAER-35,
USDA, 1967.
    * Projections assume a population growth rate of 2.5 percent a year. Compound
growth rates in grain production are for 1964–65 to 1970 and to 1980. Per capita consumption growth rates vary as follows: 1964–65 to 1980 I, 0.3 percent; and 1964–65 to
1980 IV, 0.6 percent.

Abel and Rojko recently made estimates of production, consumption, and net imports of grain in the less developed countries under alternative assumptions for 1970 and 1980 (Table
1.2).[4] Their study shows how per capita food consumption rises
as production, income, and demand for food increases. They
deal with economic demands rather than needs as measured by
diets considered nutritionally desirable.

The study by Abel and Rojko shows that with continuation
of historical trends in production and consumption and a population growth rate of 2.5 percent a year, net imports of grain by
the less developed countries would increase from 14 million tons
in 1964–65 to about 20 million tons in 1970. However if growth
rates in grain production in India and Pakistan increase in the
next few years as now seems likely, net imports by the less developed countries would increase to only 16 million tons in 1970.

Net imports of grain by the less developed countries could
be as large as 38 million tons in 1980 or as low as 6 million tons,
depending upon growth rates in production and per capita consumption. If historical trends in grain production and consumption continue, net imports would total about 38 million tons. On
the other hand, if the growth rate in grain production increases

---

[4] Martin E. Abel and Anthony S. Rojko, *The World Food Situation,
Prospects for World Grain Production, Consumption and Trade*, FAER-35,
USDA, 1967.

to 3.6 percent a year over the 1965–80 period and per capita consumption increases .6 percent a year, net imports of grain by the less developed countries would be only 6 million tons in 1980. Of course a growth rate in per capita food consumption of only .6 percent a year would not be large enough to correct nutritional deficiencies in diets of the less developed countries. However it would be large enough to meet economic demands for food that likely will be generated from economic growth and rising incomes.

Long-term changes in population, food production, consumption, and trade cannot be forecast very precisely. However significant projections were presented recently by Thorkil Kristensen, Secretary-General of the Organization for Economic Cooperation and Development.[5] He concludes that the developed countries have a comparative advantage in agriculture because they have larger areas of fertile land per person than do the less developed countries. He points out that it is much easier to transfer industrial production technology than it is to transfer advanced agricultural technology from the developed to the developing countries. Abundant supplies of labor at relatively low wage rates should contribute to low-cost industrial production in the developing countries. Recent trends in world trade in agricultural products will continue, according to Kristensen's projections for 1980 and for 2000. The developed countries would export 10 percent of the food they produce and the less developed countries would import about 13 percent of the food they consume in 1980. In the year 2000, the developed countries would export 23 percent of the food they produce, while the less developed countries would import about 20 percent of the food they consume. These changes would take place even though food production increases more rapidly in the less developed countries than in the developed. According to these projections, the less developed countries will make shifts in trade patterns similar to those made years ago by Japan and now in process in Taiwan. Of course if the less developed countries are to become large net importers of agricultural products on a commercial basis they would need large export markets for industrial products in the developed countries.

## IMPLICATIONS FOR DEVELOPED COUNTRIES

The net import requirements for food of the less developed countries that likely will arise because of rising economic de-

---

[5] Thorkil Kristensen, "The Approaches and Findings of Economics," *Int. Jour. of Agrarian Affairs,* May 1967, Oxford Univ. Press.

mands caused by population growth and higher per capita incomes are small, compared with food production capacity of the developed countries. In fact the study by Abel and Rojko shows that the developed countries could meet net import requirements of the less developed countries for grain, meet expected demand for grain within their countries, and still have unused grain production capacity in 1980. They show that world surplus grain production capacity may be 30 to 34 million metric tons in 1980 with continuation of historical trends. The grain surplus could go even higher if the less developed countries do a better job of increasing their food production than they have in the past.

It must be recognized that many developing countries will face difficulties in financing food imports out of foreign exchange earnings. Growth in economic demand for food within the developing countries does not necessarily mean growth in effective import demand. Developing countries need large imports of capital goods to achieve industrial development. Use of scarce foreign exchange to import food may retard economic growth. A large part of the food imports by the developing countries probably will need to continue to be under food aid programs. How the developed countries can equitably share the costs of food aid programs is a question that needs to be faced.

As pointed out earlier, net imports of food required by the developing countries to correct nutritional deficiencies likely will be much larger than those required to meet economic demands resulting from population growth and rising incomes. Food aid programs of the developed countries could be expanded to help meet these nutritional shortages. However, careful planning of food aid programs will be essential to make certain that food aid imports do not interfere with economic incentives to expand food production in the less developed countries.

The less developed countries have large physical potentials for expanding food production. Crop yields in these countries generally are low. Agricultural technicians report that several countries are on the verge of breakthrough in achieving higher crop yields. For example, Aresvik reports that new high yielding varieties of dwarf wheats, dwarf rice, and synthetic maize which are highly responsive to fertilizer will greatly increase grain production in West Pakistan in the next few years.[6] He points out that introduction of new crop varieties and improved use of water and fertilizer caused the average annual rate of growth in

---

[6] Odvar Aresvik, *Strategy and Outlook for Agricultural Development in West Pakistan*. Agr. Dept., Gov. of West Pakistan, Lahore, July 1967.

agricultural production in West Pakistan to increase to 3.8 percent in 1960–65 from only 2.1 percent a year in 1955–60 and 1 percent in 1950–55. The new higher yielding varieties also are expected to greatly increase crop yields in India. Obviously, it will be desirable that the developing countries take advantage of opportunities to expand agricultural production and that imports of food not depress prices to farmers in these countries.

To sum up briefly, it should be evident that world population growth and food requirements cannot be forecast very precisely. Thus far, food production has kept pace with population growth in most developing countries. However, it has not increased rapidly enough to meet nutritional requirements or economic demands generated from rising incomes. Population growth likely will remain high for the next 20 years, perhaps close to 2.5 percent a year because reductions in death rates will offset reductions in birth rates. There is little evidence yet that birth rates have begun to decline except in a few small countries like South Korea and Taiwan. Increases in per capita food consumption of 1 to 1.5 percent a year over the next 20 years are needed to provide nutritionally adequate diets. Food supplies will need to increase about 4 percent a year in the less developed countries to meet needs for population growth and dietary improvements. Some acceleration in food production growth rates may be achieved in the less developed countries. But it seems likely that these countries will require larger imports in the next 20 years than in the last few years if they are to meet economic demands for food resulting from population and income growth. Food imports required by the less developed countries are well within the capacity of developed countries to supply. In fact, the developed countries likely will continue to face problems of surplus agricultural production capacity even with larger commercial and concessional food exports to the developing countries.

# CHAPTER TWO

# Commercial Food Demand and Government-Sponsored Shipments

## ROBERT L. TONTZ

COMMERCIAL DEMAND as expressed by the wish to buy plus the ability to buy has been the most effective means to date in getting the world's food produced and distributed. In recent decades, however, shipments of food under Government-sponsored programs have been made on a generous scale to help feed the world's hungry and to develop markets for commercial demand. The NACM (North American Common Market), the discussion subject of this conference, has in the aggregate relied heavily on commercial demand as well as food aid shipments in distributing its food abroad.

World production resources can provide enough food to feed the world in the forseeable future, but the world's distribution resources, as measured by commercial demand, are not yet adequate.

The purpose of this chapter is to contribute background information to help solve the significant problem of world food distribution by evaluating prospective commercial demand and food aid shipments of a North American Common Market. As

ROBERT L. TONTZ, Trade Statistics and Analysis Branch, Foreign Development and Trade Division, United States Department of Agriculture. The author gratefully acknowledges the helpful suggestions of H. G. Hirsch and I. E. Lemon, Agricultural Economists of the Trade Statistics and Analysis Branch.

such, the discussion will include: (a) growth and changing patterns of world food trade; (b) the parameters of North America's food trade; (c) analysis of the role of North America's food sales for dollars and food aid shipments; and (d) food grain projections for North America.

Before discussing the growth and changing patterns of world food trade, let us look at some economic dimensions of a North American Common Market—assuming that we had such an economic entity. As shown in Figure 2.1 the gross national product would be $800 billion; agricultural exports $8 billion; population 260 million; and value of agricultural production $56 billion.

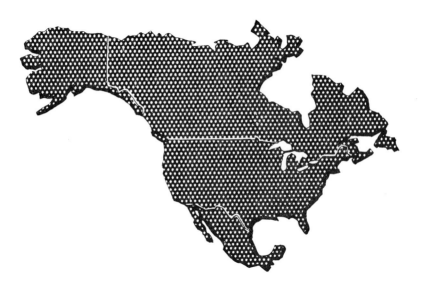

GROSS NATIONAL PRODUCT ..... $8 HUNDRED BILLION

AGRICULTURAL EXPORTS .................. $8 BILLION

POPULATION ........................ 260 MILLION

VALUE OF AGRICULTURAL PRODUCTS ...... $56 BILLION

*Fig. 2.1—A North American Common Market.*

## GROWTH AND CHANGING PATTERNS
## OF WORLD FOOD TRADE

A number of noteworthy changes have occurred in the pattern of world food trade that merit attention in providing a basis for better understanding of future developments.

First, although food is becoming scarce relative to population in the underdeveloped countries, its relative importance in world trade has historically decreased. For example, a half century ago the value of world food trade was a little over one-fourth the value of world trade. Today it equals approximately 13 percent. The fact that income elasticity of food generally is a declining function of real per capita income has been a major causal force in the decreasing significance of food imports relative to other imports of a nonfood type. This development has been most pronounced in the higher income industrialized countries. The relatively high demand elasticities for tropical beverages such as coffee, compared with other foods, particularly cereals, help explain the changes in relative shares of world trade for these commodities. Studies show that the income elasticity of demand (quantity) for coffee ranges from 0.3 for North America to 0.5 for Western Europe. In contrast, the income elasticity of demand for cereals ranges from 0.02 for Southern Europe to 0.32 for Northwestern Europe.[1]

A further reason which may help explain the declining relative significance of food in world trade is the major improvement in food technology which has taken place. Such technological improvements along with changes in the structure and operation of food-related industries have reduced the amount of raw food materials per physical unit of consumed food. An example of this is the development of soluble coffee and tea. It has been estimated that at least 30 percent less green coffee is used to make a cup of instant coffee than one of the regular roasted variety.

Besides improvements in food technology, improvements in farm technology have also contributed to a decline in the relative importance of food in world trade. In addition to the well-known achievements of North American agriculture, particularly the United States and Canada, similar developments, although not yet as pronounced, have taken place in Western Europe. Such changes in agriculture have resulted in a reduction in costs

---

[1] Eric Thorbecke and John B. Condliffe, in *Food—One Tool in International Economic Development,* Iowa State Univ. Press, Ames, 1962, p. 192.

TABLE 2.1
WORLD EXPORTS OF FOOD AT 1965 PRICES BY MAJOR COMMODITY GROUPS

| Commodity Group | 1913 | 1937 | 1965 |
|---|---|---|---|
| | *(million dollars)* | | |
| Cereals | 4,781 | 3,311 | 6,763 |
| Livestock products | 3,087 | 3,379 | 6,724 |
| Beverages (tea, coffee, cocoa) | 1,482 | 1,417 | 3,434 |
| Oilseeds and fats | 2,013 | 1,914 | 2,338 |
| Fruits and vegetables | 1,203 | 1,432 | 2,245 |
| Sugar | 1,235 | 937 | 1,894 |
| Other food and drink | 1,032 | 1,174 | 2,219* |
| Total food | 14,833 | 13,564 | 25,617† |

Source: Data for 1913 nad 1937 were compiled from P. Lamartine Yates, *Forty Years of Foreign Trade*, Macmillan Co., New York, 1959, pp. 63 and 224: data for 1965 were compiled from FAO, *Trade Yearbook 1966*. The value figures from Yates were adjusted by the index of U.S. wholesale prices to reflect the 1965 price level.
 * Estimated.
 † Partially estimated.

of resource inputs per unit of product output through the use of more capital intensive (less labor intensive) production methods. Increased output can, therefore, occur with a smaller labor force. The rise in agricultural efficiency in Western Europe was greatly aided also by protectionist policies, such as the stress on self-sufficiency aimed to correct an imbalance of foreign payments and price support policies designed to stabilize incomes, but which may have tended also to stimulate domestic production. The latter also occurred in North America, especially the United States.

In general, agricultural protectionism in the industrialized world has discriminated against and thereby impeded the growth of exports by producers in competing temperate-zone materials, such as cereals, meat and dairy products, as well as by producers of sugar and oilseeds.[2]

The declining relative importance of food in world trade should not obscure the fact that in an absolute sense the value of world trade in food has increased over time. Although such trade may not have kept pace with world population growth, as compared to half a century ago, it has shown gains in the past three decades. Significant increases in world trade as measured by the value of such trade at 1965 prices took place for beverages, livestock products, and fruits and vegetables, along with less significant gains for cereals, sugar, and oilseeds and fats (Table 2.1).

---

[2] See FAO, *The State of Food and Agriculture,* 1956 (Rome: 1957), Ch. III; United Nations, ECC, *Economic Survey of Europe,* 1960 (Geneva: 1961), Ch. III; GATT, *Trends in International Trade,* a Report by Panel of Experts (Geneva: 1958), Ch. IV.

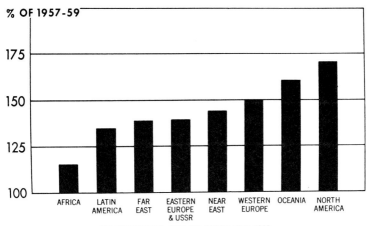

FAO. THE STATE OF FOOD AND AGRICULTURE, 1966.

U.S. DEPARTMENT OF AGRICULTURE                    NEG. ERS 5373 67(9) ECONOMIC RESEARCH SERVICE

*Fig. 2.2—Food and feed exports, by region, 1963–65 average.*

Other indicators of the growing absolute value of food in world trade, reflecting the growth of world population and the increase in demand, are indices of export and import values.

The annual value of world food and feed exports in 1963–65 was nearly two-fifths larger than for the three-year average of 1957–59. As shown in Figure 2.2 the developed countries, that is, North America, Oceania, and Western Europe had the largest export increases ranging from 50 percent for Western Europe to 71 percent for North America. Increases in exports were lower for the developing countries with Africa reporting a 16 percent gain, while Latin America and the Far East had increases ranging from 30 to 50 percent.

Figure 2.3 indicates that increases in import values of world food and feed were inversely correlated with gains in values of exports for the developed countries. North America, for example, registered a 15 percent increase in average value of food and feed imports in 1963–65 as compared to 1957–59, while food and feed exports increased 71 percent. Imports also increased less in Oceania and Western Europe than exports. Increases in import values of food and feed for the developing countries, however, were generally correlated with, but larger than, increases in exports. Africa, which evidenced the smallest increase in export value with 16 percent had a 29 percent gain in import value while the Far East, which had a 44 percent gain in export

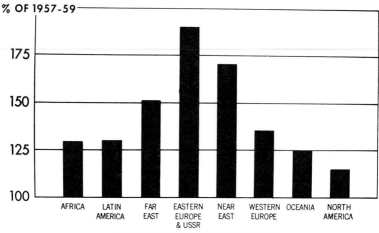

FAO, THE STATE OF FOOD AND AGRICULTURE, 1966

U.S. DEPARTMENT OF AGRICULTURE                    NEG. ERS 5372-67(9) ECONOMIC RESEARCH SER

*Fig. 2.3—Food and feed imports, by region, 1963–65 average.*

value, showed a 71 percent increase in import value of food and feed.

## NORTH AMERICA'S FOOD TRADE

The magnitude of North America's food trade is so great, its structural makeup is so varied, and its destinations and origins are so widespread that a sketch of its parameters is helpful for obtaining a better perspective for evaluating and recommending changes designed to seek improvements in policies and programs affecting it.

As shown in Figure 2.4, North America's food exports to the world are roughly one-third the value of its nonfood exports to the world. Intra-North American food exports, however, are relatively much less important than intra-North American nonfood exports, equaling one-tenth the value of the latter. The rising significance of intra-North American nonfood trade has come about from a sharp upward trend since the 1940's, reflecting rapid industrial growth and increasing per capita incomes, particularly in the United States and Canada.

Food exports to the rest of the world from North America, one of the world's leading food exporting regions, equaled a record $5.4 billion annually in 1963–65 (Table 2.2). This total

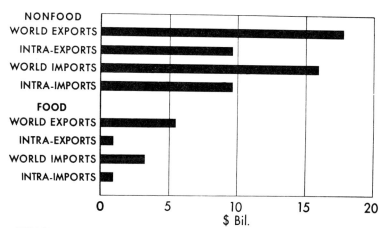

UNITED NATIONS, COMMODITY TRADE STATISTICS, SERIES D, 1963-65, AND INTERNATIONAL MONETARY FUND, DIRECTION OF TRADE, 1964-65.

U. S. DEPARTMENT OF AGRICULTURE                                    NEG. ERS 5377-67(9) ECONOMIC RESEARCH SERVICE

*Fig. 2.4—Trade of North America, food and nonfood, 1963–65 average.*

excludes trade among the three countries: The United States, Canada, and Mexico.

Grains and preparations equaling $3.5 billion accounted for over 64 percent of North America's food exports to the world. Other important commodity groups ranged in value from $22 million for sugar and some honey, to $639 million for oilseeds and related products.

North America is the world's leading exporter of cereals, accounting annually in 1961–65 for 63 percent of the world's wheat and flour exports, 57 percent of the world's corn exports, and 32 percent of the world's barley exports. At the same time, it contributed 17 percent of the world's rice exports exceeded only by Thailand and Burma, each of which exported slightly over one-fifth of the world's total (Table 2.3).

Although the United States currently exports the largest part of North American cereals, Canada plays a significant role in exports of wheat. Further, it ranks third among the world's barley exporters despite a sizable decline in its contribution since the 1950's. Mexico is a nominal exporter of wheat and rice and an occasional exporter of corn and barley.

In view of the significant export role of the United States in the North American and world grain market let us examine some of the developments contributing to this role.

TABLE 2.2

FOOD TRADE OF NORTH AMERICA WITH REST OF WORLD: VALUE BY COMMODITY GROUP, AVERAGE 1963–65

| Food Group | Exports | | | | Imports | | | | Net Trade |
|---|---|---|---|---|---|---|---|---|---|
| | United States | Canada | Mexico | Total | United States | Canada | Mexico | Total | |
| | *(million dollars)* | | | | | | | | |
| Animals and animal products (excluding fats and oils) | 331.4 | 50.3 | 0.2 | 381.9 | 465.0 | 28.3 | 1.4 | 494.7 | −112.8 |
| Grains and preparations | 2,500.5 | 934.8 | 54.4 | 3,489.7 | 10.8 | 5.7 | 2.0 | 18.5 | 3,471.2 |
| Fruits and nuts | 191.5 | 11.1 | 2.7 | 205.3 | 254.3 | 72.5 | 0.7 | 327.5 | −122.2 |
| Vegetables | 93.2 | 19.1 | 4.5 | 116.8 | 77.9 | 9.3 | 0.2 | 87.4 | 29.4 |
| Sugar and honey | 8.7 | 5.8 | 7.7 | 22.2 | 471.7 | 92.8 | 0.2 | 564.7 | −542.5 |
| Coffee, cocoa, and tea | 27.2 | 1.8 | 9.1 | 38.1 | 1,214.3 | 91.1 | 0.1 | 1,305.5 | −1,267.4 |
| Animal feeds | 196.6 | 33.2 | 0.5 | 230.3 | 36.7 | 0.6 | 4.6 | 41.9 | 188.4 |
| Fats and oils | 218.5 | 4.0 | | 222.5 | 82.2 | 10.0 | 0.5 | 92.7 | 129.8 |
| Oilseeds, nuts, and kernels | 567.9 | 69.2 | 1.8 | 638.9 | 50.7 | 3.2 | | 53.9 | 585.0 |
| Other | 61.7 | 9.8 | 1.2 | 72.7 | 162.1 | 23.1 | 5.0 | 190.2 | −117.5 |
| Total food | 4,197.2 | 1,139.1 | 82.1 | 5,418.4 | 2,825.7 | 335.6 | 14.7 | 3,177.0 | 2,241.4 |

Source: Compiled from United Nations, *Commodity Trade Statistics*, Series D, 1963–65; data exclude intra-trade, and therefore are less, particularly for the United States, than summarized in the United States commercial and food aid table ihtne following section of this chapter.

The growth of U.S. cereal exports as compared with cereal production shows that the latter has more than kept pace with domestic demand in the United States since the 1930's. The increase in U.S. output reflected the gains in the nation's agricultural productivity, especially noteworthy in the food and feed crop sector which have far exceeded the gains in the livestock sector. The gains can be traced in great part to U.S. agricultural policy which has promoted a rapid technological advance in agriculture and, of course, to the favorable market conditions which have existed during many of the years since the late 1930's. Demand has also increased because of increases in population and incomes, but the inferior status of such commodities as wheat and the relatively low income elasticity of demand for food at the farm level have caused this growth to be much slower than the growth in supply.

In contrast to Government agricultural policy in the United States, the policies adopted in the U.S.S.R. and its satellites and in Argentina were designed until recently to furnish the means for industrialization and a redistribution of income at the expense of the agricultural sector, while conditions in India were influenced greatly by the sharp increase in population after World War I. Pressure from the demand side in the U.S.S.R. and Argentina became more serious because of the distinctive effects which Government policy had upon producers.[3] After 1953, these countries adopted less restrictive policies; Argentina, however, has not to date been able to recapture the share of world wheat exports which it held in the 1930's. In the U.S.S.R., India, and Pakistan, the demand for food has increased more rapidly than the supply, with the result that exports have been reduced and imports of some magnitude have been necessary for many years.[4] The more rapid increase in demand has come about because of relatively large increases and internal shifts in population, programs favoring domestic consumers, and a relatively high income elasticity of demand for food as compared to the United States.

Grains and beverages, principally coffee, which occupy the leading export and import roles in North American food trade

---

[3] Robert M. Stern, "A Century of Food Exports," Chap. 14, *Foreign Agricultural Trade: Selected Readings,* The Iowa State Univ. Press, Ames, 1966.

[4] The U.S.S.R. has been an intermittent importer since 1963. In 1966 the U.S.S.R. signed an agreement with Canada to purchase 335 million bushels of wheat over a three-year period.

## TABLE 2.3

### A. Wheat*

| Country | 1909–13 | 1924–28 | 1934–38 | 1952–56 | 1961–65 |
|---|---|---|---|---|---|
| | | | (percent) | | |
| North America | 27.1 | 57.3 | 35.9 | 64.8 | 62.9 |
| United States | 14.5 | 22.1 | 8.0 | 33.5 | 39.3 |
| Canada | 12.6 | 35.2 | 27.9 | 31.3 | 23.1 |
| Mexico | ... | ... | † | † | 0.5 |
| Australia | 6.9 | 10.6 | 16.4 | 9.8 | 11.9 |
| USSR (Russia) | 22.3 | 2.1 | 4.2 | 2.6 | 7.6 |
| Argentina | 13.2 | 16.8 | 19.3 | 8.8 | 6.4 |
| Danube countries | 15.8 | 4.2 | 7.6 | 1.1 | 0.5 |
| India | 7.1 | 2.1 | 1.6 | ... | ... |
| Other | 7.6 | 6.9 | 15.0 | 12.9 | 10.8 |
| Total | 100.0 | 100.0 | 100.0 | 100.0 | 100.0 |
| Metric tons (000's) | 19,696 | 23,852 | 17,332 | 27,142 | 51,065 |

### B. Rice

| Country | 1909–13 | 1924–28 | 1934–38 | 1952–56 | 1961–65 |
|---|---|---|---|---|---|
| | | | (percent) | | |
| North America | ... | ... | 0.8 | 13.8 | 17.4 |
| United States | ... | ... | 0.7 | 13.8 | 17.2 |
| Canada | ... | ... | ... | † | ... |
| Mexico | ... | ... | 0.1 | † | 0.2 |
| Thailand | ... | ... | 14.4 | 24.8 | 23.3 |
| Burma | ... | ... | 31.8 | 28.5 | 22.2 |
| China (Mainland) | ... | ... | 0.2 | 5.9 | 9.2 |
| Cambodia | ... | ... | 13.7‡ | 3.6‡ | 4.9 |
| U.A.R. (Egypt) | ... | ... | 1.0 | 1.8 | 4.7 |
| Italy | ... | ... | 1.5 | 4.9 | 2.1 |
| Pakistan | ... | ... | 4.1 | 2.1 | 1.9 |
| Taiwan | ... | ... | 7.0 | 1.9 | 1.8 |
| Vietnam Republic | ... | ... | ... | ... | 1.7 |
| Other | ... | ... | 25.5 | 12.7 | 10.8 |
| Total | ... | ... | 100.0 | 100.0 | 100.0 |
| Metric tons (000's) | ... | ... | 9,650 | 5,044 | 6,945 |

### C. Corn

| Country | 1909–13 | 1924–28 | 1934–38 | 1952–56 | 1961–65 |
|---|---|---|---|---|---|
| | | | (percent) | | |
| North America | 16.2 | 5.7 | 8.3 | 50.8 | 57.1 |
| United States | 16.2 | 5.7 | 8.0 | 50.3 | 55.5 |
| Canada | ... | ... | † | 0.3 | † |
| Mexico | ... | ... | 0.3 | 0.2 | 1.6 |
| Argentina | 43.2 | 64.1 | 65.0 | 19.9 | 13.0 |
| Danube countries | 23.9 | 18.1 | 11.5 | 7.3 | 5.6 |
| USSR (Russia) | 11.2 | 1.7 | 0.3 | 1.5 | 3.5 |
| Other | 5.5 | 10.4 | 14.9 | 20.5 | 20.8 |
| Total | 100.0 | 100.0 | 100.0 | 100.0 | 100.0 |
| Metric tons (000's) | 6,800 | 8,452 | 100,049 | 5,386 | 20,454 |

TABLE 2.3 (continued)

| Country | 1909–13 | 1924–28 | 1934–38 | 1952–56 | 1961–65 |
|---|---|---|---|---|---|
| | | | D. Barley | | |
| | | | (*percent*) | | |
| North America | 5.2 | 39.7 | 18.8 | 49.0 | 31.8 |
| United States | 3.3 | 19.6 | 7.9 | 16.9 | 21.7 |
| Canada | 1.9 | 20.1 | 10.9 | 32.0 | 10.1 |
| Mexico | ... | ... | † | 0.1 | ... |
| USSR (Russia) | 67.1 | 8.8 | 11.7 | 3.1 | 13.6 |
| Australia | ... | 0.9 | 2.7 | 8.3 | 7.1 |
| Argentina | 0.3 | 5.5 | 12.6 | 8.2 | 3.4 |
| Danube countries | 12.2 | 15.2 | 12.6 | 0.2 | 0.3 |
| Other | 15.2 | 29.9 | 41.6 | 31.2 | 43.8 |
| Total | 100.0 | 100.0 | 100.0 | 100.0 | 100.0 |
| Metric tons (000's) | 5,536 | 3,451 | 2,655 | 5,900 | 7,045 |

Sources: Data for wheat, corn, and barley from 1909–13 through 1934–38 adapted from Robert M. Stern, *World Food Exports and United States Agricultural Policies*, Ph.D. dissertation, Columbia Univ., 1958. Figures were compiled originally from the following sources: 1909–13 and 1924–28–International Institute of Agriculture (L.B. Bacon and F. C. Schloemer), *World Trade in Agricultural Products* (Rome, 1940), and *International Yearbook of Agricultural Statistics 1928–29* (Rome, 1929); FAO, *Grain*, Commodity Ser. Bull. 18 (Washington, 1950); 1934–38–see 1909–14 and 1924–28 above, also, FAO, *Yearbook of Food and Agricultural Statistics, 1955*, Part 2 (Rome, 1956); 1952–56–FAO, *Yearbook of Food and Agricultural Statistics, 1957*, Part 2 (Rome, 1958); 1961–65–*Trade Yearbook, 1966* (Rome, 1967).
* Includes wheat equivalent of wheat flour.
† Less than 0.05 percent.
‡ Indochina: Cambodia, Laos, and Vietnam.

with the rest of the world play a much less prominent role in intra-North American trade.

The leading United States' exports in the context of the North American framework are fruits and vegetables, feed grains, animal feeds, animal products, and oilseeds to Canada; and animal products and grains to Mexico.

Canada's leading food exports are feeder steers, barley, feed wheat, animal feeds, and fruits and vegetables to the United States.

Mexico's main food exports include sugar and some honey to the United States; coffee and fruits and vegetables to the United States and Canada; stocker steers to the United States; and oilseeds to Canada.

## NORTH AMERICA'S FOOD SALES FOR DOLLARS AND FOOD AID

Foreign trade in the classical sense that individual traders operate atomistically and avail themselves of an unrestricted exchange market through which to convert currencies, according to one writer, has not existed for many years and probably will not exist in the future. He further points out that trade is called commercial by some if there are no direct controls, no increasing or variable tariffs, no domestic taxes, subsidies, or other intervention, no discrimination among types of transactions or areas, and no quantitative restrictions.[5]

The market economies of the world include substantial exceptions to these conditions that must be fulfilled to be classified as institutions of commercial trade. As used in this chapter, commercial trade refers to those foreign exports for which dollar payments are obtained and exclude, therefore, sales under Government-financed programs.

Appraising U.S. agricultural export opportunities, Bachman properly emphasizes that there is a distinct difference between needs and effective demand for food exports.[6] Although a large part of the world's population is ill fed, the extent to which the needs of the ill fed are reflected in food imports is severely restricted by low incomes and limited external financial reserves available in the less developed countries. This restriction is reflected in the fact that North America's food exports to the world are largely commercial sales for dollars rather than food aid shipments.

Nearly three-fourths of North America's food exports are sold for dollars through regular commercial channels. Yearly dollar sales abroad of food in 1963–66 from the United States—the world's major aid exporter—were a record $3.4 billion and accounted for all of the increase in U.S. food exports since 1949–50 (Table 2.4).

Largest gains in U.S. food exports for dollars in recent years have come from feed grains and oilseeds. United States feed grain and soybean exports for dollars have more than doubled since 1960. Feed grains and soybeans account for over 40 percent of U.S. food exports for dollars. Significant dollar gains have also been achieved in U.S. exports of fruits and vegetables.

A major reason for the rapid growth in the world feed grain market is the expansion that rising incomes have stimulated in

---

[5] George L. Mehren, "Commercial Export Markets for Farm Products," Chap. 18, Foreign Agricultural Trade: Selected Readings, Iowa State Univ. Press, Ames, 1966.
[6] Kenneth L. Bachman, "U.S. Agricultural Export Opportunities," talk presented at Southwestern Conference on Agricultural Policy and Development, Baton Rouge, La., Apr. 27, 1966.

TABLE 2.4

U.S. Food Aid Exports, Commercial Food Exports, and Total Food Exports Classified by Commodity; Value by Fiscal Year Averages, 1949–50 to 1963–66

| Commodity | 1949–50 | 1951–54 | 1955–58 | 1959–62 | 1963–66 |
|---|---|---|---|---|---|
| | | | *(million dollars)* | | |
| Wheat and Wheat | | | | | |
| Products | 994 | 733 | 702 | 1,033 | 1,358 |
| Food aid | 798* | 214* | 457 | 703 | 931 |
| Commercial | 196 | 519 | 245 | 330 | 427 |
| Feed Grains (incl. | | | | | |
| products) | 278 | 324 | 364 | 607 | 994 |
| Food aid | 211 | 83 | 157 | 153 | 106 |
| Commercial | 67 | 241 | 207 | 454 | 888 |
| Rice | 77 | 134 | 111 | 128 | 201 |
| Food aid | NA† | NA | 54 | 61 | 75 |
| Commercial | NA | NA | 57 | 67 | 126 |
| Oilseeds and Products | 219 | 214 | 432 | 584 | 998 |
| Food aid | 187‡ | 35‡ | 104 | 128 | 124 |
| Commercial | 32 | 179 | 328 | 456 | 874 |
| Animal Products (incl. | | | | | |
| dairy) | 328 | 272 | 426 | 382 | 488 |
| Food aid | 57 | 31 | 196 | 73 | 132 |
| Commercial | 271 | 241 | 230 | 309 | 356 |
| Fruits and Vegetables | 194 | 230 | 338 | 391 | 455 |
| Food aid | NA | NA | 19 | 3 | 4 |
| Commercial | NA | NA | 319 | 388 | 451 |
| Other | 122 | 136 | 158 | 141 | 246 |
| Food aid | NA | NA | 2 | . . . | 2 |
| Commercial | NA | NA | 156 | 141 | 244 |
| Total | 2,212 | 2,043 | 2,531 | 3,266 | 4,740 |
| Food aid | 1,407 | 407 | 989 | 1,121 | 1,374 |
| Commercial | 805 | 1,636 | 1,542 | 2,145 | 3,366 |

Source: Trade Statistics and Analysis Branch, Foreign Development and Trade Division, USDA.
* Bread grains included wheat, wheat flour, and rye.
† NA—Not available.
‡ Fats, oils, and oilseeds.

livestock and poultry industries, especially those of Western Europe and Japan.

As shown in Figure 2.5, U.S. food exports in the fiscal year that ended June 30, with the exception of wheat and flour, consisted mainly of commercial sales for dollars. Major nonfood agricultural items such as cotton and tobacco were moved abroad also largely by commercial sales rather than under the authority of Government-program shipments.

In Figure 2.6 we note that the major foreign customers for U.S. agricultural exports, with the exception of India, are the industrialized countries. Japan stands alone as the leading market outlet. Japan and five other countries—Canada, India, West

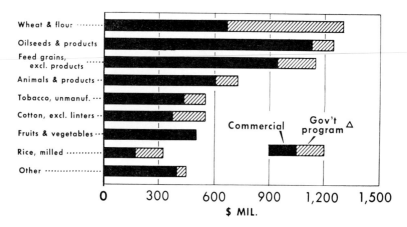

Δ GOVERNMENT - FINANCED PROGRAMS, P.L. 83 - 480 AND P.L. 87 - 195.

U. S. DEPARTMENT OF AGRICULTURE    NEG. ERS 2906 - 67 (9)    ECONOMIC RESEARCH SERVICE

Fig. 2.5—U.S. agricultural exports, by commodity group, 1967 (year ending June 30).

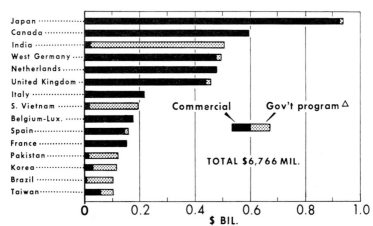

DATA NOT ADJUSTED FOR INTRANSIT SHIPMENTS; U.S. SHIPMENTS THROUGH CANADIAN PORTS, FOR EXAMPLE, WERE $116 MILLION.    Δ GOVERNMENT–FINANCED PROGRAMS, P.L. 83–480 AND P.L. 87–195.

U. S. DEPARTMENT OF AGRICULTURE    NEG. ERS 5340 - 67 (9)    ECONOMIC RESEARCH SERVICE

Fig. 2.6—U.S. agricultural exports, by country, 1967 (year ending June 30).

Germany, the Netherlands, and the United Kingdom—accounted for approximately half of total U.S. agricultural exports in the fiscal year 1967. Except for India, all are largely dollar customers.

## UNITED STATES FOOD AID EXPORTS

Food aid exports from North America come, for the most part, from the United States. Canada supplies some food aid and Mexico, until recently, was a food aid recipient of the United States.

About one-fourth of U.S. food exports go to friendly, dollar-short, developing countries under specified Government-financed programs. United States food aid exports equaled $1.4 billion annually in 1963–66. These programs, often referred to as Food-for-Peace programs, operate mainly under P. L. 480—the Agricultural Trade Development and Assistance Act of 1954. They use four major approaches: sales for foreign currencies; donations to provide disaster relief, promote economic development, or help needy persons; barter; and long-term supply and dollar credit sales.

Wheat and products have been the major commodities supplied under food aid programs representing over two-thirds of the total value in recent years.

United States food exports, both commercial sales and Government program shipments (aid exports), benefit from export payment assistance from the United States Government. The purpose of this assistance for certain price-supported commodities is to make the prices of the commodities competitive in world trade. Such assistance may be needed for these price-supported commodities when domestic prices are higher than world prices. Assistance amounts to a payment to the exporter that bridges the gap between the world price and the domestic price, enabling him to offer the commodity in foreign trade at the lower export market price. Export payment assistance, which is not included in the value of U.S. exports, is estimated at about $300 million for the fiscal year 1967. It benefited about $1.4 billion worth of commercial dollar exports and slightly over $0.8 billion worth of exports under Government-financed programs.

In the fiscal year 1967, wheat (including flour) and rice were the principal U.S. food commodities assisted. Other food and nonfood commodities that received assistance included flaxseed, linseed oil, tobacco, peanuts, and a limited quantity of grain sorghums. In addition a small quantity of nonfat dry milk was sold at reduced prices for foreign school lunch programs. In the current fiscal year export payment assistance is limited mainly to wheat and flour among the major export commodities.

Food aid can play an important intermediate role in providing external resources to fill the gaps that exist because of rapid increases in food demands where the country lacks the foreign exchange reserves to finance the food and other imports needed for continued economic development. Public Law 480 sales for local currency and long-term loans help alleviate the problems of balance of payments and food-price fueled inflation. By doing this, it provides a basis for continued growth in the economy. Over the longer run, however, promotion of more rapid economic growth in the less developed countries offers a more promising way of meeting the world's food deficits. This, in turn, leads to larger purchases for dollars.

### CANADIAN FOOD AID EXPORTS

Canada ranks second to the United States as a supplier of food aid for emergency and development purposes. Most of the Canadian food assistance since 1951 has been under the Colombo Plan for Cooperative Economic Development in South and Southeast Asia. This plan was developed in 1950 as a Commonwealth Project, with Australia, Britain, Canada, and New Zealand as original donor countries. These countries were joined by the United States and Canada. Recipients under the plan include most of the countries of South and Southeast Asia.

Although Canada has no legislative authority for food aid, the Parliament votes funds to be used by the External Aid Office for this purpose. In the case of food exported under the Colombo Plan, the recipient countries establish counterpart funds in local currencies, which are used for economic development purposes agreed upon between the two countries.

In 1963–66, Canadian food aid equaled about $15 million annually (Table 2.5). Canadian shipments were about 1 percent of the annual value of U.S. food aid shipments. Aid to India, the largest recipient, continued to consist almost entirely of wheat, but some milk, flour, and dry peas were also supplied. During 1967, Canadian food aid was reported at an annual rate of $100 million, equaling about 7 percent of the value of U.S. food aid.

TABLE 2.5

CANADIAN FOOD AID EXPORTS, COMMERCIAL FOOD EXPORTS, AND TOTAL FOOD
EXPORTS, CLASSIFIED BY COMMODITY: VALUE BY ANNUAL AVERAGES
1955–58, 1959–62, 1963–66

| Commodity | 1955–58 | 1959–62 | 1963–66 |
|---|---|---|---|
| | | *(million dollars)* * | |
| Wheat and Wheat Flour | 529.0 | 585.9 | 931.1 |
| Food aid | 5.6 | 16.3 | 13.2 |
| Commercial | 523.4 | 569.6 | 917.9 |
| Dairy Products | 15.0 | 25.3 | 31.6 |
| Food aid | . . . | . . . | 0.3 |
| Commercial | 15.0 | 25.3 | 31.3 |
| Other | 645.4 | 520.3 | 536.5 |
| Food aid | . . . | . . . | 1.1 |
| Commercial | 645.4 | 520.3 | 535.4 |
| Total | 1,189.4 | 1,131.5 | 1,499.2 |
| Food aid | 5.6 | 16.3 | 14.6 |
| Commercial | 1,183.8 | 1,115.2 | 1,484.6 |

Source: Data for total exports for calendar years 1955 and 1956 were compiled from
*Trade of Canada;* data for calendar years 1957–66 were summarized from United Nations,
*Commodity Trade Statistics.* Statistics on food aid on an April–March fiscal year basis
were furnished by R. H. Roberts, U.S. Agricultural Attaché to Canada, and W. S. Hill-
house, Canadian Agricultural Attaché to the United States, as originally compiled by
the Canadian External Aid Office.
* In terms of U.S. dollars.

## MEXICAN FOOD AID IMPORTS

Since the beginning of P. L. 480 in 1954, U.S. exports of farm
products to Mexico have been for the most part commercial sales
for dollars. United States food aid exports, excluding other agricultural exports, to Mexico averaged $8 million annually in 1963–
66 (Table 2.6). In the fiscal year 1967, all U.S. agricultural exports to Mexico were commercial sales for dollars. Mexico has
ranked in 9th to 11th place as a dollar market for agricultural
commodities from the United States.

The donations programs with Mexico were terminated June
30, 1965, by agreement with the Government of Mexico, primarily as a result of Mexico's more favorable economic situation.
Mexican production of wheat and corn have increased substantially since 1963. These commodities were the principal
items supplied under the donations programs.

## FOOD GRAIN PROJECTIONS FOR NORTH AMERICA

Having analyzed the dimensions of North America's commercial
sales of food for dollars and food aid, let us turn now to future

TABLE 2.6

U.S. FOOD AID EXPORTS, COMMERCIAL FOOD EXPORTS, AND TOTAL FOOD EXPORTS
TO MEXICO CLASSIFIED BY COMMODITY: VALUE BY FISCAL YEAR AVERAGES
1956–57 TO 1963–66

| Commodity | 1956–58 * | 1959–62 | 1963–66 |
|---|---|---|---|
| | *(million dollars)* | | |
| Wheat and Wheat Products | 3 | 1 | 2 |
| Food aid | 3 | † | 2 |
| Commercial | . . . | 1 | † |
| Feed Grains (incl. products) | 33 | 9 | 17 |
| Food aid | 7 | 4 | 1 |
| Commercial | 26 | 5 | 16 |
| Rice | † | 1 | 1 |
| Food aid | † | † | . . . |
| Commercial | † | 1 | 1 |
| Oilseeds and Products | 4 | 5 | 6 |
| Food aid | . . . | † | 2 |
| Commercial | 4 | 5 | 4 |
| Animal Products (incl. dairy) | 19 | 16 | 19 |
| Food aid | † | 1 | 3 |
| Commercial | 19 | 15 | 16 |
| Fruits and Vegetables | 6 | 10 | 7 |
| Food aid | † | † | † |
| Commercial | 6 | 10 | 7 |
| Other | 9 | 7 | 13 |
| Food aid | . . . | . . . | . . . |
| Commercial | 9 | 7 | 13 |
| Total | 74 | 49 | 65 |
| Food aid | 10 | 5 | 8 |
| Commercial | 64 | 44 | 57 |

Source: Trade Statistics and Analysis Branch, Foreign Development and Trade
Division, ERS, USDA.
\* Three-year average.
† Less than $500,000.

trade prospects. Since grains represent the major food export of
North America and, in view of the fact that grains constitute a
large share of the world's food supply either directly or indirectly,
the discussion will be focused on projections for coarse grains and
wheat in the first instance and then on all grains.

The "Adjusted Trends" long-range projections of the World
Food Supply Panel of the President's Science Advisory Committee show that commercial demand prospects while favorable for
coarse grains are less favorable for wheat.[7]

Export projections of coarse grains for North America for
1980 equal about 54 million metric tons. This is an almost three-
fold increase above average exports for 1964–65. Most of these

[7] "Projected Trends of Trade in Agricultural Products," Chap. 2, *The
World Food Problem,* a Report of the President's Science Advisory Commit-
tee, Vol. II, Report of the Panel on the World Food Supply, The White
House, May 1967.

projected North American exports—95 percent—represent U.S. exports.

The principal importers of North America's projected coarse grain exports for 1980 are the other developed countries including those of Western Europe along with Japan. These developed countries, for the most part commercial dollar buyers, would import 48.1 million metric tons—approximately 90 percent of the projected export total of North America. The developing countries—likely concessional importers—would take most of the remainder; Communist Asia would also be a nominal importer (Table 2.7).

The coarse grain projections are based on the assumption that the demand for meat will continue to grow in Western Europe and Japan. To satisfy this demand, grain input per unit of pork and poultry is assumed to increase. Higher prices for beef, however, are expected to encourage consumers to shift to pork and poultry.

Net trade (export) projections of wheat and flour (wheat equivalent) for North America by 1980 come to 46.4 million metric tons annually. The export increase, while substantially less than for coarse grains, represents a significant 50 percent rise over shipments for 1964–65. Both the United States and Canada would play important roles in the increase, with the United States contributing 29.5 million metric tons, Canada 16.5 million, and Mexico 0.4 million (Table 2.8).

However, this overall increase would take place while the net wheat imports of Europe, U.S.S.R., and Japan would decline from an annual level of 13.6 million tons in 1964–65 to 11.1 million tons in 1980. The return of the U.S.S.R. to an export position—at about the same 5 million-ton level as during 1959–61—is the major factor. Also, Oceania is expected to increase its wheat exports from 6.3 million in 1964–65 to 10 million tons in 1980. With all these areas part of the developed world, a new dimension is projected for wheat and flour trade for 1980. This is the shift of the developed countries outside of North America as a group to a net exporter from a net importer basis. By 1980 these other developed countries as a group are projected to export 3.1 million metric tons, whereas in 1964–65 they imported 3.1 million metric tons.

Net wheat imports of the developing countries are projected at 39.5 million metric tons for 1980–70 percent above 1964–65. A total of 10 million metric tons is projected for Communist Asia—nearly 100 percent higher than for 1964–65. It is clear that

## TABLE 2.7

### Coarse Grains: World Production, Net Trade, and Domestic Disappearance by Regions, Average 1959–61, 1964–65, and 1980 Projected

| Region | Production* | | | Net Trade† | | | Domestic Disappearance | | |
|---|---|---|---|---|---|---|---|---|---|
| | 1959–61 | 1964–65‡ | 1980 | 1959–61 | 1964–65 | 1980 | 1959–61 | 1964–55 | 1980 |
| | | | | *(1,000 metric tons)* | | | | | |
| North America | 151,988 | 145,787 | 267,300 | −11,363 | −18,719 | −54,100 | 134,712 | 142,285 | 213,200 |
| United States | 135,551 | 125,879 | 234,400 | −10,536 | −17,275 | −52,000 | 118,139 | 122,540 | 182,400 |
| Canada | 11,010 | 11,677 | 20,000 | −716 | −633 | −2,000 | 11,126 | 12,325 | 18,000 |
| Mexico | 5,427 | 8,231 | 12,900 | −111 | −811 | −100 | 5,447 | 7,420 | 12,800 |
| Other Developed Countries§ | 160,459 | 171,612 | 238,200 | 11,462 | 16,119 | 48,100 | 170,818 | 189,200 | 286,300 |
| Developing Countries | 80,367 | 83,321 | 138,800 | 173 | 434 | 5,500 | 81,025 | 83,755 | 143,300 |
| Communist Asia | 37,603 | 46,000 | 65,500 | 398 | 412 | 500 | 38,001 | 46,412 | 66,000 |
| World Total | 430,417 | 446,720 | 709,800 | 670 | −1,754 | ... | 424,555 | 461,652 | 708,800 |

Source: Compiled from Tables 2–18, p. 166; and 2–23, p. 171 of *The World Food Problem*, Volume II, The White House, May 1967.
* Calendar year 1964.
† Plus indicates net imports; minus indicates net exports.
‡ Total includes 30,100 tons to countries unspecified.
§ Includes River Plate; Northern, Southern, and Eastern Europe; U.S.S.R.; South Africa; Japan; and Oceania.

## TABLE 2.8

WHEAT AND FLOUR (WHEAT EQUIVALENT): WORLD PRODUCTION, NET TRADE, AND DOMESTIC DISAPPEARANCE BY REGIONS, AVERAGE 1959–61, 1964–65, AND 1980 PROJECTED

| Region | Production | | | Net Trade* | | | Domestic Disappearance | | |
|---|---|---|---|---|---|---|---|---|---|
| | 1959–61 | 1964–65† | 1980 | 1959–61 | 1964–65 | 1980 | 1959–61 | 1964–55 | 1980 |
| | | | | (1,000 metric tons) | | | | | |
| North America | 45,734 | 53,267 | 76,800 | −24,978 | −31,706 | −46,400 | 21,542 | 23,249 | 30,400 |
| United States | 33,684 | 35,126 | 51,500 | −16,012 | −19,510 | −29,510 | 16,202 | 17,848 | 22,000 |
| Canada | 10,764 | 16,341 | 21,800 | −8,970 | −11,816 | −16,500 | 3,962 | 3,981 | 5,300 |
| Mexico | 1,286 | 1,800 | 3,500 | 4 | −380 | −400 | 1,378 | 1,420 | 3,100 |
| Other Developed Countries ‡ | 118,120 | 142,692 | 164,500 | 6,467 | 3,132 | −3,100 | 125,417 | 141,390 | 161,400 |
| Developing Countries | 35,677 | 36,492 | 58,800 | 15,630 | 23,371 | 39,500 | 49,280 | 60,543 | 98,300 |
| Communist Asia | 21,930 | 22,500 | 28,000 | 1,273 | 5,120 | 10,000 | 24,247 | 26,620 | 38,000 |
| World Total | 221,461 | 254,951 | 328,100 | −1,608 | −83 | ... | 220,486 | 251,802 | 328,100 |

Source: Compiled from Tables 2–16, p. 162; and 2–23, p. 171 of *The World Food Problem*, Volume II, The White House, May 1967.
* Plus indicates net imports; minus indicates net exports.
† Calendar year 1964.
‡ Includes River Plate; Northern, Southern, and Eastern Europe; U.S.S.R.; South Africa; Japan; and Oceania.

export prospects for commercial demand for wheat and flour in the future are far less bright than for coarse grains since the projected increases call for increased exports from the developed countries and increased imports by the developing countries. Mainland China (Communist Asia), however, could well continue as a dollar market for Canadian exports.

Besides the World Food Supply Panel's Adjusted Trend projection just discussed, Abel and Rojko make projections for the developed and the less developed world, subdividing the latter with respect to grain-importing and grain-exporting nations.[8] They then combine the various elements to determine the grain prospects for the world. This approach enables them to evaluate supply-and-demand prospects in each and to assess the projected trend for the trade in grains. Their projections for the developed countries are based on productive capacity. Thus they show that the developed countries in 1980 will have more than adequate food production capacity to provide for the increased food import needs of the less developed countries. This contrasts with the approach of the World Food Supply Panel. That approach results in a balance of world trade, that is, exports equal imports.

Abel and Rojko present two assumptions based upon recent historical grain production and consumption trends in the less developed countries. Another assumption is based on moderate improvement, while a further assumption assumes rapid improvement over historical trends. All assumptions use the same rate of population increase, but different rates of increase in per capita consumption are used depending on the levels of economic development.

For the developed world only one set of projections was made. This is based on the most likely rates of growth and grain production and consumption, assuming world market prices remain at about the average levels of the past three years.

Under the three more likely of their four assumptions, basic to projecting net trade for the less developed countries for 1980, world grain production capacity exceeds demand by 30 to 39 metric tons. This would be the amount left over after supplying world demand and including the import needs of the less developed importing countries of 52 to 58 million metric tons by 1980 (Table 2.9). Most of this would likely be wheat and a substantial part of this probably would be aid shipments. Roughly, the grain import needs of 1980 would be nearly double those in

[8] Martin E. Abel and Anthony S. Rojko, *World Food Situation, Prospects for World Grain Production, Consumption and Trade*, FAER-35, USDA, 1967.

## TABLE 2.9

### Net Trade in Grains, 1964–65, and Under Alternative Projections for 1980, Classified by Selected World Regions

| Region | 1964–65* | 1980 Alternatives | | | |
|---|---|---|---|---|---|
| | | Historical trend I | Historical trend II | Moderate improvement in production | Rapid improvement in production |
| | | *(million metric tons)* | | | |
| All less developed countries | 13.7 | 38.5 | 34.3 | 29.7 | 5.8 |
| (Less developed importing countries) | (29.0) | (58.5) | (54.3) | (52.2) | (28.3) |
| Developed countries† | −20.3 | −77.6 | −77.6 | −77.6 | −77.6 |
| Communist Asia | 4.9 | 9.0 | 9.0 | 9.0 | 9.0 |
| World Total† | −1.7 | −30.1 | −34.3 | −38.9 | −62.8 |

Source: Compiled from Martin E. Abel and Anthony S. Rojko, *World Food Situation* . . . , FAER-35, pp. 12 and 19, USDA, 1967. Minus indicates net exports; plus indicates net imports.
* Year beginning July 1 for wheat and coarse grains, following calendar year for rice; negative numbers mean either a world surplus or an increase in stocks.
† Negative numbers indicate net exports, world surplus, or increase in stocks.

1964–65. Under the assumption of rapid improvement, grain output rises at an annual rate of 4 percent a year. The grain importing countries would need to import 28 million tons of grain, only 5.8 million tons more than the less developed grain exporters would be shipping out. Commercial sales would largely supplant sales under concessional Government programs because of the rapid agricultural and economic growth. The authors feel that there is little likelihood that this rapid rate of improvement will materialize in such a short span of years.

## SUMMARY AND CONCLUSIONS

1. Food has declined in relative importance in world trade. One of the major causal forces for this development is the fact that income elasticity of food in general is a declining function of increasing real per capita income.
2. World food trade has not kept pace with world population growth. Currently, world food trade per capita is below the level of a half century ago. Compared with the depressed world food trade level of the 1930's, the recent volume of world food trade reflects both population and per capita growth.
3. Indices of increases in import values of food and feed for the developed countries in recent years were inversely correlated with indices of increases in export values. The indices of increases in values of food and feed exports were larger for the developed countries than they were for the underdeveloped countries.
4. The growth of North America's grain exports in world trade has been the major contributing factor to North America's preeminence in world food exports.
5. North America is one of the world's leading importers of food. Coffee from Latin America is the principal food import and represents a major source of foreign exchange earnings for the Latin American countries.
6. The intra-North American trade pattern in food differs from the pattern of North America's trade with the rest of the world. The leading food commodities in intra-North American trade are fruits, nuts, vegetables, animals, and animal products.
7. The United States' share of world wheat exports has increased since the late 1930's. The growth in the U.S. share has accelerated since the inauguration of P. L. 480 shipments

in the 1950's. Canada's share has declined; however, its exports have gained in an expanding world market.

8.  Commercial sales for dollars account for over three-fourths of North America's annual food exports. Food shipments under Government-financed programs (aid shipments) consist principally of wheat from the United States to the less developed countries.

9.  Long-term projections for grain, the main source of the world's food, show that future dollar sales prospects are much more favorable for feed grains than for wheat. Other North American food commodities such as oilseeds, fruits, and vegetables also have favorable future export prospects as dollar earners.

# CHAPTER THREE

# Potential Food Production Possibilities

## ARTHUR B. MACKIE

A MOST DISTURBING PROBLEM of our time is the apparent inability of some less developed countries to produce enough food to keep pace with their growing population. This phenomenon is probably the most publicized disparity, although by no means the only one, between the developed and less developed world.

The problems of wide disparities in levels of development, income, and agricultural productivity between nations, as between regions within nations, have increasingly concerned economists and policy makers in the postwar period. No doubt, the world would be a better place to live if it were not for all the economic disparities that are created by different rates of economic growth. These disparities lead to paradoxical situations in that populations are increasing most rapidly in those countries that can least afford to have additional mouths to feed. Because of the wide disparities in levels of income, rapid rates of economic growth in the low income countries may in fact fail to narrow the absolute income gap between the less developed and the developed countries even though the latter may be growing at a slower rate. What this means is that the less developed countries will have to run faster than the developed countries just to keep from losing more ground in the years ahead. It is

ARTHUR B. MACKIE, Economic Development Branch, Foreign Development and Trade Division, United States Department of Agriculture.

paradoxical in that prices of agricultural exports of less developed countries have tended to fall relative to the prices of
their imports, thereby decreasing their import capabilities and
often the capacity of less developed countries to generate a more
rapid rate of national economic growth, where rapid rates of
growth are most needed. Production, capital accumulation, and
capital formation have proceeded more slowly in those countries
where productivity and additional capital inputs are most urgent-
ly needed to increase agricultural productivity. It is paradoxical
in that productivity is lagging in agriculture where its increase is
most imperative and, in relative terms, is lowest where the proportion engaged in agriculture is highest.[1] Finally, it is paradoxical in that increases in agricultural production are most common
where stocks of food are already excessive, thereby creating surpluses and deficits on the world scene. Under these disparities,
and I have mentioned only some of them, food deficits in some
countries are causing a sharp diminution in the world's food reserves. It is also stimulating many professional and political
leaders to take another look at the world's food production and
distribution possibilities.

This chapter will (a) review the past and current situations
in world grain production as an index of food production for the
world and its major subregions, (b) point up some of the major
implications of these trends in relation to future needs, (c)
examine the chances for stepping up agricultural or grain production in the less developed countries, and (d) indicate some of
the implications of improvements in grain production in the less
developed countries on agricultural exports and production in
the developed countries, particularly for North America.

Grain production will be used as a proxy measure for food
production because most of man's food comes directly or indirectly from grains. Trends in production and utilization of
grains should fairly well represent trends in the total food
situation.

## POPULATION, INCOME, AND FOOD PRODUCTION

The relationship between economic growth and agricultural development is a very complex one—it probably cannot be measured in precise mathematical terms. However, even though this
relationship is rather an undefined concept, there is general agree-

---

[1] David Horowitz, *Hemispheres North and South, Economic Disparity
Among Nations,* Johns Hopkins Press, Baltimore, 1966.

ment that the two are positively correlated. That is, rising agricultural productivity and agricultural development usually go hand in hand and both are essential ingredients of the growth process. In other words the self-perpetuating forces of economic growth can be released only by greater productivity. And in the less developed countries, this usually means the agricultural sector since it is the largest sector.

There are many factors that tend to work against efforts to increase productivity in less developed countries. Malnutrition and food shortages are powerful enemies of rising productivity and therefore of economic growth and economic development generally.[2]

The data in Table 3.1 on growth rates in population, income, and grain production for the world and its three major subregions—developed, centrally planned, and less developed countries—show the importance of increasing population on growth in per capita availability of grain supplies. You will note that I am using the per capita growth rate in grain production as an index of food shortfalls and the need for drawdowns on the food reserves of the developed countries. On a global basis, grain production has just barely managed to keep ahead of population since 1954. During this period, the developed countries have been the primary source of net additions to world available grain supplies. The less developed and centrally planned countries have both taken their turns at drawing down the world grain reserves during the period 1954–66.

## TRENDS IN FOOD PRODUCTION

World food production is currently increasing about 2.4 percent per year.[3] At this rate, the world's food supply has slightly exceeded the growth in population during the sixties. Were it not for the fact that world demand for food has been increasing at the rate of about 4 percent per year during this period because of rising population and income, the current food crisis would probably not exist. This situation would be especially true if the performance of grain production in some of the less developed countries had continued to increase at the historical rate rather than fall off rather sharply in 1965 and 1966 (Fig. 3.1.)

---

[2] *Ibid.*, pp. 24–36.
[3] Martin E. Abel and Anthony S. Rojko, *World Food Situation, Prospects for World Grain Production, Consumption and Trade*, FAER-35, USDA, 1967.

TABLE 3.1

COMPARISONS OF GROWTH RATES IN POPULATION, INCOME, AND GRAIN
PRODUCTION 1954–66

| Item | Developed Countries* | Centrally Planned Countries* | Less Developed Countries* | World |
|---|---|---|---|---|
| | (percent growth rate) | | | |
| **Population** | | | | |
| 1954–60 | 1.2 | 2.2 | 2.2 | 2.2 |
| 1960–66 | 1.2 | 2.1 | 2.3 | 2.3 |
| 1954–66 | 1.2 | 2.0 | 2.2 | 2.2 |
| **Total Income** | | | | |
| 1954–60 | 3.9 | 2.5† | 3.4 | 2.9 |
| 1960–66 | 4.9 | 3.0† | 4.1 | 4.6 |
| 1954–66 | 4.4 | 2.8† | 3.8 | 3.6 |
| **Per Capita** | | | | |
| 1954–60 | 2.7 | 0.3† | 1.4 | 0.7 |
| 1960–66 | 3.7 | 0.9† | 1.8 | 2.3 |
| 1954–66 | 3.2 | 0.8† | 1.6 | 1.4 |
| **Total Grain Production** | | | | |
| 1954–60 | 3.3 | 1.1 | 2.3 | 2.4 |
| 1960–66 | 2.4 | 2.7 | 1.8 | 2.5 |
| 1954–66 | 2.6 | 1.8 | 2.0 | 2.4 |
| **Per Capita** | | | | |
| 1954–60 | 2.0 | −1.1 | 0.1 | 0.2 |
| 1960–66 | 1.2 | 0.6 | −0.5 | 0.2 |
| 1954–66 | 1.4 | −0.2 | −0.2 | 0.2 |

* For countries included in these regions, see the footnotes to Table 3.2.
† Based on limited information.

## HISTORICAL TRENDS

Over this past decade world grain production has increased about
2.4 percent per year (Table 3.2), while the world's population increased about 2.2 percent per year. The growth rate in grain production was about the same in both the developed and less developed countries.

However, there was a marked difference between developed
and less developed countries in per capita grain production,
which takes into account the rate of growth in population. Per
capita grain production in the developed countries grew about
1.4 percent per year from 1954–1966, while per capita grain production remained almost constant in the less developed and centrally planned countries. Thus, as a group the less developed and
centrally planned countries only managed to keep pace with
their increase in population (Fig. 3.1).

Within the broad group of less developed countries, there
were divergencies in performance. For example, over the 1954–

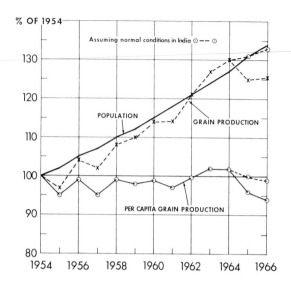

*Fig. 3.1—Indices of population and grain production in less developed countries.*

66 period grain production materially exceeded the growth in population in Southeast Asia and in Mexico. The performance of five countries in Southeast Asia with a combined population of 82 million (Table 3.2) equaled that of the developed countries, while the production performance of Mexico far exceeded, in terms of growth rate, that of the developed countries. Other gainers in the food production-population race were the countries in Other East Asia, Other Asia, East Africa, and Central America. The losers in the food-population race were West and South Asia, North and West Africa, and the Caribbean. The countries of South America as a group just maintained the status quo. In terms of population, the losers outnumbered the gainers 958 million to 594 million.[4] They also outproduced the gainers 133 million metric tons to 108 million metric tons. However, on the per capita bases, the gainers faired much better, producing .18 metric tons to .14 metric tons for the losers.

The data in Table 3.3 and in Figure 3.2 illustrate the rela-

---

[4] The countries in South America were included in the gainers in this example.

TABLE 3.2

Changes in World Population and Grain Production, 1954–55 to 1965–66

| Region* | Population | | Total Grain Production | | Per Capita Grain Production | | Growth Rate Grain Production | | |
|---|---|---|---|---|---|---|---|---|---|
| | 1954–55 | 1965–66 | 1954–55 | 1965–66 | 1954–55 | 1965–66 | Population | Total | Per capita |
| | (million) | | (million metric tons) | | (metric tons) | | (percent) | | |
| Developed Countries | 588.9 | 671.4 | 265.7 | 353.3 | .451 | .526 | 1.2 | 2.6 | 1.4 |
| Centrally Planned Countries | 933.8 | 1,157.9 | 258.6 | 313.0 | .277 | .270 | 2.0 | 1.8 | −0.2 |
| Less Developed Countries Developing | 1,194.9 | 1,562.5 | 189.5 | 240.8 | .159 | .154 | 2.4 | 2.2 | −0.2 |
| Asia | | | | | | | | | |
| West | 66.9 | 89.0 | 17.4 | 22.3 | .260 | .251 | 2.6 | 2.3 | −0.3 |
| South | 504.9 | 645.8 | 74.3 | 86.0 | .147 | .133 | 2.2 | 1.3 | −0.9 |
| Southeast | 62.3 | 82.3 | 12.3 | 18.8 | .197 | .228 | 2.6 | 3.9 | 1.3 |
| Other East | 57.3 | 79.0 | 8.6 | 12.0 | .150 | .152 | 3.0 | 3.1 | 0.1 |
| Other Asia | 94.4 | 121.3 | 10.4 | 14.2 | .110 | .117 | 2.3 | 2.9 | 0.6 |
| Africa | | | | | | | | | |
| North | 58.0 | 75.7 | 12.2 | 11.6 | .210 | .153 | 2.4 | 0.4 | −2.8 |
| West | 100.9 | 134.3 | 9.9 | 12.5 | .098 | .093 | 2.6 | 2.1 | −0.5 |
| East | 67.1 | 85.4 | 8.1 | 11.2 | .121 | .131 | 2.2 | 3.0 | 0.8 |
| Latin America | | | | | | | | | |
| South | 124.6 | 168.3 | 28.6 | 38.7 | .230 | .230 | 2.8 | 2.8 | .0 |
| Central (excluding Mexico) | 10.3 | 14.6 | 1.5 | 2.2 | .145 | .151 | 3.2 | 3.5 | 0.3 |
| Caribbean | 18.1 | 23.0 | .6 | .6 | .033 | .026 | 2.3 | | −2.3 |
| Mexico | 30.2 | 43.4 | 5.7 | 10.8 | .189 | .249 | 3.4 | 6.0 | 2.5 |
| World | 2,717.6 | 3,391.8 | 713.8 | 907.1 | .263 | .267 | 2.2 | 2.4 | 0.2 |

* Developed countries include: Canada, United States, Japan, Australia, New Zealand, Republic of South Africa, Western Europe. Centrally planned countries include: U.S.S.R., Albania, Bulgaria, China, Czechoslovakia, Germany (E.), Hungary, Mongolia, North Korea, North Vietnam, Poland, Romania, Yugoslavia. West Asia includes: Iran, Iraq, Israel, Jordan, Saudi Arabia, Syria, Turkey, Lebanon, Other Arab States. South Asia includes: Afghanistan, Bhutan, Ceylon, India, Nepal, and Pakistan. Southeast Asia includes: Burma, Cambodia, Laos, Vietnam Rep. (South), and Thailand. Other East Asia includes: Hong Kong, South Korea, Mocao, Philippines, Taiwan, Ryukyu Is., and Port. Asia. Other Asia includes: Indonesia, Malaysia, and others not elsewhere included. North Africa includes: Algeria, UAR Egypt, Libya, Morocco, Sudan, and Tunisia. West Africa includes: Angola, Cameroon, Central African Republic, Chod, Congo (Leo), Congo (Brazil), Dahomey, Gabon, Gambia, Ghana, Guinea, Ivory Coast, Liberia, Mali, Mauritania, Niger, Nigeria, Upper Volta, Port. Africa, Port. Guinea, and Togo. East Africa includes: All countries and islands not elsewhere included in Africa.

## TABLE 3.3
RELATIVE DIFFERENCES AMONG REGIONS IN PER CAPITA GRAIN PRODUCTION
PERCENT OF WORLD PER CAPITA GRAIN PRODUCTION

| Regions | Per Capita | | |
|---|---|---|---|
| | 1954–55 | 1959–61 | 1965–66 |
| | | *(percent)* | |
| North America | 336 | 367 | 377 |
| Japan and South Asia | 57 | 59 | 50 |
| Oceania | 241 | 283 | 320 |
| Western Europe | 103 | 109 | 119 |
| South Africa | 132 | 135 | 124 |
| U.S.S.R. | 168 | 170 | 168 |
| Communist Asia and North Africa | 71 | 62 | 60 |
| Eastern Europe | 164 | 190 | 204 |
| W. Africa and Other Asia and Oceania | 50 | 38 | 39 |
| West Asia and South America | 91 | 86 | 89 |
| Southeast Asia and Mexico | 74 | 81 | 88 |
| Caribbean | 12 | 12 | 9 |
| World (metric tons) | 100 = .263 | 100 = .265 | 100 = .267 |

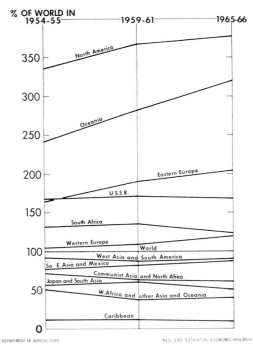

Fig. 3.2—Relative difference among regions in per capita grain production, 1959–61.

tive differences that have emerged between regions of the world in per capita grain production since 1954–66. World grain production per capita was almost constant during the 1954–66 period, being 263 kilos in 1954–55; 265 kilos in 1959–61; and 267 kilos in 1965–66. The data in Figure 3.2 for all regions are expressed in terms of percentage of the world level. On a world basis it can be seen that North America, Oceania, Eastern Europe, Western Europe, Southeast Asia, and Mexico gained ground relative to the world in per capita grain production. These regions, of course, produce the major share of the world's food—about 47 percent of the world's grain production in 1965–66.

Another way of looking at the progress in grain production is to compare one region's performance over time with its own record in some base year. Such a comparison is given in Table 3.4 in terms of indices where 1959–61 is equal to 100. Inspection of these indices reveals that 1963 and 1964 were exceptionally good years for the less developed countries, while 1965 and 1966 were exceptionally bad years. For the centrally planned countries 1966 represented a banner year—the best one in a decade.

## CURRENT FOOD PRODUCTION TRENDS

A closer look at particular regions in Table 3.4 shows that most of the loss in the recent population-food grains race can be attributed to South Asia and North Africa. North Africa, in fact, has been in an uneven downward trend in per capita grain production since 1954 with 1966 representing only a nightmare at the end of a 12-year bad dream. On the other hand, South Asia, and here I am talking predominantly about India and Pakistan, has been making slow but certain progress in per capita grain production throughout this past decade, only to be set back by bad weather in 1965 and 1966. The outlook for winning the food production race would look very dark indeed if we looked only at the data in Table 3.4 and Figure 3.1. Current estimates for India suggest that grain production has regained some of its predrought level and, hopefully, 1968 will see a return to the previous long-term upward trend in per capita grain production. Because India looms so large in the total picture of the less developed world, its progress, or lack of progress, in grain production actually sets the pace for the aggregate picture for the whole less developed free world. For example, the food-production population race for the free less developed countries

## TABLE 3.4

INDICES OF WORLD GRAIN PRODUCTION, TOTAL AND PER CAPITA, 1954–66 (1959–61 = 100)

| Region* | 1954 | 1955 | 1956 | 1957 | 1958 | 1959 | 1960 | 1961 | 1962 | 1963 | 1964 | 1965 | 1966 |
|---|---|---|---|---|---|---|---|---|---|---|---|---|---|
| *(total grain production)* | | | | | | | | | | | | | |
| World | 86 | 92 | 95 | 95 | 101 | 99 | 101 | 99 | 105 | 106 | 109 | 109 | 117 |
| Developed Countries | 82 | 88 | 88 | 89 | 99 | 99 | 105 | 95 | 103 | 108 | 104 | 111 | 114 |
| Centrally Planned Countries | 88 | 101 | 105 | 104 | 109 | 100 | 97 | 102 | 105 | 98 | 110 | 105 | 124 |
| Less Developed Countries Developing | 89 | 86 | 92 | 91 | 96 | 98 | 101 | 101 | 107 | 113 | 115 | 111 | 111 |
| *(per capita grain production)* | | | | | | | | | | | | | |
| World | 97 | 102 | 103 | 100 | 106 | 99 | 102 | 97 | 101 | 100 | 101 | 99 | 104 |
| Developed | 88 | 93 | 93 | 93 | 101 | 100 | 106 | 94 | 101 | 104 | 99 | 105 | 107 |
| Centrally Planned | 99 | 112 | 114 | 110 | 113 | 103 | 97 | 100 | 101 | 93 | 102 | 95 | 111 |
| Less Developed | 102 | 97 | 101 | 97 | 101 | 100 | 101 | 99 | 102 | 105 | 104 | 98 | 96 |
| Asia | | | | | | | | | | | | | |
| Communist | 116 | 123 | 124 | 122 | 121 | 106 | 97 | 97 | 104 | 102 | 102 | 99 | 98 |
| West | 105 | 109 | 111 | 128 | 107 | 100 | 102 | 98 | 109 | 114 | 100 | 104 | 102 |
| South | 98 | 94 | 97 | 93 | 96 | 98 | 102 | 100 | 97 | 100 | 100 | 88 | 86 |
| Southeast | 83 | 90 | 100 | 80 | 96 | 100 | 102 | 99 | 107 | 110 | 105 | 100 | 100 |
| Other East | 101 | 99 | 93 | 93 | 101 | 101 | 97 | 102 | 95 | 91 | 101 | 97 | 106 |
| Oceania & Other Asia | 112 | 99 | 97 | 95 | 103 | 99 | 105 | 97 | 108 | 99 | 104 | 115 | 110 |
| Africa | | | | | | | | | | | | | |
| North | 136 | 117 | 127 | 105 | 117 | 109 | 111 | 80 | 113 | 118 | 103 | 106 | 80 |
| West | 101 | 102 | 101 | 107 | 101 | 100 | 102 | 97 | 103 | 105 | 101 | 99 | 95 |
| East | 95 | 94 | 98 | 99 | 103 | 99 | 101 | 100 | 108 | 104 | 102 | 101 | 104 |
| Latin America | | | | | | | | | | | | | |
| South | 115 | 96 | 109 | 98 | 105 | 103 | 95 | 102 | 100 | 111 | 119 | 105 | 106 |
| Central | 110 | 110 | 109 | 100 | 100 | 101 | 100 | 99 | 109 | 106 | 108 | 108 | 122 |
| Caribbean | 106 | 104 | 112 | 109 | 98 | 105 | 103 | 92 | 91 | 76 | 75 | 79 | 78 |
| Mexico | 93 | 91 | 93 | 95 | 104 | 104 | 98 | 98 | 108 | 109 | 115 | 121 | 120 |

* See Table 3.2 for countries included in region.

as shown in Figure 3.1 is very similar to the index of grain production for South Asia as shown in Table 3.4. The dotted line
for 1965 and 1966 indicates that the drought in India may have
been only an interruption to a long-term upward trend. The
indices of per capita grain production in Table 3.4 show that
only South Asia, North Africa, and the Caribbean have fallen
behind in recent years, while all other regions have actually
recorded substantial progress.

So what we actually have is a selective food crisis rather than
a food crisis uniformly distributed throughout the less developed
world. More specifically, the stork appears to be outrunning the
plow in South Asia, Communist Asia, North and West Africa,
and the Caribbean.[5]

## IMPLICATIONS OF PRESENT TRENDS

In the light of current population growth rates, the food shortage
crisis is likely to remain critical, or almost critical, in the present
food shortage areas of South Asia, Mainland China, and North
Africa. It is in these regions where the pressure for increased food
production is greatest and probably will be hardest to achieve. In
1966 these areas or regions accounted for about 45 percent of the
world's population and 65 percent of the less developed world.
While there are, and will continue to be, food deficit problems
for some time in most of the less developed countries, the most
critical food shortages have recently been in South Asia and in
Mainland China. It is in these areas of the world where the problems of increasing food production per capita and agricultural
productivity are likely to be greatest also.

About two years ago an FAO official outlined the implications of the world food problem and indicated the nature of the
task that lay ahead if food needs of the less developed countries
were to be met. According to him:

By 1980, if present trends continue, there will be another one billion
people to be fed. It has been estimated that for every increase of 100
million in the population, an estimated 13 million tons of cereals and
more than 14 million tons of meat, milk, eggs, and fish will have to be
produced to meet pressing needs. Thus, the world's farmers will be
facing a minimum needed food production increase in the order of
130 million tons of cereals and 140 million tons of animal products, or a
33 percent increase in cereal production and 100 percent increase in

---

[5] Lester R. Brown, "The Stork Outruns the Plow," *Columbia Jour. of
World Business,* Vol. II, No. 1, Jan.–Feb. 1967.

milk, meat, eggs, and fish. It seems inconceivable that increases of this magnitude can be achieved unless far-reaching changes are made in the world's agricultural production policies, especially in those countries already feeling the heaviest pressures.[6]

Another but more recent analysis of the world food problem paints a somewhat brighter picture. According to this USDA study, by 1970 total world supply of grain will be about in balance.[7] The results of this study further conclude that by 1980, if the historical rates of increase in grain production in the grain-importing less developed countries continue, they would need to increase their grain imports from 29 million metric tons in 1964 and 1965 to between 54 and 58 million metric tons to meet minimum requirements. If this historical rate of grain production were moderately improved, the import requirements would fall to about 52 million metric tons. If a 4 percent growth rate could be achieved, which is considered unlikely, grain imports in 1980 would be about the same level as in 1964 and 1965. Finally, this study concludes that the world grain production capacity would be adequate to meet these demands. The problems that would arise would be those of getting the surplus grain produced in the developed and grain-exporting less developed countries distributed to the food deficit less developed countries through normal trade or increased aid programs. Because of these problems, the long-run solution to continued food shortages obviously lies in the increasing of production and productive capacities in the food deficit countries.

## POSSIBILITIES FOR INCREASING AGRICULTURAL PRODUCTION

According to the FAO official previously mentioned, "There appears to be no doubt that the application of man's existing knowledge to farming practice, in all its aspects, would be adequate to take care of human food needs, possibly to the end of this century."[8] There is doubt, however, that it will be applied and, especially, in those countries where the proportion engaged in agriculture is highest and where increases in agricultural production and productivity are most imperative. What this means is that since sustained increases in agricultural productivity tend

---

[6] I. E. Fischnich, "The Possibilities of Expanding Food Production by 1980," *Development Digest,* Vol. V, No. 2, July 1967.

[7] Abel and Rojko.

[8] Fischnich.

to be closely tied to general economic growth, the problem of increasing food production turns out to be as complex as the growth process itself.

The prospects for increasing grain production to meet world food needs are very promising and feasible in the developed countries. In fact, according to a recent USDA study, there probably will still be some excess productive capacity in most of the developed countries by 1980.[9] The prospects for increasing food production are also promising in some of the developing countries such as Mexico, Costa Rica, Taiwan, Thailand, Burma, and Brazil.[10] However, the outlook does not appear too bright in many of the less developed countries for increasing their grain production enough to meet their minimum requirements by 1980. This is not to say that grain production, both total and per capita, will not be increased in these countries. Rather, it means that production probably cannot be stepped up enough to offset the rising demand for food from a rapidly rising population and income.

Let us now look at the food production problem in terms of possibilities for getting increases in specific regions. To gain a better insight into the nature of the task involved I have outlined some general production goals that I have called self-sufficient grain requirement levels. These levels are based upon the production and net export or import data for all countries in 1965 and 1966. In this chapter, I will refer to the residuals between production and net imports and exports as approximate utilization or requirement levels. These levels are obviously related to the level of income and development, as well as the calorie requirements in the low income countries.

I have arranged the countries in order of their level of income and level of per capita grain production and consumption in Table 3.5 and Figure 3.3. The high income countries, as can be observed, are producing far in excess of their grain requirements of .7 metric ton per capita. Thus they are shown to be in a net export position. As we go slightly down the income scale to France and Western Europe, we find a lower per capita grain requirement for utilization and production. While France is a net exporter, Western Europe is a net importer, primarily because of its lower per capita grain production. What is assumed here is that as the per capita income level rises in Western

[9] Abel and Rojko.
[10] "Changes in Agriculture in 26 Developing Nations: 1948 to 1963," FAER-27, USDA, Nov. 1965.

TABLE 3.5

RELATIONSHIP OF GRAIN PRODUCTION AND UTILIZATION PER CAPITA TO LEVEL
OF INCOME OR DEVELOPMENT, 1965–66

| Country and Income Level* | Production | | | Approximate Utilization† | | | Net Trade Position | |
|---|---|---|---|---|---|---|---|---|
| | High | Med. | Low | High | Med. | Low | Ex-ports | Im-ports |
| | *(metric tons)* | | | *(metric tons)* | | | *(metric tons)* | |
| **High** | | | | | | | | |
| Canada | 1.81 | ... | ... | 1.14 | ... | ... | .64 | ... |
| Australia | 1.02 | ... | ... | ... | .49 | ... | .62 | ... |
| United States | .93 | ... | ... | .72 | ... | ... | .21 | ... |
| **Medium High** | | | | | | | | |
| France | ... | .56 | ... | ... | .45 | ... | .11 | ... |
| Western Europe | ... | ... | .32 | ... | .50 | ... | ... | .18 |
| **Medium** | | | | | | | | |
| Eastern Europe | ... | .55 | ... | .61 | ... | ... | ... | .06 |
| U.S.S.R. | ... | .50 | ... | .52 | ... | ... | ... | .02 |
| Japan | ... | ... | .14 | ... | .24 | ... | ... | .10 |
| **Medium Low** | | | | | | | | |
| Argentina | ... | .69 | ... | ... | ... | .21 | .48 | ... |
| Mexico | ... | ... | .25 | ... | ... | .21 | .04 | ... |
| South Africa | ... | ... | .33 | ... | .31 | ... | .02 | ... |
| **Low** | | | | | | | | |
| South Asia | ... | ... | .13‡ | ... | ... | .20 | ... | .05 |
| India | ... | ... | .13‡ | ... | ... | .19 | ... | .06 |
| Pakistan | ... | ... | .18 | ... | ... | .20 | ... | .02 |
| Southeast Asia | ... | ... | .23 | ... | ... | .18 | .05 | ... |
| Burma | ... | ... | .23 | ... | ... | .17 | .06 | ... |
| Cambodia | ... | ... | .28 | ... | ... | .19 | .09 | ... |
| Thailand | ... | ... | .24 | ... | ... | .16 | .08 | ... |
| West Asia | ... | ... | .25 | ... | .27 | ... | ... | .02 |
| Other East Asia | ... | ... | .15 | ... | ... | .18 | ... | .03 |
| Other Asia & Oceania | ... | ... | .12 | ... | ... | .16 | ... | .04 |
| North Africa | ... | ... | .15 | ... | ... | .19 | ... | .04 |
| South America | ... | ... | .23 | ... | ... | .21 | ... | .04 |
| Central America | ... | ... | .15 | ... | ... | .19 | ... | .04 |

* For countries included in regions, see footnote at bottom of Table 3.2.
† Includes approximate consumption requirements for self-sufficiency at this level of income; it also includes stocks when appropriate. For simplicity of presentation, these requirements and/or utilization levels have been rounded up to the nearest hundredth of a metric ton. However, since these data are intended to portray only an approximate self-sufficient level of grain requirements, they need not necessarily coincide exactly with other published estimates of consumption.
‡ Due to a 2-year drought in India, production fell from .15 metric tons per capita in 1963 and 1964 to .13 metric tons per capita.

Europe and approaches the level of North America, grain utilization is likely also to rise. That is, the shaded areas in Figure 3.3 indicating approximate grain requirements in 1965–66 would be moved upward with increased income. These higher levels of utilization are reflected in the 1980 estimated requirements in Table 3.6 for all regions. If per capita grain production does not keep pace with this increased utilization by 1980, imports will

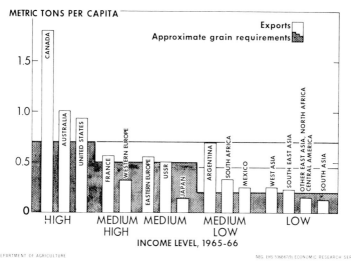

U.S. DEPARTMENT OF AGRICULTURE NEG. ERS 5366(7)9) ECONOMIC RESEARCH SERVICE

*Fig. 3.3—Grain production and utilization per capita related to level of income or development, 1965–66.*

also rise in Western Europe. Even with a continuation of its 1960–66 growth rate in grain production to 1980, Western Europe would still take 35 years to reach self-sufficiency if her grain requirements inched upward during this time.

At present France is in a net export position. With a current per capita growth rate in grain production of 3 percent per year since 1960 and a probable growth rate projected at 2 percent per year per capita, France does not appear to be in danger of losing her current net export position between now and 1980 (Table 3.6). You will note that I have assumed that grain requirements will rise from .45 to .6 metric ton by 1980 as shown in Table 3.6. A slower rate of increase in requirements with current production levels would probably not be consistent with economic growth and trade policies.

Moving farther down the income scale, we see that in Eastern Europe and U.S.S.R., per capita grain production was about equal to that of France. But, because of their higher level of grain utilization or requirements,[11] these countries were forced into a small net import position during the 1960's when short-

[11] These data appear to overstate the utilization levels for Eastern Europe when compared to Western Europe. In the absence of more reliable data, I have assumed the production data, as reported, to be correct even though logic would suggest a small downward adjustment is needed.

# TABLE 3.6
## RELATION OF GRAIN PRODUCTION AND UTILIZATION PER CAPITA UNDER DIFFERENT PRODUCTION ASSUMPTIONS TO LENGTH OF TIME TO OBTAIN SELF-SUFFICIENCY

| Country and Income Level* | 1960-66 Growth Rate | 1965-66 Level | Probable Growth Rate to 1980 Per capita | Probable Growth Rate to 1980 Total | Estimated 1980 Self-sufficiency Requirements‡ | Years To Gain Self-sufficiency With 1960-66 growth rate | Years To Gain Self-sufficiency With probable growth rate |
|---|---|---|---|---|---|---|---|
| | (percent) | (metric tons) | (percent) | (percent) | (metric tons) | (member) | (member) |
| **High** | | | | | | | |
| Canada | 3.1 | 1.80 | 2.0 | 4.0 | .8 | Exporter | Exporter |
| Australia | 2.3 | 1.85 | 2.0 | 4.1 | .5 | Exporter | Exporter |
| United States | 0.0 | .92 | 1.0 | 3.6 | .8 | Exporter | Exporter |
| **Medium High** | | | | | | | |
| France | 3.0 | .56 | 2.0 | 3.3 | .6 | 2 | 4 |
| Western Europe (include France) | 1.8 | .32 | 1.5 | 2.5 | .6 | 35 | 42 |
| **Medium** | | | | | | | |
| Eastern Europe | 1.3 | .55 | 1.5 | 2.2 | .6 | 7 | 6 |
| U.S.S.R. | 1.7 | .50 | 1.5 | 3.1 | .6 | 11 | 12 |
| Japan | -2.7 | .14 | 1.0 | 2.0 | .3 | Importer | Importer |
| **Medium Low** | | | | | | | |
| Argentina | 0.0 | .69 | 0.5 | 2.1 | .3 | Exporter | Exporter |
| Mexico | 3.1 | .25 | 2.0 | 5.2 | .3 | 6 | 9 |
| South Africa | -0.1 | .33 | 1.0 | 3.4 | .4 | Importer | 19 |
| **Low** | | | | | | | |
| South Asia | -2.3 | .13 (15)† | 1.0 | 3.0 | .2 | Importer | 50+ (29)† |
| India | -2.4 | .13 (15)† | 1.0 | 3.3 | .2 | Importer | 50+ (29)† |
| Pakistan | 0.2 | .17 | 1.0 | 4.0 | .2 | Importer | 16 |
| Southeast Asia | 0.1 | .23 | 0.5 | 2.9 | .2 | Exporter | Exporter |
| Burma | 0.0 | .23 | 0.5 | 2.5 | .2 | Exporter | Exporter |
| Cambodia | 0.0 | .28 | 0.5 | 3.5 | .2 | Exporter | Exporter |
| Thailand | 2.2 | .24 | 2.0 | 5.0 | .2 | Exporter | Exporter‡ |
| West Asia | 0.4 | .25 | 0.5 | 2.9 | .3 | 45 | 37 |
| Other East Asia | 0.2 | .15 | 0.5 | 3.6 | .2 | 50+ | 40+ |
| Other Asia & Oceania | 1.9 | .12 | 1.3 | 3.6 | .2 | 28 | 40 |
| North Africa | -1.3 | .15 | .5 | 2.8 | .3 | Importer | Importer |
| South America | 0.9 | .23 | 1.0 | 3.7 | .3 | 30 | 26 |
| Central America | 2.3 | .15 | 2.0 | 4.7 | .2 | 8 | 10 |

* For countries included in regions, see Table 3.2.
† Without drought in India, production would probably have been .15 metric tons, which was what they attained in 1963 and 1964.
‡ Based in part on data found in Martin E. Abel and Anthony S. Rojko, *World Food Situation, Prospects for World Grain Production, Conservation and Trade,*" FAER-35, USDA, 1967.

falls appeared in their production. The current net export position for Eastern Europe suggests that these countries, as a group,
are operating about at self-sufficient levels. A probable growth
rate of about 1.5 percent per year between now and 1980 would
leave them in about the same relative position, as their per capita
grain utilization is projected to rise very slowly. However, a
faster growth rate in per capita grain production than 1.5 percent
per year would enable them to maintain a small net export position; that is, provided their per capita grain utilization did not
exceed .6 of metric ton by 1980.

Japan has had a decline in her per capita grain production
since 1960. Consequently, her grain imports have increased
during this period to keep pace with her grain utilization level
which has moved upward with the rapid rise in per capita income
level. A projected increase in per capita grain production of
about 1 percent per year would be far from adequate to meet her
rising level of grain utilization. Yet, a higher growth rate than 1
percent does not appear to be feasible in light of her performance
since 1960. The recent decline in the per capita growth rate in
grain production would suggest that an even slower growth rate,
or at least a leveling off of the recent decline, would be more
realistic. Thus Japan is expected to remain indefinitely as a net
grain importer.

In the medium-low income group of countries, Argentina
and the Republic of South Africa are projected to slightly increase their per capita grain production between now and 1980.
Even at this slow rate of increase, their per capita level of grain
utilization will probably remain rather low—about .3 metric ton
per capita. At this projected level of utilization, Argentina will
still be able to export over half her production. While South
Africa will probably still have to import some grain, she is likely
to remain a net grain importer unless she is able to step up greatly her per capita grain production beyond the 1 percent rate
projected to 1980 (Table 3.6).

Mexico, on the other hand, has only recently passed from a
net grain import to a net grain export position, primarily because
of her rapid growth rate in grain production since 1960. Should
this rate be maintained until 1980, she would still be able to out-
produce her own growing utilization level and, thereby, enjoy a
modest net export position by 1980. However, if her per capita
growth rate falls to about 2 percent annually, her relatively small
net export position would remain nearly unchanged. This conclusion is based upon an extrapolation of growth rates of production and utilization as shown in Table 3.6.

We come now to the low income countries. One or two things become rather apparent from the data in Tables 3.5 and 3.6: (a) the production and utilization levels are rather uniformly low, being around .2 metric ton per capita, and (b) the majority of the countries and regions will still have to rely on imports in 1980 even with increased rates of per capita grain production.[12] In other words, only the countries of Southeast Asia are expected to remain net grain exporters while the other less developed countries will fall far short of reaching their estimated self-sufficient levels of about .2 metric ton per capita in 1980. Only Central America appears to have a fighting chance to achieve self-sufficiency in grain production in about 8 years with a continuation of the 1960–66 growth rate. However, this goal could be reached within 10 years with a growth rate of 2 percent per year, which would represent a slight slackening in the present growth rate of 2.3 percent.

West Asia, because of its higher level of grain utilization than other less developed countries, appears to be an exception to the general case being explored. An examination of the production and consumption data for these countries shows a higher historical dependency upon grain than other less developed countries. Even though they are shown in a net export position in Figure 3.3, they are actually net importers, as shown in Table 3.5. Actually, a fourth general requirement level in Figure 3.3 should be drawn for these countries at .3 metric ton per capita. You will note that I have projected this level of utilization for these countries in Table 3.6 for 1980. At their present slow growth rate in per capita grain production, they are likely to remain net grain importers until the end of this century—unless, of course, something can be done to step up their grain production.

Perhaps I should point out one more thing about the prospects of increasing grain production in South Asia. From an examination of the data earlier in Table 3.3, it would seem that two bad crop years in India, which dropped her per capita grain production from .15 to .13 metric ton, were an exception to the long-term trend. The present prospects in India strongly indicate that production may be on the rebound. However, unless India experiences at least a moderate improvement in her grain production, per capita grain production will fail to increase. Should total grain production undergo a rapid improvement between now and 1980 to about 4 percent per year, it would still take

---

[12] Abel and Rojko.

about 30 years for India to obtain the goal of self-sufficiency in food grain production. However, at this rate of growth India would be able to greatly reduce her level of grain imports by 1980.[13]

The 1967 monsoon season has brought the best rains to India in three years, raising the hopes of Indian officials for a grain crop that may surpass the 1964–65 record of 88.9 million metric tons. However, with population growing at 12 million a year (one year's increase in India equals Australia's total population), India will continue to face rapid increases in food demand.

To help foster greater food production, India is (a) increasing domestic fertilizer production, (b) instituting a policy of forward pricing or at least announcing preseason price support levels for farm products, and (c) expanding her information and extension programs to help educate her farmers to adopt modern farming methods. During 1967 and 1968, India plans to invest about $533 million in agriculture—an increase of 42 percent over 1966. It is hoped that these policies will not only increase the production on existing acres but will also make a start on a program that is designed to bring about 10 million additional acres into cultivation by 1970–71.

The problems of increasing grain production have been large, but increased investments in irrigation and other advances in adaptable farm technologies hold out the promise of increased production potentials in India. Among some of these adaptable technologies are the development of new varieties for India's major cereal crops—rice, wheat, jowar, bajar, and maize. These new varieties may do for India what corn hybrids did for Midwestern agriculture in the United States in the 1940's. From 1940–41 to 1954–55 U.S. corn production for grain grew 1.4 percent per year, accelerated to 6.7 percent from 1954–55 to 1959–60, before being reduced to less than 1.0 percent since 1959–60 by the acreage-control program. During this time, yields per acre more than doubled. It will take technological breakthroughs of this nature if India is to achieve a rapid improvement in her grain production of about 4 percent per year. Should she be able to achieve a 5 percent growth rate in grain production, her goal of self-sufficiency in grain production could be achieved within less than a decade. Such an attainment, which appears unlikely, would help India meet new needs from a population and per capita income growth. It would also enable

---

[13] *Ibid.*, pp. 16–17.

her to gain the necessary growth momentum required to carry her to within reach of self-sufficiency in food grains in the near-term future.

## IMPLICATIONS FOR NORTH AMERICAN AGRICULTURE

The results of recent studies of the world food production and utilization prospects suggest a continued near-term dependency of some less developed countries upon the productive capacity of the high income exporting countries for a vital part of the grain supply. It also suggests that the farmers of North America and Australia will have a vital interest in the success of economic growth programs and efforts in less developed countries in raising their own agricultural productivity and levels of income. This statement may sound paradoxical at first but a closer examination of the data shows that where countries are able to achieve high rates of economic growth, their imports of agricultural products have also increased.[14] And, since North America and Australia are the major sources of grain supplies, the rapidly developing countries will continue to look to these grain exporting countries for a major proportion of their increased imports.

Increasing food and grain production in the less developed countries will probably not materially affect Western Europe as it is likely to remain a grain importer. However, increased production in the less developed countries is likely to have an impact on world grain trade, grain prices, and rate of growth in grain production in North America and Australia. This impact would be felt more upon food grain rather than feed grain production. The world demand for feed grains will continue to be in Western Europe and Japan where rising incomes will step up the demand for meat and livestock products—the production of which is likely to rely more heavily in the future on grains rather than forage. Some demand for feed grains will probably continue to develop in the rapidly growing developing countries as they pass through higher stages of economic development, but this demand is not likely to expand too rapidly in the near-term future.

Improvements in food grain production in the less developed countries will have major implications for the United States.

[14] Arthur B. Mackie, "Foreign Economic Growth and Market Potentials for U.S. Agricultural Products," FAER-24, USDA, Apr. 1965. See also, John R. Schaub and Arthur B. Mackie, "U.S. Agricultural Exports and Foreign Economic Growth," *Agr. Econ. Res.*, Vol. XIX, No. 2.

Programs to raise farm incomes and production will have to be adjusted to meet different types of demand growing out of rising incomes abroad, thereby affecting the composition of production for commercial exports and the nature and level of future food aid. I will not elaborate on these implications since, I believe, these subjects will be covered in subsequent chapters. However, I would like to say that a solution to the world food problem is likely to involve a greater cooperation among countries to achieve a more optimum utilization of the world's resources. Such cooperation will have to take place at many levels—international monetary and trade policies, international production and marketing programs, international programs to facilitate capital and labor mobility, international agricultural research and educational programs, as well as international aid programs. The adoption of some, or all, of these programs will involve a higher degree of integration of efforts and markets than currently exists.

# PART TWO

# Capacity of North American Agriculture

# CHAPTER FOUR

# Trends and Capacity
# of United States Agriculture

EARL O. HEADY, LEO V. MAYER
and A. GORDON BALL

THE NORTH AMERICAN CONTINENT is today the most adequately fed of the world's continents. The question of whether it can feed itself in a relevant planning period is not the pressing problem of the day. It can do so readily, even though some problems of food distribution and policies to assure adequate diets for all do exist within the continent and all nations of it. The more important questions over the long run are: To what extent can this continent help meet the world food gap and will it need to fully use its resources to do so?

In the past many projections of world food needs have been compared with estimates of potential food supplies for the future. Under conventional demographic projections, the picture is dark and every element of potential supply would be required to meet potential demand for world food in the decades ahead. This prospect will certainly come into being if world populations follow the past exponential population trends and no great breakthrough is attained on the cheap physical synthesis of foods from abundant raw materials. This is the danger, but it need not be the outcome. The variables relating to population growth

EARL O. HEADY, Department of Economics and Center for Agricultural and Economic Development, Iowa State University; LEO V. MAYER, Department of Economics, Iowa State University; A. GORDON BALL, Department of Economics, Iowa State University.

can be altered, just as can those relating to food supply. One prospect in this century is that the demand for food, through family planning, can be bent as much toward a given potential food supply as vice versa.[1] This is the promise of the century, but it will not be attained without more active policies on family planning in the less developed countries. And even then, food supplies may be inadequate by the end of the century.

Along this line, Kristensen and recent OECD studies suggest a mammoth food gap by the year 2000, with the burden for meeting it falling on the developed countries.[2] Kristensen argues that the comparative advantage in food production lies with the developed countries while the advantage in certain other labor-intensive goods rests with the underdeveloped countries where food is now relatively short. Further, the greatest acreage of arable land is in the developed countries while the majority of the people are in the underdeveloped countries. He concludes that the developed world should produce food and trade for nonfood items of the less developed countries.

While it is not necessarily true that the overall comparative advantage in food production need rest with the developed countries over the long run, this will likely remain true for the next generation. Over this period, population growth will be large because the modern technologies of birth control cannot be effectively disseminated in a shorter time. Thus we can look forward to several stages in the efficient development of food supplies for the world.[3] Different world regions will enjoy relatively different comparative advantages during these periods or stages and there is no reason—except lack of efficient policies—why the less developed countries cannot "arrive at their day." Still, over the rest of this century, the comparative advantage will rest with regions such as North America and Oceania. In the short run of a decade and a half, Secretary Freeman's recent proposal may prevail—the world food problem in the 1980's may

---

[1] For example, see Donald J. Bogue, "The Prospects for World Population Control," *Alternatives for Balancing World Food Production and Needs,* Center for Agricultural and Economic Development, Iowa State Univ. Press, Ames, 1967, pp. 72–85.

[2] Thorkil Kristensen, "The Findings of Economists," Paper presented at the 13th Conference of Agricultural Economists, Sydney, Australia, Aug. 21–30, 1967.

[3] Cf. Earl O. Heady and John F. Timmons, "Objectives, Achievements, and Hazards of the U.S. Food Aid and Agricultural Development Programs in Relation to Domestic Policy," *Alternatives for Balancing World Food Production and Needs,* Center for Agricultural and Economic Development, Iowa State Univ. Press, Ames, 1967, pp. 172–86.

still be one of distribution rather than productive capacity. Whether his optimistic projections of world food balances (which will be reviewed in detail later in this chapter) are realistic is open to discussion. However, ongoing increases in agricultural productivity in the United States are strong evidence that the United States will be able to supply greatly increased quantities to the food-short nations of the world over the next decade or two. Our aim in this chapter is to indicate the magnitude of increased exports which the United States could provide if the need arose.

## SOURCES OF INCREASED FOOD PRODUCTION

While it appears trite to observe that our potential production depends upon land and technology, this is still true, especially for grain. In recent years, the flow of new technology into agriculture has increased, along with a substitution for land. The result is that land resources have been in relative abundance in the United States for three decades, allowing the United States to be largely free from that kind of worry. The 1958 inventory of land resources, designed to determine the total land available and the types of investments needed to continue an abundant acreage of cropland in the United States, indicates that our supply is still large relative to domestic demand and to effective or potential exports. As summarized in Table 4.1, a large quantity of potential cropland in the United States is not now being used to produce crops. Out of the nearly 806 million acres of land in classes I through IV, which are generally defined as including all land available for crop use, only 422 million acres were used for crops in 1958. Even less is so used now because of production control policies. Of Class I land which is considered almost problem free, only 27.4 out of a total of 36.2 million acres were used for crops. Considerable expansion could be made in production with only a small investment on this land.

If large-scale expansion of agricultural production in the United States became a long-run objective, a much larger proportion of the total 806 million acres could be brought under cultivation with more intensive production through appropriate investments in erosion control, drainage, irrigation, and other land improvement measures. Some notion of the types of investments required is given in Table 4.2. Erosion hazard is the greatest deterrent to use of more land for crops. Of the 806 million acres potentially available for crops, 52.5 percent have problems

## TABLE 4.1

LAND AVAILABLE FOR CROP USE IN THE UNITED STATES BY LAND CAPABILITY CLASSES WITH MAJOR LIMITATIONS WITHIN EACH CLASS

| Class of Land and Limitations Restricting Use | Crop-land | Pasture range | Forest— wood-land | Other land | Total land |
|---|---|---|---|---|---|
| | | | *(thousand acres)* | | |
| Total Land Available for Crops* | 422,020 | 167,183 | 182,407 | 34,189 | 805,797 |
| Class I | 27,418 | 3,939 | 3,570 | 1,247 | 36,174 |
| Class II | 192,807 | 42,837 | 43,158 | 11,275 | 290,077 |
| Erosion control needed | 99,327 | 22,824 | 21,249 | 6,382 | 149,782 |
| Drainage problems exist | 58,038 | 9,226 | 15,617 | 3,473 | 86,354 |
| Other soil problems exist | 20,881 | 5,003 | 6,071 | 1,140 | 33,095 |
| Climatic problems exist | 14,561 | 5,784 | 221 | 281 | 20,847 |
| Class III | 152,885 | 66,547 | 77,573 | 13,839 | 310,843 |
| Erosion control needed | 95,350 | 44,884 | 31,390 | 6,331 | 177,954 |
| Drainage problems exist | 27,448 | 10,581 | 30,363 | 5,343 | 73,735 |
| Other soil problems exist | 22,312 | 8,110 | 15,705 | 2,077 | 48,205 |
| Climatic problems exist | 7,775 | 2,972 | 115 | 88 | 10,949 |
| Class IV | 48,910 | 53,860 | 58,106 | 7,828 | 168,703 |
| Erosion control needed | 31,930 | 33,530 | 26,375 | 4,047 | 95,883 |
| Drainage problems exist | 4,995 | 4,913 | 15,541 | 2,088 | 27,536 |
| Other soil problems exist | 10,115 | 13,276 | 16,052 | 1,665 | 41,108 |
| Climatic problems exist | 1,870 | 2,140 | 137 | 28 | 4,176 |

Source: USDA, *Basic Statistics of the National Inventory of Soil and Water Conservation Needs*, Stat. Bull. 317, Aug. 1962.
* Includes Class I through IV land only.

## TABLE 4.2

PROPORTION OF LAND AVAILABLE FOR CROPS AFFECTED BY DIFFERENT LAND-USE LIMITATIONS

| Type of Limitation and Improvement Needed for Crop Use | Crop-land | Pasture range | Forest— wood-land | Other land | Total land |
|---|---|---|---|---|---|
| | | | *(percent)* | | |
| Total Land Available for Crops* | 100.0 | 100.0 | 100.0 | 100.0 | 100.0 |
| Problem free (Class I) | 6.5 | 2.4 | 2.0 | 3.6 | 4.5 |
| Erosion control needed | 53.8 | 60.5 | 43.3 | 49.0 | 52.5 |
| Drainage problems exist | 21.4 | 14.8 | 33.7 | 31.9 | 23.3 |
| Other soil problems exist | 12.6 | 15.8 | 20.7 | 14.3 | 15.2 |
| Climatic problems exist | 5.7 | 6.5 | 0.3 | 1.2 | 4.5 |

Source: USDA, *Basic Statistics of the National Inventory of Soil and Water Conservation Needs*, Stat. Bull. 317, Aug. 1962.
* Includes Class I through IV land only.

of erosion control. Drainage problems are the major limitation restricting use on 23.3 percent. Thus investments in these two programs alone, if expanded adequately, could affect over 75 percent of the total land available for crops. Additional land resources are available in the United States in the event that world food demands require an expansion in grain production, and if the return on the investment in land reclamation and improvement can be brought to an appropriate level. Of course, if more water could be made available for irrigation, the opportunities are vast.

However, even the present U.S. land base for crops provides considerable room for expanding output. Currently, under supply control programs, we have around 50 million acres of cropland held in idleness. Idle acreage increased from 1956 through 1966 as is shown in Figure 4.1. As idle cropland increased, total land used for crop production declined—from 377 million acres in 1950 to 332 million acres in 1966. Acreages of feed grains, wheat, and cotton each declined over the period. Soybeans expanded somewhat as some land released from other crops was used for this purpose. In addition, cropping practices also released land for other uses. Continuous row cropping in the hu-

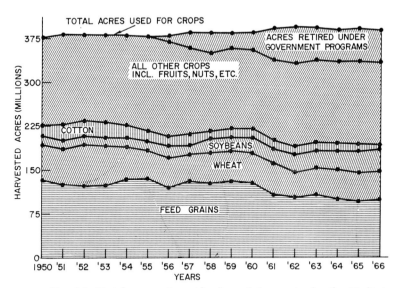

Fig. 4.1—Total acres of cropland used for crops in the United States for the period 1950–66, with the acres retired under government programs indicated for the period 1956–66.

mid areas of the United States, with rotation hays and legumes no longer used as production practices, allowed an increase in available land. This source of additional land freed around 15 million acres for crop use over the period 1950–66. Nine million acres of this land is located in the major Corn Belt states, thus affecting the potential production of feed grains and land retired under government programs.

In addition to these major factors affecting the land available for crops in the United States, the output from each acre affects the total quantity produced. Yield increases in the past have resulted from the efforts of three main groups: (a) farmers who have been willing and financially able to adopt new capital using production technology, (b) a public sector dedicated to improving the efficiency of agricultural production processes, and (c) a private sector which has excelled in supplying new commercial inputs to farms at low real prices. Each of these groups, favored or forced by economic incentives and competition, has contributed toward increased crop yields and output. Each can be expected to continue its efforts at an accelerated rate in a growing commercialization of farming. In addition, impending farm changes will further affect adoption rates of both known technology and future innovation. Some of these more important changes are: (a) the retirement of older farm operators which will accelerate because of their present high average age. As younger farmers take over the cropland released, they will adopt new technology such as continuous row cropping, narrow row planting, heavier fertilizer application, and use of appropriate herbicides and insecticides. Also, younger farmers in general will have less secure capital positions and more need to maximize net income. (b) In addition to increased retirements, projected high employment levels in the remainder of the economy will provide alternative employment opportunities for the inefficient producer who, because of a weak capital position or for other reasons, finds himself unable to compete in the farm industry. As he leaves, his farm will likely be taken over by someone capable of operating it at more nearly an economic optimum, using a plan of operation based on a different capital position, and able and willing to seek out innovations.

As these changes take place on the farms of the nation, the use of modern production technology will become more widespread. The large variation between farms in fertilizer use, for example, will tend to disappear. The variation in seeding rates between farms will also decrease. In general, the new generation

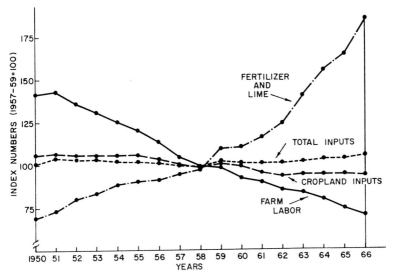

*Fig. 4.2—Trends in input use in U.S. agriculture, 1950–66.*

of farm operators will be more willing not only to make single changes in farm production techniques but also to program a more complete set of changes for increasing yields. These changes in the farm industry, along with a substantial amount of new technology available for the coming years, provide reason for optimism in the outlook for a continued uptrend in crop yields and an increasing amount of food which can be supplied to the rest of the world in the short run.

These changes on individual farms of the United States are already moving at a relentless pace. Fertilizer use has been increasing phenomenally. In fact if one source were to be chosen over others for the greater levels of output, it is the increased use of fertilizer.[4] The point is emphasized in Figure 4.2, showing trends in major input use over the period 1950–66. Total inputs have remained almost constant over the last 15 years. Farm labor has declined to 60 percent of its 1957–59 average. Fertilizer and lime use has nearly tripled.

As a result of the many changes taking place in U.S. agriculture, output of grain has increased considerably over the last 15 years even though acreage has been reduced through govern-

---

[4] For example, see Earl O. Heady and Ludwig Auer, "Imputation of Production to Technologies," *Jour. of Farm Econ.*, Vol. 17, pp. 117–30.

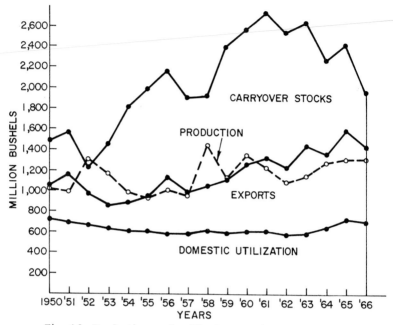

*Fig. 4.3—Production and utilization of wheat by years 1950–66, with stocks at end of marketing year.*

ment policies. Indeed over most of that period the United States has been concerned with surplus stocks of government-held grain. As is evident in Figure 4.3 for wheat and Figure 4.4 for feed grains, production exceeded domestic and export use during most of the 1950's. The excess of production over utilization in any given year was quite small, but the result was a slow buildup of stocks of grains, particularly feed grains. Variability of wheat yields and production caused wheat to be more erratic, with wheat production exceeding use by nearly 40 percent in 1958. A large increase in stocks resulted.

Adequate means for controlling output of grains were finally agreed upon early in the 1960's. The result was a slow decline in total stocks. Then two successive years of poor growing weather in India in 1965–66 also caused a further reduction. In response, through policy measures, larger acreages of most grain crops were produced in the United States in 1967. In general the magnitude of these crops also supports the thesis that the immediate potential of the United States to supply additional quantities of grain to the world is still large—so large in fact

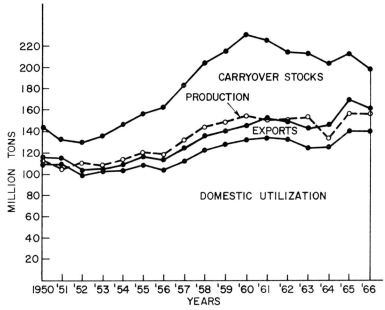

*Fig. 4.4—Production and utilization of feed grains by years 1950–66, with stocks at end of feed year.*

that wheat and feed grain acreage has again been reduced for 1968.

If nothing else, the information in Figures 4.3 and 4.4 reminds us that the rate of supply increase need not exceed demand growth by much to bring forth large potential surpluses plus the need for huge public expenditures to curtail output. As we point out later, when we evaluate U.S. food capacity in terms of implied world food needs, it is more sensible to invest in aids directed at population control than to invest too rapidly in expanding supply with complementary investment for restraining this same supply. Rather than to overinvest in land improvement in the short run, other policies should be emphasized. The potential land base will still be there when it is needed.

## PROJECTING THE CAPACITY OF U.S. AGRICULTURE

The capacity of U.S. agriculture has received a great deal of attention over the last 20 years from both research and policy-making persons. Almost every major study projecting the future

## TABLE 4.3

### Projected and Actual Acre Yields of Grains, United States: 1950, 1965, 1975, and 1980

| | 1950 | | 1965 | | | 1975 | | | | 1980 |
| | Proj.* | Actual | Proj.† | Actual | Proj.‡ | Proj.§ "B" | Proj.§ "A" | Proj.‖ attainable | Proj.‖ maximum | Proj.¶ |
|---|---|---|---|---|---|---|---|---|---|---|
| Wheat (bu.) | 13.3 | 16.5 | 14.6 | 26.5 | 23 | 19.8 | 25.0 | 24 | 27 | 25 |
| Corn (bu.) | 33.8 | 37.6 | 35.8 | 73.8 | 51 | 55.0 | 80.0 | 53 | 61 | 57 |
| Oats (bu.) | | | 36.5 | 50.2 | 39 | 42.0 | 60.0 | 42 | 52 | 44 |
| Barley (bu.) | | | | 42.9 | 32 | | | 35 | 42 | 37 |
| Gr. Sorghum (bu.) | | | | 51.6 | 32 | 26.6 | 32.0 | 35 | 42 | 37 |
| Soybeans (bu.) | 22.5 | 21.7 | 21.9 | 24.5 | 24 | 26.3 | 32.9 | 26 | 30 | 27 |
| Potatoes (cwt.) | 88.8 | 152.6 | 114.0 | 207.0 | | 164.4 | 227.4 | 208 | 276 | 221 |
| Cotton (lb.) | 261.0 | 269.0 | 315.0 | 526.0 | 480 | 401.8 | 500.0 | 495 | 616 | 539 |
| Tobacco (lb.) | 1,023.0 | 1,269.0 | 1,200.0 | 1,898.0 | | 1,378.0 | 1,566.0 | 1,422 | 1,541 | 1.453 |

Source: D. Gale Johnson, "Prospects of Food Supply in Highly Developed Regions," *Food—One Tool in International Economic Development*, Iowa State Univ. Press, 1962. Johnson noted that he was indebted to James Bonnen, Michigan State Univ., for bringing together most of the material included in the table.

\* USDA, "What Peace Can Mean to American Farmers; Postwar Agriculture and Employment," Misc. Pub. 562, May 1945.

† "Long-Range Agricultural Policy: A Study of Selected Trends and Factors Relating to the Long-Range Prospects for Agriculture," Committee on Agriculture, U.S. House of Representatives, 80th Cong., 2nd Sess., Washington, D.C., March 1948, p. 46.

‡ USDA, "Farm Production Trends, Prospects, and Programs," Agr. Inf. Bull. 239, May 1961, p. 92.

§ "Resources for Freedom: A Report to the President's Materials Policy Commission" (The Paley Commission), June 1952, Vol. V, p. 66. The "A" yield estimate "based on the assumption that all commercial agriculture of the U.S. is organized and managed to make full use of all available technology where such use would add more to farm receipts than to expenses." The "B" estimate was formulated on the basis of "a projection to 1975 of the yield likely to come about from such application of available techniques as can reasonably be expected on the basis of past experience."

‖ USDA, "Our Farm Production Potential, 1975," Agr. Inf. Bull. 233, Sept. 1960, p. 6. "*The economic maximum yield* is based on full, efficient economic application of presently known technology under assumed economic conditions. *Economic attainable yields* are yields that would be expected by 1975, from actual application by farmers of presently known technology." (*Ibid.*, p. 3).

¶ USDA, "Land and Water Potentials and Future Requirements for Water," A Report to the Senate Select Committee on National Water Resources, 86th Cong., 1st Sess., Committee Print 12, Dec. 1959, p. 28.

capacity of American agriculture has erred on the side of under-estimation, as indicated by the summary of those studies in Table 4.3. In a study completed in 1945, the USDA projected crop yields and resulting farm capacity for 1950. All yield esti-mates except soybeans were below yields recorded, wheat by almost 25 percent. In 1948 USDA projected yields for 1965. The margin of error was greaterh tan in the 1945 estimates, with projected corn yields being only half of actual 1965 yields. Pro-jections completed in 1961 for 1965, given the perspective of the 1950's, were much closer but still estimated corn yield at only 51 bushels per acre while the recorded yield turned out to be 73.8 bushels per acre. While yields for individual years do deviate from trend lines, due to weather and other variables, it is still obvious that yield projections for the past have uniformly underestimated realization.

A number of studies with projections for 1975 have been completed. Two such studies reported in Table 4.3 estimated yields on both an "attainable" and a "maximum" basis. Even the maximum yield estimates for 1975 have already either been surpassed or will be as early as 1970.

The first published projections for 1980 to indicate future land and water requirements were completed by the USDA in 1959 at the request of Congress. Again, almost all of these yield projections for 1980 had been surpassed by 1965 and the 1980 projected yields will certainly fall far short of those realized for that date.

We have reviewed previous studies to indicate that they have generally underestimated technological change and the level of realized yields and potential production. As a result, policy makers were quite unprepared for the sharp upturn in output which came during the 1950's. Fortunately, demand levels also increased by more than expected amounts. Thus the gap between actual production and utilization was smaller than the gap between projected levels of output and levels actually recorded.

## 1980 CAPACITY ESTIMATES
## ON THE PRESENT CROPLAND BASE

We have also just completed a study which projects 1980 farm output, supposing an efficient or optimal interregional allocation of production within the nation. Hence, we hope that the previ-ous review of underestimates provides a framework for evaluating the rather large potential output which we project for 1980, if all previously used cropland is returned to production.[5] The following assumptions underlie our estimates: (a) The U.S. population for 1980 will be 243.4 million persons. (b) Per capita incomes will increase in real terms at the rate indicated in 1950–65 trends, with an additional increase of 40 percent between 1965 and 1980. (c) The land base available for major crops, which has been expanding in recent years, will be equivalent in acres to that used (both for crops and land retirement) in 1965. (d) Technological improvements will continue at rates realized over the period 1948–65, a rate which is conservative relative to technological improvement in the last decade. (e) Agriculture will operate in an atmosphere of interfarm and interregional competition which allows production to locate in areas of greatest economic advantage.

With the technological improvements and changes in farm structure outlined previously, yields per acre are projected to increase to the following level by 1980:

| | |
|---|---|
| Wheat | 32.2 bushels |
| Corn | 99.4 bushels |
| Oats | 59.1 bushels |
| Barley | 48.1 bushels |
| Grain sorghum | 61.8 bushels |
| Soybeans | 29.3 bushels |
| Cotton | 754.0 pounds |
| Tobacco | 2715.0 pounds |

We consider these 1980 yield estimates to be conservative, considering both the previous tendency for projections to underestimate realized yields and the base period upon which our projections rest.

**CROP PRODUCTION**

With a cropland base at 1965 levels for major crops, yields at the above levels, and a market structure encouraging efficient allocation of crops among farms and regions, output of crops could increase greatly. The projected level of output of each major crop is indicated in Table 4.4. Wheat production, using 88.7 million acres of cropland, would be 246 percent of the annual

[5] Earl O. Heady and Leo V. Mayer, *Food Needs and U.S. Agriculture in 1980*, Technical Report No. 1, National Advisory Commission on Food and Fiber, Washington, D.C., 1967.

TABLE 4.4

INDEX NUMBERS OF MAJOR CROPS AND LIVESTOCK COMMODITIES FOR 1964, 1965,
1966, AND PROJECTED VALUES FOR 1980, ASSUMING MAXIMUM CROP PRODUCTION

|  | Actual | | | Projected |
|---|---|---|---|---|
|  | 1964 | 1965 | 1966 | 1980 |
|  | | *(1957–59 = 100)* | | |
| Total Output * | 112 | 113 | 112 | 157 |
| Crops | 109 | 117 | 110 | 176 |
| Wheat | 109 | 112 | 111 | 246 |
| Feed grains | 95 | 112 | 111 | 162 |
| Oilseeds † | 131 | 152 | 156 | 224 |
| Cotton | 124 | 121 | 78 | 140 |
| Tobacco | 128 | 107 | 107 | 117 |
| Livestock | 113 | 110 | 113 | 144 |
| Beef and veal | 128 | 125 | 129 | 182 |
| Pork | 103 | 92 | 97 | 120 |
| Lamb and mutton | 81 | 74 | 77 | 107 |
| Broilers | 142 | 147 | 169 | 230 |
| Farm chickens | 84 | 81 | 84 | 78 |
| Turkeys | 132 | 138 | 152 | 208 |
| Milk | 103 | 101 | 98 | 113 |
| Eggs | 105 | 106 | 107 | 114 |

\* Total output was calculated for those commodities listed.
† Includes soybeans and cottonseed.

1957–59 average output. Total 1980 potential wheat production
is estimated at 2.9 billion bushels if maximum production is
sought on the 1965 cropland base. Over 2.1 billion bushels
would be available for export under these conditions.

Feed grain production could also increase substantially.
With all cropland allocated to its most economically suitable
use, 1980 feed grain tonnage could increase to 162 percent of the
annual 1957–59 average. In contrast to wheat, this 1980 quantity
of feed grain could be produced on slightly less cropland than
was used in either 1965 or 1966. In essence, production of feed
grains could increase by 50 percent between 1965 and 1980 without an increase in acreage. Part of this increase would come
from higher yields and a shift in land use among regions on a
fuller comparative-advantage basis, but an additional source is
the continued shift from oats to corn production. Acre for acre,
corn would produce nearly three times more tonnage of grain
on the average than oats. Thus by 1980 the continued shift of
feed grain land from oats to corn will allow a greater tonnage of
feed grains on the same or smaller acreage.

Oilseed production is projected to total 224 percent of the
1957–59 annual average by 1980. Although seemingly large, 1966

production had already risen 56 percent above the average
1957–59 output. At the projected level of output, soybean
acreage would total 58.6 million acres. Cotton acreage would be
only 9.7 million acres, thus causing cottonseed to make up a
smaller proportion of total oilseeds than at present. Since soybeans yield nearly twice the oilseed tonnage per acre as cottonseed, the same acres again would produce more oilseeds under
the greater proportion of soybeans.

Cotton-lint production was estimated to increase to 140
percent of the 1957–59 annual output. The 9.7 million acres
could, however, produce 17.3 million bales as production shifts
toward the higher yielding areas of the Southwest and some
technological improvement takes place. An increase in irrigated
acreage in the Southwest will also affect total production.

Tobacco production is projected to increase to 117 percent
of the 1957–59 annual average. Under increased yields, the
acreage required for 1980 would be smaller than the 1964–65
annual average.

### LIVESTOCK PRODUCTION

Estimates of livestock production were also completed, assuming capacity grain production. Increases are based on three
factors: (a) population growth, (b) increases in real income, and
(c) changes in the response of consumers to changes in real income, that is, changes in the income elasticity of demand. On
this basis, beef production is projected to increase to 182 percent
of 1957–59 annual levels. This level of production exceeds the
1966 level by 50 percent.

Pork production is expected to increase by a smaller proportion than beef. The projected production is only 20 percent
greater than 1957–59 annual levels, but this is consistent with
past trends since both 1965 and 1966 were below 1957–59 levels.

Projections for broiler production parallel that for beef.
Total production is projected 230 percent above 1957–59 annual
levels. This gain will come as the proportion of production
from farm chickens continues to lag and broilers fill a larger
proportion of the market. In addition, the competitiveness of
broiler prices and changing demand patterns allow a continuation of past trends in per capita production and consumption.

Turkey production is expected to double by 1980, as compared to the average production for the 1957–59 period. The

trend toward year-round consumption of turkey, and away from its use only as a holiday specialty, will allow the greater production to be readily absorbed.

Both milk and egg production are projected to grow at a slower rate than population. Per capita consumption of each product is projected to decline. As a result, total production will grow slowly. With increased output per milk cow and per hen, fewer resources will be needed for both of these commodity groups by 1980.

In general, livestock production is projected to increase through 1980 in response to the larger population and higher per capita incomes. However, if demand for these commodities should increase at even faster rates in the United States, livestock production could easily be expanded simply by reducing feed grain exports from the level of 70 million tons. (Feed grain exports were 29 and 21 million tons in 1965 and 1966 respectively.) We would expect market encouragement of lower grain prices, and thus greater livestock production, under the potential production of an efficient agriculture implying optimal interregional allocations of crop production. Even then, grain production potential in the United States is still large enough to allow large increases in exports.

### RESOURCE REQUIREMENTS

With agricultural output increased to capacity levels on the current cropland base, and with the structural transformation of agriculture continuing, various changes would take place in the resources used by U.S. agriculture. Labor use would continue to decline. Capital use, by contrast, would increase substantially. According to our projections, 1980 man-hour requirements for agriculture would decline 31 percent below 1965 levels, or from 8 billion in 1965 to 5.5 billion in 1980. This decline in man-hours would be associated with a 40 percent reduction in farm laborers, even if only recent mobility rates continue. (National and regional projections on man-hours are shown in Table 4.5.)

At a regional level the largest decreases in man-hours occur in the Delta and Appalachian regions. Mechanization of agriculture in these regions, as well as shifts in production to other areas, causes a large decline in man-hours used. The Northeast region likewise has a sharp decline in farm man-hours, but urbanization is the major cause here. Least affected are the South-

TABLE 4.5

Man-hour Requirements for Maximum Levels of Production in Agriculture in 1980 With Total Man-hours Used in 1965 for Comparison

| Region | Percent Change All Farmwork 1965–80 | All Farmwork* | | All Livestock | | All Crops | |
|---|---|---|---|---|---|---|---|
| | | 1965 | 1980 | 1965 | 1980 | 1965 | 1980 |
| | *(percent)* | *(million man-hours)* | | | | | |
| United States | −31.0 | 7,976 | 5,501 | 3,066 | 2,210 | 3,798 | 2,654 |
| Northeast | −35.2 | 627 | 406 | 314 | 202 | 226 | 157 |
| Lake States | −27.6 | 849 | 615 | 452 | 320 | 284 | 230 |
| Corn Belt | −32.6 | 1,309 | 882 | 658 | 474 | 448 | 293 |
| N. Plains | −25.4 | 630 | 470 | 290 | 225 | 240 | 180 |
| Appalachian | −39.5 | 1,157 | 700 | 341 | 226 | 658 | 394 |
| Southeast | −36.6 | 801 | 508 | 219 | 169 | 484 | 289 |
| Delta States | −48.4 | 594 | 304 | 179 | 135 | 340 | 139 |
| S. Plains | −19.5 | 709 | 571 | 247 | 156 | 353 | 340 |
| Mountain | −18.7 | 470 | 382 | 174 | 143 | 230 | 195 |
| Pacific | −20.1 | 830 | 663 | 192 | 160 | 535 | 437 |

* All farmwork includes man-hours used on crops, livestock, and overhead.

ern Plains, Mountain, and Pacific regions which are moderately
well adjusted to modern agricultural technologies and hence
show a smaller decline in labor used by 1980.

In contrast, capital values and use would rise substantially
if output rose to the capacity levels on the current cropland base
by 1980. Greatest increases would be in land and building values, but machinery and equipment values also would rise substantially. As indicated in Table 4.6, according to our estimates,
total assets for land and building, machinery and equipment,
and livestock inventories would increase 187 percent over the
1965 values.

At the regional level, capacity production on the current
cropland base would have greatest effect on asset values in the
Lake States, the Corn Belt, Southeast and Delta States. Other
regions would increase farming assets by a smaller amount and
we could expect considerable interregional shifts in the allocation
of agriculture's capital resources.

## CONSISTENCY OF ESTIMATES

While our projections are based on a combination of regression
estimates of yield trends and programming models of efficient
production, they agree generally, if we consider differences in
the proportion of acreage allocation to various crops in the two

TABLE 4.6

CAPITAL REQUIREMENTS FOR MAJOR CATEGORIES OF CAPITAL FOR MAXIMUM
LEVELS OF PRODUCTION IN AGRICULTURE IN 1980 WITH 1965 TOTALS FOR
COMPARISON

| Region | Percent Change Total Capital 1965–80 | Total Capital | | Land and buildings | Projected 1980 Value of | |
|---|---|---|---|---|---|---|
| | | 1965 | 1980 | | Machinery and equipment | Livestock inventories |
| | | *(million dollars)* | | | | |
| United States | +187.3 | 198,890 | 571,391 | 501,727 | 47,945 | 21,719 |
| Northeast | + 49.9 | 10,924 | 16,379 | 11,238 | 3,950 | 1,191 |
| Lake States | +313.8 | 16,065 | 66,473 | 56,212 | 8,065 | 2,196 |
| Corn Belt | +371.1 | 45,044 | 212,177 | 195,702 | 11,592 | 4,883 |
| N. Plains | +167.5 | 23,043 | 61,630 | 49,450 | 8,582 | 3,598 |
| Appalachian | + 84.8 | 15,022 | 27,760 | 22,659 | 3,736 | 1,365 |
| Southeast | +292.9 | 12,597 | 49,498 | 46,218 | 2,154 | 1,126 |
| Delta States | +216.7 | 9,191 | 29,109 | 26,917 | 1,327 | 865 |
| S. Plains | + 57.0 | 24,154 | 37,924 | 32,793 | 2,906 | 2,225 |
| Mountain | + 69.5 | 16,989 | 28,790 | 23,469 | 2,803 | 2,518 |
| Pacific | + 61.1 | 25,862 | 41,651 | 37,069 | 2,830 | 1,752 |

studies, with projections by Daly and Egbert[6] and Abel and Rojko.[7] The Daly-Egbert estimates based on a regression model of the U.S. agricultural economy are presented in Table 4.7. The results, which assume all diverted land in production by 1980 and without use of the added output specified, correspond closely in total output with our estimates for 1980.

The results from the recent Abel-Rojko study are, aside from a few differences in crops included, almost identical with our own. We estimate that feed grains and wheat in the United States might use 183 million acres of land and produce 311 million tons of grain under a 1980 efficient agriculture. Their estimates are for 186 million acres of grain—including rye, rice, and buckwheat—and production of 315 million tons of grain. However, compared to their 109.5 million tons, our projections indicate 123.8 million tons of grain available for export. The difference arises from assumptions in domestic rates of grain utilization relating to demand alternatives for livestock products, rates of livestock-feed conversion efficiencies, and use of grain for industrial products, seed, and other purposes.

Given the consistency of these estimates for 1980, the capac-

[6] Cf. R. F. Daly and A. C. Egbert, "Statistical Supplement to a Look Ahead for Food and Agriculture," *Agr. Econ. Res.*, Jan. 1966.

[7] Martin E. Abel and Anthony S. Rojko, *World Food Situation, Prospects for World Grain Production, Consumption and Trade*, FAER-35, USDA, 1967.

TABLE 4.7

FARM OUTPUT AND RELATED DATA, SELECTED YEARS AND PROJECTIONS FOR 1980

|  | Averages | | Actual | Projected 1980 |
|---|---|---|---|---|
|  | 1949–51 | 1959–61 | 1964 | II* |
|  | *(1957–59 = 100)* | | | |
| Farm Output | 87 | 105 | 112 | 160 |
| Crop Production | 91 | 106 | 109 | 172 |
| Feed grains | 79 | 105 | 97 | 191 |
| Hay | 88 | 101 | 105 | 129 |
| Food grains | 88 | 106 | 114 | 178 |
| Cotton | 112 | 117 | 124 | 184 |
| Oil crops | 66 | 108 | 128 | 249 |
| Livestock Production | 88 | 104 | 113 | 147 |
| Meat animals | 89 | 105 | 116 | 160 |
| Dairy products | 93 | 101 | 105 | 119 |
| Poultry products | 78 | 107 | 118 | 152 |
| Cropland Used for Crops | 107 | 98 | 94 | 106 |
| Crop Production Per Acre † | 85 | 108 | 116 | 162 |

Source: R. F. Daly and A. C. Egbert, "Statistical Supplement to a Look Ahead for Food and Agriculture," *Agr. Econ. Res.*, Jan. 1966.
* Production with all diverted cropland planted to crops, use of added production not specified.
† Index of crop production per acre is a ratio of total crop production to total land used for crops.

ity utilization of land resources in U.S. agriculture thus appears to provide a substantial (and conservative) cushion on which enlarged exports of grain might be based. That potential production levels may not be needed through 1980 is a major inference which stems from these data and the Abel-Rojko analysis. They suggest that all less developed countries—including India and Pakistan—may show only moderate increases in effective food demand when viewed with ". . . a more realistic set of economic demands than those based on what might be considered nutritionally desirable."[8] The less developed countries imported 20.7 million metric tons of grain annually in the period 1959–61, one-third on a concessional basis; they imported 29.0 million metric tons of grain annually in 1964–65, one-half on a concessional basis. As shown from USDA projections in Table 4.8, these countries are predicted to require imports of 30.7 million metric tons per year by 1970 if rates of increase in grain production are generally at 1956–66 levels. By 1980 they will require around 54.3 million metric tons of imported grains under similar assumptions. Even if their productivity improves substantially by 1980, these countries will still require imports of 1964–65 magnitude.

[8] *Ibid.*, p. 24.

## TABLE 4.8

WORLD GRAIN PRODUCTION AND TRADE, 1959–61 AVERAGE, 1964–65, AND PROJECTIONS TO 1970 AND 1980

| Country or Region | 1959–61 Average | | 1964–65 | | 1970 Projection II‡ | | 1980 Projection II‡ | |
|---|---|---|---|---|---|---|---|---|
| | Production* | Net imports† | Production* | Net imports† | Production | Net imports | Production | Net imports |
| | *(million metric)* | | | | | | | |
| Less Developed Countries: | | | | | | | | |
| India | 67.6 | 4.0 | 73.6 | 6.6 | 87.0 | 6.0 | 106.1 | 16.5 |
| Pakistan | 15.5 | 1.2 | 17.5 | 1.6 | 20.6 | 2.2 | 27.4 | 3.3 |
| Other less developed countries, excluding grain exporters | 105.7 | 15.5 | 118.0 | 20.8 | 138.0 | 22.5 | 180.0 | 34.5 |
| Subtotal | 188.8 | 20.7 | 209.1 | 29.0 | 245.6 | 30.7 | 313.5 | 54.3 |
| Net grain exporters§ | 33.1 | − 9.4 | 45.2 | −15.3 | 50.2 | −14.9 | 68.0 | − 20.0 |
| Total, less developed countries | 221.9 | 11.3 | 254.3 | 13.7 | 295.8 | 15.8 | 381.5 | 34.3 |
| Developed Countries: | | | | | | | | |
| United States‖ | 170.4 | −27.5 | 159.7 | −38.2 | 217.1 | −54.8 | 315.0 | −109.5 |
| Developed exporters (less U.S.)¶ | 59.5 | −18.0 | 73.4 | −26.6 | 92.5 | −36.5 | 115.0 | − 42.5 |
| Other developed free world | 83.1 | 32.8 | 89.2 | 37.0 | 92.5 | 58.5 | 106.8 | 73.2 |
| Eastern Europe (incl. U.S.S.R.) | 156.2 | − .1 | 171.6 | 7.5 | 192.6 | 4.3 | 230.2 | 1.2 |
| Total, developed countries | 469.2 | −12.8 | 493.9 | −20.3 | 594.7 | −28.5 | 767.0 | − 77.6 |
| Communist Asia | 117.6 | .7 | 130.8 | 4.9 | 150.0 | 5.7 | 183.5 | 9.0 |
| World Total§ | 808.7 | − .8 | 879.0 | − 1.7 | 1,040.5 | − 7.0 | 1,332.0 | − 34.3 |

Source: Martin E. Abel and Anthony S. Rojko, *World Food Situation, Prospects for World Grain Production, Consumption and Trade,* FAER-35, USDA, 1967.
* Calendar year basis.
† Year beginning July 1 for wheat and coarse grains, following calendar year for rice; negative numbers mean either a world surplus or an increase in stocks.
‡ For 1970, assumes 1954–66 rate of growth in production with normative evaluation of the impact of agricultural policies and development plans. For 1980, production growth rates are 2.5 percent per year for grain importers, 3.1 percent per year for grain exporters, and 2.6 percent per year for less developed countries, using the above 1970 estimates as a base level of production.
§ Argentina, Mexico, Burma, Cambodia, and Thailand.
‖ Grain production in the United States is based on harvested acreages of 150 million in 1964, 158 million in 1970, and 186 million in 1980.
¶ Canada, Australia, France, and Republic of South Africa.

Under the Abel-Rojko estimates of requirements in 1970, imports of the less developed countries could be met from a U.S. grain acreage of 158 million, as compared to 150 million acres harvested in the 1964–65 crop year. If the less developed countries continued to increase grain production at only historical rates, their requirements of 1980 could be met and surpluses would exist if the United States harvested 186 million acres of grain. (The United States harvested about 165 million acres of grain in 1967.) Even at the lower trends of grain production in the less developed countries, the world could have a surplus grain production of 34.3 metric tons in 1980—supposing the United States put all of its present cropland base in production and attained the specified trend levels in technological improvement. This compares with a world annual grain surplus of .8 million metric tons in the 1959–61 period and 1.7 million metric tons annually in the 1964–65 period.

We believe it is likely that the effective world food demand could be expected to exceed the Abel-Rojko levels by 1980, thus tempering the grain surplus potential suggested above. Perhaps demand by 1980 will be larger than these sets of projections imply. But we also believe the projections of U.S. food production potential to be low, especially if extended over the next quarter century and considering our total potential cropland base—and any possibilities of greater international cooperation in water supplies. The data we present above are conservative estimates of potential U.S. grain production capacity because they do not include the acreage of land not now in crop production but which could be so diverted with the types of investment suggested in Table 4.2. Upchurch estimates that 150 million additional acres from our total agricultural supply could be converted readily from other uses to crops at an investment of $30–50 billion in irrigation, drainage, clearing, and auxiliary investment.[9] Given the previous projections from the 1965 land base and the potential for increasing cropland by 50 percent by improving land and shifting it from such uses as pasture and forestry, the total output of U.S. agriculture could be doubled easily in 25 years. And, if the demand price were sufficiently high to draw forth the appropriate amounts of capital in fertilizer, irrigation, and other inputs, output of grain could increase by

---

[9] M. L. Upchurch, "The Capacity of the United States To Supply Food for Developing Countries," *Alternatives for Balancing World Food Production and Needs,* Center for Agricultural and Economic Development, Iowa State Univ. Press, Ames, 1967, pp. 215–23.

150 percent in the next quarter century. A large amount of this, a greater proportion than at the present, would be available for export.

## INSTITUTIONAL RESTRAINTS
## AND PRODUCTION SHIFTS

Of course any policy for U.S. agriculture which allows all current cropland to be used in its most efficient interfarm and interregional use, the basis of our own study, would cause considerable shift in the location of production.[10] Feed grain production would become concentrated more in favorable soil and rainfall regions. Wheat would adapt similarly to regions of advantage in the Central Plains. In any policy of less than maximum land use with land use restrictions removed, land previously used for wheat would shift to grass in marginal areas of the Northern and Southern Plains. With tardy technological improvement, much land in the Southeast would shift to grass and trees; but with a "catching up" on technology, this region would take over more of the nation's feed grain and soybean production and substitute some for wheat and small grain in marginal producing regions of the Plains.

Under a common market for North America, similar shifts would take place among the three countries. Feed wheat from Canada might replace part of the feed grain from marginal areas of the United States. Several of our models of less than capacity use of U.S. agriculture resulted in a large use of wheat in western areas of the United States. Up to a quarter of a billion bushels of wheat were indicated for feed use when land resources were in excess. Given a greater freedom of movement among the three countries, competitive pressures would likely cause changes of the nature suggested by our results. Wheat from the Prairie Provinces of Canada could move south to supply some feed needs in the western United States, while further development of feed grain production in the eastern Corn Belt and Southeast could move to the eastern provinces of Canada. But changes in do-

---

[10] For example, see the details for the 150 regions used in our set of projections (Heady and Mayer). For other details indicating interregional shifts implied in an optimized agricultural pattern, see Earl O. Heady and Melvin Skold, *Projection of U.S. Agricultural Capacity and Interregional Adjustment in Production and Land Use,* Iowa Agr. Exp. Sta. Bull. 539; and Earl O. Heady and Norman Whittlesey, *A Programming Analysis of Interregional Competition and Surplus Capacity of American Agriculture,* Iowa Agr. Exp. Sta. Bull. 538.

mestic policies, including the transport subsidy in Canada, would likely concentrate greater grain production for feed and livestock in both the Prairie Provinces of Canada and the southeastern United States (supposing a complete structural and technological transformation of the latter region).

## SUMMARY

The short-run problem in the United States is not that additional production capacity is lacking. More nearly it is the danger that too many people will be carried away with the long-run prospects for world food and will be encouraged to spend too much too soon in expanding our agricultural plant. The producing capacity is there for a large-scale expansion in output and exports, just as it is in countries such as Canada and Australia. And rather than overinvest in this direction in the short run, with the cause thus laid to continue costly farm programs to contain output and support prices in the near term, we would be better advised to divert some of the investment to aid in population control and family planning throughout the world. Our underdeveloped land can always be put into production when it is needed and world demand promises the payoff which merits the investment. The decision to help aid population control is not similarly a two-way road. No feasible method will exist for returning from a doubled population in 35 years to one which would be possible if we implemented appropriate population planning and policy at the present. Thus our conclusions are: adequate production capacity exists for short-run needs, both on this continent and others; the solution to the long-run problem lies in greater investments in population control rather than in an expanded production potential for U.S. agriculture alone.

# CHAPTER FIVE

# Trends and Capacity
# of Mexican Agriculture

EDMUNDO FLORES

THE DEVELOPMENT of systems for the collection, analysis, evaluation, and diffusion of agricultural statistics in Mexico has failed to keep pace with the rapid development of the agricultural sector and shows a considerable lag. Available statistics make it possible to reconstruct within reasonable margins of reliability the past performance of the sector—a rather elementary ex post proposition; but they are inadequate and insufficient to perform the more sophisticated and demanding tasks normally expected today from contemporary statistics, such as input-output analysis, cost-benefit analysis, and adequate short-, medium-, and long-term forecasts.

The spectacular growth of Mexican agriculture during the last three decades has attracted a large number of foreign observers, among whom are some highly qualified specialists who, understandably, came to Mexico inoculated by professional doses of pragmatic skepticism. Some of these experts worked for international organizations such as FAO, ILO, and the International Bank for Reconstruction and Development; others worked for the several research-supporting foundations or for research institutes; and, finally, a rather large group consisted of graduate students in search of original truths for their doctoral dissertations. Invariably, all of them had to make their peace with

EDMUNDO FLORES, Universidad Nacional Autónoma de México.

Mexican statistics since that was the only way to acquire a quantitative notion of what made our agricultural system work. The clash between underdeveloped statistics and overdeveloped analysts produced a number of reports in which Mexican statistics were subjected to all imaginable criticisms, tests, and adjustments and emerged substantially undamaged, largely because they are an immovable limiting factor.

There are in Mexico two main sources of agricultural statistics: the census taken every ten years by the Dirección General de Estadística, a bureau of the Ministry of Industry and Trade; and the continuous series on agricultural production published since 1925 by the Dirección General de Economía Agrícola, a bureau of the Ministry of Agriculture. Rather than using raw data and making my own adjustments, I have preferred to rely in most cases on data as published in reports available in English and written by foreign observers. One important exception is the report *Projections of Supply of and Demand for Agricultural Products in Mexico to 1965, 1970 and 1975.* This study was proposed by the USDA as part of an evaluation of long-term prospects of supply and demand for agricultural products in approximately 40 countries, as authorized by P.L. 480. The study was carried out under an agreement signed by the Mexican Ministry of Agriculture, the Economic Research Service of the USDA, and the Bank of Mexico (the Central Bank), and was sponsored, additionally, by the Mexican Ministry of Finance. This report is the most important single attempt to forecast the course of Mexico's agricultural development, and I take it as the main point of reference in these remarks on the future trends and capacity of Mexican agriculture.

## THE PERFORMANCE OF AGRICULTURE
## SINCE 1940

Agricultural output in Mexico has increased at a sustained high average rate during the last three decades. While GNP has grown at an average rate of 6 percent annually, the agricultural product has increased at 5.4 percent. Table 5.1 shows data assembled by Folke Dovring for eight Latin American countries, where he links two series of index numbers from FAO which go from 1934 to 1965. These index numbers show that Mexico has trebled gross agricultural production in less than three decades, while at the same time the other seven countries have

TABLE 5.1

FAO Indices of Agricultural Production, 1934–39 to 1964–65, Countries in Latin America for Which Long-term Series Are Available

| Country | Average 1952–53 to 1956–57 (index base 1934–38 = 100) | Average 1962–63 to 1964–65 (index base 1952–53 to 1956–57 = 100) | Average 1962–63 to 1964–65 (index base 1934–38 = 100) * |
|---|---|---|---|
| Argentina | 114 | 117 | 133 |
| Brazil | 139 | 141 | 196 |
| Chile | 135 | 123 | 166 |
| Colombia | 180 | 126 | 227 |
| Cuba | 147 | 104 | 153 |
| Mexico | 192 | 169 | 324 |
| Peru | 152 | 127 | 193 |
| Uruguay | 138 | 98 | 135 |

Source: Folke Dovring, *Land Reform and Productivity: the Mexican Case, a Preliminary Analysis*, Dept. of Agr. Econ., Agr. Exp. Sta., Univ. of Illinois, Nov. 1966, p. 4.
* Linked index.

remained relatively stagnant.[1] Tables 5.2 and 5.3 show similar results for Mexican agriculture.

Reed Hertford, a graduate student from the University of Chicago who has been studying Mexican agriculture for several years, concludes happily after he relates all the difficulties he met handling Mexican statistics:

These data point rather uniformly to the following facts: (i) over the past quarter of a century Mexico's growth in crop production ranks within the top three of twenty-six countries recently studied by ERS/ USDA;[2] its crop yield increases were exceeded probably by only Israel, Taiwan, Yugoslavia, and Sudan over the same period; (ii) crop production increases were greater in the forties than the fifties, though the yield performance of the latter period outstretched the earlier period; (iii) by far the largest gains in production, acreage, and yields were made in the five states of the Pacific North bordering the Ocean; (iv) the largest increases in production, acreage, and yields came from export crops (bananas, coffee, cotton, garbanzo, garlic, henequen, and tomatoes. . . .[3]

There is no agreement on the causes that account for the phenomenal growth of the Mexican economy. Mexicans gener-

[1] Folke Dovring, *Land Reform and Productivity: the Mexican Case, a Preliminary Analysis*, Dept. Agr. Econ., Agr. Exp. Sta., Univ. of Illinois, Nov. 1966, p. 4.
[2] USDA, *Changes in Agriculture in Twenty-Six Developing Nations, 1948 to 1963*, FAER-27, 1965.
[3] Reed Hertford, *Mexican Agricultural Development: A Progress Report*, Univ. of Chicago, Apr. 1966. Mimeo.

TABLE 5.2

INDEX NUMBERS OF CROP PRODUCTION, MEXICO, 1929–65

| Year | Physical Production* | | |
|------|---------------|--------|----------|
|      | Domestic use | Export | All crops |
| 1929 | 100 | 100 | 100 |
| 1939 | 148 | 117 | 137 |
| 1949 | 254 | 210 | 239 |
| 1959 | 379 | 397 | 386 |
| 1965 | 523 | 534 | 527 |

Source: *Current Economic Position and Prospects of Mexico* (in five volumes), Internatl. Bank for Reconstruction and Development, Internatl. Dev. Assn., Oct. 26, 1966, p. Annex 7, Part I. The index numbers are based on 25 principal crops grown in Mexico, 16 principally used for domestic consumption and 9 which have been historically considered as export crops. The 25 crops represent close to 90 percent of the country's total crop production. Individual crop data for the years 1929–59 were obtained from the respective agricultural census reports. Those for 1965 are preliminary data from the Direccion General de Economia Agricola, except the estimates for corn and beans which were adjusted by the mission.
* Weighted by average prices 1929–65.

ally attribute it to the 1910–17 revolution and to the ensuing land reform and public works policies, which broke the feudal stalemate of the long Díaz epoch and released powerful developmental forces that led to political stability, to industrial and urban growth, and to the modernization of the agricultural sector. But while the identification of the reasons behind general growth is controversial, there is little argument about the main components of agricultural development, namely: (a) the expansion of acreage caused by the irrigation and road construction policies which opened up lands previously idle; (b) massive shifts in land utilization, from extensive crop production and cattle breeding, which were stimulated by increased demand from urban-industrial expansion, by modern communications, and by favorable prices within the country and abroad; and finally and more recently (c) increases in productivity generated

TABLE 5.3

INDEX NUMBERS OF CROP YIELDS, MEXICO, 1929–65

| Year | Crop Yields* | | |
|------|-------------|--------|-----------|
|      | Domestic use | Export | All crops |
| 1929 | 100 | 100 | 100 |
| 1939 | 113 | 106 | 113 |
| 1949 | 151 | 137 | 150 |
| 1959 | 163 | 162 | 163 |
| 1965 | 198 | 216 | 199 |

Source: *Current Economic Position and Prospects of Mexico* (in five volumes), Internatl. Bank for Reconstruction and Development, Internatl. Dev. Assn., Oct. 26, 1966.
* Weighted by average area harvested.

by the spread of modern technology and research—hybrids, antibiotics, fertilizers, fungicides, herbicides, machinery, food processing and packaging, etc.

Quantification of the share attributable to each component is, of course, difficult, since all these different families of innovation pervade the whole process, overlap, and reinforce each other cumulatively. But, despite difficulties, it seems essential to have some sort of an idea—or perhaps even a theory—of the role played by each one of these agents of growth in order to estimate their future availability and their effects on future production.

## THE EXPANSION OF ACREAGE BY IRRIGATION

The construction of dams and other irrigation facilities initiated in 1926 has absorbed over 90 percent of public investment in the agricultural sector since this policy went into high gear during the early forties. (Incidentally, this policy also gave massive impetus to the development of the construction industry.) At present, over 2.5 million hectares are in irrigation districts, under the administration of the Ministry of Hydraulic Resources, and between 1 and 2 million hectares are privately irrigated.

Between 1940 and 1964 an average of approximately 56,000 hectares a year of new land were irrigated. Total cumulative outlay amounts to 8.200 million pesos (at 1960 prices). Costs per irrigated hectare have been relatively low.

Concerning the future of irrigation, it is often argued that the construction of new dams is going to become increasingly costly since the easy and inexpensive possibilities received early attention. This "diminishing-returns syndrome" in the light of the present technological explosion, which certainly has caught up in Mexico, seems out of place if one brings to mind the fact that the multiple uses of irrigation—flood control, energy, etc.—spread costs over many benefits. But here we meet one of the many imponderables which, whether we like it or not, will mar our projections.

Venezian and Gamble attribute about 40 percent of the increase of output to the expansion of harvested acreage.[4] For a quantitative view of the increases in acreage by irrigation, see Tables 5.4, 5.5, 5.6, and 5.7.

---

[4] Eduardo Venezian and William K. Gamble, *A Review of Mexican Agricultural Development, 1950–1965*, Office of International Agricultural Development, N.Y. State College of Agriculture, Cornell Univ., Ithaca.

## TABLE 5.4
### Index Numbers of Area Harvested, Mexico, 1929–65

| | Area Harvested* | | |
| Year | Domestic use | Export | All crops |
|---|---|---|---|
| 1929 | 100 | 100 | 100 |
| 1939 | 122 | 93 | 118 |
| 1949 | 153 | 149 | 152 |
| 1959 | 191 | 226 | 195 |
| 1965 | 203 | 230 | 206 |

Source: *Current Economic Position and Prospect of Mexico* (in five volumes), Internatl. Bank for Reconstruction and Development, Internatl. Dev. Assn., Oct. 26, 1966. Coverage, basic source materials, and adjustments are the same as for Table 5.2.
\* Unweighted.

## TABLE 5.5
### Expansion of Irrigation, by Regions

| | New Land Area Put Under Irrigation by the Government (1,000 ha.) | | | |
| Region | Before 1946 | 1947–52 | 1953–60 | Total 1947–60 |
|---|---|---|---|---|
| P. North | 150.5 | 129.1 | 333.9 | 463.0 |
| North | 154.2 | 126.2 | 140.9 | 267.1 |
| Central | 113.4 | 98.3 | 102.0 | 200.3 |
| P. South | 1.4 | 28.0 | 10.4 | 38.4 |
| Gulf | .4 | 4.9 | 22.5 | 27.4 |

Source: Eduardo Venezian and William K. Gamble, *A Review of Mexican Agricultural Development, 1950–1965*, Office of Internatl. Agr. Dev., N.Y. State College of Agriculture, Cornell Univ., Ithaca, p. 16. Adapted from Secretaria de Recursos Hidraulicos, *Informe de Labores, 1960–61*, Mexico, 1962.

### TABLE 5.6
MAIN CROPS GROWN UNDER IRRIGATION, 1960

| Crop | Area Under Irrigation (1,000 ha.) | Percent of Total Crop Area | Percent of Total Irrigated Area |
|---|---|---|---|
| Corn | 629.4 | 9.2 | 26.9 |
| Cotton | 603.7 | 80.3 | 25.8 |
| Wheat | 578.1 | 68.3 | 24.7 |
| Sugarcane | 106.1 | 35.2 | 4.5 |
| Beans* | 76.0 | 10.3 | 3.2 |
| Alfalfa | 57.6 | 70.2 | 2.5 |
| Rice | 53.6 | 55.7 | 2.3 |
| Other | 236.1 | –0– | 10.1 |
| Total | 2,350.6 | –0– | 100.0 |

Source: Venezian and Gamble. Censo Agropecuario, 1960.
* Excludes beans planted together with corn.

### TABLE 5.7
CONTRIBUTION OF AREA AND YIELD INCREMENTS TO AGRICULTURAL OUTPUT, 1949–51 TO 1962–64

| Crop | % Due to Area Expansion | | % Due to Yield Increment | | % Due to Yield and Area Combined | | Total % Increase in Vol. of Prod. | |
|---|---|---|---|---|---|---|---|---|
| | Ac-tual | Rela-tive | Ac-tual | Rela-tive | Ac-tual | Rela-tive | Ac-tual | Rela-tive |
| Corn | 60 | 55.0 | 27 | 24.8 | 22 | 20.2 | 109 | 100 |
| Beans | 96 | 47.5 | 50 | 24.8 | 56 | 27.7 | 202 | 100 |
| Cotton | 8 | 8.1 | 83 | 83.8 | 8 | 8.1 | 99 | 100 |
| Wheat | 30 | 14.6 | 106 | 51.4 | 70 | 34.0 | 206 | 100 |
| Sugar | 84 | 80.8 | 11 | 10.6 | 9 | 8.6 | 104 | 100 |
| Coffee | 96 | 81.2 | 10 | 8.5 | 11 | 9.4 | 117 | 100 |

Source: Venezian and Gamble, p. 13.

### SHIFTS IN LAND UTILIZATION

Highway construction also has had high priority in public expenditure (and has added additional impulse to the development of the construction industry). The construction, since 1926, of a highway network exceeding 60,000 kilometers has linked agricultural regions with consumption centers and ports. Thus highways and urban-industrial expansion have generated huge external economies, stimulated shifts toward more intensive land utilization patterns, and made accessible lands which were either idle or were operated merely for subsistence.

For example, a recent survey of the *ejidos* (an agrarian community which has received and holds land in accordance with the land-reform legislation) of the state of Mexico—a state adjacent to Mexico City—showed that despite widespread fragmentation of land tenure caused by the land reform in an area of very high population density, the dairy cattle population even in small *ejidos* had increased considerably because of the proximity of Mexico City and the fresh milk demand of its 7 million population.[5]

There are no estimates of the effect that the spread of urbanization and communications has had upon the expansion of acreage and the increase of productivity, but there is no doubt that such shifts have contributed substantially to create a more intensive, diversified, and efficient pattern of land utilization.[6] The breakdown of a "cellular" spatial system to form a more nearly integrated one with regional specialization has characterized agricultural-urban development in many regions of the country.

### DOMESTIC PRICE SUPPORTS

Mexico began its price support policies in 1937. Initially, this policy sought to lower the prices of basic foods and favored urban consumers at the expense of farmers. In recent years, however, prices have been raised generally above the world market level, and the terms of trade have tended to favor the agricultural sector. At present, the price support agency CONASUPO (Compañía Nacional de Subsistencias Populares) supports the prices

---

[5] *Los Ejidos del Estado de México.* Catálogo. Gobierno del Estado de México. Dirección de Agricultura y Ganadería. Toluca, México. MCMLVIII.

[6] Edmundo Flores, "The Significance of Land-Use Changes in the Economic Development of Mexico," *Land Economics,* May 1959, Vol. XXXV, No. 2.

of corn, wheat, beans, rice, sorghum, and chili. Approximately half of the wheat crop, 10 percent of the corn crop, and marginal quantities of the other products are marketed through CONASUPO.

The price support policy has been successful. Mexico had been traditionally a wheat importer, and it had to import corn frequently. In 1950 domestic wheat production was less than 600,000 tons, and more than 400,000 tons were imported. In 1966 production was 2,445,000, and 648,000 tons were exported to the UAR and Poland. Corn exports also began. About one million tons of the 1964 crop were exported; in 1965 exports amounted to 600,000 tons, and last year they were around 800,000 tons.

The agricultural sector has shown also sensitivity toward world prices. Favorable prices abroad have stimulated production. In 1950–55 cotton production increased twofold, due largely to favorable competitive conditions created by the price-support policies of the United States, which caused an "umbrella effect." Since then, cotton has been the leading agricultural export commodity. Likewise the withdrawal of Cuba from the U.S. market acted as a powerful incentive to increase sugarcane production from about 16 million tons in 1960 to around 24 million tons in 1966. Sugar exports reached the half million mark and domestic consumption increased 35 percent.

### INCREASES IN PRODUCTIVITY GENERATED BY THE SPREAD OF MODERN TECHNOLOGY COMBINED WITH THE INCENTIVES OF AN EXPANDING MARKET

Tables 5.3 and 5.7 show the increase in productivity of Mexican agriculture. Roughly, average agricultural productivity doubled in three and a half decades. Obviously, these spectacular gains were the result of a cumulative process of mutually reinforcing innovation which originated in many sectors: sweeping land reform; the reorganization of technical education to prepare agronomists to work both as technicians in the field and laboratory and as civil servants in charge of devising and implementing the policies of the central government; the training of graduate students abroad; the spread of live, exciting nationalism which inoculated Mexican experts against the temptations which cause the brain-drain; the public works policies of the administration; and the joint work of the Rockefeller and Ford Foundations and the Ministry of Agriculture's research agency INIA (Instituto Nacional de Investigaciónes Agrícolas). These, and many other changes in the power structure, in the stratification of society, in the patterns of income distribution and the distribution of opportunity provided the stimuli to improve agricultural performance.

Take wheat for instance. At the beginning of the last decade stem-rust resistant wheat varieties were developed. These varieties, however, did not yield more than 3.5 tons per hectare but, since then, the use of short-straw wheat based on the Norin varieties developed in Japan has increased yields notably. These short-straw varieties have the great advantage of not lodging even after heavy applications of fertilizer and, in addition, are insensitive to differences in photoperiodism. Thus they have a wide range of adaptability to different physical and climatic environments.

National average yields thus increased from 800 kilograms per hectare in 1940 to more than 2.5 metric tons in 1964; and yields of up to 8 tons per hectare are not unusual.

Table 5.8 shows the increase in consumption of fertilizer in Mexico, Table 5.9 shows the production of improved seeds, and Table 5.10 shows the contribution of yield increments to output.

## PROJECTIONS OF OUTPUT TO 1975

In 1966 the Ministry of Agriculture, the Ministry of the Treasury, and the Central Bank, with assistance from the USDA, published a report, the main conclusions of which were:

The gross national product at 1960 prices is projected at the annual rate of increase of 6 percent for the 1961–70 period and 7 percent for the 1971–75 period, increasing from 156 billion pesos in 1960 to 392

TABLE 5.8

Consumption of Fertilizers, 1948–61

(1,000 tons of nutrient elements)

| Fertilizer | 1948–52 | 1956 | 1957 | 1958 | 1959 | 1960 | 1961 |
|---|---|---|---|---|---|---|---|
| Nitrates | 10.4 | 44.4 | 53.8 | 72.0 | 85.7 | 95.1 | 110.7 |
| % change | 100 | 427 | 517 | 692 | 824 | 914 | 1064 |
| Phosphates | 8.9 | 26.9 | 35.0 | 29.6 | 32.7 | 34.0 | 37.7 |
| % change | 100 | 302 | 393 | 332 | 367 | 382 | 424 |
| Potassium | 2.2 | 6.2 | 9.4 | 16.3 | 14.4 | 14.2 | 17.0 |
| % change | 100 | 282 | 427 | 741 | 655 | 645 | 773 |

Source: 1948–52 *FAO Production Yearbook, 1960.* 1956–61 Consejo de Recursos Naturales no Renovables, *Fertilizantes, Situacion Actual y Consumo Potencial, Mexico, 1963.*

## TABLE 5.9
### Improved Seed Production in Mexico (selected crops)

| Crop | Period* | Seed Production (tons)* |
|------|---------|------------------------|
| Corn | 1949, 1950 | 4,500.0 |
| | 1951, 1952 | 5,700.0 |
| | 1953, 1954 | 6,200.0 |
| | 1955, 1956 | 10,198.0 |
| | 1957, 1958 | 5,976.0 |
| | 1959, 1960 | 13,668.0 |
| | 1961, 1962 | 14,723.0 |
| Wheat | 1959–60 | 20.0 |
| | 1960–61 | 409.4 |
| | 1061–62 | 6,508.1 |
| Beans | 1959–60 | 93.0 |
| | 1960–61 | 90.0 |
| Sorghum | 1959–60 | 165.5 |
| | 1960–61 | 79.2 |
| | 1961–62 | 153.0 |

Source: Productora Nacional de Semillas, S.A.G., *Quince anos de Produccion de Semillas de Alta Calidad, Mexico, 1962.*
* For corn, each period includes the total production of 2 years; for other crops, the period and production correspond to 1 year.

## TABLE 5.10
### Changes in the Coefficients of the Production Function in Agriculture

| Region | Labor | Capital Inputs | Land | Advanced Inputs |
|--------|-------|----------------|------|-----------------|
| North | | | | |
| 1950 | −.10 | −.03 | .26 | .56 |
| 1960 | .15 | .21 | .62 | .12 |
| Gulf | | | | |
| 1950 | −.51 | .04 | .93 | .63 |
| 1960 | .32 | .19 | .23 | .19 |
| North Pacific | | | | |
| 1950 | −.25 | .05 | .46 | .47 |
| 1960 | .01 | .34 | .37 | .19 |
| South Pacific | | | | |
| 1950 | −.33 | .07 | .40 | .60 |
| 1960 | −.02 | −.30 | .51 | .91 |
| Center | | | | |
| 1950 | −.10 | .04 | .28 | .53 |
| 1960 | .00 | .31 | .42 | .26 |
| All Regions | | | | |
| 1950 | −.29 | −.001 | .41 | .58 |
| 1960 | .08 | .08 | .55 | .47 |

Source: Banco de Mexico, S. A., Division de Desarrollo Economico, Departmento de Estudios Economicos.

billion pesos in 1975. The population growth is projected to increase at an annual rate of 3.6 percent, going from 36 million persons in 1960 to 61 million persons in 1975. Per capita gross national income is projected to increase from 5,310 pesos in 1960 to 6,430 pesos in 1975, an annual rate of increase of 2.7 percent.

Rural population as a percentage of the total population is expected to decrease from about 50 percent in 1960 to 36 percent in 1975. As Mexico industrializes rapidly and an increasing proportion of the labor force is occupied in nonagricultural activities, the agricultural sector must nevertheless continue to expand and to contribute to the overall economy. In order to achieve the projected rate of growth of gross national product, total agricultural product should increase at 4.0 percent annually in 1961–70 and at 4.5 percent annually between 1971 and 1975. These rates of increase are consistent with the requirement that industrial output would rise over the same periods at annual rates of 6.9 and 8.2 percent, respectively, and they should do much to stimulate the market for manufactured products and to raise living conditions in the rural sector.

However, the overall projections of agricultural output that result from aggregating individual commodity production prospects in this study are 4.0 percent for 1961–70, but only 3.3 percent in 1971–75, which underlines the continued need for allocating more resources to the expansion of Mexican agriculture (see Tables 5.11, 5.12, 5.13, and 5.14).

The individual agricultural projections indicate also that crop and livestock output will increase between 1961 and 1975 at a rate slightly

TABLE 5.11
THE MEXICAN ECONOMY IN 1970–1975

| | Share of Product | | | Growth Rates | |
|---|---|---|---|---|---|
| | 1965 | 1970 | 1975 | 1966–70 | 1971–75 |
| Agriculture | 16.0 | 15.0 | 14.4 | 5.3 | 5.5 |
| Mining and quarrying | 1.6 | 1.4 | 1.3 | 4.9 | 5.2 |
| Petroleum and coal | 3.8 | 3.9 | 4.2 | 6.8 | 8.1 |
| Foodstuffs, beverages, and tobacco | 5.3 | 4.9 | 4.5 | 4.6 | 4.9 |
| Textile and leather products | 3.4 | 3.3 | 3.2 | 6.1 | 5.8 |
| Wood and paper products | 1.7 | 1.8 | 1.9 | 7.4 | 8.4 |
| Chemical and rubber products | 2.2 | 2.3 | 2.4 | 7.3 | 7.7 |
| Manufactured nonmetallic mineral products | 0.9 | 0.9 | 1.0 | 6.3 | 7.9 |
| Basic metal industries | 1.6 | 1.8 | 2.0 | 8.4 | 9.1 |
| Machinery and metallic products | 4.3 | 4.7 | 5.3 | 9.6 | 9.6 |
| Construction | 4.8 | 5.0 | 5.2 | 6.1 | 7.2 |
| Electricity | 1.1 | 1.1 | 1.2 | 6.6 | 7.3 |
| Commerce | 32.6 | 31.8 | 31.2 | 6.2 | 6.0 |
| Transportation | 3.6 | 3.7 | 3.7 | 6.9 | 6.9 |
| Services | 17.1 | 18.4 | 18.5 | 7.3 | 6.4 |
| | 100.0 | 100.0 | 100.0 | 6.2 | 6.2 |

Source: Banco de Mexico, S. A., Departamento de Estudios Economicos.

## TABLE 5.12
### Projection of Private Consumption

| Producing Sector | 1961–70 Growth Rate |
|---|---|
| | (*percent*) |
| Agriculture | 5.2 |
| Petroleum and coal | 7.2 |
| Foodstuffs, beverages, and tobacco | 4.4 |
| Textile and leather products | 5.9 |
| Wood and paper products | 9.3 |
| Chemical and rubber products | 7.6 |
| Manufactured nonmetallic mineral products | 8.8 |
| Machinery and metallic products | 9.1 |
| Electricity | 7.2 |
| Commerce | 5.7 |
| Transportation | 7.2 |
| Services | 7.3 |
| Weighted Average | 6.2 |

Source: Banco de Mexico, S. A., Encuesta de Ingreso y Gastos Familiares, Oficina de Proyecciones Agricolas.

## TABLE 5.13
### Current Government Expenditures
(millions of 1960 pesos)

| | 1960 | 1970 |
|---|---|---|
| Agriculture | 13 | 23 |
| Mining and quarrying | 1 | 2 |
| Petroleum and coal | 116 | 208 |
| Foodstuffs, beverages, and tobacco | 42 | 75 |
| Textile and leather products | 23 | 41 |
| Wood and paper products | 117 | 209 |
| Chemical and rubber products | 217 | 389 |
| Manufactured nonmetallic mineral products | 24 | 43 |
| Machinery and metallic products | 281 | 503 |
| Construction | 28 | 50 |
| Electricity | 179 | 320 |
| Commerce | 222 | 397 |
| Transportation | 180 | 322 |
| Services | 277 | 496 |
|     Domestic goods and services | 1,837 | 3,287 |
|     Imports | 168 | 221 |
|     Investments | 3,571 | 6,062 |
|     Wages and salaries | 7,204 | 13,023 |
| Total | 12,843 | 22,593 |

Source: Banco de Mexico, S. A., Departamento de Estudios Economicos.

## TABLE 5.14

(thousands of workers)

| Year | Total | Agricultural | Other | Percentage of Total Agricultural | Other |
|------|-------|--------------|-------|--------------|-------|
| 1930 | 4,981 | 3,580 | 1,401 | 71.9 | 28.1 |
| 1940 | 5,426 | 3,763 | 1,663 | 69.4 | 30.6 |
| 1950 | 7,208 | 4,650 | 2,550 | 64.5 | 35.5 |
| 1960 | 9,297 | 5,481 | 3,816 | 59.0 | 41.0 |
| Projections: | | | | | |
| 1970 | 12,086 | 6,362 | 5,724 | 52.6 | 47.3 |
| 1980 | 15,711 | 7,125 | 8,586 | 45.4 | 54.6 |
| 1990 | 20,424 | 7,545 | 12,879 | 36.9 | 63.1 |
| 2000 | 26,551 | 7,233 | 19,318 | 27.2 | 72.8 |

Source: Folke Dovring, "Papel de la Agricultura en las Poblaciones en Crecimiento," *El Trimestre Economico* 136, Octubre Diciembre de 1967.

## TABLE 5.15

ANNUAL RATES OF GROWTH OF CROP AND LIVESTOCK OUTPUT, 1941–64 AND
PROJECTIONS TO 1965, 1970, AND 1975

| Years | Crop and Livestock Production | Crop Production | Livestock Production |
|-------|-------------------------------|-----------------|----------------------|
| | (*millions of 1960 pesos*) | | |
| 1940 | 9,585 | 4,414 | 5,171 |
| 1950 | 16,381 | 9,700 | 6,681 |
| 1955 | 21,573 | 13,610 | 7,963 |
| 1960 | 25,082 | 14,841 | 10,241 |
| 1961 | 25,868 | 15,227 | 10,641 |
| 1962 | 27,189 | 16,191 | 10,998 |
| 1963 | 27,755 | 16,432 | 11,323 |
| 1964 | 29,483 | 17,763 | 11,720 |
| Projections | | | |
| 1965 | 31,708 | 20,004 | 11,807 |
| 1970 | 38,740 | 24,367 | 14,373 |
| 1975 | 45,520 | 28,214 | 17,306 |
| | (*percent*) | | |
| Average Rates of Growth | | | |
| 1940–50 | 5.5 | 8.2 | 2.6 |
| 1951–60 | 4.4 | 4.3 | 4.4 |
| 1951–55 | 5.4 | 6.3 | 3.7 |
| 1956–60 | 3.1 | 1.8 | 5.2 |
| 1961–63 | 3.4 | 3.5 | 3.4 |
| Projections | | | |
| 1961–65 | 4.8 | 6.2 | 2.9 |
| 1961–75 | 4.1 | 4.4 | 3.6 |
| 1961–70 | 4.4 | 5.1 | 3.4 |
| 1966–70 | 4.1 | 4.0 | 4.0 |
| 1971–75 | 3.3 | 3.0 | 3.8 |

Source: Bank of Mexico, Office for the Study of Agricultural Projections. From 1941 to 1964, based on series used for estimating gross national product. Terminal years indicated are three-year averages.

lower than that of aggregate demand for farm products. While output is projected to grow at an annual rate of 4.0 percent in 1961–70, the sum of projected domestic and external demand is expected to rise by 4.2 percent per year. Between 1971 and 1975 output will grow at 3.3 percent, whereas total demand will increase 4.3 percent (Table 5.15). This increase means that output will fall short of demand by 3.3 percent in 1970 and 8.0 percent in 1975, as compared with only 1.1 percent in 1960, when the difference was met out of imports.

In general, the foreseeable deficits will be larger in 1975 than in 1970, and in most cases in 1975 they will also be proportionately greater in relation to total estimated demand. The principal deficits in output with respect to total demand are the following: vegetables (15 percent in 1970 and 24 percent in 1975), fruits (16 and 25 percent), oilseeds (8 and 19 percent), sorghum (9 and 11 percent), chickpeas (26 and 36 percent), and barley (16 and 15 percent).

The main foreseeable surpluses are the following: wheat (37 percent in 1970 and 32 percent in 1975), rice (10 and 22 percent), beans (10 and 19 percent), and coffee (17 and 10 percent). Possible external demand has not been allowed for in the case of wheat, rice, and beans; in the case of coffee, the surplus is a net surplus after taking into account foreign demand.

With regard to the remaining commodities, principally corn, cotton, and sugarcane, the imbalances between production and total demand will not be significant; there will be relatively small surpluses in the case of corn and cotton, and a relatively small deficit in the case of sugarcane.

On the whole, given the foreseeable changes in average yields, the excess in output will be equivalent to a surplus of 1,044,000 hectares in harvested area in 1970 and 960,000 hectares in 1975, whereas the shortfalls in output of certain commodities will require 379,000 hectares in 1970 and 675,000 in 1975. This suggests an apparent availability of land for deficit crops, although subject to restrictions derived on the one hand from the actual technical possibility of crop substitution and, on the other hand, from social and economic factors influencing the degree of flexibility in the structure of output. A high proportion of the harvest area that would be in surplus—as much as 45 percent in 1970 and 30 percent in 1975—relates to corn, but represents only 7 and 4 percent, respectively, of the total projected crop area for this product. In the case of beans, it would account for 15 percent of the surplus area in 1970 and 34 percent in 1975, which is 9 and 19 percent, respectively, of the harvest area of this crop. Broadly speaking, the surplus area for corn and beans could not be easily allocated to other crops. Wheat involves 28 percent of the surplus area in 1970 and 28 percent in 1975, which is in turn 37 and 32 percent of the crop area for this product. The rest of the gross surplus in crop area—12 percent in 1970 and 8 percent in 1975—is accounted for by rice, coffee, and cotton. Insofar as wheat, cotton, and coffee are concerned, it would be possible to shift part of the surplus area to other crops for which deficits are now foreseen.

In relation to domestic demand, the most important deficit in the supply of animal products in 1970 and 1975 will be that expected with regard to beef cattle. To the extent that this deficit may be met out of livestock and meat normally exported, the possibilities offered by foreign markets will not be fully used. The deficit with respect to pork will also be relatively important, while that relating to other animal products can be expected to be secondary.

Underlying the overall prospects and the particular imbalances foreseen for individual commodities is changing pattern of domestic consumption and of external demand. As incomes rise and the proportion of urban population increases, the share of food consumption in family expenditure will tend to decline. Within food consumption, *per capita* consumption of corn and beans is expected to fall, and that of wheat and sugar to increase at a slow pace, whereas expenditure on meat, dairy products, fruits, vegetables, coffee, and others is expected to rise, in some cases rapidly. Domestic demand for certain agricultural products as feed and as inputs for manufacturing—corn, barley, chickpeas, oilseeds, sugar, cotton, tobacco—will grow more rapidly than in the past. Foreign demand prospects are not on the whole favorable for some of Mexico's main agricultural exports—cotton, coffee, sugar, livestock, and henequen—but are expected to be more dynamic for frozen beef, as well as fruits and vegetables, for which the United States is the main market.[7]

I have indulged in such a long quotation for two reasons. First, because it comes from the most elaborate and authoritative source in the field of agricultural prediction in Mexico. Second, because enough time has elapsed since it was published to warrant the assertion that it is substantially wrong. Many of the goals set for 1975 have already been surpassed. In 1966 sorghum, corn, sugarcane, wheat, strawberries, and at least ten other products exceeded the goals originally set for 1975. Any similarity between what goes on in the field and the projection seems therefore coincidental. Failure may be attributable above all to the understandable wish on the part of its authors to remain on the bureaucratic safe side of this agricultural roulette.

On the other hand, let me say that if by some unhappy miscasting I had been in charge of this orthodox type of projection, in all probability I would have incurred the same mistakes for the very same reasons as our anonymous authors. By this I am trying to say that the game of forecasting long-term, sectorial growth in backward—or more or less developing—countries is a bad game to play. Inadequate statistics, refined analytical tools and prejudices which do not fit the object of analysis, heavy political pressures and, above all, a very imprecise notion of the dynamics of local growth make this task as futile and frustrating as trying to wage conventional war under guerrilla conditions.

---

[7] *Supply and Demand Projections for Agricultural Products in Mexico to 1970 and 1975,* Secretaría de Agricultura y Ganadería, Secretaría de Hacienda y Crédito Público, Banco de México, S.A. México, D. F., Sept. 1965.

When so often in the field I see the many transformations going on in Mexican agriculture, I realize that modernization, diversification, and integration between agriculture and animal husbandry and between agriculture and industrial and urban activities, are taking place so fast and successfully that anticipating annual rates of growth of around 7 percent for the whole sector does not seem as improbable as it surely would look solely from a statistical viewpoint. Since it is obvious that a continuously expanding part of the agricultural sector is becoming increasingly sensitive to changes in domestic and foreign demand, important shifts may be predicted away from cotton, coffee, sugarcane, and wheat into fresh vegetables, fruits, and beef, for all of which there is a huge market in the United States, Canada, the Caribbean, and even Europe. Development of the dairy industry to satisfy growing domestic needs is also a sure bet.

To conclude, if capital availability and high prices for agricultural products are assumed, there is no foreseeable impediment for total output and yields of Mexican agriculture to grow steadily in the cumulative causation manner of Gunnar Myrdal at even higher rates than those registered during the last three decades.

# CHAPTER SIX

# Comparative Analysis of Canadian and United States Productivity

## LUDWIG AUER

In INTERNATIONAL COMPARISONS of economic performance, Canada ranks high among countries of the world. In comparison with the United States, however, Canada lags behind. For decades labor productivity in Canada, measured in real income per person, has been from 20 to 30 percent lower than in the United States. This gap in productivity performance persists in spite of the fact that capital investment per worker in Canada is equally high and capital facilities even higher. The causes for this gap are not so much related to quantity of resource inputs, but more so to quality of resource use. Exploratory studies of the Economic Council show that educational attainment of the population and returns to scale in manufacturing are likely to account for a significant part of this gap in productivity performance.

Our objective here is to compare the productivity performance of Canadian and U.S. agriculture. We wish to determine if there is a significant productivity gap between the agricultural industries of the two countries. If so, we intend to measure the magnitude of this gap. We wish to determine also what changes have taken place over time, and how changes in resource use and technology have contributed to advances in labor productivity in both countries. We begin with historic trends in labor

LUDWIG AUER, Economic Council of Canada.

productivity ratios. From there we proceed to examine: (a) levels of resource inputs, (b) growth in labor productivity, and (c) the contribution of individual resources and technology to growth. In addition we shall examine certain aspects of crop yield technology, land use, and specialization.

## LABOR PRODUCTIVITY COMPARISONS

Labor productivity ratios have frequently been used for the description of economic performance.[1] Statistically, they measure labor productivity in terms of output per man, a measure at once attractive because of its conceptual simplicity and meaningful because improvement in labor productivity is a necessary condition for economic progress. In comparing labor productivity of Canadian to U.S. agriculture we consider two measures: (a) the gross value of production per man, and (b) the net value of production per man. The first is simply total value of agricultural production per worker. The second is this value of production per worker minus all expenditures on nonfarm inputs, and therefore more nearly corresponds to a "value-added" concept. It is an attempt to exclude productivity gains due to the use of inputs from other sectors.

    Annual comparisons of Canadian and U.S. labor productivity in agriculture show clearly that there is a very significant gap between the two countries. Over the past two decades labor productivity in Canadian agriculture, measured in terms of *gross* value of production per man, has been approximately only 65 percent of U.S. productivity. Measured in terms of *net* value of production per man, labor productivity has been in the neighborhood of 75 percent. As one might expect, the net-value comparison is somewhat more favorable for Canadian agriculture as it discounts against greater use of purchased inputs in the United States. As shown in Figure 6.1, annual comparisons of Canadian and U.S. labor productivity fluctuate considerably from year to year but these are largely random variations attributable to more or less favorable weather conditions. Also the effects of Canadian-U.S. dollar exchange ratios have been ignored and consequently our labor productivity comparisons are at times more favorable for Canada than they would have been otherwise.[2] We tenta-

---

[1] For definition of terms see Appendix at the end of this chapter.

[2] For further details on labor productivity comparison, see Appendix at the end of this chapter.

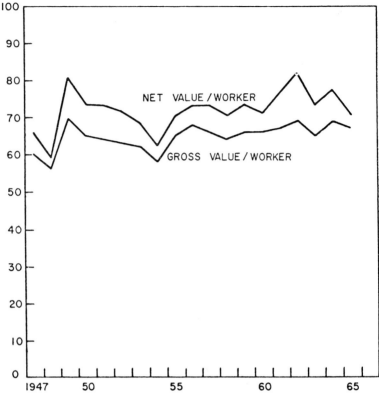

*Fig. 6.1—Labor productivity in Canadian agriculture in percent of U.S. agriculture in terms of gross and net values per worker—in current dollars. (Estimates based on Dominion Bureau of Statistics and USDA Statistics. For definition of gross and net values, see Appendix at the end of this chapter.)*

tively conclude that labor productivity in Canadian agriculture is from 25 to 35 percent lower than in U.S. agriculture.

## RESOURCE INPUTS PER WORKER

As is evident from the preceding discussion, part of the productivity gap between Canada and the United States can be explained by the fact that farmers in the United States buy more inputs from the manufacturing sector. We might, therefore, be tempted to hypothesize that U.S. agriculture is more efficient than Canadian agriculture because it is more highly mechanized. However, a comparison of resource inputs, stratified by type of

TABLE 6.1
RESOURCE INPUTS PER WORKER IN CANADIAN AND U.S. AGRICULTURE,
ANNUAL AVERAGES, 1961–65

| Resource Description | Canada (1949 dollars) | United States (1949 dollars) |
|---|---|---|
| Land and Buildings | 568 | 1,031 |
| Labor | ... | ... |
| Capital Inputs | 2,443 | 4,277 |
| Related to: | | |
| Mechanization | 960 | 1,230 |
| Crop yield technology | 198 | 445 |
| Livestock yield technology | 733 | 1,976 |
| Miscellaneous operating expenses | 413 | 465 |
| Taxes | 139 | 161 |
| Constant Dollar Value of Production (output) | 5,299 | 8,394 |

input, shows that differences in capital inputs related to yield technology are far greater than differences in mechanization. Whereas U.S. expenditures on machinery inputs per worker are not quite 30 percent higher than in Canada, expenditures on yield technology, in both crop and livestock production, are more than 100 percent higher (Table 6.1). Correspondingly the ratios of inputs in machinery to yield technology differ between the two countries; whereas in the United States expenditures on yield technology are nearly twice the amount spent on mechanization, in Canada they are less than the amount spent on mechanization. This then suggests that labor productivity in U.S. agriculture is greater primarily due to more intensive application of yield technology and to a lesser extent due to mechanization.

Over the years there have been significant changes in agricultural resource use and output per worker. From 1947 to 1965, total capital inputs and output per worker have more than doubled in both countries. To examine these changes in resource use, in technology and labor productivity we turn to econometric analysis. For the interested reader a formal description of concepts and techniques of estimation follows. A more "convenient" summary is presented later.

## CONCEPTUAL FRAMEWORK

We assume aggregate production of an industry can be described by function (1) where $Y$ is output and $X_1, \ldots, X_n$ are the resource inputs. To quantify the contribution

$$Y = f(X_1, \ldots, X_n) \tag{1}$$

of changes in resource use to output, we recognize the dynamic elements of production by dating all changes in resource use and by incorporating technological changes explicitly. We make no assumptions regarding returns to scale, neutral, or non-neutral technological change. We assume only that aggregate production can be described by a set of variables with finite and continuous derivatives of all orders which converge upon expansion. In purely definitional form such changes in production can be described by (2). Applying Taylor's expansion we obtain (3) and after rearrangement (4).

$$Y_{t+1} - Y_t = f(X_{1, t+1}, \ldots, X_{n, t+1}) - f(X_{1, t}, \ldots, X_{n, t}) \tag{2}$$

Accordingly the contribution of the $i$th resource input to growth in output is quantified in terms of the change $\Delta X_i$, its marginal productivity $\partial Y / \partial X_i$, and a series

$$Y_{t+1} - Y_t = \sum_i^n \Delta X_i \left( \frac{\partial Y}{\partial X_i} \right)_t + \frac{1}{2}! \sum_i^n \sum_j^n \Delta X_i \Delta X_j \left( \frac{\partial^2 Y}{\partial X_i \partial X_j} \right)_t + \frac{1}{3}! \sum_i \sum_j \sum_k \ldots$$

$$Y_{t+1} - Y_t = \Delta X_1 \left( \frac{\partial Y}{\partial X_1} \right)_t + \frac{1}{2}! \sum_j \Delta X_j \left( \frac{\partial^2 Y}{\partial X_1 \partial X_j} \right)_t + \frac{1}{3}! \sum_j \sum_k \ldots \tag{4}$$

$$\vdots \qquad\qquad\qquad\qquad \vdots$$

$$= \Delta X_n \left( \frac{\partial Y}{\partial X_n} \right)_t + \frac{1}{2}! \sum_j \Delta X_j \left( \frac{\partial^2 Y}{\partial X_n \partial Y_j} \right)_t + \frac{1}{3}! \sum_j \sum_k \ldots$$

of higher order terms which essentially describe interaction effects with other resources.

While application of this approach is valid irrespective of the type of function, we choose an exponential production function because of its simplicity and applicability. In general form, this function is described in (5) where

$$Y_t = a(t) \prod_i^n X_{it}^{b_i(t)} \quad \text{where} \quad \prod_i^n X_i^{b_i} = X_1^{b_1} \ldots X_n^{b_n} \tag{5}$$

$Y$ is output and $X_{it}$ are resource inputs at time $t$, and the coefficient $a(t)$ and the production elasticities $b_i(t)$ are functions of time.

To accommodate technological advances in this production function framework, we consider two approaches. The first allows for *neutral* technological change, the second for *non-neutral* changes. To represent neutral technological change we follow Tinbergen's proposition and insert an exponential shift variable for term $a(t)$ in (5) as in (6). Resource inputs are allowed to vary but production elasticities are assumed to remain constant. This formulation implies that technological change shifts marginal and average productivities of all resource inputs equiproportionately (1, p. 111).

$$Y = a(t) \; \Pi \, X_i^{\,b_i} \text{ where } a(t) = A_o e^{vt} \tag{6}$$

$$Y = a_o \, \Pi \, X_i^{\,b_i(t)} \text{ where } b_{i,t} = b_{oi} + b_{1i}\, t + b_{wi}\, b_{i,t-1} \tag{7}$$

The second approach allows for changes in production elasticities over time as in (7). As production elasticities change, marginal rates of substitution among resources change and thus we account for non-neutral technological changes.

If we were to estimate the production function parameters in (6) and (7) for all variables simultaneously, problems of multicollinearity would arise and distort our results. These problems could be quite serious since we are interested in disaggregate analysis. Instead we employ a short-cut method which is related to Denison's approach.[3] It assumes that employment of resources tends toward equilibrium levels where marginal costs are equal to or equiproportionate to marginal returns. In perfect equilibrium, marginal costs equal marginal revenue and therefore production elasticities of individual resource inputs are equal to their factor shares as in (8). In case of the Cobb-Douglas function the production elasticities

$$e_i = \frac{\partial Y}{Y} \bigg/ \frac{\partial X_i}{X_i} = \frac{X P_{xi}}{y P_y} \tag{8}$$

are equal to the exponents $b_i$. As a first hypothesis we may assume that the equilibrium factor shares remain unchanged over

---

[3] At the time of write-up, computer analysis of changes in labor productivity under the assumption of non-neutral technological change was incomplete and hence will not be presented here.

the years and obtain estimates for the elasticity parameters by averaging their annual values. However, if factor shares change significantly over time, and this is likely to occur in agriculture, a production function model which ignores such changes is quite unrealistic. We therefore may estimate the time trends of these factor shares, allowing at the same time for adjustment lags as indicated in (7) above. Results of these two types of estimating equations can be interpreted as "range estimates" of the contribution of changes in resource use and advances in technology to growth. The contribution of these changes to growth in labor productivity is then evaluated by dividing both sides of production function by labor inputs and then applying Taylor's expansion as described earlier.

### SUMMARY OF ESTIMATING PROCEDURES

For analysis of changes in production we distinguish between changes in levels of resource inputs and changes in the rates of output over inputs. To impute the contribution of changes in resource inputs we multiply their annual changes (measured in constant dollars) by their corresponding factor shares in output (in current dollars). We then compute the remainder, the annual ratios of output over the weighted product of inputs, and attribute it to technological change. Under conditions of economic equilibrium this is equivalent to derivation of a Cobb-Douglas type production function described in (9) where the $X$-variables denote resource input levels, the $b$-exponents are the factor shares or production elasticities, and the

$$Y = a(t) X_1^{b_1} X_2^{b_2} \ldots X_{15}^{b_{15}} \tag{9}$$

$$\frac{Y}{X_4} = a(t) X_1^{b_1} X_2^{b_2} \ldots \frac{X_4}{X_4} \ldots X_{15}^{b_{15}} \tag{10}$$

variable $a(t)$ estimates improvement in resources use through advances in technology. Estimates of labor productivity are obtained by dividing both sides of equation (9) by the labor input variable, here denoted by $X_4$, as in (10). This estimating procedure is based on a specific set of assumptions. By altering some of these assumptions, for example, taking time trends of factor shares into account, different results are obtained. While resource productivities will change over time, estimates of annual growth rates averaged over the length of the period are likely to remain unchanged. Here we will only present "average" values.

A summary of average annual factor shares generally reflects the differences in resource inputs per worker in both countries. In conformance with earlier results Canadian factor shares are significantly lower in land and buildings, and in capital inputs related to yield technology. By contrast Canada's share in labor inputs (measured in terms of total farm labor paid at hired-labor wage rates) is much higher than in the United States, that is, 46 percent in Canada versus 30 percent in the United States. This is in spite of the fact that Canadian farmers spent a somewhat larger proportion on mechanization than U.S. farmers (Table 6.2).

## GROWTH IN LABOR PRODUCTIVITY

Advances in labor productivity in agriculture have occurred at a remarkable pace. Compared to 1947, productivity levels in 1965 were two to three times higher. Our task is to determine the source of these changes and to find out why Canada has continuously lagged behind the United States. For this purpose we use our previously derived production estimates which closely resemble the actual data (Fig. 6.2).

## SOURCES OF GROWTH

To simplify, we express the contribution of changes in resource use and technology to growth in terms of average annual growth

TABLE 6.2

FACTOR SHARES (OR PRODUCTION ELASTICITIES) OF RESOURCE INPUTS IN AGRICULTURAL OUTPUT, ANNUAL AVERAGES, CANADA AND THE UNITED STATES, 1947–65

| Resource Description | Canada | United States |
|---|---|---|
| Land and Buildings | .169 | .180 |
| Labor | .464 | .305 |
| Capital Inputs | .508 | .537 |
| Related to: | | |
|     Mechanization | .235 | .183 |
|     Crop yield technology | .027 | .052 |
|     Livestock yield technology | .145 | .211 |
|     Miscellaneous operating expenses | .056 | .054 |
|     Taxes | .045 | .037 |
| Total | 1.141 | 1.022 |

Source: Based on Dominion Bureau of Statistics and USDA Statistics; for details on estimation procedures, see Appendix at the end of this chapter.

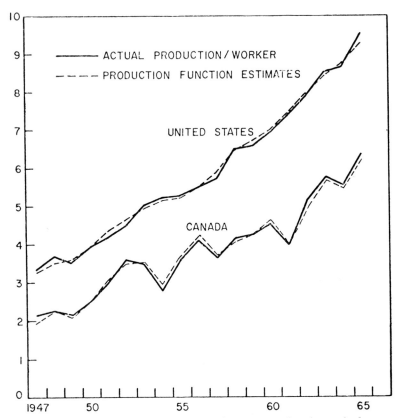

Fig. 6.2—*Gross value of production per worker in agriculture, Canada and the United States—constant dollars in thousands. (From Dominion Bureau of Statistics and USDA Statistics.)*

rates. Overall growth rates in gross output per worker for Canada and the United States are 5.44 and 5.94 percent per year respectively (Table 6.3). Considering that at the outset Canada's level of productivity was significantly lower than that of the United States and that Canada's growth rate has not been greater than that of the United States, the relative disadvantage has essentially remained unchanged over the past two decades. Canadian farmers would need to increase their labor productivity today (measured in terms of gross output per worker) by 50 percent to reach U.S. levels of productivity (Fig. 6.2).

Among major input categories, changes in land and buildings have contributed least to productivity increase, an estimated

TABLE 6.3

CONTRIBUTION OF CHANGES IN RESOURCE INPUTS AND TECHNOLOGY TO GROWTH
IN LABOR PRODUCTIVITY, ANNUAL AVERAGES IN PERCENT, CANADA AND THE
UNITED STATES, 1947–65

| Resource Description | Canada | United States |
|---|---|---|
| Land and Buildings | .10 | .17 |
|   Interest on real estate | .08 | .15 |
|   Depreciation of buildings | .02 | .05 |
|   Building repairs | .00* | −.03 |
| Labor | 1.95 | 2.62 |
| Capital | 1.56 | 1.63 |
|   Inputs related to mechanization | .87 | .62 |
|     Interest on machinery investment | .07 | .16 |
|     Machinery depreciation | .20 | .31 |
|     Machinery operating expenses | .60 | .15 |
|   Inputs related to yield technology in crop production | .25 | .18 |
|     Fertilizer | .16 | .17 |
|     Lime | .00* | .00* |
|     Seed, purchased | .09 | .01 |
|   Inputs related to yield technology in livestock production | .07 | .70 |
|     Interest on livestock investment | .00* | .03 |
|     Livestock, purchased | .05 | .23 |
|     Feed, purchased | .02 | .44 |
|   Miscellaneous operating expenses | .37 | .17 |
|   Taxes | −.00* | −.04 |
| Other Technological Change | 1.83 | 1.52 |
| Average Annual Rate of Growth in Labor Productivity | 5.44 | 5.94 |

Source: Based on Dominion Bureau of Statistics and USDA Statistics; for details on estimation procedures, see Appendix at the end of this chapter.
* Smaller than .005 percent.

.10 percent per year in Canada and .17 percent in the United States. Much more significant are the changes induced by other capital expenditures. We categorize these "other" expenditures into several groups: (a) capital inputs related to mechanization (interest on machinery investment, machinery depreciation, machinery operating expenses), (b) capital inputs related to yield technology in crop production (expenditures on fertilizer, lime, and seed), (c) capital inputs related to yield technology in live-stock production (interest on livestock investment, purchases of livestock and feed), (d) miscellaneous operating expenses, and (e) taxes. They account for more than one quarter of the growth rates in both countries. In the United States, inputs related to yield technology and, in Canada, inputs related to mechanization make up the largest portion of these capital inputs. Aside from these capital inputs, other changes in technology, not readily quantified, have contributed very significantly. They may cover crop variety and livestock improvements introduced by universities and federal agencies; they may include improved farm management practices, regional specialization, farm size distribution, and numerous other items not represented here.

By far the most significant contribution to growth in labor productivity has come through adjustments of the labor force itself. Today fewer farmers produce more than was produced two decades ago. Even if total volume of production had not increased, the mere fact that fewer farmers are able to produce the same output reflects increased productivity. Rates of outmigration from agriculture have been very similar in both countries (Fig. 6.3), a reduction of nearly 50 percent of the agricultural labor force over the past two decades. Our estimates suggest that the contribution of outmigration to growth is nearly 25 percent greater in the United States than in Canada. This is not because of a more rapid rate of outmigration but because farm labor is higher priced in the United States, and hence greater

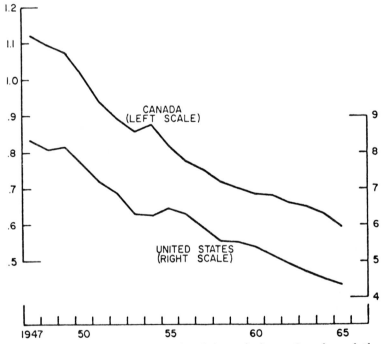

Fig. 6.3—Labor force employed in agriculture, Canada and the United States—in millions. (From Dominion Bureau of Statistics.)

gains are derived for each unit of labor saved in agricultural production.

## MARGINAL VALUE PRODUCTIVITIES

After inputing growth in labor productivity to changes in resource use, technology, and structural shifts in manpower, it would be appropriate to go one step further and identify the forces behind these changes. This is a far more difficult task. Because of its complexity and our lack of knowledge, we can only touch upon this question. If, as before, we assume that farmers react to economic incentive patterns, then prices and marginal productivities should serve as relevant indicators. To simplify, we combine prices and marginal productivities in marginal *value* productivities. Marginal value productivities indicate what dollar returns we may expect from each additional dollar spent. We hypothesize that the higher the marginal value productivity of a resource at the outset the more of that resource should be used over time relative to others. Employing this criterion, our analysis indicates that incentives for investment in Canadian agriculture were strong for mechanization and crop yield technology but weak for investment in land and buildings (Table 6.4). Over the years these incentives have declined in the area of mechanization but are still strong in inputs related to yield technology. In a general way this corresponds to the growth pattern of Canadian agriculture. Capital inputs related to mechanization and crop yield technology ranked higher in contribution to growth than inputs related to livestock production and real estate, but of the two, mechanization was far more important.

An equivalent analysis of U.S. data does not show such close correspondence. Our estimates of marginal productivities are high for mechanization and low for most others (Table 6.5). Contribution to growth, however, is low for mechanization and high for yield technology, especially in livestock production (Table 6.3). This is not as we would expect it.

We might speculate at this point that government policies have had a decisive influence. During the period of excess production the United States Government encouraged farmers to take land out of grain production. This in turn induced farmers to increase crop yields on the remaining acreage and to feed more to livestock. The Canadian Government, on the other hand, instituted a system of grain delivery quotas based on grain acreage. This, in turn, induced farmers to enlarge farm size and, there-

TABLE 6.4

MARGINAL VALUE PRODUCTIVITIES IMPUTED TO RESOURCE INPUTS (IN CURRENT DOLLARS), ANNUAL AVERAGES, CANADA, 1947–51 AND 1961–65

| Resource Description | Canada | | Economic Incentive To Increase Input |
|---|---|---|---|
| | 1947–51 | 1961–65 | |
| Land and Buildings | | | |
| Interest on real estate | 1.06 | 1.08 | weak |
| Depreciation of buildings | 1.02 | 1.06 | weak |
| Building repairs | 1.07 | 1.05 | weak |
| Labor | .99 | 1.03 | weak |
| Capital | | | |
| Inputs related to mechanization | | | |
| Interest on machinery investment | 1.91 | 1.12 | strong |
| Machinery depreciation | 1.94 | 1.12 | strong |
| Machinery operating expenses | 1.40 | 1.06 | strong |
| Inputs related to yield technology in crop production | | | |
| Fertilizer | 1.33 | 1.75 | strong |
| Lime | .92 | .90 | weak |
| Seed, purchased | 4.02 | 1.37 | strong |
| Inputs related to yield technology in livestock production | | | |
| Interest on livestock investment | 1.03 | 1.03 | weak |
| Livestock, purchased | 1.17 | 1.10 | intermediate |
| Feed, purchased | .99 | 1.02 | weak |
| Miscellaneous operating expenses | 1.20 | 1.08 | intermediate |
| Taxes | 1.51 | 1.06 | . . . |

Source: Based on Dominion Bureau of Statistics and USDA Statistics; for details on estimation procedures, see Appendix at the end of this chapter.

fore, Canadian farmers invested more in mechanization. This is a plausible hypothesis[4] and it probably accounts for part of this difference in resource allocation.

As a partial test of this hypothesis we examine changes in production of principal crops by observing crop acreage, shifts among crops, and changes in crop yields. We let production $Q$ be a function of total cropland $A$, relative crop

$$Q = A \sum_{i}^{n} \frac{A_i}{A} \cdot \frac{Q_i}{A_i} \text{ where } A = \sum_{i}^{n} A_i \tag{11}$$

acres $A_i/A$ and quantity produced per acre $Q_i/A_i$ where subscript $i$ refers to individual crops as in equation (11). A third-term Taylor expansion of this expression, as before, will enable

---

[4] The author is indebted to Dr. J. A. Dawson of the staff of the Economic Council of Canada for suggesting this hypothesis.

TABLE 6.5

MARGINAL VALUE PRODUCTIVITIES IMPUTED TO RESOURCE INPUTS (IN CURRENT DOLLARS), ANNUAL AVERAGES, UNITED STATES, 1947–51 AND 1961–65

| Resource Description | United States | | Economic Incentive To Increase Input |
|---|---|---|---|
| | 1947–51 | 1961–65 | |
| Land and Buildings | | | |
| Interest on real estate | 1.01 | 1.00 | weak |
| Depreciation of buildings | 1.10 | 1.06 | weak |
| Building repairs | 1.16 | .92 | weak |
| Labor | 1.03 | 1.02 | weak |
| Capital | | | |
| Inputs related to mechanization | | | |
| Interest on machinery investment | 1.90 | 1.16 | strong |
| Machinery depreciation | 2.12 | 1.05 | strong |
| Machinery operating expenses | 1.60 | .93 | strong |
| Inputs related to yield technology in crop production | | | |
| Fertilizer | 1.20 | 1.06 | intermediate |
| Lime | .86 | 1.01 | weak |
| Seed, purchased | 1.03 | 1.01 | weak |
| Inputs related to yield technology in livestock production | | | |
| Interest on livestock investment | 1.03 | .97 | weak |
| Livestock, purchased | .96 | 1.02 | weak |
| Feed, purchased | 1.00 | .99 | weak |
| Miscellaneous operating expenses | 1.10 | 1.04 | weak |
| Taxes | 1.01 | 1.01 | . . . |

Source: Based on Dominion Bureau of Statistics and USDA Statistics; for details on estimation procedures, see Appendix at the end of this chapter.

us to impute changes in volume of production to each variable. Results of this analysis confirm the hypothesis. In Canada acreage expansion increased production; in the United States acreage reductions slowed down the rate of production expansion. Shifts among crops contributed little to change but changes in yield were significant. In Canada higher yields accounted for 70 percent of the expansion; in the United States they accounted for 171 percent and more than compensated for negative effects of acreage reduction and shifts among crops.

## CROP YIELD TECHNOLOGY

It would be unrealistic to attribute these differential patterns of growth of the two countries to government policy alone. Interactions between crop yields and climatic conditions have probably played an important role. In Canada crop production is centered in the Prairie Provinces where the growing season is

TABLE 6.6

CUMULATIVE CHANGES IN VOLUME OF PRODUCTION OF PRINCIPAL CROPS IMPUTED
TO CHANGES IN ACREAGE, SHIFTS IN CROPS AND YIELDS, CANADA AND THE
UNITED STATES, 1947–65

|  | Canada | | United States | |
|---|---|---|---|---|
| 1947 Acreage in Million Acres | 60.0 | | 308.4 | |
| 1965 Acreage in Million Acres | 61.9 | | 265.5 | |
| 1947 Production in Million Dollars | 1,815.5 | | 11,854.0 | |
| 1965 Production in Million Dollars | 2,274.1 | | 15,085.2 | |
| 1947–65 Change in Million Dollars | 458.6 | 100% | 3,231.2 | 100% |
| Attributed to: | | | | |
| Changes in acres in million dollars | +133.5 | +29% | −2,070.4 | − 64% |
| Shifts in crops in million dollars | + 6.1 | + 1% | − 222.8 | − 7% |
| Changes in yield in million dollars | +319.0 | +70% | +5,524.4 | +171% |

Source: Based on Dominion Bureau of Statistics and USDA Statistics; for details on
estimation procedures, see Appendix at the end of this chapter.

short, precipitation is sparse, and farmers specialize in the production of food grains. In the United States, agricultural production is centered in the Corn Belt states where climatic conditions favor production of feed grains, especially corn. Corn
yields are much higher than wheat yields and are increasing at
a faster rate. In 1960, for example, U.S. "trend" yields of corn
were approximately 54 bushels compared to 23 bushels for wheat.
Corn yields were increasing at an annual rate of about 1⅓
bushels whereas wheat yields were increasing at a rate of less
than half a bushel. In Canada comparative yields for corn were
20 percent higher than in the United States (64.4 bu. vs. 53.6 bu.)
but for wheat they were nearly 15 percent lower (20.1 bu. vs. 23.0
bu.), annual yield increases were equally high for corn (1.37 bu.
vs. 1.33 bu.) but lower again for wheat (0.13 bu. vs. 0.41 bu.). In
the United States, corn acreage is larger than wheat acreage. In
Canada wheat acreage accounts for over 40 percent of the cropland acreage and corn acreage accounts for less than 2 percent
of the cropland. Climatic conditions do not favor production of
corn in Canada and it is rarely grown in the Prairie Provinces.
Consequently, Canadian farmers benefit little from the advances
in corn production. A comparative summary of crop yields
quickly reveals that Canada has, at the moment, no ready substitute for corn and relies very heavily on the lower-yielding
small grains (Table 6.7).

Even if we allow for the differences in the relative importance of wheat and corn between the two countries, Canada is
still at a disadvantage. Applying the same estimation techniques
as before we determine how Canada's crop production would

TABLE 6.7

COMPARATIVE YIELDS AND YIELD CHANGES OF SELECTED CROPS, CANADA AND
THE UNITED STATES, 1939–63

| | 1960 "Trend" Yield | | Annual Change | |
| --- | --- | --- | --- | --- |
| | Canada | United States | Canada | United States |
| Food Grains (in bushels) | | | | |
| Wheat | 20.1 | 23.0 | .13 | .41** |
| Rye | 16.7 | 17.0 | .21** | .33** |
| Feed Grains (in bushels) | | | | |
| Corn | 64.4 | 53.5 | 1.37** | 1.33** |
| Oats | 40.6 | 40.8 | .55** | .54** |
| Barley | 28.0 | 31.4 | .04 | .45** |
| Grain sorghum | ... | 34.6 | ... | 1.20** |
| Tame Hay (in tons) | 1.8 | 1.8 | .01† | .02** |
| Oilseeds (in bushels) | | | | |
| Soybeans | ... | 23.3 | ... | .28** |
| Flaxseed | 9.6 | 8.8 | .12* | −.02 |
| Special Crops (in bushels) | | | | |
| Potatoes | 144.7 | 192.0 | 3.54** | 5.76** |
| Cotton (in pounds) | ... | 454.7 | ... | 11.67** |

Source: Based on Dominion Bureau of Statistics and USDA Statistics; for details on estimation procedures, see Appendix at the end of this chapter.
* Tested statistically significant at the 5 percent level.
** Tested statistically significant at the 1 percent level.
† Tested statistically significant at the 10 percent level.

have advanced had it been possible to apply U.S. yield technology. For this comparison we select six crops for which we have comparable yield trend coefficients: wheat, oats, barley, flaxseed, corn, and tame hay. Had these crops been produced under U.S. technology in Canada, the impact of changes in acreage would have been slightly larger, shifts between crops would have had a lesser effect, but changes in yield would have contributed nearly twice as much. Canada would have had a slight advantage at the outset but would have lost it soon and been surpassed by a 10 percent margin toward the end of the period (Table 6.8). In part this reflects the fact that most of the Canadian wheat is *spring* wheat whereas most of the U.S. wheat is *winter* wheat, and spring wheat normally yields less than winter wheat. If in addition we allow for this difference, for example by comparing crop production in Saskatchewan to that of North Dakota, Canada barely maintains an absolute advantage in crop yield technology.

There are indications that Canada's yield technology in livestock production is at a similar disadvantage. Instead of examining various livestock enterprises we turn to aggregate analysis. To assess the relative importance of yield technology and mechanization, in both crop and livestock production, we reduce

TABLE 6.8

CHANGES IN VOLUME OF PRODUCTION OF SIX CROPS PRODUCED IN CANADA UNDER
SIMULATED U.S. CONDITIONS, 1947–65

| | Yield Technology | | | |
|---|---|---|---|---|
| | Canada | | United States | |
| 1947 Acreage in Million Acres | 54.9 | | 54.9 | |
| 1965 Acreage in Million Acres | 58.7 | | 58.7 | |
| 1947 Production in Million Dollars | 1,649.5 | | 1,597.3 | |
| 1965 Production in Million Dollars | 2,061.9 | | 2,318.1 | |
| 1947–65 Change in Million Dollars | 412.4 | 100% | 720.8 | 100% |
| Attributed to: | | | | |
| Changes in acres in million dollars | 127.3 | 31% | 137.1 | 19% |
| Shifts in crops in million dollars | 21.6 | 5% | 14.9 | 2% |
| Changes in yield in million dollars | 263.5 | 64% | 568.7 | 79% |

Source: Based on Dominion Bureau of Statistics and USDA Statistics; for details
on estimation procedures, see Appendix at the end of this chapter.

all changes in labor productivity to two variables: one measures
yield technology in terms of total value of production per acre,
the other measures mechanization in terms of crop acres per
man. We evaluate annual changes in both variables by Taylor's
expansion, cumulate these annual changes from 1947 to 1965,
and find that in Canada yield technology contributed only one-
third as much as mechanization whereas in the United States
yield technology contributed more than mechanization to growth
in labor productivity (Table 6.9). These results confirm those
obtained earlier. Compared to the United States, Canada has
advanced in the area of mechanization but has not kept pace in
yield technology.

To conclude, we suggest that Canada may need to examine
her policy in agricultural research and development.

It does not follow from our analysis that mechanization is
not the most desirable direction of development for Canadian

TABLE 6.9

CUMULATIVE CHANGES IN LABOR PRODUCTIVITY IMPUTED TO YIELD TECHNOLOGY
AND MECHANIZATION, CANADA AND THE UNITED STATES, 1947–65

| | Canada (1949 dollars) | | United States (1949 dollars) | |
|---|---|---|---|---|
| Yield Technology (production/acre) | 833 | 23% | 3,251 | 53% |
| Mechanization (acres/worker) | 2,755 | 77% | 2,925 | 47% |
| Total (production/worker) | 3,588 | 100% | 6,176 | 100% |

Source: Based on Dominion Bureau of Statistics and USDA Statistics; for details on
estimation procedures, see Appendix at the end of this chapter.

agriculture. It indicates, however, that significant gains in labor productivity could be derived from more rapid advances in yield technology. As yields increase, the volume of production is likely to expand. Because of inelastic demand on the domestic market, this could depress farm income unless Canada shifts more into export markets. This might require that Canada's production pattern more nearly adjusts to international demand patterns for food and feed grains. To the extent that crop yields may advance in different regions of the country at different rates, regional advantages may be lost or gained and adjustment problems intensified or solved. Failure to expand exports as increases in agricultural production exceed population growth could necessitate more rapid adjustment of the agricultural labor force. In view of these potential gains and problems, it would be most desirable to examine these questions in greater depth, evaluate costs and benefits of alternative solutions, and then arrive at an optimal policy.

# APPENDIX

## DEFINITION OF TERMS

*Gross value of production per worker =*
(Cash receipts from farm marketings of livestock and production)
+ (Cash receipts from marketings of crops)
+ (Value of farm products consumed directly in farm household)

Government payments, rental value of dwelling, and nonfarm income have been excluded from data sets of both countries. Data have been converted from current to constant dollars by deflating component data sets. No allowance has been made for fluctuations in Canadian/United States currency exchange rates.

Canadian data, in addition, have been adjusted for inventory changes and weather effects.

The number of workers, the denominator of the labor productivity ratio, refers to persons employed in the agricultural labor force, aged 14 years and over.

*Net value of production per worker =*
Gross value of production per worker minus
(Operating expenses [fertilizer, lime, seed, feed, and livestock

purchases, and miscellaneous expenditures] + [building repairs and depreciation of buildings and machinery] )/number of workers in agricultural labor force.

## ADDITIONAL INFORMATION CONCERNING TABLES

Table 6.1 — The Resource Description of this table is based on a more detailed breakdown:

    I. Land and buildings
        1. Interest on real estate
        2. Depreciation of buildings
        3. Building repairs
    II. Labor
    III. Capital
        Farm purchases of inputs related to mechanization
            1. Interest on machinery investment
            2. Machinery depreciation
            3. Machinery operating expenses
        Farm purchases of inputs related to yield technology in crop production
            1. Fertilizer
            2. Lime
            3. Seed, purchased
        Farm purchases of inputs related to yield technology in livestock production
            1. Interest on livestock investment
            2. Livestock, purchased
            3. Feed, purchased
        Miscellaneous operating expenses
        Taxes
    IV. Constant dollar value of product is gross value of production in 1949 dollars.

Table 6.2 — Factor shares or production elasticities of resource inputs are computed as annual ratios of current values of output over current values of inputs, summed and averaged over the period 1947–65.

Table 6.3 — These estimates are production function estimates. They are derived from function (10) in the text by application of Taylor's expansion. It can be shown that in this case the expression for annual percentage changes in output reduces to:

$$r_y = r_a + r_1 b_1 + r_2 b_2 + \ldots + r_n b_n + \ldots$$

where $r_y$, $r_a$, $r_1$, $\ldots r_n$ are annual percentage changes of output, neutral technological change, and individual resource inputs, and the $b_i$ coefficients are production elasticities. Averaging annual estimates over the period of years provides us with annual average estimates.

Tables 6.4 and 6.5 — Marginal value productivities are defined by:

$$\text{MVP} = \frac{\partial Y}{\partial X_i} \frac{P_y}{P_{x_i}} = b_i\, Y\, P_y\, /\, X_i\, P_{x_i}$$

where $b_i$ are production elasticities, $Y$ is output, and $X_i$ is input $i$, all measured in current dollars. The production elasticities are estimated in accordance with function (7) in the text.

Table 6.6 — Cumulative changes in volume of production of principal crops were imputed to changes in acreage, shifts in crops and yields as described by function (11) in the text. Principal crops include 12 crops of Canada (wheat, oats, barley, rye, flaxseed, corn for grain, tame hay, potatoes, sugar beets, mixed grains, field roots, and fodder corn) and 9 crops of the United States (wheat, oats, all corn, soybeans, tame hay, barley, flaxseed, grain sorghum, and cotton). Canadian acreages refer to seeded acres, U.S. acreages refer to harvested acres.

Table 6.7 — Estimates are linear trend line coefficients of the function:

$$Y = a + bt + u$$

where $Y$ is yield, $a$ the base yield, $b$ the annual yield increase, and $u$ is an error term.

Table 6.8 — Estimated as described above (Table 6.6) but only 6 crops are included (wheat, oats, barley, corn, flaxseed, and tame hay). For "simulating U.S. conditions," U.S. trend-yield coefficients were substituted for Canadian trend-yield coefficients.

Table 6.9 — Estimated by Taylor's expansion of the expression:

$$\frac{Q}{M} = \frac{A}{M} \cdot \frac{Q}{A}$$

where $Q$ is volume of production (in constant dollars), $M$ is size of labor force, and $A$ is cropland acreage. Cropland acreage of Canada includes 18 crops; cropland acreage of the United States includes 59 crops.

## REFERENCES

(1)  Brown, M., *On the Theory and Measurement of Technological Change,* Cambridge Univ. Press, 1966.

(2)  Denison, E. F., "The Sources of Economic Growth in the United States and the Alternative Before Us," Committee for Econ. Dev., Supplementary Paper 13, Jan. 1962.

(3)  Dunlop, J. T., and V. P. Diatchenko, *Labor Productivity,* McGraw-Hill Book Co., 1964.

# PART THREE

# Economic Integration of North American Agriculture

# CHAPTER SEVEN

# Implications of a North American Common Commodity Market

## ALEX F. McCALLA

IN THIS CHAPTER I will restrict my discussion to a qualitative analysis of the implications of the integration of the Canadian and U.S. grain-livestock sectors, constrained by domestic as well as international policy objectives. I will discuss the question of including Mexico in the union, some issues regarding food aid and domestic policy objectives, and a definition of a common market and a summary of the barriers to its accomplishment.

### SOME BASIC QUESTIONS AND DEFINITIONS

#### THE INCLUSION OF MEXICO

This chapter is the first to explicitly discuss the combining of Mexican, U.S., and Canadian agricultures into one of several forms of economic integration. I feel compelled, therefore, to raise a reservation as to the reality of including Mexico in such a unit. I introduce the reservation on three grounds. First, in the postwar period, the economic integration of sovereign states in various forms of economic union has occurred between countries at generally similar stages of economic development. The

ALEX F. McCALLA, Department of Agricultural Economics, Agricultural Experiment Station, and the Giannini Foundation, University of California, Davis. The author expresses thanks for assistance in the preparation of this chapter to Gordon A. King and Stanley Detering.

European Economic Community (EEC) and the European Free Trade Area (EFTA) are groupings of generally industrialized developed nations. The Central American Common Market (CACM) and the Latin American Free Trade Area (LAFTA), of which Mexico is already a member, are groupings of developing nations where agriculture is dominant but industrialization is sought through expanded markets. Further, in all four cases most, if not all, sectors of the economy are included in the unions.

While the absence of a historical example does not prove that an integration of the agricultures of a developing and two developed nations is not feasible, it does suggest that integration is more likely between nations at similar stages of economic development. Second, while in broadest terms the overall economic objective of all nations is to sustain a rapid rate of per capita income growth, the dominance of this objective is much greater in developing nations. Developed nations such as the United States give at least verbal recognition of this dominance. If there is a consensus on any point in the theory of economic development, it is that rapid income growth is accomplished by the generation of off-farm employment opportunities, coupled with increased agricultural productivity. All economic policy, including trade, should be so directed. Restrictive trade policies administered with this goal in mind may offer positive contributions to economic development. Mexican trade policy as presently constituted seeks, as an integral part of development policy, to foster agricultural self-sufficiency in essential food products, to promote import substitution, and to lessen the dependence of Mexico on a single source of import supply, namely the United States (25). All of these are accepted development goals. The removal of Mexico's present complex and generally high agricultural import restrictions would represent a drastic change in Mexican development policy and the results of this change should be evaluated against Mexican development objectives rather than global food aid objectives. Third, it would certainly be incongruous if the creation of a North American Common Market, for the explicit purpose of contributing food aid to developing nations, could potentially damage the development process of one of these nations. For these reasons, I shall give only limited consideration to Mexico as a participant in the common market.

## FOOD AID AS THE SOLE GOAL

The above discussion also begs the question of the relevance of the goal of expanded food aid as the sole or even major objective of agricultural integration. It is not my purpose to engage in a definitive discussion of the role of food aid in economic development but, rather, I simply wish to emphasize certain propositions which should be borne in mind.

1.  The multiplying of population projections by minimum nutritional requirements to compute world food needs and setting this against biological production projections is an economically naive way to approach the question (21, p. 322). Quite clearly budget, price, and technical questions also contribute to the determination of effective demand (8, pp. 100–109).
2.  The long-run solution to the world food problem lies with the control of population and the expansion of food production in the developing countries (13, Chap. 7; 23).
3.  The most effective form of economic assistance to developing nations, by developed nations, is the transfer of productive resources (14). Food aid is an inefficient way of transferring these resources (12, pp. 3–4) and may hinder increases in indigenous food production (10, 11).
4.  The effective constraints on the availability of food aid is more likely to be the ability of developing nations to absorb it and willingness of the developed nations to finance it rather than the production potential of developed nations, particularly the United States and Canada (1, 9). In the light of these considerations it will be more meaningful to consider food aid as a demand component determined by national and international political and economic objectives rather than as unlimited need which requires all-out North American food production. Thus for the purposes of this chapter food aid will be considered as a part of the broader objective of international economic assistance which, in interaction with other national objectives, determines agricultural policy.

## POSSIBLE OBJECTIVES OF A COMMON COMMODITY MARKET

If the above limitations are accepted, then it is necessary to consider other motivations besides expanded food aid which could motivate varying degrees of economic integration of the agricultures of Canada and the United States. One broad objective of a total integration could be to improve the welfare of both participants. Clearly other unions have been economically motivated by the potential increases in efficiency, national income, and welfare accruing from economic integration.[1] Thus the overall objective of North American integration could be expressed as the improvement of the welfare, that is, per capita income, of Canadians and Americans. This implies optimum resource allocation consistent with goals of equity in income distribution, growth, stability, employment, and balance of payments. The goal of agricultural integration then could be expressed as the improvement of the welfare of North American farmers. Canadian-American agricultural integration would realistically have roughly the same objectives as are presently held for domestic agricultures; namely price stability, income equity, and technological adjustments. Further, as domestic agricultural programs are constrained by food price, budget, export, and international assistance objectives so, probably, would be any form of agricultural integration. It is against these objectives, then, that the benefits and losses arising from integration should be judged. Because food aid represents only a partial objective of U.S. and Canadian policy, it would be also only a partial objective of the economic unit. Finally, it should be clear that for a total judgement of the welfare effects of integration, nonagricultural effects also should be considered but I will leave this discussion to others.

## THE NATURE OF A COMMON COMMODITY MARKET

In the postwar period, a substantial literature on the theory of economic integration has developed (2, 3, 16, 20, 22, 26). Similarly, much has been written on the progress and prospects for existing or proposed economic combinations of varying sorts such as the EEC, EFTA, LAFTA, and CACM (5, 28). Balassa (3, p. 25) has proposed the following hierarchy of degrees of integration: A free trade area exists when sovereign nations agree to reduce or remove tariffs and trade barriers among themselves, but pursue independent trade policies with respect to third countries; a customs union is a free trade area but with a common external tariff established toward third countries; a common market is a

---

[1] See, for example, Article 2 of the Rome Treaty quoted in (27, p. 31); also see (5, pp. 1–4).

customs union supplemented by the removal of restrictions on resource movements; an economic union is a common market with some degree of harmonization of economic and social policies; and economic integration is defined as full unification of all economic policies under a supranational authority.

But none of these is acceptable for the purposes at hand. The customs union definition is not sufficient for two reasons. First, in the area of agriculture, trade restrictions among Canada, Mexico, and the United States are not distinct trade policies but are, in general, integral parts of domestic agricultural programs. Thus, to remove restrictions on agricultural trade without harmonizing domestic agricultural policies is a highly unlikely proposition. Second, North America is a net surplus area in some commodities, notably grains, and a deficit area in other commodities, such as livestock products. These circumstances create particular problems in defining what would be a common external trade policy. It is sufficient to say here that the problems of the rationalization of individual country agricultural policies in the EEC, and the absence of the attempt in EFTA, coupled with the potential problems likely to arise in the North American context, require that the definition of a common commodity market be more embracing than that of a customs union. It is clear that any workable integration would require some harmonization of domestic policies as well. Thus, I shall define a common commodity market as containing the following elements.

1. The removal of tariff and nontariff restrictions to the movement of agricultural commodities between the participating members.
2. The establishment of a common external trade policy toward third countries. This policy must, of necessity, in addition to common tariffs on imports, contain a common export policy.
3. The harmonization of domestic agricultural policies to become consistent with the commonly held goals of national economies discussed above.

### OBSTACLES TO A COMMON MARKET

The following summary review of import restrictions is presented to clearly show that such restrictions, in general, exist as parts of domestic programs. *United States* restrictions on agricultural products are composed of: (a) simple tariffs on vegetables, certain meat and meat products, oilseeds, oilseed products, and all grains except wheat; (b) combinations of tariffs and absolute quotas on wheat, beef and veal, dairy products, sugar, and tobacco; (c) variable tariffs on successive quotas on live animals; (d) seasonal tariffs on certain fruits and vegetables; (e) progressively increasing tariffs with increasing degrees of processing of agricultural products. *Canadian* restrictions are composed of: (a) simple tariffs on meat, meat products, tobacco, and oilseeds; (b) tariffs and licensing requirements on all grains; (c) absolute quotas and tariffs on sugar and certain dairy products; (d) seasonal tariffs on most competing fruits and vegetables; (e) absolute prohibition of butter and margarine imports; (f) increasing tariff rates with the degree of processing. *Mexican* import regulations are complex and consist of five components: (a) an import license required on all agricultural imports; (b) a specific duty expressed on per unit of gross weight (product plus containers); (c) an ad valorem duty as a percentage of the official Mexican valuation; (d) the official valuation, which is arbitrarily determined and can be used to increase protection simply by setting it above CIF prices at the border; (e) a 3 percent surtax on the sum of the duties computed above.

Actual trade restrictions for selected agricultural commodities are given in Table 7.1. While it is difficult to judge the protectiveness of a tariff by its absolute magnitude, some general propositions can be stated.

1. With the exception of corn, restrictions on grain trade are high and this conclusion is substantiated by the small volume of inter-North American trade that occurs.
2. With the exception of dairy products, restrictions on livestock and meat trade between Canada and the United States are low. Mexico, however, prohibits imports of live cattle and hogs and their products. In addition Mexico applies substantial export taxes on the export of live cattle.
3. Relative to U.S. and Canadian rates, Mexican duties are high as one would expect from our earlier discussion of Mexican development policy.
4. In general, high import restrictions coincide with the existence of domestic price support programs.

In *Canada,* the Canadian Wheat Board, a compulsory crown marketing board for Prairie grains, utilizes quotas to control the marketing of grains at Board-determined prices. The Canadian Livestock Feed Board operates a transport and storage subsidiza-

TABLE 7.1

Barriers to Agricultural Trade in North America; Selected Products (cents (U.S.) per 100 lbs.)

| Item | Entering Canada | Entering United States | Entering Mexico* |
|---|---|---|---|
| Wheat | † | 37.5 on quota of 800,000 bu. | 83.0† |
| Barley | 15.6† | 15.6 | 60.4† |
| Oats | 11.1† | 11.1 | 105.8† |
| Corn | 14.3† | 44.6 | 7.2† |
| Cattle for breeding | Free | Free | Free |
| Live cattle: | | | Live animals for slaughter are |
| < 200 lbs. | 150 | 150 up to 200,000 head | prohibited |
| | | 250 over 200,000 head | |
| 200–700 lbs. | 150 | 250 | |
| > 700 lbs. | 150 | 150 up to 400,000 head | |
| | | 250 over 200,000 head | |
| Peef and veal | 300 | 300; plus quotas for Australia, New Zealand, | Prohibited |
| | | and Ireland | |
| Fresh pork | 50 | 50 | Prohibited |
| Ham | 175 | 200; 300 in airtight containers | Prohibited |
| Bacon | Free | 200 | Prohibited |
| Chickens, live | (12½% ad valorem) | 200 | 8 cents/head† |
| Chicken meat | 500 | 300 | NA‡ |
| Turkeys, live | (12½% ad valorem) | 200 | 18 cents/head† |
| Turkey meat | 500–1,000 | 850 | NA‡ |
| Potatoes | 37.5 | 37.5 to 45 million lbs.; 75 over | 161† |
| Apples, fresh | Free | Free | 1,429† |
| Oranges | Free | 100 | 638 |
| Tomatoes | Seasonal | 210 Mar. 1–July 14; Sept. 1–Nov. 14 | 131† |
| | | 150 July 15–Aug. 31; Nov. 15–Feb. 28 | 705† |
| Butter | Prohibited | 70–140 quotas and seasonal | |

Source: United States: U.S. Office of the Special Representative of Trade Negotiations, *General Agreement on Tariffs and Trade, 1964–67 Trade Conference*, Report on U.S. Negotiations, Vol. II, Part 1, Washington, 1967. Canada: G. A. MacEachern and D. L. MacFarlane, "The Relative Position of Canadian Agriculture in World Trade," in *Proceedings of Conference on International Trade and Canadian Agriculture*, Ottawa: Queen's Printer, 1966, pp. 77–203. Mexico: Derived from Mexican Import Tariff as provided by Bureau of International Commerce, U.S. Dept. of Commerce, Aug. 1967.

* These rates are computed by applying the specific duty, ad valorem rate, and surtax to the published Mexican official valuation and converting to U.S. dollars at the official rate of 12.5 pesos = 1 dollar.
† Requires license in addition to tariff.
‡ NA–Not available.

tion program for feed grains moving from the Prairies to British Columbia and Eastern Canada. These two agencies control import licenses for grains. Freight rates on export-destined Prairie wheat are fixed under the Crows Nest Pass Rates and are substantially lower than comparable domestic or U.S. freight rates (24, p. 15). The prices of several other commodities, including hogs and eggs, are supported under the Agricultural Prices Stabilization Act. A recently enacted Dairy Policy heavily supports the dairy industry in conjunction with provincial fluid milk regulations. In the *United States,* programs using combinations of diversion payments, loan rates, and income payments exist for wheat, feed grains, cotton, rice, and tobacco. For wheat, export subsidies are paid. No direct livestock programs exist—except for dairy—where prices are supported by both federal and state programs. Many federal and state marketing orders exist for fruits and vegetables. In *Mexico,* minimum prices are fixed for many products and provincial production quotas are set. Included in this group are grains and livestock. These programs, in conjunction with import restrictions, accomplish domestic price support.

## SUMMARY OF THE APPROACH TAKEN

The above lengthy introductory remarks serve as a basis for confining the remainder of this paper to a discussion of the implications of integration mainly as they affect Canadian and U.S. agricultures. Further, food aid is considered as only one component of international demand which is determined by the willingness of the donors to finance it. The common market is considered in the light of domestic as well as international objectives. Finally, the analysis is limited to the grain-livestock sector excluding dairy. This is done for practical reasons of manageability, but it can be argued that this sector accounts for a majority of gross farm income in both countries. It also provides an illustration of both surplus export products and products where self-sufficiency or deficits exist.

## A QUALITATIVE ANALYSIS OF A COMMON MARKET

When I began to explore the literature of international trade and customs union theory for an appropriate model to analyze the effect of the removal of barriers to agricultural trade, I was disappointed to find that author after author shied away from the issue, for example (4, p. 125). After I had attempted to analyze the question, I knew why they had done so. Clearly the complexness and interrelatedness of social and economic issues in the area of agricultural policy and trade makes definitive economic conclusions difficult, if not impossible. Thus my approach has been to select a few commodities and explore in a pedestrian, partial, static framework some of the implications of changes in relations between Canada and the United States. Model I assumes that trade restrictions only have been removed and explores the compatability of existing programs with integration. Model II adjusts those programs which are clearly incompatible to make them compatible with joint objectives.

## MODEL I
### Removal of Trade Barriers Only

Let me make the following assumptions regarding a Canadian-American union as a beginning point:

1.  Assume that all barriers to trade in grains, livestock, and meat products are removed, with the result that prices in the two countries would be equalized except for space, time, and form differences in products.
2.  Assume that a common external tariff is established toward third countries which is equal to the average of individual country tariffs, giving as much protection as before, and that export subsidies, as a general policy, are not followed.
3.  Assume that the demand for grains has four components: (a) inelastic domestic demand; (b) relatively inelastic international commercial demand, given importer's domestic farm programs; (c) food aid demand which is jointly determined by recipient's needs and donor's budget constraints; and (d) the demand for strategic reserves. In total, the demand for wheat is assumed to be inelastic; the demand for feed grains is less inelastic and is derived from the demand for meat which may approach unitary elasticity.
4.  Assume that both countries hold fast to the goal of farm income maintenance as constrained by broader goals of low food prices, export expansion, and limited direct budgetary expenditure on agricultural support. These constraints would result in farm prices remaining constant or falling.
5.  Assume that existing individual country programs continue,

though this is a shaky assumption with respect to certain Canadian programs, as the analysis attempts to show.

The immediate effect of the removal of trade barriers would be on absolute and relative prices of products of the grain-livestock sector. This can be termed the *price effect*. Given that we can say something about the direction of the price changes, and also something about the *trade effect*, the *production effect*, and the *consumption effect*. However, our ability to reach definite conclusions by this form of qualitative analysis is severely limited by cross effects within the sector. Ultimately the outcome is an empirical question requiring detailed knowledge of elasticities—price, cross, and income—of demand and supply, production, and transport costs. But let us not be deterred from saying something by the absence of facts.

## PRICE EFFECTS

*Wheat.*—The removal of barriers to wheat trade would likely induce a flow of hard red spring wheat from Canada into the U.S. domestic market and would result in an equalization of market prices for comparable quality wheat. This equalized price would be the lower Canadian or world price. Even given the dominance of Canada and the United States in the world wheat market (17), it would be difficult for them to raise world prices. Further, the present direction of U.S. policy is to be competitive in the world market without the use of export subsidies. However, the slight fall (given the present price spread) in U.S. market prices would have little effect on producer or miller prices, given producers income payments and the miller certificate. The net effect on wheat prices would be a small decline in U.S. prices and constant prices in Canada.

*Feed Grains.*—The dominance of the United States in the North American and world markets would make it likely that feed grain prices would equalize at U.S. levels. In the simplest context, this would mean that Canadian feed grain prices would fall at most by the amount of the Canadian tariff. Kerr (15) has argued that Eastern Canadian feed grain prices, as established by the Canadian Wheat Board, are at, or just below, U.S. prices plus tranport and tariff costs. The removal of the tariff of 8 cents per pushel on U.S. corn would force the Board to lower prices by that amount. Given the Board's one-price policy, prices in Western Canada would also fall by the amount of the tariff. Further, if Western feed grain prices are determined by Ontario prices less transport, then the subsidy on feed grain shipments has the effect of holding Western prices up by at least part of the amount of the subsidy (about $4.80 per ton or 11.5 cents per bushel of barley). Thus, given the licensing requirement plus tariffs on feed grain imports into Western Canada, Western feed grain prices in general are higher than comparable prices across the border. The removal of import restrictions, coupled with the continuance of the freight subsidy, could result in U.S. producers selling in the Canadian market and reaping the benefit of the freight subsidy paid for by the Canadian taxpayer. If the cost of transport to Winnipeg plus the subsidy is less than the cost of transport to, for example, Chicago, the U.S. producer would sell in the Canadian market. This shows the inconsistency of the feed freight subsidization with integration. If the subsidy is set high enough to cause Western grain to move east, it would offer American producers in border areas similar alternatives. If the subsidy were set so low that U.S. corn became cheaper than barley, it would be nonoperative. It seems likely that feed grain prices in Eastern Canada would fall by the amount of the tariff, and feed grain prices in Western Canada would fall by the amount of the tariff and some portion of the subsidy if the latter were discontinued. In general, Western Canadian feed grain prices would adjust to "freight under" Chicago.

*Livestock and Meat.*—In general, Canada and the United States already represent a unified market for livestock and livestock products (6, 18). Existing tariffs on meat and meat products are in general equal in both directions and their removal would not alter relative prices in the two countries. Where Canadian tariffs were higher—as on chicken meat—Canadian prices would fall at most by the amount of the net difference in tariffs (in this case, 2 cents per pound). Removal of variable tariffs and quotas on Mexican and Canadian feeder cattle would tend to raise prices in the Canadian market. But in general, integration would have little immediate impact on livestock prices in either country.

TRADE EFFECTS

The most significant trade effect of the removal of barriers would be the shipment of hard red spring Canadian wheat into the U.S. domestic milling market. The United States consumes for food about 500 million bushels of wheat per year while producing about 200 million bushels of hard spring wheat, other than durum. That difference presently is filled by hard red winters. If red spring wheat has more desirable milling attributes as is generally presumed, then potentially Canadian spring wheat could displace red winter wheat in U.S. milling mixes. Suppose, for the sake of argument, that 200 million bushels of Canadian wheat were sold in the U.S. market. In normal years, this quantity, coupled with Canadian consumption, would exhaust grades 1, 2, and 3 Northern (in 1965–66 Canada produced 281 million bushels in these grades). If the Western European market is the next highest quality-demanding market, then Canadian sales there could decline because of the non-availability of higher grade wheat, assuming no immediate supply increase in Canada. If the Western European market were all lost because of the shipments to the United States, it is possible that U.S. red winters would replace Canadian wheat in these markets. In fact, in general it is likely that U.S. wheat would replace Canadian wheat in any markets lost by Canada. The only case under which this would not occur would be where Canada substituted the U.S. market for the Red Chinese market. It is possible that Canada would attempt to substitute her least certain market—Red China—for the more certain U.S. market. If this were to occur, then the reduction in Canadian sales to Red China would not be replaced by U.S. sales and would represent a net loss of markets for the United States. This would put downward pressure on prices or require further acreage restrictions to maintain prices. While the above is all speculation, it is clear that a substantial adjustment in wheat trade flows would likely occur as a result of integration.

Trade in feed grains would change, if any, in the direction of increased exports of U.S. corn to the Eastern Canadian market. Trade flows of livestock and livestock products initially would not change significantly.

PRODUCTION EFFECTS

Short-run production effects with integration would be induced by changes in relative product and input prices. The above analysis suggested that, in Canada, the price of feed grains relative to wheat would fall by at least the amount of the tariff. This would tend to cause a shift in Western Canadian acreage from feed grains to wheat and expand Canadian wheat supplies. In the United States, relative prices of feed grains and wheat were expected to change marginally in the same direction, but U.S. production would still be determined largely by the wheat and feed grain programs. Livestock production would be unaffected in the United States and stimulated in Canada by the fall in feed grain prices. However, the more interesting situation with respect to Canadian livestock production would result from the discontinuance of the feed freight subsidy program and this will be discussed in the next section.

## CONSUMPTION EFFECTS

The commodity price changes predicted above would probably not be large. Thus, given increasing margins between producer and consumer prices, one would expect little effect on consumer prices but, to the extent food prices would be affected, it would be downward, especially meat prices in Canada, inducing expanded consumption.

Given the above effects of the removal of trade restrictions between Canada and the United States, what would be the consistency of existing domestic programs with integration? In Canada, most programs would encounter problems. The *modus operandi* of the Canadian Wheat Board—initial prices, final payments, and acreage marketing quotas—depends on its monopoly position. The availability of an alternative U.S. cash market would make the Board's operations more difficult. Similarly the U.S. wheat program would have to be adjusted so that certificate payments on domestic consumption went only to U.S. producers. The broader implication is that given a common wheat market, common wheat policy would be a virtual necessity. The Crows Nest Pass Rates would likely have to be discontinued as transshipment of U.S. wheat through Canada would clearly be profitable, given existing rates. It is unlikely that Canadian railways and the Canadian taxpayer would long subsidize U.S. wheat producers. The same result occurs under feed freight subsidy and it, too, would likely be altered. Thus feed grain policy would also have to be harmonized with the U.S. feed grain program. Finally, P.L. 480 would have to be adjusted to allow Canadian sharing in food aid costs—especially if free trade resulted in net loss of commercial markets for U.S. wheat.

## MODEL II
### *Removal of Trade Barriers and Policy Harmonization*

Quite clearly free trade without policy harmonization would be unlikely. The remainder of this chapter is devoted to a brief discussion of the effects of one possible set of harmonized policies. These are presented, not as a prediction of a likely set, but rather are formulated on the basis of adjusting only those policies which were shown to be inconsistent in Model I. Suppose the following sort of joint program existed. For wheat, assume a program which determines jointly projected demand requirements including food aid and allocates production on the basis of acreage and/or marketing quotas. Income support might be accomplished by income payments shared by the two governments on the basis of production. Freight rates are equalized and exports are not subsidized.[2] The implication of such a program would be that Canada would share in the cost of food aid and in the responsibility for production control. For feed grains, assume the total discontinuance of the feed freight subsidy and the application of the U.S. feed grain program to Canada. For livestock, assume no price programs in either country.

The major impact of such a set of programs would be on the location of the production of grains and livestock. Concerning the effects of the discontinuance of the feed freight subsidy, Kerr (15) has argued that the discontinuance of this subsidy program in the absence of any other changes would result in a shift of livestock feeding from Eastern Canada to Western Canada. With integration as well as the cessation of the subsidy program, a more complex adjustment could occur. Feed grain prices in Eastern Canada would fall by the amount of the tariff. But feed grain prices in Western Canada would fall by the amount of the tariff plus some portion of the subsidy. Thus Western feed grain prices would fall relative to Eastern prices and induce two simultaneous reactions. First, given constant wheat prices, an increase in wheat acreage at the expense of feed grains would occur. Second, the expansion of livestock feeding in the West would be stimulated. These shifts would induce secondary price responses tending to reduce the wheat-feed grain price ratio, and equilibrium would ultimately depend on the profitability of wheat versus livestock. The discontinuance of the subsidy program would affect about 50 to 60 million bushels of oats and barley which could be fed in the West. Eastern Canadian livestock production under integration would likely decline and the source of feed in-shipments, if any, for the dairy and other livestock would likely be the Midwestern United States. Meat imports to

---

[2] An interesting problem in a common external policy would result from the U.S. embargo on sales to Red China.

Eastern Canada would come from either the United States or Western Canada, depending on relative costs of transport.

Ultimately the total adjustments in North American agriculture would depend on the comparative advantage of different regions in the production of particular commodities and on the form of the farm programs jointly decided upon. If one accepts the analysis of Campbell (7) and MacEachern and MacFarlane (19), Canada has a comparative advantage in producing wheat and the United States in producing feed grains, especially corn, and it is adjustments in this direction that the above analysis would suggest. Livestock production would be spatially distributed on the basis of costs of production and transport and demand. This pattern is an empirical question and is beyond the scope of this chapter.

## GENERAL IMPLICATIONS OF THE ANALYSIS

It may be presumptuous to attempt to draw conclusions on the basis of the above discussion, but let me suggest some general implications.

1. The potential agricultural output of North American agriculture would not be greatly altered by integration. Short-run output expansion as a result of the removal of restrictions contained in U.S. farm programs would greatly swamp any integration effects. This is so because Canadian agriculture has expanded acreage rapidly in the past six years. This does not say that total output of both Canadian and U.S. agriculture could not be expanded by raising price levels, but this approach I have argued to be unrealistic.
2. Integration would, however, require harmonization of domestic policies and would require Canada to share in food aid and the cost of supply control now borne by the United States. Thus politically one might find some justification in considering integration in the context of food aid because it might be one means of forcing other nations—in this case Canada—to share in food aid costs.
3. Production patterns would be altered substantially more in Canada than in the United States as a result of integration and/or domestic policy changes. The location of Canadian livestock feeding and the composition of Western Canadian grain output would be altered by changes in relative prices.

The effects on the United States would be small—as one would expect—given the dominant size of U.S. agriculture in the union.

4. Finally, I must emphasize the limitations of the analysis and the needs for more definitive studies. Clearly there would be implications of integration for other agricultural products—tobacco, dairy, fruits, and vegetables—to name a few, but these have not been discussed. Changes in the international market for grains could greatly affect future production patterns, but these have not been considered. Ultimately the prediction of the configuration of North American agriculture with integration would depend on considerations of costs, supply, demand, and policy. In essence, it is an empirical question requiring much additional research.

## REFERENCES

(1) Abel, M. E., and A. S. Rojko, *World Food Situation: Prospects for World Grain Production, Consumption and Trade,* FAER-35, USDA, 1967.

(2) Balassa, B. A., *The Theory of Economic Integration,* Homewood, Ill.: Richard D. Irwin, 1961.

(3) ———, "Toward a Theory of Economic Integration," M. S. Wionczek (ed.), *Latin American Economic Integration,* New York: Frederick A. Praeger, 1966, pp. 21–31.

(4) ———, and M. E. Kreinin, "Trade Liberalization Under the 'Kennedy Round': The Static Effects," *Rev. Econ. and Stat.* 49(2):125–37, May 1967.

(5) Benoit, Emile, *Europe at Sixes and Sevens,* New York: Columbia Univ. Press, 1961.

(6) Boswell, A. N., and G. A. MacEachern, "Determinants of Change in the North American Feeder-Cattle Economy," *Canadian Jour. Agr. Econ.* 15(1):54–65, 1967.

(7) Campbell, D. R., "Alternatives and Opportunities for Canada in International Trade in Agricultural Products," Proceedings of *Conference on International Trade and Canadian Agriculture,* Ottawa: Queen's Printer, 1966, pp. 397–441.

(8) Cochrane, W. W., *The City Man's Guide to the Farm Problem,* Minneapolis: Univ. of Minnesota Press, 1965.

(9) Daly, R. F., and A. C. Egbert, "A Look Ahead for Food and Agriculture," *Agr. Econ. Res.* 17(1):1–9 plus supplement, June 1966.

(10) Falcon, W., "Farmer Response to Price in Subsistence Economy," *Amer. Econ. Rev.* 54:580–91, May 1964.

(11) Fisher, Franklin N., "A Theoretical Analysis of the Impact of Food Surplus Disposal on Agricultural Production in Recipient Countries," *Jour. Farm Econ.* 45(4):863–75, Nov. 1963.

(12) FitzGerald, D. A., *Operational and Administrative Problems of Food Aid,* World Food Program Study No. 4, Rome: Food and Agriculture Organization of the United Nations, 1965.

(13) Heady, E. O., *Agricultural Problems and Policies of Developed Countries,* Oslo: Johansen and Nielsen, 1966.

(14) Johnson, H. G., *Economic Policies Towards Less Developed Countries,* Washington, D.C.: The Brookings Institution, 1967.

(15) Kerr, T. C., *An Economic Analysis of the Feed Freight Assistance Policy,* Ottawa: Agricultural Economics Research Council of Canada, 1966.

(16) Lipsey, R. G., "The Theory of Customs Unions: A General Survey," *Econ. Jour.* 70(279):496–513, Sept. 1960.

(17) McCalla, Alex F., "A Duopoly Model of World Wheat Pricing," *Jour. Farm Econ.* 48:711–27, Aug. 1966.

(18) ———, "Implications for Canada of United States Farm Policies," *Jour. Farm Econ.,* Dec. 1967.

(19) MacEachern, Gordon A., and David L. MacFarlane, "The Relative Position of Canadian Agriculture in World Trade," Proceedings of *Conference on International Trade and Canadian Agriculture,* Ottawa: Queen's Printer, 1966, pp. 77–203.

(20) Meade, J. E., *The Theory of Customs Unions,* Amsterdam: North Holland Publishing Co., 1956.

(21) Schultz, T. W., "Increasing World Food Supplies: The Economic Requirements," *Proceedings of the National Academy of Sciences* 56(2):322–27, Aug. 1966.

(22) Scitovsky, T. de, *Economic Theory and Western European Integration,* London: Allen and Unwin, 1958.

(23) Sen, B. R., "War on World Hunger—The Next Phase," New York: Address to National Convocation on "World Hunger" conducted by the National Industrial Conference Board, Sept. 12, 1967.

(24) U.S. Department of Agriculture, *Canadian Wheat Marketing,* Foreign Agricultural Service, July 1962, FAS-M-140.

(25) U.S. Department of Commerce, "Foreign Trade Regulation of Mexico," Overseas Business Report 66–62, Oct. 1966.

(26) Viner, Jacob, *The Customs Union Issue,* New York: Carnegie Endowment for International Peace, 1950.

(27) Weil, G. L., *A Handbook of the European Economic Community,* New York: Frederick A. Praeger, 1965.

(28) Wionczek, M. S. (ed.), *Latin American Economic Integration,* New York: Frederick A. Praeger, 1966.

# CHAPTER EIGHT

# Implications of an Unrestricted Pooling of North American Agricultural Resources

## R. E. CAPEL, J. C. GILSON, and T. D. HARRIS

RESOURCE USE EFFICIENCY in agriculture has been of long-standing concern from an intranational point of view. A great number of studies in both Canada and the United States have indicated that considerable gain could be made by a change of the resource mix within given areas and by a reallocation of resources among agricultural regions within the two nations. To date, very little effort has been made to assess the possibilities associated with the reallocation of resources between the agricultural industries of Canada and the United States.[1]

Questions associated with the concept of a common market in North America are being debated, certainly in Canada at the present time, with a great deal of vigor. One group contends that a more liberal trading arrangement, indeed a common market, between Canada and the United States would be of great mutual benefit to both countries. Johnson estimates that

R. E. CAPEL, Department of Agricultural Economics, University of Manitoba; J. CLAYTON GILSON, Department of Agricultural Economics, University of Manitoba; T. D. HARRIS, Department of Agricultural Economics, University of Manitoba.

[1] A notable exception was the study made by D. Gale Johnson. See D. Gale Johnson, *Income and Resource Effects of Canadian and United States Farm Policies: A Comparison*, presented as the J. S. McLean Memorial Lecture at the Ontario Agricultural College, Guelph, April 23, 1959.

Canadian protection is reducing Canadian national income by about 4½ percent.[2] He contends that

> . . . the long-run historical trend has been towards increased interdependence of the two economies—economic integration in a broad sense—the forces of continental geography and the rapid growth of the United States triumphing over the intentions of tariff policy . . . a movement towards regional integration comparable to the formation of the European Common Market, an integration essentially founded on the combination of American capital and Canadian resources.[3]

The effect on Canada of North American tariffs has been most recently calculated as being a loss of about 10½ percent of the Canadian gross national product.[4]

Another large and articulate group in Canada argues for a greater degree of economic nationalism; import quotas, higher tariffs, and a more stringent control over foreign investment in Canadian industries are being advocated.[5] Judging from the protests which are raised from time to time by various interest groups in the United States, not all persons in that country are in favor of an unrestricted pooling of commodities and resources.

Still others believe that we have a virtually unrestricted pooling of resources between Canada and the United States at the present time, tariffs and import restrictions notwithstanding. They point to the $2.7 billion of Canadian investment in the United States and the $17.9 billion (1961) of American investment in Canada. They cite the large flow of agricultural products both ways across the Canadian-U.S. boundary. In 1963, for example, the United States exported $618.3 million worth of agricultural products to Canada and in return imported $173.6 million worth of agricultural products from Canada. Large quantities of chemical fertilizers are exported from Canada to the United States and there is a reciprocal flow of millions of dollars worth of farm machinery and equipment.

One writer on the topic believes that market forces in North

---

[2] H. G. Johnson, *The Canadian Quandary*, McGraw-Hill, Toronto, 1965, p. 125.

[3] *Ibid.*, p. 152.

[4] R. Wonnacott and P. Wonnacott, *Free Trade Between the United States and Canada: The Potential Economic Effects*, Harvard Univ. Press, Cambridge, Mass., 1967.

[5] The extent of American investment in Canada was closely analyzed by A. E. Safarian, *Foreign Ownership of Canadian Industry*, McGraw-Hill, Toronto, 1966.

America bring about an extremely close relationship between Canada and the United States:[6]

The population of North America is so extremely mobile, and the freedom of movement between Canada and the United States, in both directions, is so great, that the two countries should properly be regarded, if not as a single reservoir of population at least as two reservoirs so closely related that the same natural economic forces will operate upon both of them at the same time . . . the continent of North America (north of the Mexican border) constitutes practically a single economy, broken only by the boundary line with its persistent possibility of government interference.

Many find the "reservoir" theory to be a plausible explanation of the relationship. Canada is frequently viewed as a microcosm of the United States insofar as most economic matters are concerned—the Canadian economy is commonly viewed as roughly 10 percent of the economy in the United States.

Of course such a theory is far too simple as a basis for the examination of the present topic, but there can be no doubt of the long-standing interdependence on matters relating to agriculture. The Homestead legislation which was enacted in Canada in 1872 was a close parallel of the Homestead Act which was legislated earlier in the United States. Many of the earlier settlers in Western Canada came from the midwestern states. It is estimated that 113,364 farmers from the United States migrated into Canada between 1915 and 1920.[7] In the early part of the present century, Canadian and American agricultural officials were in very close contact with respect to the development of farm credit legislation.[8] It is not a coincidence that the cooperative farm credit legislation which was enacted in the United States in 1917 was accompanied by the establishment of similar cooperative farm credit institutions in Canada during the same year.

The relationship between Canada and the United States on agricultural matters has not always been a completely harmonious one. During the last two decades, for example, both countries have had some strong differences of opinion on the wheat export market. Canadian farmers were alarmed about the sub-

---

[6] B. K. Sandwell, "The Canadian People," *Canada's Tomorrow*, G. P. Gilmour (ed.), The Macmillan Co. of Canada, Toronto, 1954.

[7] *Canada Year Books*, 1915–1919/20.

[8] *Circular 35*, Farm Credit Administration, Washington, D.C., 1961. Seven officials from Canada joined with representatives from the United States in 1913 to make a detailed study of farm credit systems in Europe.

sidized sales of wheat from the United States under P.L. 480 during the mid-fifties while American farmers have found it difficult during recent years to reconcile their production control programs with the unrestricted sales of Canadian wheat to Russia and China. At the present time Canadian officials are very disturbed about the sharp decline in wheat prices, the main cause of which many attribute to marketing policies in the United States.[9] In other areas, too, conflicts of interest have developed between the two countries. For example, during recent years increasing concern has been expressed over the purchase of farmland in Saskatchewan by American investors.[10]

While there are unique differences between Canada and the United States, there are also some very striking similarities. Nowhere is the similarity greater than between the agricultural industries of the two countries. In general one might suggest that the similarity leads to a predominantly competitive rather than a complementary relationship. Of the $186.8 million worth of agricultural products imported into the United States from Canada in 1964, only $8.4 million were classed as complementary to those produced in the United States.[11] Unfortunately, no similar classification is available for the flow of agricultural products into Canada from the United States, although perhaps Canadian imports, which include more fruits and vegetables, are more complementary with her own products.

There are many important economic and political ramifications to the unrestricted pooling of agricultural resources in North America. Before probing this question further, however, a brief survey will be made of the agricultural resources of the two countries.

## LAND RESOURCES

In 1959 the total land in farms in the United States amounted to 1.12 billion acres of which 311 million acres were classified as cropland (Table 8.1). In 1961 Canada had 172 million acres of farmland of which approximately 103 million acres

---

[9] J. Schriener, "Wheat-War Rumblings Could Mean Trouble for Tariff Deal," *The Financial Post*, Sept. 16, 1967.

[10] A recent study in Saskatchewan indicated that an increasing number of farmers from the United States have invested in farmland in the southern part of the province. See J. A. Brown, *Purchases and Ownership of Saskatchewan Farm Lands by Individuals and Companies of the United States, to December 31, 1964*. Saskatchewan Dept. of Agr., Regina, July 1965.

[11] *Agricultural Statistics 1966*, USDA, Washington, D.C., 1966, p. 605.

TABLE 8.1
TOTAL LAND IN FARMS, SIZE OF FARM, AND VALUE OF REAL ESTATE PER ACRE,
CANADA AND THE UNITED STATES

| | United States | | | | Canada | | | |
|---|---|---|---|---|---|---|---|---|
| Year | Total area in farms | Crop-land | Area per farm | Value of real es-tate/ac. | Total area in farms | Crop-land | Area per farm | Value of real es-tate/ac. |
| | *(mil. ac.)* | | *(acres)* | *($)* | *(mil. ac.)* | | *(acres)* | *($)* |
| 1940 | 1,061 | 321 | 174 | 32 | ... | ... | ... | ... |
| 1941 | ... | ... | ... | ... | 174 | 91.6 | 237 | 17 |
| 1950 | 1,159 | 344 | 215 | 65 | ... | ... | ... | ... |
| 1951 | ... | ... | ... | ... | 174 | 96.8 | 279 | 32 |
| 1959 | 1,120 | 311 | 302 | 111 | ... | ... | ... | ... |
| 1961 | ... | ... | ... | ... | 172 | 103.4 | 359 | 50 |

Source: USDA, *Agricultural Statistics 1966*, U.S. Dept. of Commerce, Bureau of the Census, *Statistical Abstract of the United States, 1965*; DBS: *Census of Canada*, 1941, 1951, 1961.

were utilized as cropland. Accordingly, the amount of cropland per capita in the United States amounts to approximately 1.6 acres as compared to 8.6 acres per capita in Canada at the present time.

Farm size in Canada, measured in acres, is generally larger than that in the United States (Table 8.1). For example, in 1959 the average land area per farm in Canada was 359 acres as compared to 302 acres in the United States. On the other hand, value of real estate per acre tends to be considerably higher in the United States. The value of real estate per acre of farmland in the United States was $111 in 1959 as compared to $50 per acre in Canada in 1961.

Thus in comparing the agricultural land bases of Canada and the United States, one cannot ignore the substitutability of capital inputs for land. While no attempt has been made in this study to provide empirical estimates of the substitution of capital for land, it is generally recognized that this is becoming an extremely important aspect of agricultural production in North America.[12]

By far the greatest difference between Canada and the United States as far as the farmland resource is concerned is the impact of government policies. The chronic surpluses which appear to have characterized U.S. agriculture for the past three

[12] See, for example, D. B. Ibach, "Economic Potentials of Agricultural Production," *Dynamics of Land Use: Needed Adjustment*, Iowa State Univ. Press, Ames, 1961, p. 132. Ibach estimates, for example, that one ton of plant nutrients will substitute for about 5.1 acres in corn production and about 7.9 acres in hay production in the United States by 1980.

decades have led to a heavy reliance on policies designed to withdraw land from agricultural production. The national acreage allotments for basic commodities and the Soil Bank program in the United States have no parallel in Canada.[13] While the national acreage allotment for wheat in the United States was reduced from 55 million acres in 1963 to 49.5 million acres in 1964, wheat acreage in Canada increased from 27 to 29 million acres. It would not be surprising under these circumstances if many of the American farmers who have invested in Canadian farm lands in recent years have also had part of their land in the Soil Bank program in the United States.

Without comprehensive empirical study of the matter, it is difficult to anticipate what the specific effects of an unrestricted pooling of resources would be on the land use pattern of Canada and the United States. There can be little doubt, however, that major adjustments would be called for in terms of the land use policies which have been followed by both countries during the past two decades. The problems involved in rationalizing agricultural land use on a continental basis may be anticipated to some extent from the experience of the European Common Market Countries.[14] It seems probable that a common commodity market would have a far greater impact on land use in Canada and the United States than would a mere pooling of resources. Unlike labor and capital, which can be transferred at some cost from one region of the continent to another, land can be changed only in terms of its use rather than its location.

## LABOR

The economic, political, and cultural forces which dominated life in the early days in Canada and the United States appear to have dictated the same general type of farm organization in both countries. Each country has supported the basic objective of the "family farm." The family farm concept has traditionally implied that the labor, capital, and management resources were supplied or owned by the farm operator and his family. It is interesting to note that vertical integration and contract farming

---

[13] On the other hand, it should be recognized that exclusive of possible development of organic soils, Canada's reserves of potentially arable land likely total about 42 million acres. See *Conference Background Papers,* "Resources For Tomorrow," Vol. I, Queen's Printer, Ottawa, 1961.

[14] See, for example, S. Sinclair, *The Common Agricultural Policy of the E.E.C. and Its Implications for Canada's Exports,* sponsored by The Canadian Trade Committee, Private Planning Association of Canada, Montreal, 1964.

TABLE 8.2
FARMS CLASSIFIED BY TENURE OF OPERATOR, CANADA, 1961,
AND UNITED STATES, 1959

| Tenure | Canada, 1961 (percent of total) | United States, 1959 (percent of total) |
|---|---|---|
| Owner | 72.9 | 57.1 |
| Tenant | 5.8 | 19.8 |
| Part owner/part tenant | 20.9 | 22.5 |
| Manager | 0.4 | 0.6 |
| Total | 100.0 | 100.0 |

Source: *Census of Canada,* Agriculture 1961; U.S. Dept. of Commerce, *Statistical Abstract of the United States, 1965.*

are viewed similarly by both Canadian and American farmers—as a threat to their traditional way of life. In spite of the similar traditions and objectives, however, significant differences have appeared in the farm tenure pattern of the two countries.

A significantly higher proportion of the farmers in the United States are classified as tenants compared to Canada (Table 8.2). On the other hand, nearly three-fourths of the farmers in Canada are classified as owner operators, compared to approximately 60 percent in the United States. Both the part owner-part tenant operator and the part-time owner operator are growing in importance in both countries. Also, it appears that the growing capital requirements of farming are forcing farmers in both Canada and the United States to turn to a part owner-part tenant type of arrangement to expand their size of operation.[15]

There are also some striking parallels in the trends and adjustments taking place in the farm population in Canada and the United States (Fig. 8.1). Of the total population of 191.5 million persons in the United States in 1964, 12.9 million were living on farms. During the same year in Canada 1.7 million persons out of a total population of 19.3 million were included in the farm population.

Since World War II the number of persons living on farms has declined enormously in both Canada and the United States. During the sixteen-year period 1949–64, the farm population in both countries declined by a total of 12.6 million persons. The decline in the farm population relative to the total population has been very similar for both countries (Fig. 8.1). It is estimated

[15] A. G. Ball, "The Economic Opportunities for Tomorrow's Commercial Farmers," Canadian Agricultural Economics Society Workshop Proceedings, *Meeting the Needs of Tomorrow's Commercial Farmers,* Winnipeg, 1966.

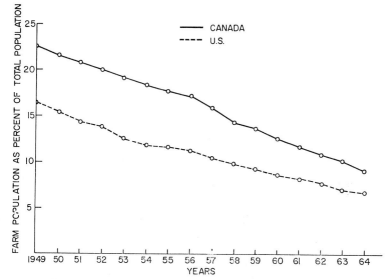

*Fig. 8.1—Farm population as a percent of total population, Canada and the United States. (From the U.S. Department of Commerce,* Statistical Abstract of the United States, 1965; *and the* Dominion Bureau of Statistics, Census of Canada, *1951 and 1961.*

that slightly over 6 percent of the total population in Canada live on farms at present while the corresponding figure for the United States is even lower. The Fourth Annual Review of the Economic Council of Canada anticipates that the farm labor force in Canada will represent approximately 4.3 percent of the total labor force in Canada by 1975.[16] The National Advisory Commission on Food and Fiber in the United States anticipates a reduction of probably 40 percent in the number of people employed in agriculture by 1980, leaving the farm labor force around 3½ percent of the total labor force at that time.[17]

## CAPITAL

The capital investment in farms in the United States is substantially higher than the investment in Canadian farms (Table 8.3). In 1957 the average farm assets per farm in the United

---

[16] Economic Council of Canada, Fourth Annual Review, *The Canadian Economy From the 1960's to the 1970's,* Queen's Printer, Ottawa, Sept. 1967.

[17] *Food and Fiber for the Future,* Report of the National Advisory Commission on Food and Fiber, U.S. Government Printing Office, Washington, D.C., July 1967.

TABLE 8.3

Total Number of Farms and Average Farm Assets Per Farm, Canada and
United States, Selected Years

| Year | United States | | | Canada | | |
|---|---|---|---|---|---|---|
| | Total no. of farms | Total farm assets | Ave. farm assets per farm | Total no. of farms | Total farm assets | Ave. farm assets per farm |
| | *(thou.)* | *($billion)* | *($)* | *(thou.)* | *($billion)* | *($)* |
| 1957 | 4,372 | 141.6 | 32,388 | 537 | 10.8 | 20,186 |
| 1960 | 3,949 | 167.8 | 42,492 | 481 | 12.7 | 26,362 |
| 1963 | 3,573 | 183.3 | 51,301 | 451 | 14.5 | 32,239 |
| 1965 | 3,374 | 199.0 | 58,980 | 430 | 17.3 | 40,186 |

Source: USDA, *Agricultural Statistics, 1966;* DBS, Handbook of Agricultural Statistics, Part II, *Farm Income,* 1962–63.

States amounted to $32,388 compared to $20,186 per farm in Canada. By 1965 the capital investment per farm in the United States was $58,980 while the corresponding figure for Canada had increased to $40,186.

Farmers in the United States appear to have a relatively higher proportion of their total farm assets invested in land and buildings as compared to those in Canada (Table 8.4). In 1964 approximately 79 percent of the total farm assets in the United States were land and buildings, compared to 67.6 percent for Canada.

It is interesting to note that the net worth position of farmers in Canada and the United States was very similar. Total farm debt in Canada in 1964 was $2.6 billion or 16.5 percent of the total investment in farm assets compared to $34.9 billion and 18.2 percent, respectively, for the United States.

TABLE 8.4

Farm Assets and Debt, Canada and the United States, 1964

| Item | United States | | Canada | |
|---|---|---|---|---|
| | Total | % of Total | Total | % of Total |
| *(assets)* | *($billion)* | | *($billion)* | |
| Real estate | 150.7 | 79.1 | 10.7 | 67.6 |
| Livestock | 15.7 | 8.3 | 2.2 | 13.8 |
| Machinery | 24.1 | 12.6 | 2.9 | 18.6 |
| Total farm assets | 190.5 | 100.0 | 15.8 | 100.0 |
| Total debt | 34.9 | . . . | 2.6 | . . . |

Source: USDA, ERS, *The Balance Sheet of Agriculture,* 1965; R. S. Rust, "Farm Credit Expansion in Canada," *Canadian Farm Economics,* I (Apr. 1966), 23–26.

The national average investment in farms tends to obscure the tremendous variation which exists within and among various agricultural regions of both countries. In Quebec, for example, only 2 percent of the farmers had an investment in their farms of over $50,000 in 1961. In Alberta, on the other hand, about 21 percent of the farmers had an investment in their businesses in excess of $50,000. Similar variations are found among different agricultural regions of the United States.[18]

One of the most significant aspects of farming in both Canada and the United States is the increasing quantity of farm inputs purchased off the farm. This is the basis for the rapid expansion in the farm supply industry in each country. Between 1949 and 1965 the average production expenses per farm in the United States increased from $3,142 to $9,110. For the same period of time in Canada, average production expenses per farm increased from $1,911 to $5,994. Measured another way, farm production expenses in the United States in 1959 averaged $23 per acre of farmland as compared to $12 per acre of farmland in Canada in 1961. It appears that farmers in the United States have a considerably higher production expense than Canadian farmers. These expenses also appear to absorb a somewhat higher proportion of the farm gross income in the United States than in Canada (Fig. 8.2). For example, 70.7 percent of the farm gross income in the United States in 1964 went for production expenses as compared to 65.4 percent in Canada. Thus for the period 1960–64, the gross income per dollar of production expenses amounted to $1.45 in the United States and $1.55 in Canada.

## RETURNS TO FARM RESOURCES

Gale Johnson's comparative analysis of farm incomes in Canada and the United States indicated that the average income per farm worker in Canada was 81.1 percent of that in the United States during the period 1953–57.[19] For the same period, Johnson found that the average income per farm worker in the Prairie Provinces was 72.5 percent of that for Montana and North Dakota; the average income per farm worker in Ontario was 91 percent of that in Michigan and 90 percent of that in Minnesota. On the other hand, in 1951–52 farm income in the

---

[18] *Structural Changes in Commercial Agriculture*, Center for Agricultural and Economic Adjustment, CAED Report 24, Ames, Iowa, 1965.

[19] D. Gale Johnson.

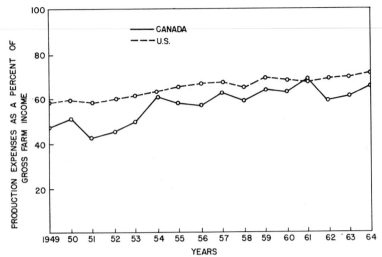

*Fig. 8.2—Production expenses as a percent of gross farm income, Canada and the United States. (From the U.S. Department of Agriculture, Agricultural Statistics, 1966; and the Dominion Bureau of Statistics Handbook of Agricultural Statistics, Part II, Farm Income, 1926–65.)*

Prairie Provinces was 103.6 percent of that in Montana and North Dakota. However, farm income per worker in the Prairie Provinces amounted to 149.2 of the corresponding figure in Ontario, indicating that the regional income differences within the country may be considerably larger than those between corresponding regions of Canada and the United States.

The authors have made a more recent comparative analysis of the two countries using per capita personal income (Table 8.5). The analysis indicated that the per capita personal income for persons on farms in Canada amounted to an average of 71.6 percent of the corresponding figure in the United States during the period 1949–65. However, the ratio ranged from a low of 56.2 percent in 1954 to a high of 84 percent in 1963 (Fig. 8.3).

The farm to nonfarm income ratio in Canada ranged from a low of 39.7 percent in 1957 to a high of 67.9 percent in 1965 (Table 8.6). In the United States the farm to nonfarm income ratio ranged from a high of 59 percent in 1951 to a low of 45.2 percent in 1956. In general, farm income relative to nonfarm income in Canada tended to be higher than the corresponding ratio in the United States during the periods 1951–53 and 1962–65 (Fig. 8.4).

TABLE 8.5

PERSONAL INCOME PER CAPITA, FARM AND NONFARM, CANADA AND THE UNITED STATES

| Year | United States Per Capita Personal Income | | | | | Canada Per Capita Personal Income | | | | |
|---|---|---|---|---|---|---|---|---|---|---|
| | Persons on farms | | | Persons not on farms | Total population | Persons on farms | | | Persons not on farms | Total population |
| | From farming | From nonfarm sources | From all sources | | | From farming | From nonfarm sources | From all sources | | |
| | | | (dollars) | | | | | (dollars) | | |
| 1949 | 549 | 256 | 805 | 1,501 | 1,389 | 452 | 117 | 569 | 1,092 | 972 |
| 1950 | 612 | 272 | 884 | 1,611 | 1,501 | 390 | 130 | 520 | 1,127 | 994 |
| 1951 | 740 | 297 | 1,037 | 1,759 | 1,657 | 668 | 149 | 817 | 1,212 | 1,130 |
| 1952 | 706 | 309 | 1,015 | 1,852 | 1,735 | 666 | 156 | 822 | 1,302 | 1,206 |
| 1953 | 672 | 324 | 996 | 1,921 | 1,806 | 562 | 183 | 745 | 1,352 | 1,123 |
| 1954 | 658 | 312 | 970 | 1,895 | 1,787 | 359 | 186 | 545 | 1,357 | 1,208 |
| 1955 | 597 | 325 | 922 | 2,006 | 1,881 | 432 | 192 | 624 | 1,397 | 1,260 |
| 1956 | 600 | 352 | 952 | 2,108 | 1,980 | 521 | 203 | 724 | 1,492 | 1,361 |
| 1957 | 625 | 375 | 1,000 | 2,171 | 2,050 | 391 | 226 | 617 | 1,553 | 1,404 |
| 1958 | 747 | 390 | 1,137 | 2,176 | 2,074 | 481 | 248 | 729 | 1,582 | 1,456 |
| 1959 | 664 | 425 | 1,089 | 2,277 | 2,166 | 473 | 274 | 747 | 1,613 | 1,495 |
| 1960 | 733 | 461 | 1,194 | 2,314 | 2,217 | 523 | 294 | 817 | 1,645 | 1,541 |
| 1961 | 819 | 468 | 1,287 | 2,352 | 2,266 | 459 | 320 | 779 | 1,668 | 1,564 |
| 1962 | 850 | 490 | 1,340 | 2,455 | 2,369 | 727 | 351 | 1,078 | 1,739 | 1,666 |
| 1963 | 899 | 504 | 1,403 | 2,535 | 2,455 | 802 | 377 | 1,179 | 1,803 | 1,738 |
| 1964 | 860 | 521 | 1,381 | 2,666 | 2,579 | 715 | 409 | 1,124 | 1,897 | 1,821 |
| 1965 | 1,112 | 552 | 1,664 | 2,821 | 2,748 | 931 | 454 | 1,385 | 2,039 | 1,979 |

Source: USDA, *Agricultural Statistics, 1966,* DBS, *National Accounts: Income & Expenditures,* 1926–56, 1965 and 1966.

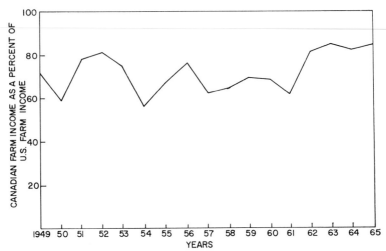

Fig. 8.3—Ratio of Canadian farm income to U.S. farm income, measured on a per capita personal income basis, 1949–65. (From the U.S. Department of Agriculture, Agricultural Statistics, 1966; and the Dominion Bureau of Statistics, National Accounts: Income and Expenditures, 1926–56, 1965, 1966.)

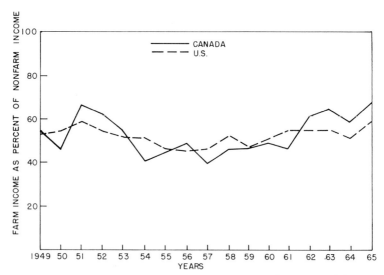

Fig. 8.4—Ratio of farm to nonfarm per capita personal income for both Canada and the United States, 1949–65. (From the U.S. Department of Agriculture, Agricultural Statistics, 1966; and the Dominion Bureau of Statistics, National Accounts: Income and Expenditures, 1926–56, 1965, 1966.)

## TABLE 8.6
### Relative Personal Income Per Capita, Farm and Nonfarm, Canada and the United States

| Year | Per Capita Personal Farm Income | | Ratio of Canadian to U.S. Farm Income | United States | | | Canada | | |
|---|---|---|---|---|---|---|---|---|---|
| | United States | Canada | | Per capita personal income | | Ratio: Farm to Nonfarm | Per capita personal income | | Ratio: Farm to Nonfarm |
| | | | | Farm | Nonfarm | | Farm | Nonfarm | |
| | ($) | ($) | (%) | ($) | ($) | (%) | ($) | ($) | (%) |
| 1949 | 805 | 569 | 70.7 | 805 | 1,501 | 53.6 | 569 | 1,092 | 52.1 |
| 1950 | 884 | 520 | 58.8 | 884 | 1,611 | 54.9 | 520 | 1,127 | 46.1 |
| 1951 | 1,037 | 817 | 78.8 | 1,037 | 1,759 | 59.0 | 817 | 1,212 | 67.4 |
| 1952 | 1,015 | 822 | 81.0 | 1,015 | 1,852 | 54.8 | 822 | 1,302 | 63.1 |
| 1953 | 996 | 745 | 74.8 | 996 | 1,921 | 51.8 | 745 | 1,352 | 55.1 |
| 1954 | 970 | 545 | 56.2 | 870 | 1,895 | 51.2 | 545 | 1,357 | 40.2 |
| 1955 | 922 | 624 | 67.7 | 922 | 2,006 | 46.0 | 624 | 1,397 | 44.7 |
| 1956 | 952 | 724 | 76.0 | 952 | 2,108 | 45.2 | 724 | 1,492 | 48.5 |
| 1957 | 1,000 | 617 | 61.7 | 1,000 | 2,171 | 46.1 | 617 | 1,553 | 39.7 |
| 1958 | 1,137 | 729 | 64.1 | 1,137 | 2,176 | 52.2 | 729 | 1,582 | 46.1 |
| 1959 | 1,089 | 747 | 68.6 | 1,089 | 2,277 | 47.8 | 747 | 1,613 | 46.3 |
| 1960 | 1,194 | 817 | 68.4 | 1,194 | 2,314 | 51.6 | 817 | 1,645 | 49.7 |
| 1961 | 1,287 | 779 | 60.5 | 1,287 | 2,352 | 54.7 | 779 | 1,668 | 46.7 |
| 1962 | 1,340 | 1,078 | 80.5 | 1,340 | 2,455 | 54.6 | 1,078 | 1,739 | 61.9 |
| 1963 | 1,403 | 1,179 | 84.0 | 1,403 | 2,535 | 55.3 | 1,179 | 1,803 | 65.4 |
| 1964 | 1,381 | 1,124 | 81.4 | 1,381 | 2,666 | 51.8 | 1,124 | 1,897 | 59.2 |
| 1965 | 1,664 | 1,385 | 83.3 | 1,664 | 2,821 | 58.9 | 1,385 | 2,039 | 67.9 |

Source: USDA, *Agricultural Statistics, 1966*, DBS, *National Accounts: Income & Expenditures*, 1926–56, 1965 and 1966.

TABLE 8.7

FARM OPERATOR'S INCOME PER NORMALIZED MAN EQUIVALENT, VARIOUS
REGIONS OF CANADA

| | Regions of Canada | | | | | |
|---|---|---|---|---|---|---|
| Year | Mari-times | Quebec | Ontario | Prairies | B.C. | Canada |
| | *(dollars)* | | | | | |
| 1931–35 | − 21 | −104 | − 85 | −406 | 28 | −168 |
| 1936–40 | 64 | 58 | 141 | 148 | 282 | 119 |
| 1941–45 | 198 | 262 | 597 | 866 | 737 | 635 |
| 1946–50 | 245 | 363 | 815 | 1,429 | 631 | 904 |
| 1951–55 | 374 | 648 | 1,077 | 2,260 | 626 | 1,353 |
| 1956–60 | 483 | 516 | 920 | 1,441 | 518 | 1,046 |
| 1961–65 | 728 | 449 | 1,308 | 3,442 | 1,139 | 1,601 |

Source: S. N. Kulshreshtha, "A Valid Comparison of Farm and Nonfarm Incomes,"
unpublished Ph.D. thesis, Dept. of Agr. Econ., Univ. of Manitoba.

There is little doubt that the disparity of incomes among various agricultural regions within Canada and the United States tends to be considerably larger than the difference between the two countries. For example, for the period 1961–65, the farm operator's income per normalized man equivalent for Saskatchewan was $3,442 as compared to $1,308 for Ontario (Table 8.7). Farm income in Ontario, on the other hand, was almost three times as high as that in Quebec during the same five-year period.

The regional variation in farm income was similar for the United States (Table 8.8). For the period 1954–56 Johnson found that the average income per farm worker was $3,805 in the Pacific region and only $1,240 in the East South Central region.

TABLE 8.8

AVERAGE FARM INCOME PER FARM WORKER FOR VARIOUS REGIONS OF THE
UNITED STATES

| | Average Farm Income Per Worker | | | |
|---|---|---|---|---|
| Region | 1927–29 | 1938–40 | 1949–51 | 1954–56 |
| | *(dollars)* | | | |
| New England | 923 | 833 | 2,638 | 2,383 |
| Mid-Atlantic | 884 | 693 | 2,211 | 2,133 |
| E.N. Central | 821 | 698 | 2,580 | 2,592 |
| W.N. Central | 809 | 650 | 2,616 | 2,407 |
| S. Atlantic | 450 | 412 | 1,545 | 1,788 |
| E.S. Central | 376 | 324 | 1,148 | 1,240 |
| W.S. Central | 514 | 478 | 2,333 | 2,064 |
| Mountain | 821 | 672 | 3,149 | 2,823 |
| Pacific | 1,232 | 885 | 3,451 | 3,805 |

Source: D. Gale Johnson, "The Dimensions of the Farm Problem," *Problems and
Policies of American Agriculture,* Iowa State Univ. Press, Ames, 1961, p. 52.

If average returns, as we have calculated them, are any indication of the opportunities for a reallocation of resources within agriculture, it seems reasonable to hypothesize that much more could be gained by a reallocation of agricultural resources within rather than between the two countries. Indeed the Rural Area Development program (RAD) in the United States and the Agricultural Rehabilitation and Development Act (ARDA) in Canada have been predicated on the assumption of immense regional discrepancies within both countries in resource use efficiency and returns.

In considering the opportunities for further pooling of agricultural resources in North America, we must not ignore the powerful attraction of the urban industrial economy for the redundant or underutilized resources found in many regions of the agricultural industry in Canada and the United States. The disparity of incomes between the farm and nonfarm sectors of both countries will continue to influence the allocation of resources in agriculture.

## ECONOMICS OF POOLING RESOURCES

In the absence of trade restrictions such as tariffs and import quotas, and given a competitive mobility of production factors, the conventional marginal criteria would determine the most efficient use of agricultural resources within and between Canada and the United States. In a general sense, the land, labor, and capital resources would be allocated in such a manner that the following equilibrium conditions would hold between the agricultural industries of the two countries:

$$\frac{MVP_{L_C}}{P_{L_C}} = \frac{MVP_{C_C}}{P_{C_C}} = \frac{MVP_{S_C}}{P_{S_C}} = \frac{MVP_{L_U}}{P_{L_U}} = \frac{MVP_{C_U}}{P_{C_U}} = \frac{MVP_{S_U}}{P_{S_U}}$$

where $MVP_{L_C}$, $MVP_{C_C}$, $MVP_{S_C}$, $P_{L_C}$, $P_{C_C}$, and $P_{S_C}$ represent the marginal value productivities and the price—adjusted appropriately for mobility costs—of labor, capital, and land, respectively, in Canada, with a similar interpretation for the United States.

The limited data which are available indicate that there is

a significant disparity between Canada and the United States insofar as returns to the various agricultural resources are concerned. The data presented in the preceding section indicate that farm income per capita in Canada in the period 1949–65 was approximately 30 percent below that in the United States. Heady and Dillon also found substantial differences in the marginal returns to land, labor, and capital between the United States and Canada.[20] While there was considerable variation in the resource productivities for different regions of the continent, it did appear from the Heady and Dillon study that marginal returns to agricultural resources in Canada tended to be somewhat above those in the United States.

The reasons for the persistence of these differences are difficult to determine. One can suggest hypotheses, however, which may explain in part at least, the disparity between the two countries' resource returns. One hypothesis ascribes the disparity to the particular agricultural price and income policies adopted in the two countries. Many contend that farmers in the United States receive the benefit of much higher price supports and income subsidies than farmers in Canada. This hypothesis deserves considerably more study than it has received to date. Another hypothesis is that Canadian farmers lag behind their counterparts in the United States in technical innovation and adoption. Many possible reasons are suggested: differences in credit policies and extension services, greater involvement of marketing and supply firms in agricultural production in the United States, and a proportionately greater investment in agricultural research in the United States by public and private agencies.

In examining the causes of disparity of returns between the agricultural industries of Canada and the United States, one cannot ignore the political, institutional, and cultural factors which tend to inhibit the free movement of resources from one country to the other. Labor provides the best example. Economists are becoming increasingly aware of the powerful sociological and cultural forces which tend to keep labor much more immobile than apparent alternative economic opportunities might indicate.[21] The political difficulties associated with capital investment by residents of one country in the agricultural industry of another are well known.[22] Farmers often resent the

---

[20] E. O. Heady and J. L. Dillon, *Agricultural Production Functions,* Iowa State Univ. Press, Ames, 1961, p. 633 ff.

[21] See, for example, T. W. Schultz "Reflections on Poverty Within Agriculture," *Jour. Political Econ.,* Vol. 58 (1950), 1–15.

[22] Brown.

investment of "outside" capital in their industry whether the investment is by firms indigenous to the country or not.

Pooling of agricultural resources between Canada and the United States may be prevented by various types of tariffs and import quotas imposed on goods moving between the two countries.[23] For example, the U.S. tariff on slaughter-feeder cattle over 700 pounds imported from Canada is 1½ cents up to an annual quota of 400,000 head with a tariff of 2½ cents per pound on imports in excess of the quota. The reciprocal tariff rate for Canada is 1½ cents per pound with no quota. The Canadian tariff rate on certain animal and poultry feed supplements is presently 3½ cents per pound. The extent to which prevailing tariffs and import quotas have prevented pooling of resources is difficult to assess. Yet this is an area which requires careful examination if we are to discover the full implications of a continental integration of agricultural resource use. What the recent Kennedy Round of tariff cuts will mean to the agricultural industries of Canada and the United States has yet to be determined. There can be little doubt, however, that the Kennedy Round tariff cuts present greater opportunities for the pooling of agricultural resources between the two countries.

## IMPLICATIONS FOR RESEARCH

We have raised some questions as to how Canadian and U.S. agricultural resources could be allocated more efficiently. To carry out useful research in economic integration it is necessary to list one's assumptions with great care. Forming a common market might, for example, entail only a partial mutual tariff reduction, or it might involve complete trade liberalization with coordinated internal policies and a common currency or flexible exchange rate.

An ambitious researcher would like to predict many of the changes due to economic integration. Changes would likely occur in the mix of final products, the locations of activities at all stages of production, the degrees of vertical and horizontal integration, industry concentration, technologies, prices, consumption, and patterns of trade in both farm and nonfarm sectors within North America and with third countries. Limited time and difficulties with data would no doubt impose narrower objectives. However, for the present discussion we adopt a rather comprehensive approach.

---

[23] *The Customs Tariff and Amendments,* Office Consolidation, July 1965, Dept. Nat. Rev., Customs and Excise Div., Ottawa, Canada.

Methods available for studying adjustments due to economic integration have been discussed by Isard *et al.*[24] The methods include input-output analysis, spatial interaction models, and interregional programming. It appears that several such analytical techniques should be employed collaterally if there is to be a valid understanding of the effects of a common market.

Input-output analysis may not in itself be a very appropriate method for studying economic adjustment, but it may be one of the better ways to obtain data for interregional programming.[25] Spatial interaction models appear promising for studying effects of changing densities of activities, but are too partial to generate sufficient understanding of the effects of general economic integration.[26] Of the available methods, interregional programming, despite its limitations, facilitates a direct approach to studying the effects of pooling resources in a common market.

When this method is used, one must recognize, as did Stevens[27] and Isard,[28] that the particular objective function and set of constraints used depends partly on the researcher's hierarchy of values. There is a real danger that due to his values or beliefs, he will omit some relevant activities or constraints.

Another difficulty in using *linear* programming is the necessity to assume a set of final product prices, and perhaps also requirements which, it is supposed, will exist in the future, after the programmed adjustments have occurred. Whether or not the researcher is able to make good price and quantity predictions depends on the validity of a model or guess of his which is separate from the program. The need for such predictions may be avoided if one is willing to make more complex assumptions about demand characteristics. In this case, using a nonlinear program as, for example, the quadratic program discussed by Takayama and Judge,[29] it is possible to predict final prices and quantities by programming. If this is a more reliable method, however, the advantage must still be weighed against the added cost of computation.

The well-known linear programming assumptions of linear-

[24] Walter Isard (ed.), *Methods of Regional Analysis: An Introduction to Regional Science,* M.I.T. Press, Cambridge, Mass., 1960.

[25] Isard, pp. 309–74.

[26] Isard, pp. 493–568.

[27] Benjamin H. Stevens, "An Interregional Linear Programming Model," *Jour. Regional Sci.,* Vol. 1 (Summer 1958).

[28] Isard, pp. 413–91.

[29] T. Takayama, and G. G. Judge, "Spatial Equilibrium and Quadratic Programming," *Jour. Farm Econ.,* Vol. 46 (1964), 67–93.

ity, additivity, divisibility, finiteness, and single-valued expectations may result in misleading solutions unless due care is taken.
However, techniques exist for overcoming most of these difficulties.[30]

In addition, there are general difficulties of taxonomy and
measurement which, while well known, often tend to be given
no more than lip service. "Products," "resources," and "regions"
should be adequately homogeneous and distinct from each other.
They should be measurable with sufficient accuracy at reasonable
cost. The number of categories should be just sufficient to permit
estimation of interesting relationships, and the model should fit
the real world well enough for the problem at hand.[31]

## MODELS OF ECONOMIC INTEGRATION

Programming models of the location of production and transportation of commodities in North American agriculture have
evolved from those dealing with a single commodity or a single
locality. More recent models have applied to multicommodity
and multiregion problems and have included complexities in
transportation, resource supplies, demand characteristics, and
industry structure.

Simple transportation models focused on the savings obtainable from better use of existing transport facilities, assuming
supplies at point origins and demands at point destinations to
be either constant or perfectly elastic. The assumptions of these
models reduced their relevance when economic integration led
to new transport facilities, changes in production technology, in
product quality, absolute incomes, participation in trade with
third countries, and the like. The more aggregate the analysis,
the more interested is one in such relationships and the less useful
are these simple models.

Fox[32] and Takayama and Judge[33] developed more sophisticated transportation models of production in a vertically specialized agriculture. These models allowed for the transforma-

---

[30] For further discussion, see Earl O. Heady and Wilfred Candler, *Linear
Programming Methods*, Iowa State Univ. Press, Ames, 1958.

[31] For further discussion, see *Regional Income*, Studies in Income and
Wealth, Natl. Bur. Econ. Res., Vol. 21, 1957.

[32] Karl A. Fox and R. C. Taeuber, "Spatial Equilibrium Models of the
Livestock-Feed Economy," *Amer. Econ. Rev.*, Vol .45 (1955), 584–608; Fox and
Taeuber, "A Spatial Equilibrium Model of the Livestock-Feed Economy in
the United States," *Econometrica*, Vol. 21 (1953), 547–66.

[33] T. Takayama and G. G. Judge, "An Interregional Activity Analysis
Model," *Jour. Farm Econ.*, Vol. 46 (1964), 349–65.

tion of resources into products at locations which were optimal in view of existing costs of transport and production. We suggest an extension of such models to include the effects of economic integration on North American trade with third countries.

MODEL I

In the first model our aim is to incorporate various interdependent influences on the supply side. Flows of various primary resources are distinguished, that is, the "cost of production" of farm products is partially disaggregated. The resources are still treated as being available at given price levels. However, there is an explicit specification of their sources, the cost of transporting them, their substitutability or complementarity, and the physical or technical limits to their supplies. This is expected to generate a more refined map of the locations and levels of output of farm products.

In this formulation the North American economy is partitioned into nonagricultural and agricultural sectors, the latter being partitioned into regions. The commodities considered are the resources and products used in each sector. In the agricultural sector these are made up of "primary resources" and "agricultural products." The resources include such items as "bags of fertilizer," "acre-feet of water," and "units of machine power." The products are the food and fiber products which are demanded at the farm gate. The flexibility offered by the model within which policy variables can be considered depends on the assumption that all commodities—whether resources or products—are transportable in form and between regions at some cost between zero and infinity according to the commodity and route in question. It is assumed there are fixed and known regional endowments of primary resources, capacities for transportation and (domestic) consumption requirements, and that prices in at least one base region are fixed and known. Trade in resources and products with third countries is permitted through specified ports, trade being constrained by the capacities of the various ports. Prices between ports may vary according to the location of domestic and foreign production and consumption. Import supplies and export demands are assumed to be perfectly elastic.[34] Constraints are imposed on trade such that consumption requirements are satisfied in each region. Regional production coefficients within the North American economy are

---

[34] It may be necessary to constrain exports and imports in order to provide greater realism.

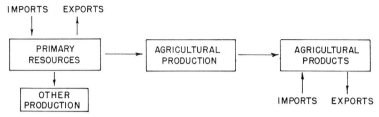

*Fig. 8.5—Definitions, assumptions, and characteristics of Model I. Imports and exports refer to commodities traded with third countries.*

assumed fixed and known. All markets are assumed to be perfectly competitive.

This model permits estimation of potential gains from relocation in space and/or changing the input mixes to produce the same farm output with fewer resources or a greater output from former input levels. The objective function of the model is to optimize in these terms.

The definitions, assumptions, and characteristics of Model I are illustrated by Figure 8.5.

The following notation is used for this model:

Let $i$, $j$ = regions; $i$, $j$, = 1, 2, . . . , $I$
which are the locations of resources, domestic consumption requirements, and trade with third countries;

$n$ = commodities in the agricultural sector: $n = 1, 2, . . . , N$
with 1, 2, . . . , $K$ = final products and
$k = K + 1, K + 2, . . . , N$ = primary resources located in the regions $j$, either as endowments or imports;

$\Theta^n$ = processes using the $n$th commodity;

$a_i^{k\theta^n}$ = quantity of the $k$th resource required per unit for the $\Theta^n$ process in region $i$;

$X_i^{\theta^n}$ = level of $\Theta^n$th process in region $i$;

$c_i^{\theta^n}$ = cost per unit of the $\Theta^n$th process in the $i$th region;

$t_{ij}^{\theta^n}$ = cost per unit of transporting the $n$th commodity from region $i$ to region $j$ given a transportation capacity between regions $T_{ij}$ which describes the existing facilities for commodity mobility (Other levels of capacity could be incorporated by parametric variations of $T_{ij}$.);

$S_i^k$ = supply of the $k$th primary resource in the $i$th region, including ports;

$D_c^k$ = quantity of the $k$th final product demanded in the $i$th region, including exports, and

$p_i^k$ = price of the $k$th final product in the $i$th region.

The objective function is to maximize income that arises from price per unit times the level of output produced in all regions less all costs of transport and production. This may be written:

$$f(x) = \sum_i \sum_k p_i^k X_i^{\theta^k} - \sum_i \sum_j \sum_n \sum_{\theta^n} t_{ij}^{\theta^n} X_{ij}^{\theta^n} - \sum_i \sum_j \sum_n \sum_{\theta^n} c_i X_i^{\theta^n}$$

The relevant constraints relate to the area dimension of the activities. Domestic and export demands are met by output which includes that which has utilized imported resources. It follows that in any one region a "net" $X_i^{\theta^K} = D_i^K$ applies, as it does in the whole economy.

The processes of agricultural production take place in any one region at positive levels of output or not at all. The level will be limited by the regional capacity. This can be written as

$$X_i^{\theta^n} \geq 0$$

The supplies of primary resources are given for regions so that

$$S_i^k \geq \sum_k \sum_j \sum_{\theta^n} a_i^{k\theta^n} X_{ji}^{\theta^n} - \sum_j \sum_{\theta^k} X_{ij}^{\theta^n}$$

**MODEL II**

Model I may be refined to take account of intermediate stages of production, specifically in this case (a) the manufacturing of farm inputs and (b) the production of intermediate agricultural resources. Previous workers who developed models of this type include Stevens,[35] Isard,[36] and Takayama and Judge.[37]

In Model I there is room only for assumptions about sup-

[35] Stevens.
[36] Isard.
[37] Takayama and Judge.

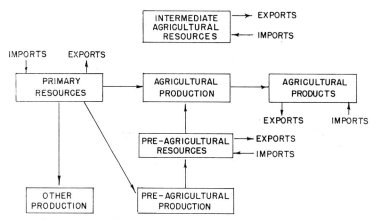

*Fig. 8.6—Definitions, assumptions, and characteristics of Model II.*

plies of the equivalents of primary resources which are embodied in manufactured inputs at the farm receiving gate. For example, in Model I no explicit account can be taken of the connection between the supply of a mineral at the mine and the supply of a fertilizer at the farm. In Model II, however, supplies of farm inputs are assumed to depend on capacities and costs of the farm supply industry in addition to endowments of primary resources. Recognition is also given to the possibility of trade with third countries in farm inputs as well as in primary resources and agricultural products.

The other refinement in the model permits explicit recognition of relationships between producers and consumers of intermediate agricultural resources. It is also assumed that there may be trade with third countries in intermediate agricultural resources.

The additional definitions and assumptions are as follows. It is assumed there is a farm supply industry which uses inorganic processes to produce "pre-agricultural" resources from primary resources. Examples of pre-agricultural resources include fuels, machinery, chemical fertilizers, herbicides, and pesticides. It is also assumed that regions may specialize vertically in agriculture, becoming net exporters or importers of intermediate agricultural resources, examples of which include seeds for planting, feed grains, and feeder cattle. These definitions and assumptions are illustrated in Figure 8.6.

Additional notation is required beyond that used in Model I, the N commodities being further partitioned as follows:

Let 1, 2, . . . , $N$ = commodities
with 1, 2, . . . , $K$ = agricultural products,
$k^2 = K+1^2, K+2^2, . . , N^2$ = intermediate agricultural resources,
$k^1 = K+1^1, K+2^1, . . , N^1$ = pre-agricultural resources,
$k^0 = K+1^0, K+2^0, . . , N^0$ = primary resources.

The objective function may be written algebraically as in Model I. However, solutions will now incorporate revenues and costs from the activities specified in connection with pre-agricultural and intermediate agricultural resources.

The mobility of the various kinds of resources will now define the constraints that apply to them. In general

$$S_i^k \geq \sum_k \sum_j \sum_{\theta^k} a_i^{k\theta^k} X_{ji}^{\theta^k} - \sum_j \sum_{\theta^k} X_{ij}^{\theta^k}$$

As before, the quantity made available in a region is just sufficient to satisfy the regional demand, while pre-agricultural and agricultural production can take place only at non-negative levels. The mix and supply conditions of the "resources" for these processes determine whether the cost constraints on a particular activity are regional or economy-wide in their impact.

## APPLICATIONS

An attempt has been made in developing this model to incorporate variables which can be treated parametrically to analyze various kinds of pooling. If effective pooling were achieved there would be a reduction in barriers that had previously increased price differentials between regions. Changing regional prices would encourage changes in long-term investments in both production and transport facilities.

The assumption that particular barriers would be lowered could be incorporated in programming the effects of alternative degrees of pooling. If this were assumed to affect production and transport capacities too, such effects could also be included. The model could then be used to predict reallocations in production, international flows of resources and products, and changes in relative prices.

Additional assumptions could be made about technological change and economies of scale, in a comparative static framework. Technological change might be accelerated or decelerated by abnormal profits, changing regional volumes of production, and changes in the degree of vertical specialization.

Such effects could be incorporated in the programmed solution in the form of assumptions about reductions in production coefficients in the forecast period compared to the present.

The structure of the model also facilitates the explicit inclusion of assumptions about the state of the economic world for the purposes of economic forecasting. For example, alternatives in population, income, and preferences could be reflected in final consumption requirements. Alternative levels of technology could be shown in the production coefficients and capacities, as could different levels of aggregate economic activity. Similarly, various prices of commodities in international trade could be considered. Government policy could be assumed to influence any of these variables and its assumed effects could be included in the way such variables were specified.

As with all static models, assumptions about the fixity of factors and the reversibility of behavioral relations must be applied carefully if adequate realism is to be attained. In addition, the model is somewhat inadequately adapted to analyzing the properties of a dynamic world since dynamic phenomena can be approximated only by the introduction of exogenous assumptions. However, while the model itself does not describe dynamic developments, it is not clear a priori that a dynamic model would be better than a comparative static use of the present one for prediction, provided good projections could be obtained of strategic exogenous variables.

# CHAPTER NINE

# Impact of Economic Integration
# on North American Agriculture

## GORDON A. KING

THE TWO PREVIOUS CHAPTERS have considered (a) the effects of a common commodity market and (b) the effects of the free flow of mobile resources among Canada, the United States, and Mexico. It has been argued, effectively in my opinion, that if the emphasis is on meeting world food needs, major attention should be directed to Canada and the United States. The purpose of this chapter, then, is to provide a framework for analyzing the combined effects of pooling of resources and common commodity markets with a goal of providing for world food needs.

### INTEGRATION AND WORLD FOOD NEEDS

As in most economic analyses, we are confronted with questions of production efficiency on the one hand and welfare considerations for producers and consumers on the other. Compromises are made in production efficiency goals to meet the political restraints of regional production and income, as in acreage allot-

GORDON A. KING, Department of Agricultural Economics, Agricultural Experiment Station, and the Giannini Foundation, University of California, Davis. The author wishes to express his appreciation to A. F. McCalla for the many helpful discussions during the preparation of this chapter and for the review comments. Also, his appreciation is given to S. Detering whose diligent research on Mexican agriculture prevented unwarranted generalizations which might have resulted from inclusion of Mexico in this discussion.

ments tied to historical bases. Consumer price policy also may be a restraint. In periods of rapid technological change, however, it is very difficult to balance off conflicting goals to achieve an optimum pattern of production subject to the desired goals of society.

A goal of meeting world food needs is an added restraint to the objective function of agricultural and foreign aid policies. Our concern is how economic integration of North America fits into this framework. Putting aside the difficult questions of economic policy harmonization, it can be argued that economic integration could result in an increased efficiency in the use of resources to meet desired objectives. Two alternatives can be stated: (a) using the same bundle of resources as at present, the level of production could be increased and could be used for food aid shipments or exports at somewhat lower prices; and (b) the present level of production could be maintained with less resources, allowing the savings thus achieved to be available for development aid.

## ECONOMIC ADJUSTMENT AND FOOD NEEDS

The question of food aid shipments has been brought into sharp economic focus by the excellent report by Abel and Rojko (1), and perhaps little more needs to be said. However, I would like to consider briefly food aid from the viewpoint of the donor and recipient nations in terms of economic adjustment and policy goals. For the United States, major food export commodities have faced inelastic domestic demand, commercial export demand limited by various restraints, and concessional sales limited by congressional budget restraints. The adoption of new technology has resulted in rapidly shifting supply curves that have been restrained by acreage controls. Policy goals include those relating to *consumer* prices and to *producer* prices and incomes. Such goals in the past have resulted in accumulations of CCC stocks of several commodities, but recent emphasis has shifted to increasing the levels of exports. With limits on commercial exports, food aid shipments have been introduced with a dual appeal: (a) to the humanitarian interest in the recipient nation consumer, and (b) to the income position of the donor nation producer.

Economic adjustment in the United States could take place by further curtailment of aggregate production and in location shifts. Fewer resources would be needed if concessional sales were discontinued or production efficiency could be improved even with current levels of food aid. Economic integration with Canada would tend to increase the adjustments required.

For the food aid recipient nation, parallel questions of economic adjustment appear. Here, however, the situation is reversed, with a rapidly shifting demand curve and a sluggish supply response. Khusro (9) provides useful insights into food problems in India with controlled producer prices and controlled consumer prices. With producer prices lower than would be true without controls, both farm sales in commercial channels and production levels are lower than would otherwise be the case. The addition of food aid supplies to his analytical framework would tend to intensify the restraint on supply response in India.[1]

The alternative of economic integration to provide increased funds available for long-term loans, technical assistance, and other measures has greater appeal to me. There is no assurance that such use would be made of savings, but it is an important possibility and one that justifies serious attention.

### TYPES OF ECONOMIC INTEGRATION

If exporters and importers agreed on a desirable level of food aid shipments, would this necessarily require integration? Balassa (2, p. 24) argues we should distinguish between *cooperation* and *integration*. Whereas both terms imply some form of economic policy harmonization, the latter requires more formal suppression of discrimination. Thus food aid shipments could be achieved through cooperation in the form of an international grains agreement.

Economic integration can take on various forms. The problem is to specify: (a) what forms of discrimination are to be eliminated among member nations, what policies are to be maintained toward nonmember nations, and what degree of economic policy harmonization is to be established; and (b) what would be the effect of alternative levels of integration on the location of production in the North American region. With such a broad scope we can do little more than indicate the relevant considerations and point to the needed research to answer such questions. The common market type of integration fits into the spectrum mid-

---

[1] Investment funds made available to the recipient nation through food aid shipments can influence development. Due to congressional reaction to the AID budget, the funds for development through food aid have the benefit of appeal to farm groups as income support for exports as well as to those concerned with development aid as such.

TABLE 9.1
TYPES OF ECONOMIC INTEGRATION

| Type | Tariffs, Quotas | | Factor Move-ment Rela-tively Free | Economic Policy | |
|------|-----------------|---|------|-----------------|---|
| | Member nations | Non-member nations | | Harmo-nized* | Uni-fied† |
| Free trade area | None | Unique | | | |
| Customs union | None | Common | | | |
| Common market | None | Common | Yes | | |
| Economic union | None | Common | Yes | Yes | |
| Total economic integration | None | Common | Yes | Yes | Yes |

Source: Based on Balassa (2).
* Harmonization of economic, monetary, fiscal, social, and countercyclical policies. A limited form would be a harmonized agricultural policy for purposes of food aid.
† Unification of economic, fiscal, and other policies with supranational authority with decisions binding for member states.

way between a free trade area and total economic integration, as indicated in Table 9.1 which summarizes ideas expressed by Balassa (2). For our problem, we lift trade restraints among member nations, set common external tariffs, allow factor movement, and harmonize agricultural and related policies to some undetermined extent.

## LOCATION AND TRADE WITH RESTRAINTS

The theoretical framework for analysis of the impact of lifting trade and factor movement restraints and agricultural policy harmonization on location is sketched out in this section, followed by commodity considerations in the next section. Major attention is given to commodity flows rather than factor flows because of arguments presented in the previous chapter by Gilson, Capel, and Harris that flows of capital and labor are essentially free between Canada and the United States. Mexico presents analytical problems because of development goals and will not be included for reasons presented by McCalla in Chapter 7.

### LOCATION ADJUSTMENTS WITH TARIFFS ELIMINATED

Consider Canada and the United States with given resource flows, trade policies, and agricultural and related policies. For convenience, assume that exports to other nations are given. We wish

to determine the effect of location of lifting tariff and quota restraints on raw products only. How can this be done? Since we
are dealing with the theoretical issues, we can suggest the use of
the Takayama-Judge (13) reformulation of the Samuelson model
to spatial general equilibrium. We consider agriculture only,
and also abstract from exchange rate and balance of payments
questions. The data needs, of course, are staggering—regional
demand functions with cross effects; transportation rates;[2] processing locations; regional production and cost functions for all
commodities, with given restraints as to resource flows; tariffs on
intermediate and final commodities; and national restraints imposed by government programs.

One measure of the impact of elimination of tariffs on raw
products would be to determine the optimum location pattern
for each country taken in isolation with current restraints. The
resulting pattern of production could then be compared with a
two-country model in which tariffs were eliminated. Later we
argue for partial models on key sectors most apt to be affected.

To simplify still further, consider a two-region, one-com-
modity model with the well-known back-to-back diagram. For
these agricultural products, a highly inelastic demand function
is appropriate and supply curves could be completely inelastic
due to government programs, but assume them to be of the usual
slope. With elimination of a tariff, the following typically might
result: For the exporting country, consumer prices would rise,
exports and production would increase. For the importing country that had removed the import tariff, price would fall, supply
decrease, and imports increase. These results then are a function
of the demand and supply elasticities and the level of the tariff,
with given constant transportation costs.

Consider the welfare implications of the above simple model.
Consumer price increases in the export country are balanced
against increased producer revenues. For the importer, consumer
prices fall, supply decreases, and the government loses revenues
from tariffs. It can be shown that some sort of compensation may
be required to assure such tariff change would be acceptable to
all parties.[3] A key issue of integration for a multicommodity
world is the means by which the gains and losses to the respective
consumers and producers in each country are to be distributed.
Thus a reduction in the tariff structure cannot realistically be

---

[2] The Canadian Freight Assistance Program would be in effect but could
be limited to Canadian-produced grain.
[3] See the discussion on gains from trade given by Kemp (7).

isolated from agricultural support programs. Further, it may be difficult to separate agricultural programs from those of the nonagricultural sector. Moreover, confining the discussion on integration to agriculture limits the potential gains from trade due to a restricted payoff matrix.

Reduction of tariffs on processed agricultural products raises complications on the line to be drawn between agricultural and nonagricultural industries.[4] The indirect effects of such changes certainly flow throughout the economy as can be shown in input-output studies. Theoretically our large model could be used to trace through the effects on long-run location of processing facilities and processed product flows.

## LOCATION ADJUSTMENTS WITH POLICY HARMONIZATION

Agricultural policies must consider production efficiency and welfare aspects as well. The regional allocation of acreages for production of certain supported crops results in cropping patterns that are nonoptimal from the viewpoint of production efficiency, as has been clearly demonstrated in a recent publication by Heady and Whittlesey (6). Thus production efficiency goals are constrained by legislation designed to maintain regional incomes at least during periods of adjustment which seem to last a considerable number of years.

The extent of differences between policy goals of Canada and the United States may not differ widely but the means of achieving these goals exhibit differences. Yet in considering economic integration, emphasis also must be given to expected future adjustments that will be made in the agricultural policy of each country. This would be especially true if Mexico had been included in these models. It is clear that Mexican development will have important implications whether included in the common market or not, as can be inferred from a study of the projections of their agriculture to 1970 and 1975 (12).

The question of the effect of policy harmonization on the location of production must be examined in detail for individual countries. However, this falls outside the scope of this chapter. Analytically, however, it should cause no particular problem above those already mentioned in connection with tariff re-

---

[4] Grubel and Johnson (4) provide a clear example of the effects of a regulation on processing location of a product of agriculture—Scotch whiskey. A labeling law requires that age cannot be advertised if reused cooperage is used in production. This regulation applied to production in the United States but not for foreign production.

straints. Given these harmonized policies, the restraints could then be specified and the location implications obtained.

One might well ask where the major economies from location shifts might occur. Would it result from each country reevaluating its own policies, with given trade restraints, or would there be important additional benefits from free trade between the two countries? Would an appropriate axiom be: Clean your home (policies) before inviting the neighbors in?

## COMMODITY LOCATION WITH INTEGRATION

We attempt here a partial ordering of commodities by the expected impact of integration on the location of production. From previous chapters it is clear what information is needed as to production and cost functions by regions, resource restraints, transfer costs, and demand interrelationships among commodities. From this framework we look at a very simple criterion that the impact of integration is a function of the restraints currently in effect.

### COMMODITIES NOT REQUIRING ANALYSIS

We expect that integration would have minimum effect for those commodities that require for commercial production unique soil-climate-water conditions that may be limited in supply in certain regions. Coffee production is an example for Canadian-U.S. integration where there would be no effect. Processing, however, may be affected by the relative import duty on raw versus processed commodity. For Mexican-U.S. integration bananas are an example of a commodity produced only in Mexico but import duties are negligible into the United States at present and integration would not be a factor affecting production.

For commodities produced for the fresh market for which the production season varies, current tariffs and restrictions are minimal between Canada and the United States. Thus the direct effect of integration would be unimportant. There may be indirect effects due to production alternatives in the various producing regions, but we limit the discussion to the direct effects as they appear from a first tentative analysis.

Processed fruits and vegetables that are produced mainly in one country would tend to have low tariffs, such as frozen asparagus for import into Canada.

## COMMODITIES REQUIRING SOME ANALYSIS

Fresh market seasonal production in which season of production coincides would be expected to have some degree of protection for the domestic producer. Thus we find seasonal tariffs on various fruit and vegetable crops between the United States and Canada.

Processed fruits and vegetables similarly tend to have higher trade restrictions than would be true for the fresh markets because of distance restraints for spoilage. Compare the U.S. tariffs on strawberries for fresh market and frozen strawberries for example.

Certain crops, such as sugar beets, tobacco, and cotton, depend to a great extent on government programs for location patterns. Take the example of sugar beets. If the United States and Canada decided to adopt a policy based on relatively free world trade in sugar, the production adjustments for both countries would be substantial for the nation and by regions of the country. For tobacco, production shifts might well occur if not restrained by farm income support considerations, and the same would be true of regional cotton production in the United States. These changes would occur mainly as policy harmonization and adjustment of quotas rather than through tariff reductions. Thus drastic effects on location could take place as we moved toward a competitive model.

## COMMODITIES FOR DETAILED ANALYSIS

The effect of trade restrictions and policies on wheat production location and trade has been discussed by McCalla in Chapter 7. Attention here will be directed to the feed-livestock complex since some interesting problems are involved relating to integration.

Location of feed grain production is influenced by regional production and cost functions, government acreage controls on feed and wheat, tariffs between the United States and Canada, an export demand, and the derived demand for poultry and livestock feeding. Transportation policies also influence the price surface, especially in Canada where the Feed Grain Assistance Program essentially flattens out the price surface across Canada for feed grains.

Location of poultry and livestock feeding is interrelated

with feed grain location, regional demand for products, tariffs on meats, live animals, dairy products, and the transportation rates for products. Government programs affect milk production more directly than other products, but the indirect effect through the feed grain programs is of importance to the extent that the regional supplies of grains are shifted.

The first question in our partial approach to this problem is to consider the differential effect on location of feeding for various classes of livestock. For the United States, Hassler (5, p. 66) provides a useful ranking of commodities as to feed grain supply versus market orientation of livestock products. The basic approach is to consider (a) the pounds of grain per pound of product—for each product; (b) the processing yield of each product for shipment (e.g., live hogs vs. pork); (c) the ratio of transfer costs for 100 pounds of product divided by the transfer costs for 100 pounds of grain. He obtains a ranking based on relative value gradients obtained by multiplying the transfer cost ratio (c) by the product conversion ratio (b), and dividing by the grain conversion factor (a). A low ratio would indicate feed grain source orientation of production and a high ratio a market orientation. Cattle feeding location also is a function of the source of feeder stock produced on range land and on imports of feeders. He considers the center of the surplus grain area as the base. Production of beef heavy feeders would be grain-supply oriented and would have the lowest ratio (.07). For the western areas the ranking is pork (.32), broilers (.60), light feeders (.71), and market milk (8.48). For eastern shipments, as we move away from the central point, the ranking is beef light feeders, pork, broilers, and market milk.

Consider now the effect of the Canadian feed transportation policy. For grains, the price surface is flattened out by the subsidized rate structure. For livestock production, the impact is greatest on products that are feed-source oriented, other things being equal. For cattle feeding, we would have to consider the sources of supply of feeder animals and regional feed conversion efficiency, for example.[5] We would expect the impact to be greatest on pork production, and this seems to be reflected in increases in Eastern Canadian hog numbers.

Now consider removal of all tariffs on imports of feeder animals into the United States from Canada and Mexico. The location of feeding would depend on (a) transportation policy

---

[5] See the analyses for Canada by Kerr (8).

of feeds, (b) tariff policy on meats, (c) production policy on grains, and (d) relative feeding efficiency by region as well as the regional demand levels. Import restrictions on feeders are not considered as very restrictive at present, and so, lifting feeder cattle tariff is considered to have minor effect of itself. But, the other policy measures might have quite substantial effects.

Now take off the trade restrictions on feed grains, harmonize transportation rates on feed grains, lift meat import restraints, and ask: What would be the impact on Eastern Canadian hog production with these three shifts toward integration? If we oversimplify to a three-region case, the factors involved are brought into perspective. Our alternatives are (a) produce hogs in Eastern Canada, using in-shipped grain (from the United States or Western Canada); (b) produce hogs in Western Canada (where grain prices are now reduced in relation to Eastern Canada without grain transportation subsidy) and ship pork to Eastern Canada; and (c) produce hogs in the Corn Belt and ship pork (Canadian-type?) to Eastern Canada. This would make a most interesting analysis if generalized to the multiregion case, and parallels exactly the analytical model used in the analysis of feedlot location by King and Schrader (10). Consideration of demand cross elasticities in a two-commodity model is suggested by Takayama and Judge (14) and, in a recent unpublished paper, Candler (3) suggests a computational procedure which makes such a quadratic model feasible to consider. Basically he suggests an iterative procedure, separating out the shipment activities from production activities, to achieve the equilibrium in all markets.

Similar analyses could be undertaken for various other poultry and livestock products. The dairy industry also would present interesting possibilities, using one of the analytical frameworks available as outlined in R. A. King (11) or in the recent study by West and Brandow (15). Location of processing industries for dairy products and other products broadens the scope of research effort with lifting tariffs on processed products as well as raw products.

## SUMMARY AND CONCLUSIONS

There is little doubt that North America is interested in helping developing countries improve their agricultural production capacity and the nutritional levels of their population. There is doubt as to the form and level of such aid, considering various budgetary and political restraints. Food aid shipments are one alternative in which domestic producers are subsidized, recipient consumers are aided, but long-run production response is restrained. If this form of aid is considered desirable, economic integration could result in increased levels of shipments with no increase in government outlays. This could result from more efficient production patterns obtained through policy harmonization and removal of trade barriers in North America. But an important alternative to food aid exists. Economic integration could result in more efficient production with the result that commercial exports might move at slightly lower prices or, more importantly, that funds currently devoted to agricultural and transportation policies could be reallocated for technical aid and other measures directed to the improvement of agriculture in the developing nations. The latter alternative should provide considerable incentive for a careful evaluation of economic integration of North American agriculture.

The question then becomes what increase in production efficiency could result from economic integration, and whether it would be due to reduction of trade restrictions or to reevaluation of policies in the attempt to harmonize and improve them. This is an empirical problem that deserves attention by the profession, and I certainly would encourage research along several lines.

One avenue might be to explore the effects of the Kennedy Round tariff reduction on trade and production patterns. A second effort might be directed to the selection of key commodity sectors for which tariff reductions and agricultural policy harmonization would be expected to have important interregional location effects. Answers would be needed as to the effect on prices, trade, production location, and income redistribution effects for farmers versus nonfarm groups and between farm groups between countries. A third effort might be directed to domestic programs with little intercountry production effect, such as the domestic cotton program as to regional location implications in the United States and the Feed Grain Assistance Program in Canada. A fourth effort, although not an exclusive category, would be to emphasize future patterns of agricultural production and trade. It is in this phase that consideration of Mexican agricultural development is of considerable importance. For example, as the income per capita increases, the demand for meat products will increase. Will the supply response of livestock producers be such that a continued flow of live animal in-shipments enters the United States, or will these animals be required for Mexican domestic consumption of meat? Or, as urban pressures for land increase in certain areas of the United States, will domestic production of vegetables be adequate, or will producers look for Mexican acreage to supply this output? There are restraints on labor and capital mobility between the United States and Mexico that provide an additional area for analysis, and such questions involve not only agricultural policies but the whole range of social legislation of the countries involved. A fifth phase might be to explore the implications for processing location due to restraints on raw versus processed products, and in this phase it would be important to consider developments on the integration of industrial as well as agricultural production activities. Whether integration takes place or not, these appear to be relevant questions to ask.

## REFERENCES

(1) Abel, M. E., and A. S. Rojko, *World Food Situation, Prospects for World Grain Production, Consumption, and Trade,* USDA, FAER-35, 1967.

(2) Balassa, B. A., "Toward a Theory of Economic Integration," M. S. Wionczek (ed.), *Latin American Economic Integration,* New York: Frederick A. Praeger, 1966, pp. 21–31.

(3) Candler, W., *Spatial Equilibrium and the Transportation Problem* (unpublished manuscript), Davis, Calif., June 1967.

(4) Grubel, H. G., and H. G. Johnson, "Nominal Tariff Rates and United States Valuation Practices: Two Case Studies," *Rev. Econ. and Stat.* 49(2):139–42, May 1967.

(5) Hassler, J. B., *The U.S. Feed Concentrate-Livestock Economy's Demand Structure, 1949–59* (with projections for 1960–70), Nebr. Agr. Exp. Sta. Res. Bull. 203, Oct. 1962.

(6) Heady, E. O., and N. K. Whittlesey, *A Programming Analysis of Interregional Competition and Surplus Capacity of American Agriculture,* Iowa Agr. and Home Econ. Exp. Sta. Bull. 538, July 1965.

(7) Kemp, M. C., *The Pure Theory of International Trade,* Englewood Cliffs: Prentice-Hall, Inc., 1964.

(8) Kerr, T. C., *An Economic Analysis of the Feed Freight Assistance Policy,* Agr. Econ. Res. Council of Canada, Sept. 1966.

(9) Khusro, A. M., "The Pricing of Food in India," *Quarterly Jour. Econ.* 81(2):271–85, May 1967.

(10) King, G. A., and L. F. Schrader, "Regional Location of Cattle Feeding—A Spatial Equilibrium Analysis," *Hilgardia* 34(10):331–416, July 1963.

(11) King, R. A. (ed.), *Interregional Competition Research Methods,* Raleigh: N.C. State Agr. Policy Inst., Series 10.

(12) Secretaría de Agricultura y Ganadería, Secretaría de Hacienda y Crédito Publico, Banco de México, S. A., *Projections of Supply of*

*and Demand for Agricultural Products in Mexico to 1965, 1970, and 1975,* Aug. 1966.

(13)  Takayama, T., and G. G. Judge, "Equilibrium Among Spatially Separated Markets: A Reformulation," *Econometrica* 32(4):510–24, Oct. 1964.

(14)  ———, "Spatial Equilibrium and Quadratic Programming," *Jour. Farm Econ.* 46(1):67–93, Feb. 1946.

(15)  West, D. A., and G. E. Brandow, *Equilibrium Prices, Production, and Shipments of Milk in the Dairy Regions of the United States, 1960,* Pa. Agr. Exp. Sta., A.E.&R.S. 49, Nov. 1964.

# PART FOUR

# Optimum Allocation of North American Resources

# CHAPTER TEN

# Water Supplies

E. KUIPER and J. MURRAY

## WATER SUPPLIES IN WESTERN CANADA

IN REVIEWING the water availability of the river systems of Western Canada, it is necessary to distinguish between average river flow and flow available for diversion. The first is simply the average river flow during the period of record. The flow available for diversion may be substantially less for several reasons. First, it may be desirable to keep a certain amount of water in the river for maintaining fish life or serving northern settlement, or other riparian rights, downstream of the point of diversion. Second, the natural river flow may fluctuate well above and below the long-term average. Hence at times the diversion works cannot handle all the available water; at other times there may not be enough water to fill the diversion system to capacity. It is evident that the ratio of flow available for diversion and average river flow depends largely on the natural stream flow fluctuation and on the amount of storage capacity that can be created in the drainage basin to even out these fluctuations. With this in mind, let us review the most important rivers in Northern Canada (see Fig. 10.1).

Nelson River: The average flow of the Nelson River at the

E. KUIPER, University of Manitoba; J. MURRAY, Department of Agricultural Engineering, University of Saskatchewan.

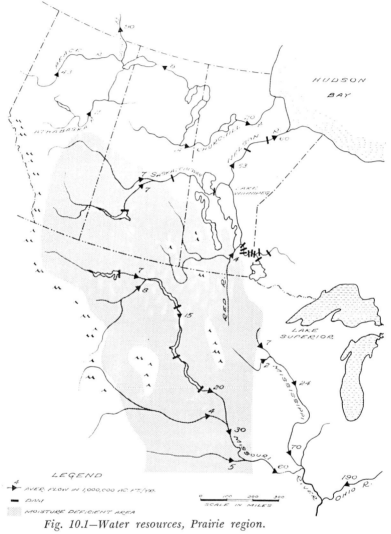

LEGEND

→4 AVER. FLOW IN 1,000,000 AC FT./YR.

▬▬ DAM

░░ MOISTURE DEFICIENT AREA

SCALE IN MILES
0    100    200    300

Fig. 10.1—Water resources, Prairie region.

outlet of Lake Winnipeg is 53 million acre-feet per year. The total storage capacity that can be created in the drainage basin (Lake of the Woods, Lac Seul, Lake Winnipeg, Lake Winnipegosis, Cedar Lake, Saskatchewan reservoirs) is in the order of 50 million acre-feet. The downstream riparian requirements on the Nelson River, other than for hydroelectric purposes, are relatively small. Hence it may be estimated that roughly 40 million acre-feet per year would be available for diversion to other places in Canada or for export.

Churchill River: The average flow of the Churchill River at Granville Falls is 20 million acre-feet per year. The total storage capacity that can be created in the drainage basin (Reindeer Lake, Granville Lake, Southern Indian Lake) is in the order of 25 million acre-feet. The downstream riparian requirements, other than hydroelectric, are relatively small. Hence the flow available for diversion may be estimated in the order of 15 million acre-feet per year.

MacKenzie River: The average flow of the MacKenzie River at Fort Simpson is about 185 million acre-feet per year. The total storage capacity that can be created in the drainage basin (Great Slave Lake, Lake Athabasca, Headwater reservoirs) is in the order of 200 million acre-feet. The downstream riparian requirements in the future are difficult to foresee. There may be extensive oil drilling; there may be other mining developments in the valley; there is a possibility of limited agricultural development; there are some fishing interests in the delta regions. However, the total of all such requirements may not amount to more than 10 million acre-feet per year. Hence the flow available for diversion may be estimated in the order of 120 million acre-feet per year.

Yukon River: The average flow of the Yukon River at the Alaskan boundary is 55 million acre-feet per year. The storage capacity that would be created by a series of high dams to divert the river flow to the south is in the order of 500 million acre-feet. Assuming that Alaska could satisfy its downstream water requirements from local stream flows, it may be estimated that practically all of the 55 million acre-feet per year is available for diversion.

British Columbia Rivers: For the present discussion it will be assumed that the waters of the Columbia River, Fraser River, Skeena River, and Stickine River with a total average of 150 million acre-feet per year are needed to satisfy local requirements and are not available for diversion to other places in Canada or the United States.

Résumé: It appears from these rough figures that the major rivers of Northern Canada have available for diversion a total flow of about 230 million acre-feet per year.

## POTENTIAL IRRIGATION DEVELOPMENT IN WESTERN CANADA

The Canadian Prairie region represents one of the largest potential food production areas in North America. It is a semiarid area, which produces a large food surplus at the present time, under rather specialized dryland farming techniques. There are recognized possibilities of increased production in the area through improved farming methods including more intensive cropping, fertilization, and improved crop varieties. However in terms of maximizing food production, which would be required for any meaningful assault on world food shortages, large increases in water use for irrigation purposes must be considered. There are many factors which affect the rate of irrigation development in Western Canada and which will necessitate difficult decisions in both the United States and Canada. The following is an attempt to outline some of the decisions which will have to be made preliminary to planning for optimized use of the water supplies of this region.

The production of meat, vegetables, and fruits represents a large segment of the agricultural industry of North America. Such products are primarily for internal use and do not represent a suitable food for export as a solution to world food shortages. In fact, growing of these items represents a highly inefficient form of food production. The quantities of these foods which must be supplied to the North American market in the future should be assessed carefully and, if one can make such an assessment, then consideration of where such crops are to be grown becomes important in terms of water use. Meat and vegetables can be produced in Canada, near the source of water supplies, and one would expect that it would be economically desirable to grow the major portion of the North American supply in Canada rather than divert water to the southern United States for use on such production. Conversely, many types of fruit production are possible only in the southern United States and expansion of that industry may be desirable. Economic considerations in both countries should eventually cause the shifts in production suggested above, but in the meantime there may be a danger that planning of water distribution systems and diversion would proceed without anticipating the eventual locations of various types of production.

In terms of food for export, one must consider increasing the production of grains and high protein products such as alfalfa and oilseed meals, all of which can be produced efficiently in Canada and the northern United States in areas relatively close to water supplies. The fact that irrigation of such crops is developing very slowly in Canada is a direct result of the inability of the world's food-short areas to buy those products at prices which would make irrigation profitable. If the world price for high protein foods and grain should rise significantly, then one would anticipate a rapidly growing demand for irrigation in Canada and this could lead to development of very large acreages in areas which are now considered to be completely unsuitable for such development. For example, should sprinkler irrigation of grain become economically feasible in Canada, the major land deficiency (poor topography) would disappear and large-scale irrigation developments could occur throughout the Prairie regions in areas where no consideration has been given previously to such a possibility. Subsequent figures listing potentially irrigable areas in the Prairie regions are based upon considerations such as these and do not, of course, reflect present-day estimates of potentially irrigable lands on the Canadian Prairies.

There are strong arguments for using irrigation water intensively on the Canadian Prairies and diverting only the balance to the regions farther south. The obvious problems of cost of water diversion and selfish interests need no discussion. However in terms of water use efficiency it should be noted that consumptive use requirements for crop production in Canada are about 60 percent of that for southern United States regions for similar yields. If one considers the percentage of water which would be lost to seepage and evaporation in long diversion systems it will be obvious that water used near the source would provide at least twice as much food as would the same quantity of water when diverted to and used in distant areas to the south.

The preceding discussion is designed as an argument for extensive Canadian development of irrigation resources. Such development is not likely in the immediate future and can be expected only when economic conditions change in such a way as to make extensive irrigation development possible. With this prospect in mind, the following estimates of possible irrigation development for Canada are presented. Presumably it will indicate the magnitude of water use which may occur in future irrigation in the Canadian Prairies.

## PREDICTING IRRIGATION DEVELOPMENT

In order to make a prediction of the eventual demand for water for irrigation purposes on the prairie region of Western Canada, one would have to consider two major factors: the land area which may eventually come under irrigation and the duty of water required for irrigation of the selected lands. In trying to establish reasonable estimates of these two factors one must attempt to predict what the economic conditions will be at some future date for which the estimate is required. Because of the difficulty, if not impossibility, of making such predictions the reliability of estimates is likely to be inversely proportional to the time being considered. It is the intention here to try to define those factors and considerations which will affect the eventual level of water use for irrigation, without considering the time when such development might occur.

### DEFINITION OF IRRIGABLE AREAS

*Climatic Need.* The relationship between available precipitation and optimum consumptive use values is the obvious starting point in defining those areas which will benefit from the application of irrigation water. The work of Laycock delineating moisture deficits for the three Prairie provinces is well known in Canada (see Fig. 10.2). Laycock has suggested that a deficit of 8 inches in a growing season will almost certainly result in crop failure. A simple relationship of seasonal rainfall divided by seasonal optimum consumptive use (R/v) will give a very similar pattern to those of Laycock and a value of R/v of 0.50 coincides closely with the 8-inch deficit. It has been suggested by Foss, PFRA Engineer, Lethbridge, that an R/v value of 0.50 is a reasonable criterion to separate areas where dryland wheat farming will be successful from areas of limited success or failure.

In the past we have tended to assess irrigability in terms of the possibility of dry-farming failure and have thus excluded areas of higher precipitation and/or lower potential consumptive use. In the future this will not be a reasonable criterion and irrigation potential will be assessed in terms of the economic return on investment. It is interesting to note that some farms

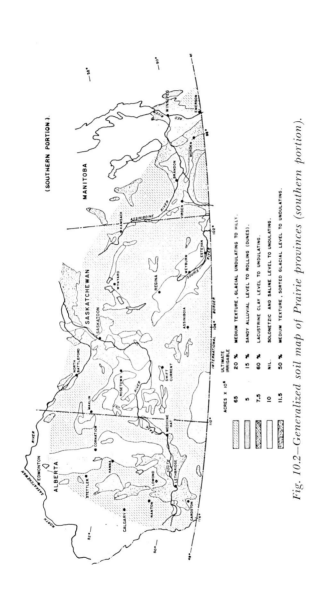

Fig. 10.2.—*Generalized soil map of Prairie provinces (southern portion).*

along the north Saskatchewan River near Prince Albert are now being irrigated by sprinkler systems. These farms are apparently showing extremely high returns on the investment involved, while sprinkler irrigation of similar crops in southern Alberta would not be considered as economically feasible. The reason is that in the Prince Albert area irrigation requirement is very low, so that the cost of applying water (labor and investment cost) on a per acre basis is about one-third of that for more arid regions. The application of water, however, results in increased yields approaching the increase for irrigation in the arid areas and, therefore, the economics of supplemental irrigation in more humid regions may be much better than the economics of full-scale irrigation in an extremely arid area. This suggests that one can ignore the level of moisture deficit insofar as irrigation in Western Canada is concerned and, therefore, all arable lands might sometime be considered as irrigable in terms of the economic value of water application.

*Irrigable Lands.* The generalized soil map of the Prairie provinces presents a very broad definition of soils in terms of their potential irrigability. Those areas shown as medium textured, sorted glacial soil are now considered to be the best irrigable soils available. Such factors as domestic and urban use, obviously unsuitable soils, and difficulty in distributing water reduce to a considerable extent the actual area of land which can be irrigated. On the basis of development in southern Alberta at this time, it would appear that a 50 percent use factor on this type of land would be a reasonable estimate. Those areas shown as solonetzic (approximately 10 million acres) may also be dealt with in rather simple terms because the soils are basically unsuitable for irrigation purposes. While one would be making a serious error to assume that all soils in this region are identical and unsuitable, it is quite obvious that the use factor would be so low as to discourage developments of the type which would require major water division and distribution systems. In other words any irrigation development would tend to be on a single farm basis, supplied with water from local sources and having no effect on the flows of the Prairie river systems.

The lacustrine clay soils (approximately 7.5 million acres) have many desirable attributes for irrigation purposes, including relatively good topography and high moisture-holding capacity. Natural drainability may be a limiting factor but experience in other heavy soil areas of Western Canada (Taber and Coaldale) has not been as bad as might be expected. The evidence to date indicates that heavy soils irrigated in Canada do not salinize as rapidly, if at all, as would similar soils in the United States where water requirements are higher. Thus it is possible that these soils could be irrigated successfully, particularly in the less arid regions. If these soils can be considered as irrigable they would probably be developed later than any of the other soils because the increase in production from irrigation would be the smallest. Because of the uniform nature of the lacustrine clay deposits, the use factor is likely to be highest of all soils considered and might reach 60 to 70 percent or something over 4 million acres.

The alluvial and aeolian sand soils (approximately 5 million acres) of the Prairies are now rated down because of topography and low soil moisture-holding capacities. Once economic conditions improve, sprinkler irrigation will become feasible and much of the topography problem will disappear. The fact that production increase from water application will be greatest on these soils is likely to lead to some early development. A land use factor for such soils is difficult to predict because there is so little experience in using them. One would expect the use factor to be relatively low because of water distribution problems on any sizable project development. As a guess one might consider an irrigation land use factor of 10 to 20 percent.

The bulk of the soils of the Prairie regions is formed on glacial till (approximately 65 million acres). The drainage problems associated with the till soils are very similar to those of the lacustrine clays but with considerably more variability. Topography problems similar to, but perhaps not as extreme as for the alluvial and aeolian sands, need also be considered. By careful selection of lands within this large area it is possible that some 10 to 20 percent might be considered as irrigable and be feasibly supplied with irrigation water. A land use factor for irrigation purposes of 20 percent would mean some 12 million acres of irrigation.

## WATER REQUIREMENTS

Water allocation to irrigated lands in Canada today is set at about 2 acre-feet per acre per year. In terms of water which eventually is used consumptively by the crops, this figure is obviously very wasteful. In fact, with present irrigation intensity, it is safe to assume that less than one-fourth of the water diverted actually goes for consumptive use or evapotranspiration. The remainder goes to canal seepage losses, evaporation in transit and storage, deep percolation, and return flow. The cost of distribution and storage works, coupled with the eventual value of water, will inevitably result in a reassessment of water requirements for irrigated land, based on minimum requirements for optimum production.

## CONSUMPTIVE USE

The obvious starting point for such an assessment is the climatic water deficit. The deficits indicated by Laycock are based on potential evapotranspiration for the full growing season. Actual crop consumptive use, even for optimum production, will be lower than this potential figure. The primary factor causing this reduction would be the length of growing season for the crops being grown. Thus it is obvious that grain will require much less water (18 inches total) than would forage (23 inches total). CDA research figures on consumptive use for optimum production are readily available. There is a further important consideration in the use of deficit figures such as those presented by Laycock. The upper quartile deficit indicates that in at least one year out of four certain deficits will occur (e.g., 8 inches in the Red River Valley). However, this high level of deficit is not likely to occur in the same year at Saskatoon and Calgary as it does at Winnipeg. Therefore there is a need to reduce the overall Prairie water requirement on the basis of expected coincidence of drought conditions.

## LEACHING REQUIREMENTS

References to leaching requirements to establish a salt balance on irrigated lands was made previously. The leaching requirement on the basis of present water quality is quite low, and in the order of about 10 percent. It is quite likely that large-scale development would lead to higher salt contents in the irrigation water and thus to an increased leaching requirement. One would, however, not expect it to go beyond 20 percent of the consumptive use requirement.

## CANAL SEEPAGE LOSSES

At the present time the losses of water in distribution systems average about 30 percent of the quantity diverted. The 1950 figures for the 17 western states of the United States confirm the magnitude of this loss. This would be a maximum figure to use in estimating future water diversions for irrigation and in fact a much lower figure is easily justified. The value of water in the future, as well as the value of land which might be damaged by canal seepage, will undoubtedly lead to a far greater use of canal lining than we have at present. Its possibilities can be seen on American irrigation projects which operate with limited water supplies, and canal losses of less than 20 percent could reasonably be expected for future developments.

To summarize the water requirements of future irrigation developments, the following estimate is presented. Of course, considerable work would have to be done to justify and/or modify the figures. Nevertheless they probably present a fairly accurate description of irrigation diversion requirements.

Assume that the water deficit, below optimum consumptive use of the crops to be grown, might average 6 inches. (It might be above 12 inches in areas of extreme drought and zero in other areas for any particular year.) Then adding a 20 percent leaching requirement and a 30 percent distribution loss would result in a net diversion requirement of about 9 inches. Since this figure represents about one-third of present diversion rates it is obvious that one should expect tremendous improvements in irrigation efficiencies of future developments.

The preceding discussion indicates the possibility of ultimately developing 20 to 25 million acres of irrigation in Western Canada. While this figure is based on a number of very hypothetical assumptions, it does represent a figure not likely to be exceeded in the foreseeable future. The actual water requirements for such an irrigation development could be estimated as high as 50 million acre-feet annually (based on present diversion rates) or as low as 25 million acre-feet (based on an assumption of high water application efficiencies).

## FUTURE WATER NEEDS IN WESTERN CANADA

When reviewing the water utilization in Western Canada from the broadest possible viewpoint, one could distinguish the following purposes of water use: (a) municipal and industrial water supply, (b) municipal and industrial waste disposal, (c) irrigation, (d) water power, (e) flood control, (f) navigation, and (g) recreation.

Regarding items d, e, f, and g, it must be noted that water

power, although an important economic aspect of water development in Western Canada, is not a consumer of water. What flows into the plant flows out of the plant. Moreover we can produce electrical energy also by steam plants or nuclear plants. Therefore water power is not going to impose any restrictions on long-term water development. Flood control does not consume water either. In fact, flood control measures, such as soil conservation, land management, and the construction of dugouts, ponds, and reservoirs, may have even a beneficial effect upon the water availability in the drainage basin. Navigation in Western Canada is of little significance but, if it should become significant, it would consume little or no water. Recreation may impose limitations on lake and reservoir fluctuations and on the permissible level of water pollution, but would not consume water.

Items a, b, and c represent the important water users. Municipal and industrial water supply is extremely important to a community, that is, the quality must be good and the quantity must be ample or economic development will be hindered. Important as this water use is, the total requirements are relatively small.

A more substantial quantity of water is needed for municipal and industrial waste disposal. Roughly speaking, the waste disposal requirements are ten times as large as the water supply requirements. Fortunately there is no consumptive use of water in carrying away the wastes of a city. Therefore if there is sufficient distance between cities, or if there is sufficient treatment of effluents, the waste disposal flow can be used over and over again.

The present water needs in Alberta, Saskatchewan, and Manitoba, with an arable area of about 100 million acres and a population of about 3 million, are roughly as follows: for industry a withdrawal of 300,000 acre-feet per year, and a return of 200,000 acre-feet; for thermal plants a withdrawal of 2 million acre-feet and a return of 1.9 million acre-feet; for municipal use a withdrawal of 300,000 acre-feet and a return of 200,000 acre-feet; for irrigation a withdrawal of 2 million acre-feet and a return of 800,000 acre-feet; for waste disposal purposes, a live stream flow of 1 million acre-feet. The sum total of the present consumptive use is in the order of 2.5 million acre-feet per year. Extrapolating present trends of population and industrial growth, it may be expected that around the turn of the century, the consumptive water demand in the Canadian Prairie region will be in the order of 5 million to 10 million acre-feet per year.

Although these quantities of water are not always available at the desired locations, they are at least available nearby. The average annual flow of the Saskatchewan River at The Pas is 15 million acre-feet; the Churchill River at Island Falls has 15 million acre-feet; the Winnipeg River and other eastern tributaries to Lake Winnipeg have 30 million acre-feet. Hence it will be relatively simple to look after the Prairie water needs for several decades to come. The trend in water development may be that first the three Prairie provinces may start using up the waters of the Saskatchewan River. After that, Alberta may use more and more water from the Saskatchewan River, the province of Saskatchewan may start diverting water from the Churchill River, and Manitoba may divert Winnipeg River water toward the southern part of its province.

This may be just the beginning of the development of the Prairie region. There are more than 300,000 square miles of rolling prairies, wooded hills, pine forests, and clear water lakes. There are abundant resources in and around the region. The climate is severe but healthful. There seems to be no reason why this region could not eventually be populated to the same density as is now being found in Western Europe or eastern North America. This would mean a total Canadian Prairie population of say 100 million.

What does such a prospect mean in terms of water requirements? A preliminary study indicated the following figures: for industry a withdrawal of 50 million acre-feet per year and a return of 45 million acre-feet; for thermal and nuclear plants a withdrawal of 125 million acre-feet and a return of 120 million acre-feet; for municipal use a withdrawal of 15 million acre-feet and a return of 10 million acre-feet; for irrigation a withdrawal of 50 million acre-feet, as was discussed in the previous section, and a return of perhaps 20 million acre-feet; for waste disposal purposes, a live stream of 35 million acre-feet. The total water requirements, after the above uses have been properly integrated, would amount to 80 million acre-feet per year.

## CANADIAN WATER EXPORT

It was estimated that the water availability in Western Canada, excluding British Columbia, exceeds 200 million acre-feet per year, while the future water demand in Western Canada will in all probability be less than 100 million acre-feet per year. Therefore for many years to come there will be a water surplus in the Canadian rivers of at least 100 million acre-feet per year.

Whether this surplus water can be used for irrigation in the U.S. prairie region depends on: (a) the engineering feasibility, (b) the economic feasibility, and (c) the political feasibility of moving large quantities of water from Northern Canada to the United States.

ENGINEERING FEASIBILITY

As far as the engineering feasibility is concerned, the University of Manitoba is undertaking a study of diversion possibilities from Northern rivers to the Canadian Prairie region and to a few selected points along the international boundary. For every diversion route, approximate cost estimates and capacity estimates are made and expressed in dollars per acre-foot of water diverted per year.

The required engineering construction needed to divert Northern Canadian rivers to selected areas in Canada and the United States would include dams, dikes, tunnels, pipelines, canals, pumping stations, and hydroelectric plants. None of these required projects would fall outside the realm of present civil engineering technology. To estimate the construction cost with any degree of precision, a mountain of work will have to be done. However, an impression of the magnitude of the cost can be gained by applying a few short-cut methods. For the purpose of cost estimating, a graph was developed, relating the cost of tunnels, pipelines, and canals to their discharge capacity. With the aid of this graph, plus unit cost figures of pumping stations and hydroelectric plants, plus topographic maps, the following possible diversion schemes have been worked out:

1. From Lake Winnipeg to the Canadian Prairies: This scheme would involve a system of reservoirs and pumping stations on the Saskatchewan River, as outlined earlier in this chapter. With the South Saskatchewan Reservoir as a distributing center, water would flow mainly by gravity over the entire Prairie regions. The cost of water at ditchside, before it enters a municipality or a farmer's field, is estimated at $10 per acre-foot.

2. From Lake Winnipeg to the U.S. boundary: This scheme would involve pumping water from Lake Winnipeg into Cedar Lake-Lake Winnipegosis-Lake Manitoba, up the Assiniboine River and Souris River. The cost of water at the boundary is estimated at $15 per acre-foot.

3. From Lake Winnipeg into the Great Lakes: This scheme would utilize first of all the waters of the Winnipeg River system

from their elevation of origin. Additional water could be pumped from Lake Winnipeg via the Winnipeg River and Rainy River to the height of land near Port Arthur, and then descend via a few hydroelectric stations into Lake Superior. This water could be used for stabilizing the levels of the Great Lakes or for diversion at Chicago into the Des Plaines River and thence into the Mississippi River. The cost of water discharged into Lake Superior is estimated at $5 per acre-foot.

4. From the Churchill River to Lake Winnipeg: After full allocation of the Nelson River flow available for diversion of 40 million acre-feet per year, another 15 million acre-feet could be obtained from the Churchill River. Most of this water could be diverted via the Sturgeon Weir River and Cedar Lake at a cost of less than $1 per acre-foot. The remainder could be diverted via the Burntwood River and pumped up via the Nelson River at a cost of $2 per acre-foot.

5. From Lake Athabasca to Lake Winnipeg: After full allocation of the Churchill River flows, the next step could be to pump water from Lake Athabasca (with an available flow of 60 million acre-feet per year), via Fond-du-Lac River and Wollaston Lake, into the headwaters of the Reindeer River and thence into Scheme 4. The estimated cost of diversion from Lake Athabasca to Lake Winnipeg comes to $5 per acre-foot.

### ECONOMIC FEASIBILITY

The above cost figures that were quoted cover only the annual charges on capital investment, plus operation and maintenance. To this Canada would have to add a certain "resource value" in order to make water export an attractive proposition. The magnitude of this resource value will depend on the economic value of the exported water in the United States and on the policy of the Canadian Government. For the sake of the present discussion let it be assumed that this resource value would be in the order of $5 to $10 per acre-foot. Thus the price of water for export at the international boundary could be anywhere from $10 to $25 per acre-foot, depending on the location, the time, and the quantity of delivery.

Of particular interest to the irrigators of the U.S. prairie region might be the possibility of importing some 50 million or 100 million acre-feet of water per year somewhere along the Alberta, Saskatchewan, or Manitoba boundary, at a price of say $25 per acre-foot. To this must be added, of course, the cost of conveying water from the boundary to its ultimate destination. This added cost could range anywhere from $10 to $50 per acre-foot, depending on the distance, elevation, and type of terrain that have to be overcome.

Now the question arises whether it would be economically justified to pay such prices for the large-scale transfer of water from Canada to the United States. At first glance it would seem that the estimated costs are out of line with prices ranging from $1 to $10 per acre-foot that are now being paid by municipalities and irrigation farmers. However it may very well be that the price structure of water will drastically change during the forthcoming decades. In order to appreciate this we must keep in mind that some 40 or 50 years from now the population in North America may be doubled, with a much higher living standard than we know now. This will require a vastly increased production of food and much greater requirements for living space, parks, lakes, air-conditioning, industrial waste dilution, and so on. In addition it may be expected that the underdeveloped and undernourished nations of the world will become more and more industrialized during the forthcoming century. Thus they will be able to pay for the vast quantities of food that are needed to feed their exploding populations. As a result it may be expected that world food prices will rise within 100 years to a level that is two to three times as high as it is now, not allowing for inflation.

It may be estimated that the average gross revenue today from irrigated cropland is in the order of $150 to $200 per acre, depending on location, type of crop, and the like. The average amount of irrigation water applied to cropland is about 5 feet, with a return flow to the river system of about 2 feet, resulting in a consumptive use of about 3 feet. Now, if the gross revenue of the land were to double, all other circumstances remaining the same, it would mean that the farmers could afford to spend an extra $50 to $70 per acre-foot of water consumed on their land.

It is very difficult to predict what the chances are that such a situation will develop. Perhaps these chances are very small. However, if it did occur, the required large-scale transfer of water from Canada to the United States would have such a tremendous influence upon the economies of both countries that it appears fully justified to explore this problem from all sides.

### POLITICAL FEASIBILITY

Apart from the engineering and economic feasibility of Canadian water export, there is the very real problem of its political feasibility. On the one hand, Canada would be concerned that perhaps after a few decades it turns out that all previous water requirement estimates are in error, and that Canada needs all its water for its own use, but that economic or political pressure from the United States would prevent Canada from closing the tap at the boundary. The United States, on the other hand, would be concerned that after having developed extensive irrigation districts on the basis of a certain water availability, the day may come that this water will stop flowing across the boundary, and that as a result the associated economy will collapse.

Whether these and other fears are realistic is relatively unimportant. What is important is that they do exist in the minds of many people and thus they form a serious obstacle to an integrated development of the water resources of North America. One way to help overcome these difficulties is through professional debate between the United States and Canada. It should be possible to find a solution to the mutual advantage of both countries, with a minimum risk and a great likelihood that it will enhance friendship and goodwill among the people of North America.

## REFERENCES

(1) Canada Department of Agriculture, *Handbook for the Classification of Irrigated Land in the Prairie Provinces,* 1964.

(2) Kuiper, E., "Canadian Water Export," *Eng. Jour.,* July 1966.

(3) ———, "Water Resources Development," Butterworths, London, 1965, 483 pp.

(4) Laycock, A. H., "Water Deficiency Patterns in the Prairie Provinces," Prairie Provinces Water Board report, Vol. 8, Regina, Saskatchewan, 1964.

# CHAPTER ELEVEN

# Alternative Uses of Water

W. J. CRADDOCK, K. W. CLARK, and R. A. GALLOP

"GLOBAL FRESH WATER needs will more than double by the year 2000 and govern man's ability to survive," stated President Johnson in his remarks to the Water For Peace Conference in May 1967. This statement and the conference to which it was addressed underscore the increased attention which is being given to water resources in recent years. While at one time water was placed in the category of free goods along with air and sunshine, this has long ceased to be the case in most parts of the world.

The industrial growth of North America over the past several decades has required large amounts of water. Concomitant with industrial expansion has come vastly improved levels of personal wealth in terms of money and leisure. The water needs of such a society are considerable, both for domestic and indirect uses such as recreation. At the same time the agricultural use of water in many parts of North America has increased at a steady rate.

These increased demands for water have created substantial pressures on the available supplies in many regions of the continent. In some areas of the United States it is now possible for one water-using activity to increase only if there is a correspond-

W. J. CRADDOCK, Department of Agricultural Economics, University of Manitoba; K. W. CLARK, Department of Plant Science, University of Manitoba; R. A. GALLOP, Department of Food Science, University of Manitoba.

ing decline in another. Discriminatory pricing of water in favor of agriculture has often resulted in a failure to reallocate water from agriculture to the growing urban sector and has led to wide discrepancies in marginal values in use. Wollman (15) has estimated that the marginal value of water in the Rio Grande Basin varies from $44 to $51 for irrigation, $212 to $307 for recreation, and $3,040 to $3,989 for industrial use.

The objective of this chapter is to assess the future use of water in food production in North America. Competing demands for water for domestic, industrial, and recreational purposes will be considered only insofar as they represent a limit to potential irrigation development. Some agronomic developments in the use of land and water which will have an impact on future irrigation expansion will be specified. The future water needs and contributions to food production of developments in the area of food technology will be briefly examined.

## ECONOMIC POTENTIAL OF IRRIGATION IN NORTH AMERICAN FOOD PRODUCTION

In the United States irrigated land on farms nearly doubled in the period 1929 to 1964, increasing from 19.6 to 36.8 million acres. It is estimated that between 5 and 8 percent of the growth in farm output between 1940 and 1960 was due to increased irrigated land (2, p. 21).

Regional changes in irrigation are even more striking. For example, in Texas irrigated acreage increased from .8 to 6.4 million acres during the period 1929–64. However, at the same time in other states, contraction in irrigation activities has taken place. Irrigated acreage in the state of Colorado declined from 3.4 to 2.7 million acres during this time.

Table 11.1 indicates the irrigated acreage for the nine western water resource regions and for a regrouping of the customary thirteen eastern water resource regions shown in Figure 11.1. The Northeast includes the New England, Chesapeake Bay, and Delaware and Hudson River regions. The Great Lakes is a combining of the Western and Eastern Great Lakes regions. The Upper Mississippi River, Lower Missouri River, and Ohio River form the Corn Belt region. The Cumberland and Tennessee River regions are included in the Southeast. This grouping of the east into six regions will in general be used throughout this chapter.

In all regions the number of irrigated acres increased be-

TABLE 11.1

IRRIGATED ACREAGE WESTERN AND EASTERN WATER RESOURCE REGIONS
SELECTED YEARS, 1939 TO 1964

| Region | 1939* | 1949* | 1954* | 1959† | 1954‡ |
|---|---|---|---|---|---|
| | *(thousand acres)* | | | | |
| Pacific Northwest | 3,305 | 3,837 | 4,353 | 4,807 | 5,348 |
| Central Pacific | 3,703 | 5,529 | 6,054 | 6,300 | |
| South Pacific | 479 | 721 | 789 | 737 | 7,210 |
| Colorado River | 2,773 | 3,485 | 2,813 | 3,025 | 3,109 |
| Great Basin | 1,168 | 1,431 | 1,935 | 1,830 | 2,120 |
| Upper Rio Grande & Pecos | 805 | 1,160 | 1,132 | 1,247 | 1,358 |
| Western Gulf | 1,078 | 3,037 | 4,432 | 4,785 | 5,430 |
| Upper Arkansas-White-Red | 591 | 1,048 | 1,409 | 2,388 | 2,656 |
| Upper Missouri | 3,690 | 4,501 | 4,622 | 6,029 | 6,309 |
| Total, western regions§ | 17,590 | 24,749 | 27,550 | 31,148 | 33,540 |
| Northeast | 19 | 84 | 189 | 193 | 272 |
| Great Lakes | 6 | 24 | 51 | 71 | 114 |
| Corn Belt | 12 | 25 | 78 | 94 | 179 |
| Southeast | 131 | 383 | 549 | 564 | 1,424 |
| Lower Mississippi | 106 | 225 | 537 | 446 | 623 |
| Lower Arkansas-White-Red | 117 | 296 | 597 | 506 | 682 |
| Total, eastern regions§ | 393 | 1,037 | 2,001 | 1,874 | 3,294 |
| Total, all regions§ | 17,983 | 25,787 | 29,552 | 33,022 | 36,834 |

* USDA (13), Table 11, p. 32.
† Ruttan (10), pp. 68, 69.
‡ Estimated by authors.
§ Totals were computed before rounding and hence may not equal the sum of the components reported here.

tween 1939 and 1954 with the exception of the Colorado River and the Upper Rio Grande and Pecos regions which showed a moderate decline between 1949 and 1954. A slight decline in irrigated acreage was experienced also between 1954 and 1959 in the Great Basin and South Pacific regions of the West, and the Lower Arkansas-White-Red and Lower Mississippi systems of the East. The estimated figures for 1964 indicate moderate increases in all of the western water resource regions and substantial increases for the eastern regions.

In Canada approximately 850,000 acres were under irrigation in 1960. This acreage has been predominantly concentrated in the four western provinces, particularly Alberta, although in recent years about 10 percent of the irrigated acreage has been located in Eastern Canada.

In 1959 approximately 7 percent of all cropland in the United States was irrigated. However the gross value of crops grown on this land was approximately 20 percent of all crop values. The significance of irrigation to the agricultural sectors

*Fig. 11.1—Water resource regions. (From the U.S. Department of Agriculture,* Land and Water Potentials and Future Requirements for Water, *p. 4.)*

in individual regions varies widely. For example, in 1954 the gross value of crop production from irrigated land, as a percentage of the value of total crop production, varied from 97.8 percent in the Colorado River region to less than 0.4 percent in the Corn Belt.[1]

In Canada irrigation is neither as important in the national agricultural picture nor in any province's agricultural industry. Less than 1 percent of the nation's improved land was irrigated in 1960. In Alberta where irrigation plays its most significant role, this figure was still only 2.7 percent. Unfortunately the corresponding contributions of irrigation to total crop values was unavailable for the Canadian data.

The historical development of irrigation in North America has been one of public and private involvement. In addition to other forms of public participation in irrigation, over 20 percent of the irrigated land in the United States in 1964 was either directly or indirectly associated with Federal Bureau of Reclamation activities. A significant proportion of this irrigated land is affiliated with large-scale multipurpose projects.

In the southern Alberta area of Canada, two-thirds of the

---

[1] Estimated from USDA (13), p. 33.

irrigation development was undertaken by the Canadian Pacific Railroad to colonize its semiarid land holdings. The development costs of the remaining one-third were backed by the Alberta government which eventually had to accept receivership of the system. The multipurpose South Saskatchewan River Dam project, which is expected eventually to support 200,000 acres of irrigation, was jointly financed by the Federal and Saskatchewan Provincial governments.

Public participation in irrigation development has been the result of economic, social, and political goals. Furthermore, because the benefits of such public expenditures have tended to accrue to a limited number of individuals there has been a major incentive for these people to try to influence favorable public decisions. The diffusion of costs, on the other hand, has obscured the consequences of a given decision by those who pay. Much irrigation development in the arid and semiarid West of the United States has also undoubtedly been facilitated by an underriding philosophy, on the part of some political leaders, that there must be some intrinsic good in making the desert bloom. This same attitude prevailed to a limited extent when the recently completed South Saskatchewan River Dam in Canada was in its formative stages.

In examining the future development of irrigation in North America one must distinguish between whether a normative or positive answer is sought. A normative assessment requires a very explicit enumeration of the goals and values of our society. What may be an optimal course of development with one set of ends in mind may not be desirable if another is more relevant. Past studies have tended to follow a positivistic approach in specifying the future of irrigation in meeting increased food needs in North America. Little attention has been given to the question of whether this is the most desirable means to increase output, taking into consideration the alternative uses of water or alternative means of expanding production.

Furthermore, there has been little distinction, either conceptually or empirically, between projections of land and water use and projections of land and water demand.[2] The terms "use," "consumption," "utilization," "requirements," "needs," and "ultimate use" are often used interchangeably and their identity with "demand" is usually clearly implied.

On the other hand the "supply" of land and water to a re-

---

[2] For a further elaboration of this point see Ciriacy-Wantrup (1).

gion is often considered to be fixed. While the physical stocks of these two resources represent obvious limitations to the future development of irrigation in North America, their potential availability is intimately dependent upon a number of economic and political considerations. Land, for example, may be fixed in physical supply, yet be transferred between alternative uses. Water, on the other hand, is highly mobile in a physical as well as economic sense.

Recognizing that past studies of land and water development have many shortcomings, we nevertheless felt it worthwhile to present the findings of two such studies for the United States to give a crude indication of the potential contribution of irrigation to future food requirements. The first study which follows the "requirements" method of projection will be compared to an analysis which was designed to put more economic content into irrigation projections. We will then outline some alternative developments which will have a bearing on future irrigation expansion as the pressures on available water supplies increase.

In 1959 the USDA (13) completed a comprehensive study of potential irrigation uses of water for the years 1980 and 2000 for the Select Committee on National Water Resources. Because of the time pressure involved in making these estimates, they did not encompass as refined an economic framework as either the USDA or many of its subsequent critics would have desired.

The analysis was done for each of three alternative levels of domestic population growth and corresponding levels of gross national product for the years 1980 and 2000.

The corresponding projections were:*

| | | 1980 | | | 2000 | | |
|---|---|---|---|---|---|---|---|
| | Unit | Low | Medium | High | Low | Medium | High |
| Population† | Mil. | 225 | 244 | 278 | 267 | 329 | 431 |
| Gross national product‡ | Bil. dol. | 960 | 1060 | 1260 | 1680 | 2220 | 3290 |

* USDA (13), Table 1, p. 22.
† Includes Armed Forces overseas.
‡ In estimated 1960 prices. For all goods this price level is 34 percent higher than the 1947–49 level. For farm goods the 1960 price is the same as in 1958, and 14 percent lower than the average level in 1947–49.

The procedure used was to first project the domestic requirements for individual farm commodities within the assumed economic framework. This was done by estimating the per capita future requirements for each major crop and livestock product and then multiplying these figures by the alternative population projections for each of the years 1980 and 2000. Estimated foreign commercial demand was added to the domestic requirements.

Three types of potential irrigation expansion were assumed. Potential I was based on a USDA appraisal of production needs and accomplishments which in part reflected the anticipated demand for the high value per acre crops typically grown on irrigated land. This acreage was then allocated to individual water resource regions in accordance with irrigation acreages in 1957.

Irrigation potential II for the eastern regions involved a straight-line projection of the 1939 to 1957 irrigation trends. For western regions, the 1980 potential was based on 1957 acreage plus U.S. Bureau of Reclamation proposed project acreages. The year 2000 estimate also included all foreseeable projects for which data were available, as listed in the 1958 report of the Commissioner of the Bureau of Reclamation.

The third irrigation potential was developed on the basis of soil suitability and a crude check of water availability. Irrigation potential III thus represented the difference between maximum physical development and the sum of potentials I and II.

Aggregate yield trends, including the influence of the irrigated acreage assumed for irrigation potential I, were established for the principal crops. These estimated yield trends were used to determine future crop production without any further land or water development. The difference between these estimates and the "required" crop production left a deficit which could be met by a combination of land use shifts, including further expansion in irrigation development. For example, for the medium domestic growth assumption in 1980, a $6.4 billion deficit in crop production and a $0.6 billion deficit in pasture production were predicted. It was estimated that the cropland imbalance could best be alleviated by shifting 25.3 million acres of grassland to cropland, increasing irrigation by 2.5 million acres (from potential II), plus several other adjustments. Land use patterns and, of particular relevance to this chapter, irrigation development, were specified for the low, medium, and high assumptions of 1980 and 2000.

As outlined above, the USDA estimates have been subjected to a considerable amount of criticism in that they do not give adequate recognition to the many dynamic interdependencies in the economy. Ruttan (10) recently completed a comprehensive analysis of the demand for irrigation with a view to incorporating a more rigorous economic framework into such projections. Several of the assumptions underlying his analysis differ from those of the USDA. His national output projection for 1980 assumes a population of 260 million, a 40 percent rise in per capita income between 1954 and 1980, and an income elasticity of demand of 0.15. While his work is a major methodological contribution to this phase of water resource economics, his empirical analysis is sufficiently detailed to merit serious consideration.

The technique used was to develop regional Cobb-Douglas production functions from county census data. Three models were developed: the "productivity," "demand," and "equilibrium" models. In the demand model, the marginal value product of irrigated land was derived from the regional production function and was equated to the cost of bringing an acre of land into production. (Two types of cost estimates were used in this study. The "full cost" assumption is the estimated cost of irrigation, assuming mid-1950 prices and no subsidies for irrigation water purchased from the public sector. The "current practice cost" reflects the actual historical prices and costs incurred by farmers for capital and operating expense inputs.) On the basis of this identity and an exogenously determined national output of farm products, regional irrigated acreages were estimated. In the equilibrium model regional input and output levels were determined simultaneously. This solution indicated the irrigated acreage which would be consistent with constant input and product prices and no change in irrigation technology.

The USDA projections made for the Select Committee on National Water Resources together with Ruttan's demand and equilibrium model solutions are given by water resource region in Table 11.2. The 1980 equilibrium model solutions given in this table were derived by constraining the estimates when either of two conditions held. First, these estimates were adjusted to reflect the future competition for water for other uses when it was in limited supply in the region. Second, if when the full cost assumption was used significant regional declines from the 1959 levels were estimated, the projected reduction in regional irrigated acreage was also constrained. This latter adjustment was intended to reflect in part the downward evaluation of land rather than its withdrawal from irrigation when its return does not equal its cost. These figures in Table 11.2 indicate the vul-

TABLE 11.2

Irrigated Acreage by Water Resource Regions for 1959 and 1964, and Projected Irrigated Acreages for 1980 and 2000 Under Alternative Assumptions

| Region | 1959* | 1964† | 1980 USDA‡ Low | 1980 USDA‡ Medium | 1980 USDA‡ High | 1980 Ruttan* Demand model (full cost) | 1980 Ruttan* Equilibrium model (restricted) | 2000 USDA‡ Low | 2000 USDA‡ Medium | 2000 USDA‡ High |
|---|---|---|---|---|---|---|---|---|---|---|
| | | | | | | *(thousand acres)* | | | | |
| Pacific Northwest | 4,807 | 5,348 | 5,022 | 5,261 | 6,342 | 5,844 | 4,326 | 5,057 | 6,579 | 7,722 |
| Central Pacific | 6,300 | 7,210 | 6,875 | 6,869 | 7,266 | 10,928 | 14,581 | 6,492 | 6,985 | 7,510 |
| South Pacific | 737 | | 827 | 816 | 921 | 2,257 | 1,311 | 707 | 843 | 1,000 |
| Colorado River | 3,025 | 3,109 | 3,283 | 3,280 | 3,327 | 1,674 | 2,723 | 3,268 | 3,340 | 3,433 |
| Great Basin | 1,830 | 2,120 | 2,242 | 2,257 | 2,315 | 1,229 | 1,647 | 2,241 | 2,320 | 2,371 |
| Upper Rio Grande & Pecos | 1,247 | 1,358 | 1,400 | 1,416 | 1,559 | 1,955 | 1,559 | 1,398 | 1,611 | 1,846 |
| Western Gulf | 4,785 | 5,430 | 5,022 | 5,126 | 6,350 | 7,137 | 4,306 | 4,981 | 6,821 | 9,012 |
| Upper Arkansas-White-Red | 2,388 | 2,656 | 1,626 | 1,681 | 2,081 | 1,698 | 2,149 | 1,642 | 2,237 | 2,871 |
| Upper Missouri | 6,029 | 6,309 | 5,500 | 6,287 | 9,118 | 4,668 | 5,426 | 5,757 | 9,709 | 12,065 |
| Total, western regions | 31,148 | 33,540 | 31,797 | 32,993 | 39,279 | 37,390 | 38,028 | 31,543 | 40,445 | 47,830 |
| Northeast | 193 | 272 | 277 | 353 | 1,155 | 3,390 | 3,482 | 235 | 1,449 | 2,997 |
| Great Lakes | 71 | 114 | 79 | 112 | 778 | 866 | 557 | 78 | 1,110 | 2,494 |
| Corn Belt | 94 | 179 | 126 | 215 | 2,897 | 215 | 215 | 150 | 4,373 | 10,301 |
| Southeast | 564 | 1,424 | 890 | 1,119 | 3,540 | 4,299 | 4,226 | 936 | 4,624 | 9,092 |
| Lower Mississippi | 446 | 623 | 883 | 918 | 1,488 | 901 | 901 | 892 | 1,763 | 2,890 |
| Lower Arkansas-White-Red | 506 | 682 | 990 | 990 | 1,464 | 2,672 | 4,050 | 990 | 1,749 | 2,887 |
| Total, eastern regions | 1,874 | 3,294 | 3,245 | 3,707 | 11,322 | 12,343 | 13,430 | 3,281 | 15,058 | 30,661 |
| Total, all regions | 33,022 | 36,834 | 35,042 | 36,700 | 50,601 | 49,733 | 51,458 | 34,824 | 55,513 | 78,491 |

* Ruttan (10), pp. 68, 69.
† Estimated by authors.
‡ USDA (13), Tables 44–46, pp. 71–73.

nerability of projections to their underlying assumptions. For example, the USDA projections, which have been derived by the same general procedure for each population level, indicate that current irrigated acreage is adequate to meet 1980 requirements if the low growth assumption holds. However, if a high rate of population increase is more realistic, then the USDA estimates that total irrigated acreage in the United States should be some 37 percent greater than the 1964 level.

The domestic growth assumptions underlying Ruttan's analysis are about an average of those used for the "medium" and "high" USDA projections. The growth of the U.S. economy during the eight years since the USDA study was undertaken would indicate that a 1980 population slightly above that incorporated in the medium projections will be realized.

The restricted equilibrium solutions correspond quite closely to the high USDA projections in terms of the totals for the eastern and western water resource regions. Within each of these two broad groupings of regions some major differences exist. Ruttan estimates that irrigated acreage in the three Pacific regions will be some 40 to 50 percent greater than the high USDA projections for 1980. On the other hand, this model projects a decline of 20 percent in irrigated acreage in the Upper Missouri by 1980. This is at odds with the USDA projection under comparison which estimates a 50 percent increase.

In view of the differences in methods used to project the regional figures such discrepancies are not unexpected. As outlined above, the USDA's estimated changes in irrigated acreage were derived from one or more of three irrigation potentials. The regional allocations of potentials I and II were based in large part on the historical configuration of irrigation development. Since the increased irrigated land in the low and medium projections consisted entirely of irrigation potentials I and II, there was a considerable effect of merely extending the past regional distribution of irrigated acreage to the years 1980 and 2000.

Both sets of projections indicate a considerable need for increased irrigation in the eastern regions. The USDA high population growth projection and the restricted equilibrium solution indicate a fourfold increase is required between 1964 and 1980 in the East. The substantial changes which have taken place in this area between 1959 and 1964 suggest that these projected acreages could be realized by the years 1980 and 2000.

Comparisons with the estimated 1964 irrigated acreages indicate that all western water resource regions are at or beyond the USDA's projected medium 1980 requirements. The Upper Arkansas-White-Red region, which surpassed both the USDA high projection and the restricted equilibrium solution in 1959, showed a further increase in irrigated acreage in 1964.

The gross value of production from the irrigated land associated with the 1980 medium projection was estimated to be 6.8 billion in terms of 1947–49 dollars. This compares to an estimated $30 billion of total crop requirements in 1980 or $5.1 billion of irrigated output in 1954. The contribution of irrigation was estimated to be $11.1 billion out of a total of $39.7 billion of crop production required for the medium 2000 projection.

No systematic projections have been made of future irrigation developments in Canada. As outlined by Kuiper and Murray in Chapter 10, the physical potential in Western Canada could be close to 25 million acres. However, in 1960 only 593,000 acres were irrigated in this region. Under existing price and cost relationships irrigated cereal and forage crops are only marginally profitable. This in part explains why an estimated 90 percent of currently irrigated land in Canada receives one application of water or less per year (8, p. 6).

The limited demand for sugar beets and specialty crops will curtail any significant expansion in irrigation for these purposes. In 1960 only 17 percent (145,070 acres) of Canada's irrigated acreage was in specialty crops. Future needs could be met by a reallocation of the acreage currently devoted to cereal and forage crops within existing irrigation projects.

The Prairie Farm Rehabilitation Administration in 1962 estimated that 2.179 million acres were irrigable in Alberta and Saskatchewan under cost and price relationships likely to prevail in the foreseeable future (7, p. 6). This figure included 470,000 acres within the South Saskatchewan River project. More recent estimates place the maximum irrigable acreage within this project at 200,000 acres (11).

Existing irrigation projects in Alberta and Saskatchewan are collecting only enough revenue to pay operating costs and minor maintenance. Given this situation it is unlikely that any major irrigation developments will be initiated in the next few years, beyond those already committed. A ten-year gestation period for large-scale projects is not unusual. On the basis of these and other considerations we would estimate that irrigated acreage in Canada will not exceed 2.0 to 2.5 million acres by the year 2000.

TABLE 11.3
PHYSICAL IRRIGATION POTENTIALS

| | Potential Irrigated Area | |
|---|---|---|
| Region | Soil suitable for irrigation* | Soil suitable for irrigation and water available† |
| | (million acres) | |
| Pacific Northwest | 7.9 | 7.9 |
| Central Pacific | 8.9 | 8.9 |
| South Pacific | 1.6 | 1.4 |
| Colorado River | 3.5 | 3.5 |
| Great Basin | 2.4 | 2.4 |
| Upper Rio Grande & Pecos | 2.4 | 1.9 |
| Western Gulf | 9.4 | 9.4 |
| Upper Arkansas-White-Red | 6.3 | 2.9 |
| Upper Missouri | 19.6 | 12.1 |
| Total, western regions | 62.0 | 50.4 |
| Northeast | 3.2 | 3.2 |
| Great Lakes | 2.6 | 2.6 |
| Corn Belt | 10.3 | 10.3 |
| Southeast | 9.2 | 9.2 |
| Lower Mississippi | 3.0 | 3.0 |
| Lower Arkansas-White-Red | 2.9 | 2.9 |
| Total, eastern regions | 31.2 | 31.2 |
| Total, all regions | 93.2 | 81.6 |

Source: USDA (13), Table 20, p. 45.
* Estimated by Agricultural Research and Soil Conservation Service. The estimates were based on the suitability of soils for irrigation with no account being given to the availability of water.
† Based on a rough preliminary check of water supply.

The USDA estimates gave explicit recognition to the maximum physical supply of irrigation in terms of land supply by not allowing regional projections to exceed the available irrigable acreage. In several regions a rough check on water supply further restricted this physical maximum. These physical restraints on further irrigation are given in Table 11.3.

While recognition was given to available water supplies little account was taken of potential increases in demand for this water by other uses or as a means to increase these regional supplies. In July 1960, Wollman (14) under the auspices of Resources for the Future completed a study for the Select Committee on National Water Resources designed to integrate a number of the studies on specific uses and supplies of water into a comprehensive coordinated analysis of future water resource development.

The results of this study indicated that five of the western water resource regions would be deficient in total water require-

TABLE 11.4

PROJECTED STREAM FLOWS AND WATER DEFICITS FOR FIVE WESTERN WATER
RESOURCE REGIONS, 1980

| | | Water Deficit | |
| Region | Maximum Flow That Can Be Maintained* | USDA (medium growth assumption)* | Ruttan-restricted equilibrium model † |
|---|---|---|---|
| | | *(million gallons per day)* | |
| South Pacific | 320 | 10,280 | 12,290 |
| Colorado River | 10,400 | 6,900 | 4,453 |
| Great Basin | 9,300 | 2,800 | 992 |
| Upper Rio Grande & Pecos | 950 | 6,350 | 6,851 |
| Upper Missouri | 26,900 | 6,700 | 4,643 |

* Wollman (14), Table 30, p. 49.
† Ruttan (10), p. 61.

ments in 1980 under the level of irrigation development projected by the USDA for the medium rate of domestic growth. Even though the irrigated acreage is projected to increase substantially in these regions between 1954 and 1980, the agricultural water losses in four of the regions are estimated to be lower in 1980 than in 1954. This reflects the importance of the projected improvements in efficiency of water use. In the Upper Missouri region it is estimated that agriculture in 1980 will require 1.2 billion gallons per day more than in 1954. These same regions are also deficient by Ruttan's restricted equilibrium model solutions. The deficits range from 10 to 12 billion gallons per day for the South Pacific region to 1 to 2 billion gallons per day in the Great Basin. These deficits together with the maximum maintainable flows for the five regions in question are given in Table 11.4.

In the year 2000 three further regions will be deficient in water under the medium USDA irrigation projections. These are the Western Great Lakes, Upper Arkansas-White-Red and Western Gulf. If one examines the quantity of water required if all physically irrigable land is used regardless of water availability, no further regions are deficient in water.[3] The deficits corresponding to this situation and for the USDA medium projections for 2000 are given in Table 11.5.

These results clearly indicate a potential future conflict between projected water uses and available water supplies in some regions of the United States. However, as the pressure on availa-

[3]This level of irrigation would be some 11.6 million acres more than the USDA high projection for the year 2000.

TABLE 11.5

PROJECTED STREAM FLOWS AND WATER DEFICITS IN WATER RESOURCE REGIONS,
MEDIUM GROWTH ASSUMPTION AND MAXIMUM FEASIBLE IRRIGABLE
ACREAGE, 2000

| | | Water Deficit | |
| Region | Maximum Flow That Can Be Maintained * | USDA medium 2000 † | Maximum irrigable acreage 2000 ‡ |
| --- | --- | --- | --- |
| | | (million gallons per day) | |
| South Pacific | 320 | 15,380 | 16,657 |
| Colorado River | 10,400 | 11,300 | 11,666 |
| Great Basin | 9,300 | 4,200 | 4,332 |
| Upper Rio Grande & Pecos | 950 | 9,350 | 11,518 |
| Western Gulf | 40,400 | 3,100 | 6,233 |
| Upper Arkansas-White-Red | 10,500 | 1,200 | 9,133 |
| Upper Missouri | 26,900 | 24,200 | 44,463 |
| Western Great Lakes | 40,000 | 19,100 | 20,168 |

* Wollman (14), Table 30, p. 49.
† Calculated from Wollman (14), Table 30, p. 49.
‡ Calculated from USDA (13), and Wollman (14).

ble supplies increases, several adjustments could take place. Large interregional water transfers from water surplus regions such as the Pacific Northwest is one possibility. Also, other alternatives are feasible which could either directly or indirectly reduce the projected regional water requirements.

The projected uses of water in 1980 for the five water-deficit regions are shown in Table 11.6. Agriculture is the largest single user of water in four of these regions. Hence any improvements in the agricultural efficiency of water use or other technological developments in either dryland or irrigation farming could considerably relieve the projected pressures on regional water supplies. Viewing the next several decades from the vantage point of the late 1960's, the contribution of agronomic developments to future crop production appears to be greater than a decade earlier when the projected irrigation requirements of the USDA were made. The introduction of new grains such as Triticale is one example. These agronomic aspects will be examined in greater detail in the second section of this chapter.

The USDA irrigation projections for 1980 were based on a 10 percent increase in efficiency of water application and a 5 percent improvement in storage and delivery efficiency over 1954.[4] This resulted in estimated application efficiencies of from 50 to 60 percent, and delivery and storage efficiencies of from 45

---

[4] A further 5 percent improvement in each of these uses was predicted for the year 2000.

## TABLE 11.6
### Projected Water Requirements in Water-Deficit Regions, 1980

| Region | Agriculture* | Mining* | Manufacturing* | Power* | Municipal | Land Treatment & Structure† | Fish and Wildlife† | Waste Dilution | Total‡ |
|---|---|---|---|---|---|---|---|---|---|
| | | | | *(million gallons per day)* | | | | | |
| South Pacific | 3,312 | 7.9 | 175 | 46.0 | 435.0 | 3 | 18 | 6,603 | 10,600 |
| Colorado River | 14,396 | 242.1 | 49 | 285.7 | 79.4 | 53 | 1,951 | 244 | 17,300 |
| Great Basin | 6,698 | 2.2 | 90 | 66.1 | 69.0 | 5 | 3,945 | 1,227 | 12,100 |
| Upper Rio Grande & Pecos | 4,964 | 27.5 | 5 | 100.0 | 31.8 | 100 | 1,101 | 970 | 7,300 |
| Upper Missouri | 15,011 | 15.9 | 58 | 107.1 | 123.6 | 658 | 13,149 | 4,477 | 33,600 |

* Wollman (14), Table 16, p. 43.
† Wollman (14), Table 21, p. 45.
‡ Wollman (14), Table 30, p. 49.

to 65 percent in the western water resource regions. These levels of efficiency are such that if the competition for water becomes acute, there is still room for considerable improvement. Research has shown that application efficiencies of up to 80 or 90 percent are possible with the proper combination of border width, stream size, and duration of irrigation (5, p. 96). A further 10 percent improvement in the efficiency of application over that predicted for 1980 would, for example, reduce the projected demand for water in the Upper Missouri region by 1.9 billion gallons per day.

As the pressures on available regional water supplies increase, nonagricultural uses of water could be sacrificed. For example, in the Upper Missouri region fish and wildlife activities are projected to require almost as much water as agriculture in 1980. In other regions a dissolved oxygen content lower than 4 milligrams per liter in the stream, or a higher level of effluent treatment, would result in lower waste dilution requirements. It is more likely, however, that as succeeding generations of the population become further removed from an agricultural origin, greater pressures of adjustment in water use will be exerted on the agricultural rather than the nonagricultural uses.

This section of the chapter has dealt with the potential of irrigation in meeting the demand for increased food output. It must be remembered that USDA projections on which parts of this section have been based follow in general what could be termed the "requirements" method of projecting. Levels of irrigation have been estimated which would support certain projected levels of output. Such methods do not encompass the tremendous capacity of the economy to adjust to changes in product prices and in the availability and cost of resources. That is, if the pressures on available water supply increase, other output increasing activities not related to irrigation might be more profitably intensified to take its place.

One method for projecting the future demand for irrigation which has not been adequately used is interregional linear programming. Such a technique would give greater recognition to the many interrelated forces which will determine the future development of irrigation. More explicit account could be given to the available supplies of restricting resources. For example, if water were the limiting resource in a particular region, the solution would indicate its marginal value in its alternative uses as well as the quantity of water associated with the marginal value.

A number of significant problems are associated with the

use of this technique to solve a problem of this magnitude, however. First, a very explicit statement of the criterion or choice indicator which is to be optimized would be required. Irrigation is often expected to fulfill a wide range of ends. It is difficult to incorporate objectives other than economic efficiency into large-scale interregional programming models.

Empirical problems would also hinder the development of such a model. A rather exhaustive set of processes would have to be incorporated. This would necessarily include both irrigation and nonirrigation activities, but perhaps also make allowance for a large number of nonagricultural uses of water. There is some question whether sufficient alternatives could be included to give the model interpretive meaning and still remain within the restrictions of computer and human data assembly capacities.

A significant research effort in this direction would be worthwhile, given the prospective water shortages of the future and extremely large investments to overcome them through interregional water transfers. It would be advisable that an analysis of this nature begin on a very aggregative basis. As the conceptual and empirical problems were overcome, the analysis could be extended by stages to encompass greater detail and to provide correspondingly more useful conclusions.

## ANTICIPATED CHANGES IN WATER USE IN FOOD PRODUCTION

### AGRONOMIC ASPECTS

The land resources in the Saskatchewan-Nelson River Basin area and the surrounding area of the Upper Missouri and Corn Belt regions have been developed to a highly productive state through dryland farming techniques, probably as efficient as any other such area in the world. Improvements in crop yields through greater use of fertilizers, herbicides, and pesticides are foreseeable, however. Significant changes in production are possible through the adoption of hybrid wheat and grains such as Triticale. Estimates of 20 bushels per acre above dryland production for irrigated wheat on the Great Plains area (6) could become the third major factor in raising aggregate yields to an average of 35 bushels of wheat per acre and 80 bushels of barley by the year 2000.

Specialty crop production will continue to command an increasing amount of irrigated acreage. Sustained yields of 15 to 30 tons of sugar beets per acre in Alberta and Manitoba may still, however, require a tariff on imported sugarcane to be profitable. In Canada beet sugar production represents only a shrinking 15 percent of total sugar usage (3). Potatoes and vegetable crops are the most profitable irrigated crops in Canada but are limited in production per acre because of a short growing season and the resulting one crop per year.

Other crops such as alfalfa which respond well to water may become dominant in the more northerly areas. Here management practices to ensure winter hardiness may permit production levels of 5 tons of hay per acre. The demand for water by such crops in the Manitoba-North Dakota area approximates 500 pounds of water to produce 1 pound of dry matter whereas in southerly areas such as Texas this value is doubled. However, up to 10 cuts of alfalfa may be harvested in the latter area compared to 3 or 4 in the more northerly climates.

To attain optimal allocation of land and water resources and maximize profit, many agronomic areas will require intensified efforts on the part of the research scientist. Weed control is most imperative. Further herbicide research is required to combat both water weeds and those species which invade perennial crops under irrigation. Insect and plant disease control on a regional basis must be further emphasized, particularly with use and reuse of water. In terms of pollution control, knowledge must be increased of the movements of insecticides, herbicides, and fertilizers to our streams.

With the advent of higher inputs of fertilizer and water for crop production, the decision making with respect to what to grow, and when and how, must become integrated with the food processor, so as to keep waste losses at a minimum that will allow efficient operation in the field and in the plant. Farm credit must facilitate purchase of irrigation equipment. Both short-term and intermediate-term capital must be more readily available from banking institutions as the production costs for seed, fertilizer, and water are in general 3 to 10 times above that required for dryland farming operations.

Groundwater supplies in the United States and Canada are inadequately inventoried. Little is known of their quality or sustainability when used in irrigation. Also, further knowledge is required on the efficiency of production of irrigated crops, particularly dwarf wheats, hybrid wheats, and new crops. The assistance of the agrometeorologist is required in estimating supplemental irrigation water requirements from climatological data and soil texture. The production function of the various crops in the Canadian Prairies and the Great Plains region with respect to the level of water use is not adequately known. It is likely that recent technological developments in methods of irrigation water application have substantially increased the efficiency of water utilization.

More agronomic studies are required to determine varieties of crops which will establish at lower soil temperatures. This is particularly true in the case of corn, one of our most efficient, yet highest, users of water. Supplemental irrigation in the eastern part of the Canadian Prairies and the subhumid areas of the Great Plains may result in a value for water in irrigation use significantly greater than that cited by Wollman (15). Research which will provide this information is necessary.

Given adequate water supplies at reasonable cost to the farmer, changes in farm production levels similar to those now experienced in the Columbia Basin irrigation project in Washington might be feasible in much of the Upper Missouri region. Here alfalfa hay is being pelleted and profitably exported to Japan. Potatoes, sugar beets, beans, wheat, peppermint, and ensiled forage crops supplying beef feedlots have jumped average gross returns to $186 per acre in an area which produced only 25 bushels of wheat every two years prior to the irrigation development. Yields per acre in this area are averaging: alfalfa hay 5.3 tons, late potatoes 404 hundredweight, sugar beets 24.7 hundredweight, wheat 90 bushels, corn 104 bushels, and onions 410 pounds.

The intensive use of alfalfa production in feeding beef cattle may delay the need to use more plant proteins or feed livestock any petroprotein synthetics until well past the turn of the century. If irrigation together with potential yield gains from the use of fertilizer, hybrid crops, and better management result in the equivalent of 100 bushels of wheat per acre, there will be little urgency to change to alternative crops grown specifically for their carbohydrate, oil, or protein contents. Research should be conducted, however, on an increasing scale on the efficient use of water in agriculture and on the fabrication of synthetic foods for emergency feeding of our increasing world population.

We have no water-pricing policy in Canada, and similarly it is often priced in a minimal manner in the United States. If the industrial and recreational values of water are substantially greater than for agriculture, the potential agricultural user would be at a distinct disadvantage in obtaining any allocation of water under a competitive market situation. Such potential competitive pressure emphasizes the need in agriculture to increase research and extension efforts in efficient use of this most valuable resource, protecting its supply and using it carefully, while striving to maintain its quality through pollution control and efficient land use management.

## FOOD TECHNOLOGY

The food industry begins and ends with water problems. The usage rates of water for the cooling, cleaning, and processing of food vary from a few hundred gallons per ton of product to several thousand gallons per ton. Wastage of water in the food industry is very considerable, and it would not be difficult to reduce the amount used per ton by about one-half. In some industries one-fifth or less of the water currently used per ton would suffice, under proper control. This wastage factor must be taken into account when estimating the potential needs of the food industry of the future.

Additional research is needed in the areas of (a) conservation of water during processing, (b) the modification of processing techniques so as to use less water and to create less wastes, and (c) to suspend less wastes in water. Methods for the partial or full reclamation of water used in food processing need to be greatly improved. Insofar as they are improved, large savings in water usage per ton will become possible.

The economic consequences are tremendous for proper conservation of the resources of the food industry, particularly its soil and its water, and of reducing the costs of creating huge volumes of troublesome wastes which have to be dealt with. The best way to control a waste problem is to not create it in the first place. The dominant effort in the food industry should be directed toward this objective rather than toward trying to deal with the types and volumes of wastes which are produced in current practice. New processes which use little or no water, and which therefore disperse little or no wastes in such water, need to be investigated and developed to an engineered stage.

The Department of Food Science at the University of Manitoba is actively involved in research in these areas in conjunction with its teaching programs and it is hoped that the proper combination of food science and technology, coupled with water and waste technology, will produce a type of graduate who will be invaluable to the future food industry. Too few research groups in the world are doing anything about these problems.

They desperately need much greater support so that we may develop a more complete understanding of what we are doing in food processing and in the control of water and waste problems. Insofar as we do this the larger processing plants, and the new plants which will undoubtedly be built by force of demand in the future, will be more soundly designed and operated with a view to the minimization of these problems. It is very likely that the pressure arising from water supply problems and problems of disposal of waste waters will lead to a complete overhaul of many food processing operations.

Those agricultural industries which can be almost completely mechanized will grow to become mass suppliers of raw materials for a food industry which to a much greater degree than at present will fractionate, purify, fabricate, and blend such raw materials as proteins, fats, carbohydrates, vitamins, spices, flavors, colors, and so on, into many thousands of items which will be tailor-made to suit the specifications of a particular submarket. The gourmet foods of today will gradually become routinely accepted. For overseas use in famine prevention and control, and in general improvement in worldwide human feeding, rations will have to be prepared which are highly nutritious, concentrated, stable, and attractive to the myriad tastes of the billions of people who will be crying out for them.

The meat analogs currently available in the United States may come to be widely used in the developed countries in replacement of meats as major sources of proteins. Other products based on protein-rich flours, requiring less sophisticated technology, could be formulated for use in overseas countries. World transport conditions will force the concentration of foodstuffs to a high degree before bulk shipment. Industrial synthesis of food constituents by chemical or microbiological methods will also be expected to expand to supply considerable quantities of very valuable minor constituents of foods, such as vitamins and some amino acids.

The foregoing gives some idea of the interrelationships between water, food processing operations, and the potential expansion of the food processing industry to the degree that world conditions and resources may demand. Critical problems impede the rapid implementation of increased food production in North America. Nor can we forget the competition which expansion of other industries will offer to water resources which are in many regions already scarce.

# REFERENCES

(1)  Ciriacy-Wantrup, S. V., "Conceptual Problems in Projecting the Demand for Land and Water," *Modern Land Policy*, Papers of the Land Economics Institute, 1958, Urbana: Univ. of Illinois Press, 1960.

(2)  Durost, D. D., and G. T. Barton, *Changing Sources of Farm Output*, USDA, Production Research Report 36, Washington, D.C., Feb. 1960.

(3)  Eaton, E. S., "Sugar and Sugar Beet Production in Canada," *Can. Farm Econ.* 2:31–36, 1967.

(4)  Fox, Irving K., "Policy Problems in the Field of Water Resources," *Water Research*, Western Resources Conference Papers, 1965, Baltimore: The Johns Hopkins Press, 1966.

(5)  Haise, Howard R., "Advances in Water Management: Key to Survival?" *Water: Development, Utilization, Conservation*, Western Resources Conference Papers, 1963, Boulder: Univ. of Colorado Press, 1964.

(6)  Hughes, William F., and A. C. Magee, *Production Practices and Specified Costs of Producing Wheat and Grain Sorghum on Irrigated Farms, Upper Texas Panhandle, 1960–61*, Tex. Agr. Exp. Sta. Bull. MP-656, 1963.

(7)  Munro, G. N., "Water Resources and Irrigation Potential in the Prairie Provinces," Paper presented to Irrigation Roundup, Lethbridge Res. Sta., Alberta, 1962.

(8)  Murray, J., *Potential Irrigation Development—Western Canadian Prairies*, Mimeo., Dept. of Agr. Eng., Univ. of Saskatchewan, Saskatoon, 1967.

(9)  Renne, R. R., "A Proper Perspective of Water in Agriculture," *Plant Environment and Efficient Water Use*, Madison, Wis.: American Society of Agronomy and Soil Science Society of America, 1966.

(10)  Ruttan, Vernon W., *The Economic Demand for Irrigated Acreage*, Baltimore: The Johns Hopkins Press, 1965.

(11)  South Saskatchewan River Development Commission, *South Saskatchewan River Development Project*, Fourth Progress Report, Regina, Saskatchewan, 1964.

(12)  U.S. Bureau of Reclamation, *Future Needs for Reclamation in the Western States*, Committee Print No. 14, Select Committee on National Water Resources, U.S. Senate, 86th Cong., 2nd Sess., Washington: U.S. Government Printing Office, 1960.

(13)  U.S. Department of Agriculture, *Land and Water Potentials and Future Requirements for Water*, Committee Print No. 12, Select Committee on National Water Resources, U.S. Senate, 86th Cong., 1st Sess., Washington: U.S. Government Printing Office, 1960.

(14)  Wollman, Nathaniel, *Water Supply and Demand*, Committee Print No. 32, Select Committee on National Water Resources, U.S. Senate, 86th Cong., 2nd Sess., Washington: U.S. Government Printing Office, 1960.

(15)  ———, *The Value of Water in Alternative Uses*, Albuquerque: Univ. of New Mexico Press, 1962.

# CHAPTER TWELVE

# Potential Uses
# of Mineral Resources

WESLEY G. SMITH, EDWIN A. HARRE,
and GERALD G. WILLIAMS

WHAT additional profitable use of mineral resources could be made by farmers of the United States, Canada, and Mexico? How much more could be used in each country if maximizing production rather than profit were the objective? What would be the prospects if the water supply were always adequate to maximize the use of minerals? How would the quantity of mineral resources used be altered if there were no Canadian or Mexican borders?

This chapter attempts to answer these questions. We will examine changes in fertilizer use by area, present estimates of crop production potentials and fertilizer requirements for selected crops by regions, and discuss change in total fertilizer production, trade, and restrictions to trade and their implications.

## TRENDS IN FERTILIZER USE
## IN NORTH AMERICA

Chemical fertilizer use in North America increased phenomenally between 1950 and 1966. Consumption of plant nutrients (N,

WESLEY G. SMITH, Agricultural Resource Development Branch, Tennessee Valley Authority; EDWIN A. HARRE, Agricultural Resource Development Branch, Tennessee Valley Authority; GERALD G. WILLIAMS, Agricultural Resource Development Branch, Tennessee Valley Authority.

$P_2O_5$ and $K_2O$) in Canada, the continental United States, and Mexico totaled 4,174,578 short tons in 1950;[1] by 1964 it had increased to 11,226,344 tons. From 1950 to 1966 fertilizer use increased 269 percent in Canada and 208 percent in the United States. Mexican consumption increased 2,636 percent between 1950 and 1964.

Nitrogen use increased more than 2,700 percent, $P_2O_5$ almost 1,900 percent, and $K_2O$ about 900 percent in Mexico between 1950 and 1964. In the United States nitrogen use increased 450 percent, $P_2O_5$ 98 percent, and $K_2O$ 190 percent between 1950 and 1966. In Canada the respective increases were 621, 212, and 179 percent. The large percentage increases in fertilizer consumption in Canada and Mexico can be attributed to higher rates of application per harvested acre and to expanding crop acreages. United States crop acreage decreased, but application rates increased.

Farmers in Canada applied 5.9 pounds of plant nutrients per harvested acre in 1950 and 19.6 pounds in 1966. The U.S. average was 23.2 pounds in 1950 and 84.6 pounds in 1966. Mexican farmers applied 12.4 pounds of nutrients per harvested acre in 1960 and 22.0 pounds in 1965.

Expenditures for fertilizer and lime by U.S. farmers increased 77 percent in the 1950–65 period.[2] Canadian farmers spent $70.1 million for fertilizer and limestone (at retail value) in 1960 and $138.6 million in 1965.[3]

## RATE OF FERTILIZATION PER HARVESTED ACRE BY REGION

In 1950 farmers in the U.S. Southeast used 77 pounds of nutrients per harvested acre, compared with only 18 pounds in the Corn Belt and less than one pound in the Northern Plains. In 1966 the Southeast applied 201 pounds of nutrients per harvested acre, while the Corn Belt used 98 pounds and the Northern Plains, 27 pounds. (See Figure 12.1 for delineated regions.)

---

[1] U.S. fertilizer consumption: 1950–65 data from *Consumption of Commercial Fertilizers and Primary Plant Nutrients in the U.S.*, USDA, ARS 41-19-7; 1966 data from *Consumption of Commercial Fertilizers in the U.S.*, USDA, SRS, SpCr 7 (5-67). Canadian fertilizer consumption: computed from annual publication, *Fertilizer Trade*, Dominion Bur. of Stat., Manufacturing and Primary Industries Div., Ottawa. Mexican fertilizer data: from *La Industria de los Fertilizantes en México, 1966;* Mexican fertilizer use data for 1966 are not available.

[2] "Fertilizer Summary Data—1966," TVA, National Fertilizer Development Center, Muscle Shoals, Ala., F67ACD3.

[3] *Farm Net Income,* Dominion Bur. of Stat., Ottawa, Canada, Sept. 1966.

*Fig. 12.1—Regional map of North America.*

From 1950 to 1966, rate of application increased from 2 to 11.3 pounds per acre in the Canadian Prairies and from 11 to 41 pounds in Central Canada. In all cases, Canadian use of fertilizer is much less than U.S. use in comparable areas. Part of this is a result of different cropping patterns, but it also appears that Canadian farmers have been slower to use fertilizer.

### REASONS FOR INCREASED USE

Some of the reasons for increased fertilizer use in the United States during this period are:

1. A favorable fertilizer-crop-price relationship. The composite price of nutrients (N, $P_2O_5$, and $K_2O$) paid by U.S. farmers decreased from an index of 100 in 1950 to 66 in 1965.[4] At the same time, the index of prices received by farmers for all crops has remained relatively constant, even though prices received for certain crops decreased.
2. As farm numbers decreased and the proportion of commercial farmers increased, more resources have come under the control of better managers who follow fertilizer recommendations.
3. Research on the economics of fertilizer use and effective educational programs by public agencies and private industry have hastened the adoption of new knowledge.
4. Government acreage restriction programs have prompted U.S. farmers to increase yields per harvested acre to maintain or increase output and incomes. This has been possible because of the high marginal return from fertilizer.
5. Government price stabilization programs have also prompted higher fertilizer use by taking out part of the uncertainty of using higher application rates.

In Canada fertilizer use is still extremely low, particularly in the Prairies. This may be due to several factors: (a) great variability in moisture conditions, resulting in more uncertainty about response to fertilizer; (b) a less favorable fertilizer-crop-price relationship than in the United States; and (c) farm prices

---

[4] Unpublished TVA data, computed from *Farm Income Situation*, USDA, 1952–65, and *Consumption of Commercial Fertilizers and Primary Plant Nutrients in the U.S.*, USDA, ARS, annual reports, 1952–64. The index of price per ton of fertilizer increased from 100 in 1950 to 110 in 1965. The difference in the two indexes is due to an increase in the amount of nutrients per ton of fertilizer.

have not been supported at high levels by the Canadian government.

## ACTUAL VERSUS RECOMMENDED FERTILIZER USE

Even though the increase in fertilizer use in the United States has been impressive, U.S. farmers were using only about one-half the amount of N, $P_2O_5$, and $K_2O$ recommended by land-grant universities as of 1963–64.[5] Had 1963 fertilizer recommendations been followed in the Canadian Prairie provinces, Gilson[6] estimates farmers would have used a minimum of 258,987 tons of N, 390,703 tons of $P_2O_5$, and 280 tons of $K_2O$. Actual use was 47,747 tons of N, 90,541 tons of $P_2O_5$, and 343 tons of $K_2O$ in 1963.

Data are not available on fertilizer use by crop in Mexico. The total amount used if average recommendations had been followed on 12 major crops was computed for the year 1962. Mexican farmers used 142,453 metric tons of N, 45,000 metric tons of $P_2O_5$, and 11,773 metric tons of $K_2O$ on *all* crops in 1962. Application at recommended rates for 12 crops would have amounted to 757,192 metric tons of N, 45,800 metric tons of $P_2O_5$, and 17,740 metric tons of $K_2O$.[7]

## ESTIMATED FERTILIZER USE AND CROP PRODUCTION POTENTIALS

Yield changes and their fluctuations over time involve such variables as increased use of fertilizers, improved cultural practices, and improved management. When acreage has been restricted, as for corn and wheat in the United States, farmers have selected their better soils to maintain or increase yields for these crops and have increased the rate of fertilization. When weather has not been a factor (for example, under irrigated conditions) progressively higher yields have occurred.

Mexican wheat yields have increased remarkably. Wheat yields also have increased dramatically in some areas of the

---

[5] *Potential Fertilizer Consumption in the U.S.*, The Sulphur Inst., Washington, D.C., and "Fertilizer Summary Data—1966."

[6] Compute from J. C. Gilson, "The Potential Growth in the Use of Fertilizer in Western Canada," Dept. Agr. Econ., Univ. of Manitoba; prepared for the Dept. of Industry and Commerce, March 1965, Table 8.

[6] Computed from J. C. Gilson, "The Potential Growth in the Use of Fertil-Secretaría de Agricultura y Ganadería, Instituto Nacional de Investigaciónes Agrícolas, México, 1965. For delineation of crops, see page 18, Table 4, of the larger study upon which this paper is based.

United States, particularly the Pacific Northwest. However, in the major wheat-producing areas of the United States, which depend almost entirely on natural rainfall, yields have increased at a slower rate. While fertilizer use has increased, it remains below the amount that can be economically justified. In the Prairies of Canada the weighted average yield of wheat was no higher in 1966 than in 1952.

Soybeans present a contrast to corn and wheat. United States acreage has expanded rapidly, but lack of knowledge in cultivating this crop has led to inconsistent yield increases.

## DESCRIPTION OF SURVEY

Information on fertilizer use by crop and its effect on yield at the farm level is extremely hard to find. In surveys, farmers are not usually asked how much N, $P_2O_5$, and $K_2O$ per acre they applied to various crops, and the resulting yield. To obtain information on possible fertilizer use and the resulting potential increases in food production, departments of agronomy or soil science in each state or provincial university in North America were contacted.[8] Each was asked to provide estimates for every major crop produced in its state or province on the following items: (a) assuming present moisture limitations, the average amount of N, $P_2O_5$, and $K_2O$ applied per acre; the average yield per acre with and without fertilizer; the amount of N, $P_2O_5$, and $K_2O$ per acre required to maximize profits at current prices and the estimated yield; and (b) assuming water for crop production was always available, the estimated amount of N, $P_2O_5$, and $K_2O$ per acre and yield required to maximize total physical production per acre. Estimates were received for each province in Canada, for 43 of the 48 states in the continental United States, and from Mexico.

## METHODOLOGY

Regional estimates of fertilizer use and crop production potentials were computed from the data received. When data were not available for a particular state within a region, the weighted average amount of N, $P_2O_5$, and $K_2O$ and yield, or data from a state with comparable conditions, were used to estimate the regional use and production of a crop. In the Arid and Desert,

[8] Appreciation is expressed to those organizations and individuals who supplied estimates for this study.

Western, and Northern Plains regions, different fertilizer use estimates usually were provided for irrigated and nonirrigated land. In the Prairie provinces fertilizer use and yield estimates, acreage, and production possibilities were separated for fallow and stubble crops and then aggregated to obtain regional totals. Average weighted crop prices received by farmers were used for each region in Canada and the United States. For the United States, current estimated prices of N, $P_2O_5$, and $K_2O$ were obtained for each region. Only one price for N, $P_2O_5$, and $K_2O$ (determined on the basis of 1964–65 data) was used for Canada, since regional differences in price could not be obtained. Neither current fertilizer nor crop prices could be obtained for Mexico.

### REGIONAL ESTIMATES

Estimated average yields per acre and crop production potentials for each region are given for the following situations: no fertilizer, current use, estimated maximum profit (optimum),[9] and maximum (physical) yield. Fertilizer requirements (in terms of total pounds of N, $P_2O_5$, and $K_2O$ per acre), total revenue and cost of fertilizer (in dollars per acre), total and actual crop production (in millions of bushels or tons), and the physical product due to fertilizer (tons of output per ton of total fertilizer nutrients applied above that obtained with no fertilizer) are also presented. Total crop production is calculated and compared with actual production. All yield and fertilizer use estimates presented in this section refer to the output farmers could produce today with known technology on acreages now cropped.

### CORN

Table 12.1 presents estimated per-acre yield potentials and fertilizer requirements by region for corn. For the Corn Belt, the yield without fertilizer is estimated to be 30 to 60 bushels per acre, with a weighted mean of 51 bushels (column 1). Total returns are estimated to be $65 per acre. For the current use situation (column 2), the estimated mean yield is 82 bushels, and the level of fertilizer application is 186 pounds of total nutrients per acre. Based on 1966 average prices in the Corn Belt, total revenue is $105 per acre and total cost of fertilizer is $12. For the maximum profit situation, the estimated yield is 105 bushels per

---

[9] The maximum profit situation is an estimated rather than a mathematically derived optimum where the marginal cost is exactly equal to marginal revenue.

TABLE 12.1
ESTIMATED YIELD, FERTILIZER USE, COSTS, AND RETURNS PER ACRE, BY REGION,
NORTH AMERICA—CORN FOR GRAIN

| | Situations | | | |
|---|---|---|---|---|
| | Moisture limiting | | | Moisture not limiting |
| | Without fertilizer | At average rate of application | For maximum profit | For maximum physical production |
| **UNITED STATES** | | | | |
| Northeast | | | | |
| Weighted mean yield (bu.) | 28 | 79 | 113 | 162 |
| Range in yield (bu.) | 26–40 | 57–100 | 110–150 | 140–175 |
| Total nutrients (lbs.) | . . . | 155 | 205 | 388 |
| Total revenue ($) | 45 | 127 | 182 | 261 |
| Cost of fertilizer ($) | . . . | 14 | 19 | 37 |
| Tons output (per ton nutrients) | . . . | 18.4 | 23.1 | 19.4 |
| Southeast | | | | |
| Weighted mean yield (bu.) | 16 | 65 | 93 | 153 |
| Range in yield (bu.) | 14–40 | 39–103 | 65–150 | 125–200 |
| Total nutrients (lbs.) | . . . | 178 | 282 | 382 |
| Total revenue ($) | 23 | 94 | 135 | 222 |
| Cost of fertilizer ($) | . . . | 16 | 26 | 35 |
| Tons output (per ton nutrients) | . . . | 15.7 | 11.2 | 20.1 |
| Corn Belt | | | | |
| Weighted mean yield (bu.) | 51 | 82 | 105 | 136 |
| Range in yield (bu.) | 30–60 | 78–84 | 95–120 | 110–200 |
| Total nutrients (lbs.) | . . . | 186 | 247 | 329 |
| Total revenue ($) | 65 | 105 | 134 | 174 |
| Cost of fertilizer ($) | . . . | 12 | 16 | 22 |
| Tons output (per ton nutrients) | . . . | 9.4 | 12.2 | 14.4 |
| Northern Plains* | | | | |
| Weighted mean yield (bu.) | 34 | 56 | 76 | 162 |
| Range in yield (bu.) | 28–48 | 38–70 | 44–120 | 52–250 |
| Total nutrients (lbs.) | . . . | 89 | 121 | 262 |
| Total revenue ($) | 44 | 77 | 91 | 100 |
| Cost of fertilizer ($) | . . . | 8 | 11 | 23 |
| Tons output (per ton nutrients) | . . . | 16.7 | 17.7 | 9.5 |
| Southern Plains | | | | |
| Weighted mean yield (bu.) | 20 | 43 | 64 | 141 |
| Range in yield (bu.) | . . . | 39–75 | 50–120 | 110–175 |
| Total nutrients (lbs.) | . . . | 113 | 185 | 297 |
| Total revenue ($) | 28 | 60 | 89 | 196 |
| Cost of fertilizer ($) | . . . | 8 | 13 | 21 |
| Tons output (per ton nutrients) | . . . | 11.2 | 13.1 | 22.8 |
| Arid and Desert† | | | | |
| Weighted mean yield (bu.) | 39 | 69 | 113 | 150 |
| Range in yield (bu.) | 35–65 | 68–75 | 100–115 | . . . |
| Total nutrients (lbs.) | . . . | 55 | 113 | 229 |
| Total revenue ($) | 57 | 101 | 166 | 220 |
| Cost of fertilizer ($) | . . . | 5 | 11 | 21 |
| Tons output (per ton nutrients) | . . . | 30.1 | 36.5 | 27.9 |

* Irrigated and nonirrigated combined.
† Irrigated only.
‡ Nonirrigated only.

TABLE 12.1 (continued)

| | Situations | | | |
|---|---|---|---|---|
| | Moisture limiting | | | Moisture not limiting |
| | Without fertilizer | At average rate of application | For maximum profit | For maximum physical production |
| UNITED STATES | | | | |
| Western * | | | | |
| Weighted mean yield (bu.) | 52 | 89 | 153 | 166 |
| Range in yield (bu.) | 40–54 | 85–90 | 95–160 | 160–200 |
| Total nutrients (lbs.) | . . . | 122 | 202 | 229 |
| Total revenue ($) | 77 | 133 | 228 | 247 |
| Cost of fertilizer ($) | . . . | 11 | 18 | 21 |
| Tons output (per ton nutrients) | . . . | 16.9 | 27.8 | 27.8 |
| CANADA | | | | |
| Central | | | | |
| Weighted mean yield (bu.) | 50 | 80 | 110 | 150 |
| Range in yield (bu.) | . . . | . . . | . . . | . . . |
| Total nutrients (lbs.) | . . . | 203 | 257 | 423 |
| Total revenue ($) | 65 | 104 | 143 | 195 |
| Cost of fertilizer ($) | . . . | 21 | 27 | 45 |
| Tons output (per ton nutrients) | . . . | 8.3 | 13.1 | 12.2 |
| MEXICO ‡ | | | | |
| Weighted mean yield (bu.) | 11 | 30 | 36 | 100 |
| Range in yield (bu.) | . . . | . . . | . . . | . . . |
| Total nutrients (lbs.) | . . . | 31 | 81 | 210 |
| Total revenue ($) | NA | NA | NA | NA |
| Cost of fertilizer ($) | NA | NA | NA | NA |
| Tons output (per ton nutrients) | . . . | 34.3 | 17.5 | 23.7 |

* Irrigated and nonirrigated combined.
† Irrigated only.
‡ Nonirrigated only.

acre; amount of total nutrients, 247 pounds; and total revenue and total cost, $134 and $16 respectively. If moisture had been adequate and maximum physical yield the objective (column 4), farmers should have applied 329 pounds of nutrients for a yield of 136 bushels per acre, which appears to be too conservative an estimate.

The physical value of fertilizer (designated tons of output per ton of applied nutrients) is estimated to be 9.4 tons for the current use situation, 12.2 tons for the maximum profit situation, and 14.4 tons for the maximum yield situation. Increasing physical returns are found when moving from the current use to the maximum profit situation because of the increase in use of improved technology and cultural practices, plus the removal of moisture restrictions when moving from the maximum profit to the maximum physical yield situation.

Estimated total corn production possibilities for each region are presented in Table 12.2. Estimated tons of N, $P_2O_5$, and $K_2O$ required for the maximum profit and maximum yield situations are presented in Table 12.2A. For example, estimated total production for the Corn Belt for the no fertilizer situation is 1,986.5 million bushels of corn, assuming the same acreage of corn for grain as in 1966. For the current use situation it is 3,200.9 million bushels and for the maximum profit and maximum yield situations it is 4,085.2 and 5,291.5 million bushels respectively. In 1966 actual production of corn in the Corn Belt amounted to 3,148.9 million bushels, indicating that the majority of farmers in that region are fertilizing corn at about the average rate computed from the survey.

The increase in physical product per ton of nutrients is higher in the Arid and Desert and Western regions of the United States than in other regions, indicating a positive interaction between fertilizer use and water. A return of 25 to 30 tons or more of corn per ton of plant nutrients applied in irrigated regions is evident, compared with about 10 to 20 tons or less where irrigation is not used.

It is obvious that there is a large potential for increased production in all regions. However, the greatest potential for increase is in Mexico because of the extremely low yields now obtained. Increased use of fertilizer in Mexico will require expanded irrigation of corn similar to that which has occurred for wheat.

Comparing data for corn production potentials by region with published average state yield data, it would appear that the estimated production potentials are reasonable. To increase yields from the estimated current use level to the maximum profit level would require, on the average, an additional $3 to $6 per acre for fertilizer in most regions. All increases in the cost of fertilizer application are much smaller than the added increase in total revenue in each region. The less favorable production areas—the Northern and Southern Plains—probably have less chance of increasing yields because of smaller profit margins and greater weather variability.

If all U.S. farmers had used the technology already known and had fertilized corn at the current use level as estimated from the survey, total corn production in 1966 would have been 4.3 billion bushels. Actual output was 4.1 billion bushels, or 95

## TABLE 12.2
### Estimated Total Crop Production Possibilities by Crop and Region, North America —Corn for Grain

| | Moisture Limiting | | | Moisture Not Limiting | Actual Production | Acreage |
|---|---|---|---|---|---|---|
| | Without fertilizer | At average rate of application | For maximum profit situation | For maximum phys. production | | |
| | (thou. bu.) | (thou. bu.) | (thou. bu.) | (thou. bu.) | (thou. bu.) | (thou. acr.) |
| United States (1966 acr. basis) | | | | | | |
| Northeast | 44,760 | 125,134 | 179,494 | 258,306 | 77,644 | 1,590 |
| Southeast | 112,412 | 467,806 | 657,512 | 1,085,885 | 314,674 | 7,101 |
| Corn Belt | 1,986,520 | 3,200,903 | 4,085,155 | 5,291,492 | 3,148,945 | 38,982 |
| Northern Plains | 271,203 | 476,886 | 567,208 | 615,470 | 494,998 | 7,741 |
| Southern Plains | 15,940 | 33,984 | 50,945 | 112,210 | 27,717 | 797 |
| Arid and Desert | 10,034 | 17,786 | 29,168 | 38,700 | 19,093 | 258 |
| Western | 12,153 | 20,773 | 35,714 | 38,796 | 20,252 | 223 |
| Canada (1964 acr. basis) | | | | | | |
| Central | 37,000 | 59,200 | 81,400 | 111,000 | 59,349 | 740 |
| Mexico (1962 acr. basis) | 168,916 | 460,680 | 552,816 | 1,535,600 | 218,055 | 238,003 |

## TABLE 12.2A
### Tons of N, P₂O₅, and K₂O Required for Maximum Profit and Maximum Yield Situations for Corn by Region as Shown in Table 12.2

| | Required for Maximum Profit Situation (tons) | | | | Required for Maximum Yield Situation (tons) | | | |
|---|---|---|---|---|---|---|---|---|
| | N | $P_2O_5$ | $K_2O$ | Total | N | $P_2O_5$ | $K_2O$ | Total |
| **United States** | | | | | | | | |
| Northeast | 67,610 | 56,980 | 51,525 | 176,615 | 140,600 | 94,378 | 97,013 | 331,991 |
| Southeast | 461,728 | 253,913 | 284,827 | 1,000,468 | 634,795 | 300,677 | 421,328 | 1,356,800 |
| Corn Belt | 2,230,954 | 1,354,659 | 1,258,009 | 4,843,622 | 3,178,710 | 1,602,265 | 1,665,363 | 6,446,338 |
| Northern Plains | 328,820 | 87,158 | 51,142 | 467,120 | 666,645 | 177,613 | 169,133 | 1,013,391 |
| Southern Plains | 45,970 | 13,854 | 13,790 | 73,614 | 71,086 | 24,432 | 22,900 | 118,418 |
| Arid and Desert | 11,257 | 3,372 | 0 | 14,629 | 22,029 | 6,688 | 0 | 28,717 |
| Western | 16,830 | 5,993 | 864 | 23,687 | 17,413 | 6,455 | 1,650 | 25,518 |
| **Canada** | | | | | | | | |
| Central | 50,450 | 25,200 | 27,000 | 102,650 | 81,500 | 43,000 | 4,450 | 128,950 |
| Mexico | 460,680 | 153,560 | 7,678 | 621,918 | 1,151,700 | 460,680 | 0 | 1,612,380 |

percent of that estimated to be possible at the present average application rate. If all corn had been fertilized at the estimated maxium profit level, total U.S. production would have been 5.6 billion bushels. At this level total fertilizer use would have amounted to 7.3 million tons of nutrients. If water had not been limited under the maximum yield situation, total production would have been 7.4 billion bushels, or 80.5 percent more than that actually produced on the 56.7 million acres used for corn for grain in 1966.

In Canada if all corn had been fertilized at the average rate in 1964, total production would have been 59.2 million bushels versus the 59.3 actually produced. Under the maximum profit situation, total production would have amounted to 81.4 million bushels. The difference between the maximum profit situation (assuming moisture limiting) and the maximum yield situation (no moisture limitations) is 29.6 million bushels.

On Mexico's nonirrigated land only, actual production in 1962 (latest year for which data were available) was 218 million bushels. Under the no fertilizer situation, total estimated production is 169 million busels. If all farmers had applied the average amount of fertilizer used by those who did use fertilizer, total production would have been 460.7 million bushels, or an increase of over 100 percent even for dryland farming. If water had not been limited and farmers had fertilized for maximum yield, estimated production would have amounted to 1.5 billion bushels for the dryland acreage alone. The potential for increased production, assuming maximum yield and no water limitations, is estimated to be over 1.3 billion bushels annually.

**WHEAT**

Unlike corn, dramatic yield increases have not occurred in wheat production over the period 1950–66, except in the western region of the United States and in Mexico. In the major wheat-producing areas of Canada and the United States (the Prairies and the Northern Plains) yields have been extremely variable over this period. To determine whether or not there has been a significant increase in yield over time, a simple linear regression was run for each region.[10] No significant yield increase over the

---

[10] Similar regressions were also run for each region for corn, oats, barley, and soybeans. Except for soybeans, a significant increase in yield at the .01 level of probability was obtained for each crop in each region in the United States, whereas a nonsignificant increase in yield was obtained for several crops and regions in Canada. See also the larger study upon which this chapter is based.

period 1950–66 was found for the Prairies; a significant response at the .01 level of probability was found for the Northern Plains.

In the Northern Plains and the Prairies, rainfall is an extremely important variable which often limits yield more than any other factor. In contrast to the more humid regions, variability in yields and rainfall (as well as low total rainfall) explains the relatively small estimated yield differences and fertilizer use for wheat (and other small grains) obtained from the survey when compared with corn (Tables 12.1 and 12.3). For example, the estimated average weighted yield of wheat in the Northern Plains for the no fertilizer situation is 19 bushels per acre; for current use, 26 bushels; and for the maximum profit, 33 bushels. For the Prairies the estimates are 22, 29, and 33 bushels per acre respectively.

Although the estimated increase in yield between the no fertilizer, current use, and maximum profit situations is relatively small, the physical return is not. For instance, as shown in Table 12.3, at the current use level a return of 9.8 tons of wheat is estimated per ton of fertilizer nutrients applied in the Northern Plains and 20.4 tons in the Prairies, which is comparable to that for corn. The increase in revenue between the no fertilizer, current use, and maximum profit situations is much larger than the increase in the cost of fertilizer. Although it is clear that wheat yields can be increased through better fertilization practices, the limiting factor in wheat production is not fertilizer per se in the major wheat-producing areas of Canada and the United States, but moisture and current inherent yield potentials. This is evident when comparing the estimated yield of wheat between the maximum profit and maximum yield situations. In regions such as the Arid and Desert, Western, and Central Canada, the estimated increase in yield is even larger for the maximum yield situation than in the Northern Plains or the Prairies. The possible increase in yield when fertilizer, improved varieties, and adequate water are available is also clearly evidenced in the case of Mexico.

Table 12.4 shows production possibilities for wheat for the various regions for each of the situations. For example, total production of wheat in the Northern Plains is estimated at 500.8 million bushels in 1966 for the no fertilizer situation. If all wheat had been fertilized at the estimated maximum profit level, output would have been 862 million bushels.

The computed total amount of fertilizer required for wheat for the maximum profit situation is 729,000 tons of nutrients

TABLE 12.3

ESTIMATED YIELD, FERTILIZER USE, COSTS AND RETURNS, PER ACRE, BY REGION,
NORTH AMERICA—WHEAT

| | Situations | | | |
|---|---|---|---|---|
| | Moisture limiting | | | Moisture not limiting |
| | Without fertilizer | At average rate of application | For maximum profit | For maximum physical production |
| **UNITED STATES** | | | | |
| Northeast | | | | |
| Weighted mean yield (bu.) | 20 | 37 | 53 | 73 |
| Range in yield (bu.) | 19–35 | 35–50 | 47–65 | 60–75 |
| Total nutrients (lbs.) | . . . | 101 | 147 | 170 |
| Total revenue ($) | 32 | 60 | 85 | 118 |
| Cost of fertilizer ($) | . . . | 9 | 14 | 16 |
| Tons output (per ton nutrients) | . . . | 9.4 | 13.3 | 12.7 |
| Southeast | | | | |
| Weighted mean yield (bu.) | 14 | 31 | 42 | 54 |
| Range in yield (bu.) | 5–21 | 23–40 | 36–50 | 42–75 |
| Total nutrients (lbs.) | . . . | 105 | 148 | 192 |
| Total revenue ($) | 22 | 49 | 67 | 86 |
| Cost of fertilizer ($) | . . . | 10 | 14 | 18 |
| Tons output (per ton nutrients) | . . . | 10.3 | 11.6 | 12.6 |
| Corn Belt | | | | |
| Weighted mean yield (bu.) | 21 | 35 | 50 | 60 |
| Range in yield (bu.) | 18–30 | 23–40 | 25–60 | 45–65 |
| Total nutrients (lbs.) | . . . | 127 | 164 | 189 |
| Total revenue ($) | 36 | 60 | 86 | 103 |
| Cost of fertilizer ($) | . . . | 8 | 11 | 12 |
| Tons output (per ton nutrients) | . . . | 6.5 | 10.5 | 12.4 |
| Northern Plains* | | | | |
| Weighted mean yield (bu.) | 19 | 26 | 33 | 58 |
| Range in yield (bu.) | 18–20 | 21–40 | 25–50 | 32–80 |
| Total nutrients (lbs.) | . . . | 40 | 56 | 133 |
| Total revenue ($) | 31 | 42 | 53 | 94 |
| Cost of fertilizer ($) | . . . | 4 | 5 | 12 |
| Tons output (per ton nutrients) | . . . | 9.8 | 14.9 | 17.4 |
| Southern Plains | | | | |
| Weighted mean yield (bu.) | 17 | 25 | 29 | 55 |
| Range in yield (bu.) | 15–20 | 20–35 | 21–50 | 40–65 |
| Total nutrients (lbs.) | . . . | 50 | 80 | 157 |
| Total revenue ($) | 27 | 40 | 46 | 87 |
| Cost of fertilizer ($) | . . . | 4 | 6 | 11 |
| Tons output (per ton nutrients) | . . . | 10.0 | 8.8 | 14.5 |
| Arid and Desert* | | | | |
| Weighted mean yield (bu.) | 23 | 30 | 40 | 86 |
| Range in yield (bu.) | 15–40 | 25–70 | 35–80 | 50–125 |
| Total nutrients (lbs.) | . . . | 23 | 61 | 155 |
| Total revenue ($) | 36 | 47 | 63 | 136 |
| Cost of fertilizer ($) | . . . | 2 | 6 | 15 |
| Tons output (per ton nutrients) | . . . | 20.7 | 17.0 | 24.6 |

TABLE 12.3 (continued)

| | Situations | | | |
| --- | --- | --- | --- | --- |
| | Moisture limiting | | | Moisture not limiting |
| | Without fertilizer | At average rate of application | For maximum profit | For maximum physical production |
| Western * | | | | |
| Weighted mean yield (bu.) | 27 | 50 | 70 | 175 |
| Range in yield (bu.) | 18–30 | 27–55 | 27–80 | 83–200 |
| Total nutrients (lbs.) | . . . | 62 | 109 | 245 |
| Total revenue ($) | 42 | 78 | 110 | 275 |
| Cost of fertilizer ($) | . . . | 6 | 10 | 22 |
| Tons output (per ton nutrients) | . . . | 22.0 | 23.6 | 36.2 |
| CANADA | | | | |
| Maritimes | | | | |
| Weighted mean yield (bu.) | 25 | 35 | 50 | 60 |
| Range in yield (bu.) | NA | NA | NA | NA |
| Total nutrients (lbs.) | . . . | 75 | 225 | 312 |
| Total revenue ($) | 43 | 60 | 86 | 103 |
| Cost of fertilizer ($) | . . . | 7 | 22 | 30 |
| Tons output (per ton nutrients) | . . . | 8.0 | 6.7 | 6.7 |
| Central | | | | |
| Weighted mean yield (bu.) | 30 | 40 | 50 | 100 |
| Range in yield (bu.) | 20–30 | 40–50 | 50–60 | NA |
| Total nutrients (lbs.) | . . . | 66 | 150 | 298 |
| Total revenue ($) | 51 | 68 | 84 | 169 |
| Cost of fertilizer ($) | . . . | 6 | 15 | 29 |
| Tons output (per ton nutrients) | . . . | 9.1 | 8.2 | 14.1 |
| Prairies † | | | | |
| Weighted mean yield (bu.) | 22 | 29 | 33 | 49 |
| Range in yield (bu.) | 20-23 | 24–32 | 30–35 | 45-60 |
| Total nutrients (lbs.) | . . . | 21 | 40 | 104 |
| Total revenue ($) | 35 | 46 | 52 | 78 |
| Cost of fertilizer ($) | . . . | 2 | 5 | 30 |
| Tons output (per ton nutrients) | . . . | 20.4 | 13.6 | 15.6 |
| Pacific | | | | |
| Weighted mean yield (bu.) | 22 | 32 | . . . | 80 |
| Range in yield (bu.) | . . . | . . . | . . . | . . . |
| Total nutrients (lbs.) | . . . | 25 | NA | NA |
| Total revenue ($) | 33 | 48 | NA | 90 |
| Cost of fertilizer ($) | . . . | 3 | NA | NA |
| Tons output (per ton nutrients) | . . . | 24.0 | NA | NA |
| MEXICO ‡ | | | | |
| Weighted mean yield (bu.) | 22 | 50 | 65 | 80 |
| Range in yield (bu.) | NA | NA | NA | NA |
| Total nutrients (lbs.) | . . . | 111 | 160 | 210 |
| Total revenue ($) | NA | NA | NA | NA |
| Cost of fertilizer ($) | NA | NA | NA | NA |
| Tons output (per ton nutrients) | . . . | 15.1 | 16.1 | 16.6 |

* Irrigated and nonirrigated combined.
† Includes both fallow and stubble.
‡ Irrigated only.

and for the maximum yield situation, 1,721,000 tons for the Northern Plains (Table 12.4A).

Data for the Prairie provinces show similar relationships. The amount of total nutrients for the maximum profit situation is 553,150 tons; for the maximum yield, 1.4 million tons.

Information similar to that presented for corn and wheat was computed for barley, oats, soybeans, grain sorghum, all hay, and alfalfa and alfalfa mixtures. A summary of production possibilities and fertilizer requirements for these crops is presented in the appendix at the end of this chapter.

## FERTILIZER PRODUCTION AND TRADE

North America is blessed with enormous supplies of the minerals needed for chemical fertilizer production. The most important are phosphate rock, potash, sulfur, and natural gas and other hydrocarbons (Table 12.5).

Phosphate rock is mined in large tonnages in the United States, but not in Mexico or Canada, although both have deposits. Reserves of sulfur, a key in phosphate fertilizer manufacture, are found in the three nations. Large reserves of potash are being mined in both the United States and Canada. Nitrogen from the atmosphere is available in virtually unlimited supply; it is combined with hydrogen in natural gas or other materials to produce ammonia, the major source of fertilizer nitrogen.

Ammonia production has soared during the past decade. Canada's output climbed from 410,000 tons in 1956 to 1,287,000 tons in 1966. In the same period, Mexico's annual production rose from 51,000 to 337,000 tons, and that of the United States from 4,078,000 to 12,156,000 tons.

In 1956 the leading area of nitrogen production in the United States was the Southeast, which produced 30 percent of the total ammonia.[11] The Southern Plains ranked second. By 1966 the Southern Plains ranked first, producing 37 percent of all ammonia, followed by the Southeast with 23 percent of the total. During this 10-year interval, the Southern Plains increased its position in both relative and absolute terms over the other regions. In Canada during this same period the Central region increased its share of production from 45 to 60 percent of the total and more than tripled production capacity.

Between 1955 and 1966 total exports of nitrogen from the

---

[11] "Fertilizer Trends," 1956 through 1967, TVA, National Fertilizer Development Center, Muscle Shoals, Ala.

## TABLE 12.4
### ESTIMATED TOTAL CROP PRODUCTION POSSIBILITIES BY CROP AND REGION, NORTH AMERICA—WHEAT

| | Moisture Limiting | | | Moisture Not Limiting | Actual Production | Acreage |
|---|---|---|---|---|---|---|
| | Without fertilizer | At average rate of application | For maximum profit situation | For maximum phys. production | | |
| | (thou. t.u.) | (thou. bu.) | (thou. bu.) | (thou. bu.) | (thou. bu.) | (thou. bu.) |
| United States (1966 acr. basis) | | | | | | |
| Northeast | 15,676 | 28,296 | 40,272 | 55,460 | 28,556 | 760 |
| Southeast | 14,387 | 33,383 | 44,956 | 57,217 | 33,569 | 1,051 |
| Corn Belt | 136,812 | 225,097 | 322,716 | 388,875 | 239,897 | 6,432 |
| Northern Plains* | 500,845 | 671,060 | 861,963 | 1,507,718 | NA | 25,908 |
| Southern Plains | 141,523 | 210,520 | 240,083 | 455,210 | 184,636 | 8,351 |
| Arid and Desert | 85,788 | 115,240 | 151,389 | 326,251 | 93,793 | 3,782 |
| Western | 89,761 | 165,770 | 232,041 | 581,585 | 124,208 | 3,321 |
| Canada (1965 acr. basis) | | | | | | |
| Maritimes | 275 | 385 | 550 | 660 | 296 | 110 |
| Central | 11,524 | 15,520 | 19,532 | 38,820 | 14,021 | 388 |
| Prairies | 606,524 | 818,816 | 919,195 | 1,373,700 | 661,000 | 27,790 |
| Pacific | 2,046 | 2,976 | | 15,580 | 2,600 | 93 |
| Mexico† (1963 acr. basis) | 21,252 | 48,300 | 62,790 | 77,280 | NA | 966 |

* Excludes nonirrigated acreage in Wyoming.
† Includes irrigated acreage only.

TABLE 12.4A

Tons of N, $P_2O_5$, and $K_2O$ Required for Maximum Profit and Maximum Yield Situations for Wheat by Region as Shown in Table 12.4

| | Required for Maximum Profit Situation | | | | Required for Maximum Yield Situation | | | |
|---|---|---|---|---|---|---|---|---|
| | N | $P_2O_5$ | $K_2O$ | Total | N | $P_2O_5$ | $K_2O$ | Total |
| | | (tons) | | | | (tons) | | |
| United States | | | | | | | | |
| Northeast | 19,520 | 19,040 | 17,280 | 55,840 | 21,620 | 21,460 | 21,460 | 64,540 |
| Southeast | 33,889 | 23,885 | 20,988 | 78,762 | 43,706 | 28,978 | 28,978 | 101,662 |
| Corn Belt | 164,727 | 200,187 | 165,907 | 530,821 | 237,493 | 185,097 | 137,306 | 559,896 |
| Northern Plains | 411,485 | 291,958 | 25,650 | 729,093 | 968,348 | 455,686 | 297,040 | 1,721,074 |
| Southern Plains | 182,548 | 115,696 | 37,813 | 336,057 | 412,412 | 152,435 | 85,088 | 649,935 |
| Arid and Desert | 88,955 | 26,739 | 0 | 115,694 | 194,970 | 96,545 | 2,205 | 293,720 |
| Western | 128,728 | 51,713 | 40 | 180,481 | 261,950 | 99,290 | 45,712 | 406,952 |
| Canada | | | | | | | | |
| Maritimes | 413 | 413 | 413 | 1,239 | 479 | 688 | 550 | 1,717 |
| Central | 9,705 | 9,705 | 9,766 | 29,176 | 19,258 | 19,758 | 19,410 | 58,426 |
| Prairies | 222,352 | 330,798 | 0 | 553,150 | 987,100 | 455,200 | 0 | 1,442,300 |
| Pacific | NA | NA | NA | NA | NA | NA | NA | NA |

TABLE 12.5
NORTH AMERICAN MINERAL RESERVES

|  | (million tons) |
| --- | --- |
| Phosphate rock | 14,100 (P$_2$O$_5$) |
| Potash | 17,950 (K$_2$O) |
| Sulfur |  |
|     Frasch | 200 (S) |
|     Petroleum & natural gas | 52 *(S) |
|     Total all sources | Enormous |
| Limestone | † |

\* Not including Canada.
† Reserves are not a limiting factor in the growth of the lime industry.

United States to Mexico increased from 29,416 to 145,593 tons.[12] This was mostly in the form of ammonia for use in the production of finished nitrogen fertilizers. United States exports of nitrogen to Canada were 17,226 tons in 1955 and 22,176 tons in 1966, reaching a high of 27,073 tons in 1965. United States imports of fertilizer nitrogen from Canada were 149,786 tons in 1955 and 216,038 in 1966, again reaching a high of 240,810 tons in 1965. Nitrogen fertilizers were not imported from Mexico by Canada or the United States during this period.

United States rock phosphate production increased from 12.2 million tons in 1950 to 34.1 million in 1966, with Florida the major producing area. Neither Canada nor Mexico mines rock phosphate. Exports of phosphate rock from the United States to Canada increased from 190,000 tons of P$_2$O$_5$ in 1955 to 711,600 tons in 1966. Exports to Mexico increased from 15,200 tons of P$_2$O$_5$ in 1955 to 108,000 tons in 1966.[13]

United States phosphate fertilizer production increased from 1.77 million tons of P$_2$O$_5$ in 1955 to 4.89 million tons in 1966.[14] During the same period, Canadian production increased from 153,000 tons to 462,000 tons. Mexican phosphate production was 21,000 metric tons of P$_2$O$_5$ in 1961 and 84,000 metric tons in 1966.

In contrast to trade in phosphate rock between the United States and Canada, U.S. exports of phosphate fertilizers to Canada have diminished since 1960, while imports from Canada have increased. In 1961 U.S. imports from Canada amounted to 65,800 tons of P$_2$O$_5$ equivalent, compared to almost 90,000 tons in 1966. United States-Mexican trade has not been great.

---

[12] Unpublished TVA estimates.
[13] *Ibid.*
[14] *Ibid.*

Neither the United States nor Canada imports phosphate fertilizers from Mexico.[15]

With respect to U.S.-Canadian trade, Canadian exports of nitrogen fertilizers to the United States are ten times greater than her imports from the United States, while Canadian imports of phosphate, mainly phosphate rock, are almost ten times greater than her exports to the United States of $P_2O_5$ as finished fertilizers.

Before 1962 all North American potash production was in the United States. Canadian production expanded from 150,000 tons of $K_2O$ in 1962 to 2 million tons in 1966. United States production increased from 2.5 million to 3.3 million tons of $K_2O$ in the same time period. Plans have been announced which would expand U.S. capacity to 4.25 million tons by 1970, while Canada's planned capacity would be 6.7 million tons.

Expansion of potash production in Canada has had a marked effect on potash trade. Prior to 1962 the United States supplied the major portion of the potash consumed in Canada. Between 1962 and 1966 U.S. exports to Canada decreased more than 90 percent. Canadian shipments of potash to the United States during the same period increased from 45,837 to 1,218,857 tons of $K_2O$. During 1955–66 Mexican imports of potash from the United States increased from 5,300 tons of $K_2O$ in 1955 to 25,400 tons in 1966. All potash consumed in Mexico is imported from the United States.

Total fertilizer trade within North America expanded greatly from 1955 to 1966. In 1955 the United States exported to Mexico the equivalent of 58,200 tons of plant nutrients (N, $P_2O_5$, and $K_2O$); in 1966 this reached 279,200 tons. United States exports to Canada were 309,100 tons of plant nutrients in 1955 and 785,600 tons in 1966. By far the greatest change in trade, however, has been the U.S. imports from Canada. In 1955 the United States imported the equivalent of 233,800 tons of nutrients from Canada, of which imports of nitrogen materials made up 64 percent of the total, and potash 2 percent. In 1966 the United States imported about 1.5 million tons, of which nitrogen materials made up 14 percent of the total, and potash 80 percent. In fact, U.S. imports of plant nutrients from Canada almost doubled between 1962 and 1963 and again between 1963 and 1965.

With the exception of Canadian exports of finished fertilizers to the United States, fertilizer trade between the nations of

---

[15] *Ibid.*

North America consists mainly of raw materials. The United States supplies phosphate rock to Canada and Mexico. Canada and Mexico supply sulfur to the United States. Canada exports potash to the United States and the United States exports to Mexico.

Sulfur production in North America totaled 5.9 million tons in 1950, all of which were produced in the United States. The 1964 total exceeded 10 million tons, divided as follows: Canada, 1.4 million tons; Mexico, 1.6 million tons; and the United States, 7.1 million tons. Between 1964 and 1965, U.S. production increased by more than 1 million tons.

The total capacity (Frasch and recovered) for North America was 14.5 million long tons as of January 1, 1967, with additional planned capacity to reach 17.2 million long tons in 1968.[16] In sulfur production, however, capacity does not always offer an indication of production capability because of depletion of the sulfur domes and the fact that recovered sulfur production from sour gas depends heavily on the availability of markets for the gas.

Between 1955 and 1966, U.S. exports of sulfur to Canada fell from 348,300 to 136,400 tons, while U.S. imports from Canada rose from 41,000 to 703,300 tons. During this same period U.S. imports of sulfur from Mexico increased from 27,000 tons in in 1955 to a high of 890,600 tons in 1964. Since then, imports have decreased to about 800,000 tons.

### TRADE RESTRICTIONS

Trade restrictions explain to some extent the patterns of trade that have developed. The United States has no import duties, tariffs, or import restrictions on fertilizer materials or materials used in the manufacture of fertilizer. Mexico has an ad valorem duty of 25 percent on export of sulfur. Calcium phosphates are imported duty free, but most other fertilizer materials require duty payments ranging from 0.01 pesos to 0.30 pesos per ton, plus an ad valorem duty ranging from about 2 percent to 80 percent, plus a 3 percent surtax.[17] Most fertilizer materials are also subject to import controls under a licensing system for countries that are not members of the Latin American Free Trade Association (LAFTA). Canada and the United States are not members.

---

[16] "Fertilizer Trends—1967," TVA, National Fertilizer Development Center, Muscle Shoals, Ala., F67ACD15.

[17] U.S. Dept. of Commerce, Bureau of International Commerce, American Republics Division; and Secretaría de Industria y Comercio, México.

Materials used exclusively for manufacture of fertilizers in Canada are duty free. A few products which might be used as fertilizers are classified in different categories, but most are duty free. An exception is ammonium nitrate. Compound or manufactured fertilizers not otherwise provided for in tariff items are dutiable at 5 percent ad valorem. By 1968, however, all formulated fertilizers and fertilizer materials for manufacture will be free of duty. There are no quotas or trade restrictions except that products must be registered and must conform to prescribed standards and labeling regulations.

### POSSIBLE EFFECTS OF ELIMINATION OF TRADE RESTRICTIONS

Because of the very low Canadian tariffs at the present time on imports of finished fertilizers from the United States, it is not anticipated that the elimination of all tariffs by 1968 will have any great effect on the amount imported by Canada. Trade in finished fertilizer products is now essentially free between Canada and the United States. If Mexico were to eliminate all barriers to trade, an increase in nitrogen fertilizer imports could be expected initially until domestic production capacity met potential demand. Exports of sulfur to the United States would probably increase to meet the present short supply situation in the United States.

## SUMMARY AND CONCLUSIONS

The main objective of this chapter was to evaluate the potential for fertilizer use in food production in North America. No attempt was made to determine fertilizer needs for all crops, since such nonfood crops as cotton and tobacco were not included. Similarly, no attempt was made to evaluate total crop production potentials for all crops or to evaluate the effect of increased production on prices or markets. All computations were based on the most recent acreage available—1966 for U.S. crops; 1964–65 for Canada; and 1962 for corn, wheat, and barley for Mexico.

Crops discussed are the main food crops produced in Canada and the United States. Several important Mexican crops were not included because of lack of data or lack of comparability with the other two countries.

We believe that the estimated potential crop yield increases and fertilizer use are realistic, although probably conservative.

Estimates computed for most crops by region fall fairly close to actual production.

It is obvious that North America has an exceedingly large capacity to produce both fertilizer and food. The facts that—(a) current levels of fertilizer use range from about one-half of recommended rates in the United States to less than one-fourth in Mexico; (b) the United States now has about 37 out of a possible 95 million acres of land under irrigation; (c) up to 2.5 million acres could be irrigated in the Prairies of Canada in the very near future and up to 10 or more million acres could be irrigated eventually; and (d) many acres of potential agricultural land in both the United States and Canada (including a very large acreage of summer fallow in the Prairie provinces) are not now used for food production—imply that the total production possibilities derived in this study based on present land use represent the lower limit of what North America actually could produce in terms of food if required.

# Chapter 12 Appendix

## APPENDIX TABLE 12.1

ESTIMATED TOTAL CROP PRODUCTION POSSIBILITIES BY CROP AND REGION, NORTH AMERICA—BARLEY

| | Moisture Limiting | | | Moisture Not Limiting | | |
| --- | --- | --- | --- | --- | --- | --- |
| | Without fertilizer | At average rate of application | For maximum profit situation | For maximum phys. production | Actual Production | Acreage |
| | *(thou. bu.)* | *(thou. bu.)* | *(thou. bu.)* | *(thou. bu.)* | *(thou. bu.)* | *(thou. bu.)* |
| United States (1966 acr. basis) | | | | | | |
| Northeast | (insufficient data to provide reliable estimates) | | | | | |
| Southeast | 4,807 | 13,329 | 19,637 | 25,850 | 12,938 | 286 |
| Corn Belt | (insufficient data to provide reliable estimates) | | | | | |
| Northern Plains | 120,157 | 153,846 | 180,580 | 313,545 | 168,788 | 5,163 |
| Southern Plains | 9,820 | 14,730 | 17,185 | 39,280 | 13,014 | 491 |
| Arid and Desert* | 18,711 | 25,953 | 33,020 | 43,644 | NA | 417 |
| Western | 46,168 | 131,045 | 166,665 | 236,682 | 104,135 | 2,132 |
| Canada (1965 acr. basis) | | | | | | |
| Maritimes | 540 | 900 | 1,620 | 1,980 | 641 | 18 |
| Central | 5,275 | 7,900 | 11,150 | 15,800 | 7,414 | 155 |
| Prairies | 199,688 | 258,345 | 303,754 | 459,280 | 202,000 | 5,741 |
| Pacific | 3,348 | 4,588 | NA | 9,300 | 4,500 | 124 |
| Mexico (1963–64 acr. basis) | 8,700 | 16,240 | 18,560 | 37,700 | NA | 580 |

* Includes irrigated acreage only.

APPENDIX TABLE 12.1A

TONS OF N, $P_2O_5$, AND $K_2O$ REQUIRED FOR MAXIMUM PROFIT AND MAXIMUM YIELD SITUATIONS
FOR BARLEY BY REGION AS SHOWN IN APPENDIX TABLE 12.1

| | Required for Maximum Profit Situation | | | | Required for Maximum Yield Situation | | | |
|---|---|---|---|---|---|---|---|---|
| | N | $P_2O_5$ | $K_2O$ | Total | N | $P_2O_5$ | $K_2O$ | Total |
| | | (tons) | | | | (tons) | | |
| United States | | | | | | | | |
| Northeast | (insufficient data for estimates to be reliable) | | | | | | | |
| Southeast | 8,838 | 8,014 | 7,438 | 24,290 | 9,787 | 8,014 | 8,014 | 25,815 |
| Corn Belt | (insufficient data for estimates to be reliable) | | | | | | | |
| Northern Plains | 57,278 | 63,206 | 19,168 | 139,652 | 86,153 | 76,278 | 37,427 | 199,858 |
| Southern Plains | 12,275 | 7,365 | 2,455 | 22,095 | 19,640 | 9,820 | 7,365 | 36,825 |
| Arid and Desert | 31,643 | 16,797 | 0 | 48,439 | 69,770 | 31,580 | 2,790 | 104,140 |
| Western | 67,255 | 32,349 | 212 | 99,816 | 108,150 | 44,080 | 8,224 | 160,454 |
| Canada | | | | | | | | |
| Maritimes | 900 | 900 | 900 | 2,700 | 1,044 | 1,500 | 1,200 | 3,744 |
| Central | 3,875 | 3,950 | 4,025 | 11,850 | 7,563 | 7,563 | 7,750 | 22,876 |
| Prairies | 96,698 | 70,843 | 0 | 167,541 | 135,325 | 123,020 | 0 | 258,345 |

## APPENDIX TABLE 12.2
### ESTIMATED TOTAL CROP PRODUCTION POSSIBILITIES BY CROP AND REGION, NORTH AMERICA—OATS

| | Moisture Limiting | | | Moisture Not Limiting | Actual Production | Acreage |
|---|---|---|---|---|---|---|
| | Without fertilizer | At average rate of application | For maximum profit situation | For maximum phys. production | | |
| | (thou. bu.) | (thou. bu.) | (thou. bu.) | (thou. bu.) | (thou. bu.) | (thou. acr.) |
| United States (1966 acr. basis) | | | | | | |
| Northeast* | NA | 54,782 | NA | 102,320 | NA | 1,019 |
| Southeast | 10,163 | 29,157 | 49,612 | 58,667 | 26,388 | 592 |
| Corn Belt | 418,333 | 572,123 | 706,913 | 761,275 | 481,362 | 9,526 |
| Northern Plains† | 168,232 | 253,116 | 309,839 | 404,101 | NA | 5,245 |
| Southern Plains | 23,490 | 32,332 | 38,185 | 101,985 | 29,953 | 914 |
| Arid and Desert | (insufficient data to provide reliable estimates) | | | | | |
| Western | 10,631 | 17,448 | 19,701 | 29,580 | 13,265 | 278 |
| Canada (1965 acr. basis) | | | | | | |
| Maritimes | 6,195 | 12,373 | 17,755 | 19,980 | 8,273 | 206 |
| Central | 106,050 | 176,350 | 242,900 | 348,950 | 131,684 | 2,745 |
| Prairies | 234,801 | 278,795 | 363,715 | 604,550 | 272,000 | 5,645 |
| Pacific | 2,400 | 3,600 | NA | 6,000 | 3,000 | 60 |
| Mexico | (insufficient data to provide reliable estimates) | | | | | |

* Includes Maryland, New Jersey, New York, Pennsylvania, and Vermont only.
† Excludes Wyoming.

## APPENDIX TABLE 12.2A

### Tons of N, $P_2O_5$, and $K_2O$ Required for Maximum Profit and Maximum Yield Situations for Oats by Region as Shown in Appendix Table 12.2

| | Required for Maximum Profit Situation | | | | Required for Maximum Yield Situation | | | |
|---|---|---|---|---|---|---|---|---|
| | N | $P_2O_5$ | $K_2O$ | Total | N | $P_2O_5$ | $K_2O$ | Total |
| | | (tons) | | | | (tons) | | |
| **United States** | | | | | | | | |
| Northeast | (insufficient data for estimates to be reliable) | | | | | | | |
| Southeast | 22,049 | 14,795 | 14,795 | 51,639 | 25,686 | 16,881 | 16,881 | 59,448 |
| Corn Belt | 208,855 | 266,443 | 191,210 | 666,508 | 289,686 | 271,471 | 199,751 | 760,908 |
| Northern Plains | 92,686 | 53,643 | 0 | 146,329 | 121,421 | 70,048 | 26,473 | 217,942 |
| Southern Plains | 24,543 | 12,860 | 4,563 | 41,966 | 49,303 | 21,885 | 6,493 | 77,681 |
| Arid and Desert | 1,798 | 1,085 | 0 | 2,883 | 8,097 | 3,339 | 0 | 11,435 |
| Western | 4,225 | 2,910 | 0 | 7,135 | 7,975 | 4,050 | 1,300 | 13,325 |
| **Canada** | | | | | | | | |
| Maritimes | 4,275 | 6,150 | 4,430 | 14,855 | 5,150 | 7,040 | 5,305 | 17,495 |
| Central | 62,800 | 62,800 | 74,450 | 200,050 | 116,863 | 113,950 | 125,600 | 356,413 |
| Prairies | 95,632 | 71,173 | 0 | 166,805 | 228,600 | 114,300 | 0 | 342,900 |
| Pacific | NA | NA | NA | NA | NA | NA | NA | NA |

## APPENDIX TABLE 12.3

### Estimated Total Crop Production Possibilities by Crop and Region, North America—Soybeans for Beans

| | Moisture Limiting | | | Moisture Not Limiting | Actual Production | Acreage |
|---|---|---|---|---|---|---|
| | Without fertilizer | At average rate of application | For maximum profit situation | For maximum phys. production | | |
| | (thou. bu.) | (thou. bu.) | (thou. bu.) | (thou. bu.) | (thou. bu.) | (thou. acr.) |
| United States (1966 acr. basis) | | | | | | |
| Northeast | 4,281 | 12,255 | 15,747 | 20,773 | 5,672 | 408 |
| Southeast | 94,497 | 136,382 | 186,058 | 242,577 | 134,923 | 5,742 |
| Corn Belt | 559,361 | 673,336 | 928,878 | 1,127,286 | 623,166 | 23,350 |
| Northern Plains | 53,033 | 62,501 | 81,263 | 165,000 | 56,121 | 2,283 |
| Southern Plains | 96,696 | 120,045 | 161,857 | 208,725 | 111,609 | 4,861 |
| Canada (1965 acr. basis) | | | | | | |
| Central | 7,950 | 9,275 | 11,925 | 15,900 | 8,030 | 265 |
| Mexico | (insufficient data to provide reliable estimates) | | | | | |

## APPENDIX TABLE 12.3A

### Tons of N, P₂O₅, and K₂O Required for Maximum Profit and Maximum Yield Situations for Soybeans by Regions as Shown in Appendix Table 12.3

| | Required for Maximum Profit Situation | | | | Required for Maximum Yield Situation | | | |
|---|---|---|---|---|---|---|---|---|
| | N | $P_2O_5$ | $K_2O$ | Total | N | $P_2O_5$ | $K_2O$ | Total |
| | | *(tons)* | | | | *(tons)* | | |
| United States | | | | | | | | |
| Northeast | 1,680 | 11,385 | 12,330 | 25,395 | 4,565 | 13,925 | 15,740 | 34,230 |
| Southeast | 3,050 | 94,816 | 144,021 | 241,887 | 7,780 | 127,623 | 189,190 | 324,593 |
| Corn Belt | 166,074 | 526,250 | 570,874 | 1,263,198 | 177,665 | 645,320 | 784,352 | 1,607,337 |
| Northern Plains | 585 | 24,725 | 30,970 | 56,280 | 49,895 | 44,795 | 75,135 | 169,825 |
| Southern Plains | 715 | 127,765 | 127,765 | 256,245 | 715 | 215,390 | 215,390 | 431,395 |
| Arid and Desert | (insufficient data for estimates to be reliable) | | | | | | | |
| Western | (insufficient data for estimates to be reliable) | | | | | | | |
| Canada | | | | | | | | |
| Maritimes | (insufficient data for estimates to be reliable) | | | | | | | |
| Central | 1,325 | 5,300 | 5,300 | 11,925 | 0 | 13,250 | 13,250 | 26,500 |
| Prairies | (insufficient data for estimates to be reliable) | | | | | | | |
| Pacific | (insufficient data for estimates to be reliable) | | | | | | | |

256

## APPENDIX TABLE 12.4

### Estimated Total Crop Production Possibilities by Crop and Region, North America—Grain Sorghum

| | Moisture Limiting | | | Moisture Not Limiting | Actual Production | Acreage |
|---|---|---|---|---|---|---|
| | Without fertilizer | At average rate of application | For maximum profit situation | For maximum phys. production | | |
| | (thou. bu.) | (thou. bu.) | (thou. bu.) | (thou. bu.) | (thou. bu.) | (thou. acr.) |
| United States (1966 acr. basis) | | | | | | |
| Southeast | 1,813 | 5,899 | 8,670 | 10,642 | 3,820 | 102 |
| Corn Belt | 8,125 | 14,721 | 23,481 | 33,640 | 13,786 | 236 |
| Northern Plains | 169,353 | 308,996 | 364,234 | 904,418 | 299,521 | 5,263 |
| Southern Plains | 191,830 | 339,660 | 434,736 | 653,839 | 334,670 | 6,140 |
| Arid and Desert | (insufficient data to provide reliable estimates) | | | | | |
| Western | 17,037 | 27,275 | 40,912 | 40,912 | 27,504 | 382 |

## APPENDIX TABLE 12.4A

Tons of N, $P_2O_5$, and $K_2O$ Required for Maximum Profit and Maximum Yield Situations for Sorghum by Region as Shown in Appendix Table 12.4

| | Required for Maximum Profit Situation | | | | Required for Maximum Yield Situation | | | |
|---|---|---|---|---|---|---|---|---|
| | N | $P_2O_5$ | $K_2O$ | Total | N | $P_2O_5$ | $K_2O$ | Total |
| | | (tons) | | | | (tons) | | |
| United States | | | | | | | | |
| Northeast | NA | NA | NA | NA | NA | NA | NA | NA |
| Southeast | 4,580 | 2,553 | 2,537 | 9,670 | 6,689 | 3,629 | 4,281 | 14,599 |
| Corn Belt | 11,575 | 9,163 | 5,930 | 26,668 | 17,348 | 11,278 | 11,095 | 39,721 |
| Northern Plains | 192,865 | 58,243 | 12,455 | 263,563 | 484,040 | 150,170 | 166,590 | 800,800 |
| Southern Plains | 354,053 | 98,911 | 37,535 | 490,499 | 726,420 | 208,810 | 97,213 | 1,032,443 |
| Arid and Desert | 19,113 | 5,189 | 0 | 24,252 | 45,655 | 15,293 | 0 | 60,948 |
| Western | 28,650 | 955 | 0 | 29,605 | 28,650 | 955 | 0 | 29,605 |

## APPENDIX TABLE 12.5

### ESTIMATED TOTAL CROP PRODUCTION POSSIBILITIES BY CROP AND REGION, NORTH AMERICA—ALL HAY

| | Moisture Limiting | | | Moisture Not Limiting | Actual Production | Acreage |
|---|---|---|---|---|---|---|
| | Without fertilizer | At average rate of application | For maximum profit situation | For maximum phys. production | | |
| | (thou. tons) | (thou. tons) | (thou. tons) | (thou. tons) | (thou. tons) | (thou. acr.) |
| **United States (1966 acr. basis)** | | | | | | |
| Northeast | (insufficient data to provide reliable estimates) | | | | | |
| Southeast | 5,011 | 15,262 | 28,915 | 40,599 | 10,565 | 7,110 |
| Corn Belt | 27,638 | 36,264 | 56,822 | 75,882 | 43,649 | 12,587 |
| Northern Plains* | 12,776 | 20,188 | 20,041 | 40,950 | NA | 11,201 |
| Southern Plains | (insufficient data to provide reliable estimates) | | | | | |
| Arid and Desert† | 4,922 | 7,399 | 13,831 | 20,453 | NA | 3,737 |
| Western‡ | 2,054 | 5,600 | 8,681 | 12,132 | NA | 2,054 |
| **Canada§ (1965 acr. basis)** | | | | | | |
| Maritimes | 730 | 1,448 | 1,986 | NA | 1,081 | 685 |
| Central | 9,615 | 16,130 | 29,160 | 45,920 | 9,588 | 6,515 |
| Prairies | (insufficient data to provide reliable estimates) | | | | | |
| Pacific | (insufficient data to provide reliable estimates) | | | | | |

* Includes irrigated acreage only in Wyoming, and excludes Kansas and Nebraska.
† Includes Colorado, Idaho, Nevada, and Utah only.
‡ Includes Oregon and Washington only.
§ Designated *tame hay* in Canada.

## APPENDIX TABLE 12.5A

Tons of N, P₂O₅, and K₂O Required for Maximum Profit and Maximum Yield Situations for All Hay by Region as Shown in Appendix Table 12.5

|  | Required for Maximum Profit Situation | | | | Required for Maximum Yield Situation | | | |
|---|---|---|---|---|---|---|---|---|
|  | N | P₂O₅ | K₂O | Total | N | P₂O₅ | K₂O | Total |
|  |  | *(tons)* | | |  | *(tons)* | | |
| United States |  |  |  |  |  |  |  |  |
| Northeast | (insufficient data for estimates to be reliable) | | | | | | | |
| Southeast | 373,888 | 244,122 | 402,238 | 1,020,248 | 635,851 | 380,491 | 585,828 | 1,602,170 |
| Corn Belt | 544,106 | 449,907 | 354,921 | 1,348,934 | 769,307 | 553,804 | 717,651 | 2,040,762 |
| Northern Plains | 378,966 | 72,959 | 3,876 | 455,801 | 817,852 | 181,897 | 111,764 | 1,111,513 |
| Southern Plains | (insufficient data for estimates to be reliable) | | | | | | | |
| Arid and Desert | 140,272 | 35,949 | 13,112 | 189,333 | 227,364 | 62,735 | 17,066 | 307,165 |
| Western | 122,755 | 84,765 | 36,796 | 244,316 | 236,368 | 146,530 | 109,825 | 492,723 |
| Canada |  |  |  |  |  |  |  |  |
| Maritimes | 28,750 | 10,950 | 25,980 | 65,680 | NA | NA | NA | NA |
| Central | 204,900 | 195,450 | 334,850 | 735,200 | 683,000 | 411,125 | 72,900 | 1,167,025 |
| Prairies | (insufficient data for estimates to be reliable) | | | | | | | |
| Pacific | (insufficient data for estimates to be reliable) | | | | | | | |

APPENDIX TABLE 12.6

ESTIMATED TOTAL CROP PRODUCTION POSSIBILITIES BY CROP AND REGION, NORTH AMERICA—ALFALFA AND ALFALFA MIXTURES

| | Moisture Limiting | | | Moisture Not Limiting | | |
| --- | --- | --- | --- | --- | --- | --- |
| | Without fertilizer | At average rate of application | For maximum profit situation | For maximum phys. production | Actual Production | Acreage |
| | *(thou. tons)* | *(thou. tons)* | *(thou. tons)* | *(thou. tons)* | *(thou. tons)* | *(thou. acr.)* |
| United States (1966 acr. basis) | | | | | | |
| Northeast | 3,981 | 7,248 | 10,663 | 13,861 | 5,610 | 2,552 |
| Southeast | 862 | 1,923 | 3,488 | 4,271 | 1,528 | 731 |
| Corn Belt | 26,277 | 36,671 | 57,098 | 76,084 | 31,336 | 11,876 |
| Northern Plains* | 14,286 | 18,976 | 23,630 | 51,796 | NA | 8,065 |
| Southern Plains | 2,082 | 2,680 | 2,917 | 6,580 | 1,997 | 825 |
| Arid and Desert | 6,000 | 10,315 | 15,981 | 23,275 | 8,374 | 2,762 |
| Western | 5,486 | 10,621 | 20,584 | 22,760 | 8,969 | 2,063 |
| Canada (1966 acr. basis) | | | | | | |
| Maritimes† | 0 | 83 | 109 | 127 | NA | 25 |
| Central | 3,949 | 6,201 | 10,520 | 13,142 | NA | 2,067 |
| Prairies | (insufficient data to provide reliable estimates) | | | | | |
| Pacific | (insufficient data to provide reliable estimates) | | | | | |
| Mexico | (insufficient data to provide reliable estimates) | | | | | |

* Includes irrigated acreage only in Wyoming.
† Includes New Brunswick and Prince Edward Island only.

APPENDIX TABLE 12.6A

Tons of N, $P_2O_5$ and $K_2O$ Required for Maximum Profit and Maximum Yield Situations for Alfalfa and Alfalfa Mixtures by Region as Shown in Appendix Table 12.6

| | Required for Maximum Profit Situation | | | | Required for Maximum Yield Situation | | | |
|---|---|---|---|---|---|---|---|---|
| | N | $P_2O_5$ | $K_2O$ | Total | N | $P_2O_5$ | $K_2O$ | Total |
| | | (tons) | | | | (tons) | | |
| United States | | | | | | | | |
| Northeast | 0 | 88,451 | 163,601 | 252,052 | 0 | 109,278 | 202,620 | 311,898 |
| Southeast | 767 | 28,682 | 58,482 | 87,931 | 449 | 43,654 | 75,334 | 119,437 |
| Corn Belt | 59,280 | 416,340 | 711,340 | 1,186,960 | 65,576 | 551,798 | 1,015,316 | 1,632,690 |
| Northern Plains | 0 | 175,705 | 54,187 | 229,892 | 86,060 | 284,345 | 180,480 | 550,885 |
| Southern Plains | 4,025 | 24,423 | 24,750 | 53,198 | 8,023 | 40,823 | 41,150 | 89,996 |
| Arid and Desert | 0 | 95,825 | 3,820 | 99,645 | 1,000 | 145,570 | 3,820 | 150,390 |
| Western | 5,290 | 40,735 | 6,273 | 52,298 | 39,675 | 85,240 | 33,705 | 158,620 |
| Canada | | | | | | | | |
| Maritimes | 394 | 789 | 2,366 | 3,549 | 394 | 1,007 | 2,608 | 4,009 |
| Central | 925 | 68,023 | 156,875 | 225,823 | 1,850 | 112,600 | 272,250 | 386,700 |
| Prairies | (insufficient data for estimates to be reliable) | | | | | | | |
| Pacific | (insufficient data for estimates to be reliable) | | | | | | | |

# CHAPTER THIRTEEN

# Implications of Free Trade in Forest Products

## JAMES G. YOHO

THE ESTABLISHMENT of a North American free trade area in forest products would probably affect the world trade picture for this large class of soil-derived products. Likewise, such an act could have a bearing on land-use patterns throughout the world, especially the long-run situation in North America.

In considering such a broad and involved problem, it is necessary to think of the trade situation for North American forest products in a worldwide context since, by accounting for 36 percent of the total volume, this continent is already the world's largest exporter of such products. North America also ranks high as an importer of forest products, accounting for one-fourth of the world's total.[1] Moreover, the flow of forest products within the region between the United States and Can-

---

JAMES G. YOHO, School of Forestry, Duke University. In the preparation of this chapter the author is particularly indebted to three people: Mr. F. L. C. Reed, Research Economist, Hedlin Menzies and Associates, Ltd., Vancouver, British Columbia; Dr. Dwight Hair, Division of Forest Economics and Marketing Research, Forest Service, USDA, Washington, D.C.; and Mr. Sperry Lea, American Director of Research, The Canadian-American Committee, National Planning Association, Washington, D.C. They took time from busy schedules to provide him with ideas and information from published and unpublished sources. Of course, they are not responsible for the interpretations or conclusions expressed in this chapter.

[1] Includes trade among the individual nations within this continent as well as trade between North America and areas outside this continent.

ada now accounts for more than one-fifth of the trade in forest products among all nations, including individual EFTA and EEC countries. And beyond this, one must also keep in mind the fact that North American forest products trade has been growing at a rapid rate even without the advantages of a free trade area. For example, during the 1958–64 period exports of forest products, mainly from Canada, increased in volume (physical volume) by 50 percent while regional imports increased by 28 percent.

Historically, trade in forest products has been a substantial source of foreign exchange for many nations but it is seldom realized that remarkable advances along these lines have been made recently by several regions of the world. Within the last decade, North America's net earnings from trade in forest products more than doubled, reaching $625 million in 1964.[2] During the same period, the Soviet Union's net forest export balance quadrupled, amounting to $430 million in 1964. During the same period, Africa emerged as the third leading earner of foreign exchange from forest products. Its net annual earnings from that source had climbed to $170 million by 1964, an increase of seventeenfold within the decade.

On the basis of this brief review of the North American and world situations, it is evident that international trade in forest products involves large, complex, and dynamic forces. Moreover, North America's deep involvement in the total world trade picture for forest products would tend to multiply the number and the impact of the interactions likely to flow from the establishment of a free trade area for such products on this continent. Accordingly, it seems inescapable that in addition to forestry, other forms of land-use activity would be influenced both directly and indirectly in the process.

## BEHIND THE ANALYTICAL DIFFICULTIES

Thus far I have been pointing to only the broad and more obvious factors that one would have to weigh in considering the probable influences on land use by free trade on a continental scale in any soil-derived product. Perhaps of greater importance, in terms of making a meaningful analysis in the case of forest products, are some of the unique aspects of forestry as a land-use activity. One of these is the fact that forest production can

---

[2] All monetary values stated in this chapter are in U.S. dollars.

range from a very intensive type of land use to an extremely extensive one in the production of identical raw timber products. Industrial forests, for instance, offer a good example of the intensive situation. They usually represent large direct per-acre outlays of capital plus large accumulations of inventory, potentially salable long before the crop is finally harvested. On the other hand, there are two typical extensive situations. One is the virgin forest which is just beyond economic reach. But of course in some cases, virgin forests have been withheld from the market for various reasons at considerable cost; thus in a few instances they may represent very intensive investments. The other extensive land-use situation is the involuntarily grown second-growth forest, produced with no direct outlay of capital except for minimal holding costs which likely would have been incurred regardless of the land use.

The relevant point here rests with the unique economic character of forestry. The essence of it is this: Forest products find their way into the normal channels of trade in varying proportions from the whole range of forest land-use intensity circumstances. This has the effect of extending the short run or market supply period for a large share of the timber supply over many years. Thus it follows that with the high proportion of extensive-use forests in North America and throughout much of the world, particularly in the underdeveloped regions, price changes for forest products (except for short-term fluctuations) tend to be gradual; hence ordinary price signals are weak in calling for intensive production or in serving as a positive force sufficient to encourage land-use adjustments toward intensive forestry.

Ironically one is led to the same general conclusion regarding the probable weakness of price signals in encouraging land-use adjustments toward forestry, under assumptions of the presence of nothing but intensive forestry with the total exclusion of extensive forestry. This follows because even under intensive forestry, with planned harvest rotations, a large share of the accumulated inventory is likely to be marketable at any given time. Thus even under idealized technical forestry, large inventory accumulations would tend to impose a dampening effect of long duration on the price increases which ordinarily would arise from decreases in the long-run supply. Accordingly, under both the actual and hypothetically extreme situations, one is led to the conclusion that, given markets which are essentially perfectly competitive, price-induced long-run investments in forestry seem very unlikely on a scale sufficient to drastically reduce the area available for agriculture.

But historically, timber growing as an economic activity has been characterized by a greater degree of direct government participation than agriculture. This participation and the policies upon which it has been based have tended, in virtually all nations, to limit market and short-run supply responses in accordance with biologically derived long-run supply capabilities which encompass both the intensive and extensive forest situations. This is quite obviously the case in respect to the prevailing management policies on U.S. National Forests. On these forests have been established rather inflexible harvesting schedules, calling for sustained annual harvests. These schedules are based largely on technical forestry considerations and hence are tied essentially to the long-term growth capacity of the land. The timber harvest from Canadian forests is generally controlled by long-term contracts which give a single private operator exclusive rights to a large area. In contrast, the U.S. system is essentially based on short-term sales contracts which cover a relatively small cutting area and are allocated on a competitive bid basis.[3]

Some idea of the impact of such government timber sales policies on the short-run supply curve for North American timber can be gleaned from the portion of the total forest inventory under direct public control. In the United States, for example, 65 percent of the softwood (the main wood of commerce) sawtimber volume is in public ownership; 54 percent actually in National Forests. In Canada 94 percent of all forest land is in public ownership, resting almost entirely with the several provincial governments. In Mexico roughly half of the forest is in public ownership, about the same as the proportion so owned in Europe exclusive of the Soviet Union. Thus one can see that the share of forest under direct public control is generally high. Regardless of the system through which government regulation is exercised over these forests, the impact on supply resulting from timber sales policies based on sustained annual fairly uniform harvests is likely to be significant in the direction of forcing a fusion of the market, short-run and long-run supply curves.

Another circumstance which makes land-use adjustments in

---

[3] This policy, particularly as it obtains to the old-growth forests of the Northwest, has been the subject of considerable debate between federal foresters and the timber-processing industries. The issue centers on the appropriate rate for reducing the accumulated forest capital and the proper but lower level of forest capital that should be maintained on the new second-growth forests.

forestry in response to ordinary and direct economic forces difficult to predict is the multiplicity of enterprises often carried on simultaneously with timber production. The conduct of nontimber enterprises on land ordinarily classed as productive forest is more common under extensive than under intensive forest use. Today, under extensive forest use, it is not uncommon for the forest enterprise to be secondary or even incidental to other uses. Yet in the aggregate, a great deal of timber is currently harvested from such lands, and it is likely to increase in the future since there appears to be a strong trend toward the ascendancy of nontimber enterprises on more and more of the extensive forest-use areas in the developed countries. Incidentally, a problem of serious concern to forestry planners in such countries, with respect to both government and private holdings, is the extent to which such lands can be counted on for future timber production.

Another current trend in North American forest land use is toward the operation of nontimber enterprises in combination with intensive forestry. At this juncture, such a management policy, known in forestry circles as "multiple-use management" is becoming increasingly popular, particularly on public lands.[4] This policy appears to be predicated on the implicit assumption that the combination of another land-use enterprise with timber production increases returns to land plus capital as well as to land alone. At the moment one would be hard pressed either to prove or disprove this assumption though justification of the commitment of large investments of public funds depends on its validity. Probably the weakest link in attempting an objective analysis of this question rests with the difficulty of developing valid demand schedules for the extra-market goods and services which are the usual output of the nontimber enterprise under public multiple-use management.

## FOREST VERSUS AGRICULTURAL LAND USE

Although the most obvious part of the land-use problem is the relationship between forestry and agriculture, I have deliberately confined this discussion to the forestry sector for good reason. The simple fact is that one could develop strong arguments on the basis of historical evidence that forestry as a land-use activity

[4] In the United States "multiple-use management" is actually specified by law (Multiple-use Act of 1960) as the policy objective for federally owned forests.

is likely to have very little limiting influence on agricultural land use under seemingly realistic price assumptions for timber products. Obviously the admission that forest land use will always remain relegated to the "effect" rather than the "causal" role in the broad agricultural land-use picture would leave little to say on the subject. But although there may be considerable general justification for such an admission, it greatly oversimplifies the story. Moreover, expectations of the future, based on unimaginative extrapolations of the past, though easy to quantify, frequently fail to recognize significant changes already under way and fall short on many other counts as well.

It would be very difficult to dispute the assertion that as a land-use activity, forestry has offered agriculture little in the way of effective competition here in North America. Our land-use history has generally followed the classic example developed by the early land economists. Forestry and grazing have been pushed farther and farther into the more remote areas or to the low-rent soils of less isolated areas; often such areas were simply the low-rent sections of individual farms. Of course in this complex evolutionary process, many mistakes were made in estimating agricultural productivity; moreover, changing economic conditions, often caused by the continuous land-use evolution itself, frequently resulted in agricultural lands again reverting to extensive forestry.

Throughout the latter part of this evolutionary period, government forestry programs were frequently active on both land-use adjustment fronts. On one margin attempts were made to keep land in forests, thereby avoiding agricultural failures. At the other margin forestry programs moved into the lee of the adjustment activity, sometimes facilitating the adjustments, sometimes simply filling the void created by agricultural abandonment. In the latter case in recent years, forest industries have been actively establishing land holdings on many parts of the continent. At both margins, the forestry efforts were at first quite extensive; but in recent years there has been a gradually accelerating shift toward more intensive practices. In the case of industrial forest investments, the shift to intensive management was particularly slow in getting started but during recent years it has been taking place at an increasingly accelerated pace. Now it is said that the average input intensity on such properties in the United States exceeds that on public lands which ranked first for many years.

This brief historical sketch of agriculture versus forestry as a land-use activity in North America leads to the question: Can we count on agriculture being able to command land away from forestry with the same ease with which such shifts have taken place in the past? Or, perhaps it would be better to phrase the question this way: Will it be possible to rely on an almost perfectly elastic supply of land from forest use for achieving a significant expansion of North American agriculture? On the basis of several very recent shifts with which I am familiar, I think the answer would have to be "yes."

But at this time these basic corollary questions can be answered only deductively and qualitatively. Moreover one is likely to be led to a somewhat biased picture of the current situation since shifts that actually take place are always more apparent than those which are deferred. Nevertheless one conclusion seems apparent when the many new forces which are emerging at the present are considered: Shifts from forestry to agriculture will be stickier than they have been in the past and they are likely to become increasingly sticky with time and with further expansions in agricultural land use.

Under past and present product price and factor cost relationships, I think there is little doubt but what most forms of agriculture would usually net a higher return per acre than forestry. But since individual and total factor input requirements are quite different for the two activities, and since future supplies of these factors are likely to vary considerably from past supplies, future per-acre profitability relationships are likely to differ considerably from those experienced in the past with *ceteris paribus* assumptions regarding product prices. Likewise, given the assumption that agriculture will continue to be a highly competitive industry while forestry trends further toward industrial oligopoly in parallel with government monopoly, increased product demands are likely to become capitalized in land values more quickly in agriculture than in forestry, thereby dampening agricultural profits relative to forestry. For these reasons one might expect the rate of return on the average investment per acre in the two activities to differ more under future expansion than is indicated by past experience.

In regard to the supply factors, it should be kept in mind that agriculture probably will continue to be more labor intensive than forestry and hence more likely to be hindered by decreases in labor supply. Also it should be remembered that forestry has adjusted to purchasing labor under ordinary increasing cost conditions while agriculture's labor supply has been more elastic or perhaps even available at decreasing costs during certain periods in many regions. The inference here is to the historical availability of farm children at zero unit cost and their inclination to become farm entrepreneurs whose input service to the enterprise has been largely labor. Of course this situation has been less pronounced in recent years but no doubt its impact will continue to be felt for some time to come.

The possibility of additional agricultural land being supplied from areas now in forest will be very greatly influenced by the physical characteristics of the latter. As pointed out earlier, North America has been experiencing a trial-and-error land-use adjustment for generations. As a result a very large share of the present forest is located on land totally unsuited for most types of farming due to topography and the like. Most of the remaining forest acreage is on land which would be costly to convert to agricultural use, hence it is likely to be unprofitable for all but the most intensive types of farming. Of course changing agricultural technology is responsible for a growing list of exceptions to this generalization. One recent outstanding example is the case of the large bottomland areas of the South, particularly those along the Mississippi River, where vast acreages of farmland, ideal for the use of new types of machinery, have been developed by clearing hardwood forests, followed by drainage. Perhaps the South's sandy coastal plains will become another example if supplemental irrigation and fertilization costs decrease sufficiently to warrant clearing. This will be an interesting case to watch since it could provide a direct large-scale confrontation between established intensive coniferous forestry and potential agricultural use.

As alluded to earlier, many economic and institutional factors have come to the front in recent years which are almost certain to furnish a restrictive influence on the future movement of land from forest to agricultural use. First is the trend toward multiple-product management on more and more forest land. Since this practice presumably adds to forest income, it is likely to deter shifts away from forest use. Also, inasmuch as production of the nontimber commodity is often called for by public policy or statute, transfer of these areas to agriculture may be virtually impossible, while timber growth and perhaps harvesting can be expected to continue on such lands.

The second new force likely to deter a shift from forestry to agriculture is entirely economic. I am thinking now of the numerous industrial investments that have been made in forest lands and timber-processing facilities since World War II. These modern investments are on a much larger scale and are considerably more intensive than ever witnessed previously on this continent. In the United States, industrial forests are usually held in fee simple ownership or leased on a long-term basis from other private owners. In Canada the processing firm ordinarily leases long-term cutting rights and assumes forest management obligations on public lands owned by the provincial governments. These arrangements support multimillion-dollar processing plants and marketing organizations which altogether represent huge sunken investments and thereby provide a private vested interest in forestry never previously experienced. Despite the fact that most estimates place the return before taxes on private investments in forest land, apart from processing, at less than 5 percent, the total industrial complex based on the forest typically earns a considerably higher return. This situation is certain to contribute substantially to the short inelasticity of the supply of new agricultural land available from forest use.

## CURRENT TRADE BARRIERS
## AND THEIR REMOVAL

International trade in forest products involving Canada and the United States presents the analyst with what might be described as both an enigma and a paradox. As a consequence, not a single definitive study has been made of the forest products trade situation which offers substantial help in making precise estimates of the impact of revised trade restrictions.

The paradoxical aspect of the situation can be seen by a very brief description of the contrasting forest products trade patterns. The United States currently is both the world's largest producer of forest products and the largest importer. Canada is the world's largest exporter of forest products and the United States is by far Canada's best customer, having bought about half of Canada's total production in recent years. Canada furnishes the United States with a majority of its imports of forest products. Of course all of these statements gloss over the great variation that exists throughout the diversified array of individual forest-derived commodities which are produced, traded, or consumed.

The enigmatic aspect of the situation rests with the fact that so little is known about either the supply or demand elasticities of individual forest products. This statement applies to both long-run and short-run considerations and also holds with respect to all of the common expressions of elasticity. Moreover, tariff barriers and other trade restrictions on the more common classes of primary forest products between Canada and the United States are already rather nominal, thereby making the impact of their removal even more difficult to anticipate.

With these problems in mind, let us make a brief rundown on the current situation and the prospects under free trade for several major classes of North American forest products. In undertaking this task, it seems advisable to continue to concentrate on the two northern countries since they account for virtually all of the present and most of the potential trade. In this discussion the round logs and bolts as they first come from the forest have been largely disregarded as a trade item. Of course the nature and source of these raw timber products are important in terms of the finished commodities that can be produced from them, but since the unit value of the round raw wood material is usually low, and inasmuch as the weight loss in further manufacture is quite high, it is seldom shipped far. Hence, except for what might be termed specialty items, round wood is usually admitted duty-free in international trade. However, one does encounter occasional export restrictions on round wood products that offer special problems.

It must be admitted that many observers with a strong interest in an individual forest product or a localized situation would quarrel with this light dismissal of the importance of round wood products in international trade. They might argue, for example, that in terms of wood volume, 14 (13.59) percent of North America's exports and 12 (12.36) percent of its imports were in round wood. Moreover they could contend that $69 million out of a net positive continental trade balance of $627 million in forest products is attributable to round wood items. Observers interested in specific situations would add to the argument by mentioning the growing exportation of coniferous sawlogs from Oregon and Washington to Japan. Such shipments totaled 5 million cubic meters in 1965. Or they might cite the growing exportation of pulpwood from Canada which now amounts to 3.3 million cubic meters with most of the recent increases going to Europe.

The above points of view, however, appear to overlook important aspects of the situation. In the case of the log exports to Japan, for example, a large share of the material has been of small diameter for which domestic U.S. markets have been weak.[5] More recently, however, Japanese buyers have been competing actively and successfully for large-size logs. In the case of Canadian pulpwood, shipments to the United States have been declining while those going to Europe have been on the increase. Cursory observation suggests that this increase is in large measure attributable to discriminatory pricing by European processors which results in higher prices for imports than for domestic pulpwood. Hence it would seem that the expansion potential of the export of pulpwood has definite limitations under such circumstances because the high marginal costs of such raw material will soon exert an increasing upward pressure on the importer's average raw material costs. It is quite possible that similar pricing policies prevail in the case of Japanese sawlog imports.

Softwood lumber is the big item in the forest products trade picture between Canada and the United States. The latter's domestic consumption of this commodity in 1965 was 34 (33.8) billion board feet with 5 (4.9) billion board feet having been imported—99 percent of it from Canada.[6] During the period 1963–65, annual Canadian softwood lumber production averaged 9.5 billion board feet of which about two-thirds was exported; three importing areas—the United States, the EEC, and the United Kingdom—bought three-fourths of Canada's export.

Spruce and Douglas fir comprised three-fifths of the board footage of U.S. softwood lumber imports in 1965. They were subject to a tariff duty of 35 cents and $1 per thousand board feet, respectively, which is typical for softwood species. On a weighted basis, taking into account grade and dressed volumes, the ad valorem equivalents on these species were 0.6 percent on the spruce and 1.6 percent on the Douglas fir. On the other hand, Canadian import duty on dressed lumber runs as high as 10 percent while rough unsurfaced material may enter free.

Both countries are now committed to reciprocal free trade for softwood lumber under the recently concluded Kennedy

[5] It should also be noted that U.S. manufacturing costs for supplying the domestic Japanese lumber market by sawing and finishing this material in Oregon or Washington would be disproportionately high due to (a) differences in the basic cost structure between the two countries, and (b) the fact that U.S. manufacturing capacity generally is not designed for, or accustomed to, handling small logs or for producing finished lumber according to foreign standards.

[6] Most of the remaining 1 percent which was imported into the United States in 1965 came from Brazil, Honduras, and Mexico, with the latter furnishing 6 million board feet.

Round which apparently erases the threat of the imposition of unilateral import quotas as sought by many U.S. firms. Based on recent history it seems unlikely that trade flows of softwood lumber will be appreciably affected in either the short or long run by the complete removal of current trade restrictions. This follows because Canadian supply cost advantages with respect to U.S. markets appear to have been attributable to lower shipping costs and less pressure on existing stumpage supplies.[7] Together these seem to outweigh any economies that could be realized from the removal of present trade barriers. The more recent stabilization of Canadian softwood exports to the United States, however, suggests that all costs between the stump and the final market (weighted according to volume shipped) for Douglas fir lumber originating in the two countries are nearly equal.

It is more difficult to generalize about hardwood lumber than about softwood lumber since the former consists of quite a conglomeration of species, each of which is often sought for a particular use. Moreover, trade in hardwood lumber between Canada and the United States has been relatively insignificant compared with the movement of softwood. However, more of a two-way flow has existed in the case of hardwoods. In 1965 Canada exported 151 (151.2) million board feet to the United States while the United States exported 85 (84.9) million board feet to Canada. A very large share of Canada's hardwood imports from the United States was oak while U.S. imports from Canada consisted mainly of beech, birch, and maple. This trade seems to reflect basic supply differences between the two nations and the fact hardwood demand is a composite of the demand for several distinctly different product services which are associated with specific species. Given these circumstances, it is unlikely that removal of all tariffs on hardwoods would have much of an impact on present trade positions despite the fact that such duties are roughly 50 percent higher than on softwoods.

Lumber which has been further manufactured into such commodities as components for prefabrication, whether it be hardwood or softwood, presents quite a different prospect than

---

[7] Contrary to common belief, the approach to stumpage appraisal involving the setting of minimum bid prices by the U.S. Forest Service does not differ basically from that practiced in connection with government cutting contracts in British Columbia, the source of most softwood shipments to the States. However, historically speaking, stumpage prices actually paid have been lower in Canada than in the Pacific Northwest in similar timber types. The longer term sales contracts employed in British Columbia may also contribute to supply cost advantages for Canadian producers although minimum stumpage prices on such sales are subject to periodic readjustment.

has just been described for ordinary rough and finished lumber. This vast array of manufactured or partially manufactured forest products, which offers many potential advantages to users, has been subjected to tariff rates very often ranging between 15 and 20 percent ad valorem; hence, complete removal of this restriction could have a significant impact on future trade. Since demand for this class of products has been on the increase and inasmuch as the further manufacture performed on such products near the raw material source would lead to freight savings, Canadian manufacturers, who generally are located farther from large U.S. markets than American producers, should experience the largest relative gains unless offset by higher unit rates on the processed material.

Plywood presents still a different story. Both Canadian and U.S. tariffs on softwood plywood have been set at 20 percent ad valorem.[8] These are among the highest rates observed by both countries for a major primary forest product that is produced in large quantities in both nations. Thus the prospects are outstanding for increased trade in this commodity following the removal of such barriers.

United States trade in plywood presents a rather strange picture. The United States produces and consumes half of the world's output of plywood and, along with the United Kingdom, it is also the world's largest importer. Most U.S. imports, however, are of hardwood species, generally from Southeast Asia or Japan, while most of the domestic production is composed of softwoods. Canadian plywood production is roughly one-eighth (12.5 percent) that of the United States with about 20 percent of the total, consisting mostly of softwood, going into export.

At the present there is virtually no trade in softwood plywood between the United States and Canada. In view of the large production and consumption of this commodity in both countries, one is inclined to attribute the lack of trade to the existence of high tariffs. Given the apparent supply advantages that have been enjoyed by Canadian lumber manufacturers[9] and

---

[8] U.S. ad valorem rates on some types of hardwood plywood are as high as 40 percent.

[9] Many authorities assume that the availability of timber of large diameters in British Columbia suitable for plywood manufacture gives Canada a greater supply advantage in plywood than in lumber. Other authorities contend that timber cutting in British Columbia already has resulted in a reduction of average log size to such an extent that neither country has an advantage in that respect. Others go beyond this with the opinion that there is a disproportionately high share of low-grade timber in British Columbia in comparison with the U.S. Pacific Northwest, thus suggesting that the latter holds the future advantage in plywood manufacture.

the arguments set forth above regarding the transportation of processed wood products, one is forced to conclude that a strong southbound flow would soon develop between the two nations if all trade restrictions were removed. However, this greatly oversimplifies the picture since Canada has tended to specialize in exterior grades while the United States has devoted most of its production to interior grades. Such a division of comparative advantages is also suggested by the present price picture for the two grades.

Turning now to the other major class of timber products—paper and paper products—we find perhaps an even greater array of commodities than in the case of wood products. Variations in unit value and effective ad valorem tariff rates are easily as great within the paper group as within the wood group. In terms of value, wood pulp and paper products, exclusive of pulpwood, account for half (50.5 percent) of the world's trade in forest products. In the case of North America, wood pulp and paper products account for approximately two and a half times (2.6 times) as much export value as wood and wood products. This doubtless reflects the decided advantage in industrial capacity and capital availability which now exists on this continent—an advantage which could pay off handsomely over the next couple of decades in the area of forest products. This follows because world consumption of paper products, which per capita is now considerably below that in North America, is expected to rise significantly with anticipated improvements in economic well being.

Wood chips, usually derived from the wastes of various wood-manufacturing processes, have been providing an increasingly larger share of the raw material for North American wood pulp manufacture. In the United States, for example, this source increased from 6 percent to 21 percent of the domestic raw material supply for the wood pulp industry during the 10-year period between 1952 and 1962. This apparently has been an important factor in stabilizing the raw material costs of the industry. Paralleling the trend just described, there have been large increases in the flow of wood chips from Canada to the United States. This, in turn, has paralleled the development of the sawmill industry in British Columbia.

Since almost all wood chips have been produced as a by-product to wood manufacture, long-term supply has been very elastic and price has been determined largely by user policy and the supply of competing materials. Currently the wood pulp industry is experiencing a very rapid growth in British Columbia, and thus it may be expected to provide an attractive local market for wood chips which probably will be sufficient to dampen further increases in this flow to the United States.

Both Canada and the United States are large exporters of wood pulp.[10] The United States is also a large net importer of wood pulp, importing over twice (2.2 times) as much tonnage as it exports; nevertheless, imports supply only 5 percent of U.S. wood pulp consumption. Nearly 90 percent of U.S. imports come from Canada, most of the balance from Scandinavia. Canada, in contrast, imports almost no wood pulp while sending over four-fifths (80.1 percent) of its export to its southern neighbor. Though U.S. exports of wood pulp have declined recently, Canada's exports across its southern border have grown at a rate of about 4 percent per annum, and most observers seem inclined to expect that this trend will continue as U.S. consumption continues to expand and as Canada continues to expand its productive capacity.

The establishment of a free trade area will have no direct effect on the movement of wood pulp between Canada and the United States since it is now a duty-free item. The advent of free trade in paper products, however, could have considerable indirect effect on wood pulp movement if it eventually results in more paper manufacturing in Canada nearer the raw material source. The prospects of this are discussed below.

Newsprint is the only major paper item that currently passes duty-free between Canada and the United States, hence presumably it would be little affected, unless indirectly, by the establishment of a free trade area. Over four-fifths (85 percent) of Canada's newsprint production already moves to U.S. markets and about three-fourths (74 percent) of U.S. consumption comes from Canada.

The tariff schedules list hundreds of paper products which bear a wide range of rates. The U.S. rates, for example, range from about 5 percent to 60 percent ad valorem but generally vary between 10 percent and 30 percent. No doubt, removal of

---

[10] Wood pulp consists of several different types of pulp made by several different processes. Though, in general, world and North American wood pulp consumption have both enjoyed a phenomenal and rather constant long-term growth, production of a few types has remained rather constant. This is attributable to the demand situation for the various final products and to the fact that newer and more efficient processes have been developed which are capable of making effective use of whatever raw wood material is most readily available.

tariff barriers on all paper products would set off a chain of complex adjustments which we will not explore in detail.

Actually, the relative comparative advantages held by either Canadian or U.S. producers for each separate class of paper products is not well understood, but it may be in order to venture a few general observations. Under open market conditions the manufacture of specialty paper products and highly processed papers tends to be market oriented. On the other hand, products such as newsprint, which require little processing and which can be mass produced for shipment to a few large consuming centers, tend to be produced near the source of wood pulp. This would lead one to assume that under a free trade arrangement, there would be a long-run tendency for the United States, with its large concentrated consumer markets, to specialize in fine and highly processed papers while Canada's smaller population and large forest resource would lead it to specialize in those products that require less intensive processing and which can be shipped in bulk quantities.

## SUMMARY AND CONCLUSIONS

Following the establishment of a free trade area for forest products, one would assume that the ensuing tariff reductions would result in a decrease in the market price and probably an increase in the consumption of the affected commodities in the importing country. Thus one important question is: How much is consumption likely to increase as a result of the expected decrease in price? From the production point of view the one most important question is: To what extent will the costs of production be influenced as output is increased in order to take advantage of the expanded market opportunities? Unfortunately, at the present in the case of forest products, we are poorly prepared to answer these and related questions as they pertain to the short run, to say nothing of the long run. We are probably in an even poorer position for estimating the short- or long-run land-use adjustments that are likely to result from shifts in forest products trade and production. Despite these handicaps it would seem to be the responsibility of this chapter to go a little beyond the judgments already ventured for individual forest products and set forth a few speculative forecasts of the North American forest economy under free trade conditions.

Assuming a continuation of past trends in economic growth, it is unlikely that significant decreases would occur in the real prices of North American primary timber products. Instead, we would probably experience a short-term stabilization of most wood products prices before these prices again resume their long-term upward trend. Lumber prices would follow this same pattern except that the eventual upward trend may be more pronounced. For the various commodities which are made directly from wood, past consumption trends are likely to continue without being influenced significantly.

Total consumption of lumber in North America would probably remain more or less stable or increase modestly while per capita consumption would continue its downward trend but perhaps at a slower rate. The opposite would be the case with prefabricated and panel products.

In the case of lumber, lumber-derived products, and plywood there has been a great deal of substitution of one of these wood products for the other. This, considered in the light of the substitution of other materials for wood, further complicates the difficulty of estimating future consumption rates for these classes of wood products.

Paper and paper products prices would likely continue to maintain their relative stability. Ultimately, however, the real prices of paper products may be influenced upward by world demands originating largely outside the continent. A long-term gradual upward trend in per capita consumption of paper products would likely be experienced for an indefinite period with total consumption almost certain to increase when one also takes into account probable population growth.

In the aggregate, the total volume of industrial timber-derived products consumed and produced in North America would likely continue to exhibit a modest upward trend.

Under the assumptions of free trade, it is also unlikely that any sudden drastic shifts in production from one North American country to another would occur. The most likely exception would be the production of softwood plywood which many authorities believe would have a tendency to shift to Canada as new capacity is added. However, as pointed out previously, it is also quite possible that most of the shifts in softwood plywood output would be toward specialization in exterior grades in Canada and interior grades in the United States.

Another area of possible sudden shift would be that of certain paper products (not paper in general). United States producers could gain a temporary advantage in Canadian markets for a few such products.

Lumber production would probably continue to decline modestly in the United States while paper production would likely continue upward but perhaps at a slower rate than in the past. On the other hand, Canadian lumber output could be expected to continue upward but more gradually than in the past. Canadian shipments of pulp and paper products (excepting fine papers) to the United States would likely increase modestly, but not nearly so significantly as increases in Canadian production, much of which could be expected to go into world trade.

This export of paper products from North America to areas overseas would likely continue to grow despite establishment of a continental free trade area here. Lumber, however, would be more likely to encounter stiff competition from the Soviet Union and thus would have a tendency to remain confined to North American markets. The Canadian plywood industry would likely continue to grow with respect to world trade while supplying its share of the significant increases which are likely to occur in the North American market.

What I have in effect been suggesting here is that, for quite some time in the future under free trade arrangements, we could expect the large forest areas of Canada to furnish at least moderate increases in output though they may be operated under extensive forestry methods.[11] It has been estimated by some observers that under such practices, Canada could conceivably triple its present output without exceeding the long-term biological capacity of its forests. But it is likely that a large share of any increment of this size will be found to lie beyond the extensive economic margin. Long-range thoughts about intensive forestry, on the other hand, must take into account the fact that the long-run inherent per-acre productivity of most Canadian forests is lower than for U.S. forests.

But how the extensive is likely to balance against the intensive in the long run offers interesting prospects for speculation. The relative outlook for these two forces holds most of the explanation for the North American land-use adjustments that can be expected as an aftermath of the establishment of a free trade area. And judging by a recent example, we may not be talking about the distant future. Within the last five years, a large Canadian firm turned down long-term cutting rights on a large area of virgin forest in British Columbia in favor of investing

---

[11] Many Canadian forests are presently operated under intensive methods and such practices are likely to spread. Nevertheless, the total area involved represents only a small share of the total forest.

heavily in intensive forestry operations in second-growth forests in Alabama.

In bringing to a close this inconclusive discussion of a very broad and difficult subject, I should reemphasize that many unknowns exist between the marketing of the final products of the forest and the standing timber from which such commodities are produced. The unknowns are multiplied many times over if the dimensions of the problem are extended to reach from future forest-products markets to the land required for long periods to produce the standing timber likely to be consumed in such markets. The unknowns grow to even more astronomical proportions when one tries to take into account the forces generated by the establishment of a free trade area between two or more large timber producing and consuming nations.

Stated as succinctly as possible, what is lacking is adequate knowledge about the supply and demand elasticities for forest products including standing timber. Very little research has been done on the subject of timber supply elasticity while the research that has been done into the elasticity of demand for forest products has been generally inconclusive. Most of the large-scale timber supply studies have estimated short-run supply simply as a physical stock and long-run supply in terms of biological growth capacity. On the demand side, a few soundly conceived studies have been undertaken but the results have been disappointing and somewhat conflicting. Their main contribution to date has been to point to the complexity of the problem and hence the need for a great deal more research effort.

Virtually all of the large national planning studies completed to date in forestry have unknowingly or by necessity greatly oversimplified the development of economic supply and demand models. Most of these studies have simply resorted to estimates of future consumption and production of forest products. That is to say, they have estimated the points of intersection of future timber supply and demand schedules without first having estimated the magnitude and shape of the curves. And as the critics have argued, the points of intersection between future timber supply and demand curves arrived at in this conceptually deficient manner have often implied very improbable supply and demand relationships, such as, for example, a perfectly elastic supply coupled with a highly inelastic and increasing demand.

But this was not meant to be a general critique on research in forest economics. I simply wanted to emphasize the fact that we are in very poor shape for estimating the impact of the removal of North American trade barriers on the continent's forest economy, much less its impact on agricultural land use.

One irrefutable conclusion regarding North American forestry emerges quite clearly. There has been a growing interdependence between Canada and the United States in the forest resource and forest products areas even though the complete removal of all trade barriers may be many years in the future. This strongly suggests that North America should be considered a single region for timber resource evaluations and planning.

This idea, most recently put forward by Zivnuska, is not new. At one time a cooperative study involving Canada and the United States was almost a reality but delays led to the plan being tabled. Since that time independent appraisals have been undertaken by each nation and new unilateral efforts are in the offing. In view of the evidence in favor of cooperative forest resource analysis and planning, one might logically question whether it is any longer possible for either nation to conduct a meaningful comprehensive forest resource analysis alone.

## REFERENCES

Algvere, Karl Viktor, *Forest Economy of the U.S.S.R.—An Analysis of Soviet Competitive Potentialities,* Royal College of Forestry, Stockholm, 1966, 449 pp., illus.

Anderson, Stuart, *Statement on Behalf of the Province of Alberta,* Natl. Forestry Conf., Montebello, Quebec, Feb. 21–24, 1966, 14 pp., mimeo.

Anonymous, *Statement on Behalf of the Province of Alberta,* Natl. Forestry Conf., Montebello, Quebec, Feb. 21–24, 1966, 3 pp., mimeo.

———, *The Pulp and Paper Industry of British Columbia,* 2nd Ed., Indus. Dev. Dept., B.C. Hydro and Power Authority, Vancouver, Canada, Oct. 1966, 68 pp.

———, *The Power of British Columbia,* Indus. Dev. Dept., B.C. Hydro and Power Authority, Vancouver, Canada, 1967, 27 pp., illus.

Boutin, Fernand, *Statement on Behalf of the Province of Quebec,* Natl. Forestry Conf., Montebello, Quebec, Feb. 21–24, 1966, 9 pp., mimeo.

Brooks, Lloyd, and H. K. Eidsvik, *Multiple Uses—Multiple Use of Forest Lands and the Year 2000,* Natl. Forestry Conf., Montebello, Quebec, Feb. 21–24, 1966, 17 pp., mimeo.

Brown, K. B., *Statement on Behalf of the Province of New Brunswick,* Natl. Forestry Conf., Montebello, Quebec, Feb. 21–24, 1966, 2 pp., mimeo.

Callahan, John C., *Food, Fibre and Hardwood Forestry Relatinships in the U.S.—With Emphasis on the Alluvial Valley of the Mississippi River,* prepared for the Natl. Adv. Comm. on Food and Fiber, Washington, D.C., Feb. 1967, 118 pp., illus.

Committee on Commerce–United States Senate, *The United States and World Trade,* GPO, Washington, D.C., 1961, 309 pp., illus.

Creighton, G. W. I., *Statement on Behalf of the Province of Nova Scotia,* Natl. Forestry Conf., Montebello, Quebec, Feb. 21–24, 1966, 2 pp., mimeo.

DeGrace, R. F., *Lumber and Plywood–The Effect of Standards on the World Position of Canadian Lumber and Plywood,* Natl. Forestry Conf., Montebello, Quebec, Feb. 21–24, 1966, 15 pp., mimeo.

Departments of Agriculture, Commerce, and the Interior, *Report of Hardwood Timber Conservation Committee,* Apr. 1967, 19 pp., illus.

Department of Forestry of Canada, *Summaries and Conclusions,* Natl. Forestry Conf., Montebello, Quebec, Feb. 21–24, 1966, 43 pp.

deVos, A., *Multiple Uses–Outdoor Recreation on Forested Land,* Natl. Forestry Conf., Montebello, Quebec, Feb. 21–24, 1966, 15 pp., mimeo.

Drysdale, D. P., *Statement on Behalf of the Province of Ontario,* Natl. Forestry Conf., Montebello, Quebec, Feb. 21–24, 1966, 10 pp., mimeo.

Food and Agriculture Organization of the United Nations, *Timber Trends and Prospects in the Asia-Pacific Region,* UN Pub., 1961, 224 pp., illus.

——, *World Forest Inventory,* UN Pub., 1963, 113 pp.

——, *European Trends and Prospects–A New Appraisal 1950–75,* UN Pub., 1964, 233 pp., illus.

——, *Yearbook of Forest Products Statistics,* UN Pub., 1966, 144 pp.

Gaudet, J. F., *Statement on Behalf of the Province of Prince Edward Island,* Natl. Forestry Conf., Montebello, Quebec, Feb. 21–24, 1966, 3 pp., mimeo.

Guttenberg, Sam, *Converting Forest Resource Statistics to Timber Supply,* Proceedings, Seventh Conf. on Southern Indus. Forest Management, pp. 46–51, Duke Univ., Durham, N.C., 1967.

Hair, D., and A. H. Ulrich, *The Demand and Price Situation for Forest Products–1966,* USDA Misc. Pub. 1045, Jan. 1967, 65 pp.

Haviland, W. E., I. B. Chenoweth, and E. T. Owens, *Fibre–Demand for Canada's Wood Fibre in 1975 and 2000,* Natl. Forestry Conf., Montebello, Quebec, Feb. 21–24, 1966, 21 pp., mimeo.

Holland, I. I., "Foreign Trade in Forest Products From the Point of View of an Importing Country: the United States," *Jour. Forestry* 60(8):538–45, Aug. 1962.

Lea, Sperry, *The U.S. Softwood Lumber Situation in a Canadian-American Perspective,* Canadian-American Comm., undated, 52 pp.

Mahood, Ian, and F. Leslie C. Reed, *Lumber and Plywood–Canada's Place in World Markets for Lumber and Plywood in 1975 and 2000,* Natl. Forestry Conf., Montebello, Quebec, Feb. 21–24, 1966, 53 pp., mimeo.

McKinnon, F. S., *Statement on Behalf of the Province of British Columbia,* Natl. Forestry Conf., Montebello, Quebec, Feb. 21–24, 1966, 2 pp., mimeo.

McMullen, D. N., *Multiple Uses–Forest Effect on Water Yield in Ontario,* Natl. Forestry Conf., Montebello, Quebec, Feb. 21–24, 1966, 12 pp., mimeo.

Naysmith, J. K., *A Statement Relating to the Yukon and Northwest Territories*, Natl. Forestry Conf., Montebello, Quebec, Feb. 21–24, 1966, 4 pp., mimeo.

Newport, Carl A., *The Outlook for Production of Lumber and Other Products in British Columbia and Prospective Trends in Shipments of these Products to the United States for the Period 1962–2000*, Pacific Northwest Forest and Range Exp. Sta., Portland, Ore., Oct. 1963, 84 pp., illus.

Parks, W. R., *Statement on Behalf of the Province of Saskatchewan*, Natl. Forestry Conf., Montebello, Quebec, Feb. 21–24, 1966, 2 pp., mimeo.

Passmore, R. C., *Multiple Uses—Wildlife in Canada's Forests*, Natl. Forestry Conf., Montebello, Quebec, Feb. 21–24, 1966, 14 pp., mimeo.

Peters, Stuart S., *Statement on Behalf of the Province of Newfoundland*, Natl. Forestry Conf., Montebello, Quebec, Feb. 21–24, 1966, 3 pp., mimeo.

Reed, F. Leslie C., *Elasticity of Demand for Wood Products*, Conf. of Western Forest Econ., Welches, Ore., Apr. 20–21, 1966, 16 pp.

Rouseau, L. Z., "Federal and Provincial Forest Policies in Canada," *The Forest Chronicle* 43(1):21–23, Mar. 1967.

Row, C., "Canadians Push Lumber Sales in U.S. Markets," *Southern Lumberman* 204(2542):27–29, Mar. 1, 1962.

U.S. Forest Service, *Timber Trends in the United States*, GPO, Washington, D.C., Forest Res. Rept. 17, 1965, 235 pp., illus.

U.S. Tariff Commission, *Summaries of Trade and Tariff Information*, GPO, TC Pub. 201, Vol. I, "Wood and Related Products I," Washington, D.C., 1967, 23 pp., illus.

————, *Tariff Schedules for Forest Products Entering the U.S.—Schedule 2—Wood and Paper; Printed Matter*, GPO, Washington, D.C., 1967, pp. 88–116.

Westoby, J. C., *World Forest Development Markets, Men and Methods*, Univ. of British Columbia, Vancouver, Canada, 1965, 16 pp.

Wilson, D. A., *Wood Products—The Supply of Timber from Canadian Forests*, Natl. Forestry Conf., Montebello, Quebec, Feb. 21–24, 1966, 34 pp., mimeo.

Zivnuska, John A., *U.S. Timber Resources in a World Economy*, The Johns Hopkins Press, Baltimore, 1967, 140 pp.

# CHAPTER FOURTEEN

# Capital and Management

## C. LEROY QUANCE and ODELL L. WALKER

GIVEN the necessary institutional arrangements, benefits from a North American Agricultural Common Market could arise from free reallocation of agricultural inputs. In modern agriculture, the major input is a set composed of different forms of nonland capital. And the management input receives emphasis because it is necessary for efficient use of sophisticated capital items.

The major issues of interest in evaluating the common market proposal with respect to capital and management inputs are implied in the following questions:

1. What are the present total and relative supplies of capital and management in the three North American countries?
2. What are the productivities and adjustment potentials of important capital inputs?
3. How would the productivity and use of capital and management be affected, assuming free resource mobility?

The issues center on (a) whether differences in amounts and productivities of capital and management exist as a necessary

C. LEROY QUANCE, Farm Production Economics Division, United States Department of Agriculture, Oklahoma State University; ODELL L. WALKER, Department of Agricultural Economics and the Graduate College, Oklahoma State University.

condition for increases in agricultural production to result from reallocating resources in and among the three countries and (b) whether potential effects on consumers, resource owners, and resource users would be acceptable to society in the three countries. Examination of data and economic theory bearing on these points is the central aim of this chapter.

## HISTORICAL PERSPECTIVE

The end of World War II marked the beginning of a new era in North American agriculture. The substitution of capital for labor in farm production received new impetus with wartime savings and technology; the substitution of mechanical power for horsepower, which began during the World War I period, was virtually complete in Canada and the United States; and Mexico began a rapid rate of industrialization (27, p. 2).

By 1943 production inputs in U.S. agriculture rose to a 1949 = 100 index of 116 and have not since greatly exceeded that level (Table 14.1). Farm inputs in Canada peaked at an index of approximately 107 in 1947, gradually declined to a low of 91 in 1957, and to date have not risen to the 1949 = 100 base. Despite this leveling off of farm inputs in the United States and Canada, farm output continued a general increase to a 1965 level of 161 and 132 in Canada and the United States respectively.

Increasing output from a fairly stable bundle of inputs

TABLE 14.1

INDEX NUMBERS OF FARM OUTPUT, INPUTS, AND PRODUCTIVITY, CANADA AND
UNITED STATES, SELECTED PERIODS, AND YEARS 1946–65.

| | Canada* | | | United States† | | |
|---|---|---|---|---|---|---|
| Year | Farm output | Production inputs | Productivity | Farm output | Production inputs | Productivity |
| 1946–50 | 106 | 102 | 104 | 98 | 115 | 85 |
| 1951–55 | 124 | 94 | 131 | 106 | 118 | 90 |
| 1956–60 | 128 | 93 | 138 | 116 | 115 | 101 |
| 1961 | 116 | 93 | 124 | 123 | 116 | 106 |
| 1962 | 144 | 94 | 154 | 124 | 116 | 107 |
| 1963 | 159 | 96 | 166 | 129 | 117 | 110 |
| 1964 | 149 | 97 | 153 | 129 | 118 | 109 |
| 1965 | 161 | 98 | 165 | 132 | 118 | 112 |

* *Canadian Farm Economics*, Vol. 2, No. 1, April 1967, Table 1.
† USDA, *Statistical Bulletin 233*, "Changes in Farm Production and Efficiency, A Summary Report, 1967," June 1967, Table 23. The U.S. data were converted from a 1957–59 = 100 base to a 1949 = 100 base to make the changes in output, inputs, and productivity comparable. However, the absolute levels of output, inputs, and productivity are not comparable.

caused overall productivity, measured as output per unit of input, to increase from 104 in the 1946–50 period to 165 in 1965 for Canadian agriculture and from 85 in 1946–50 to 112 in 1965 for the United States.

Although the total quantity of inputs in the United States and Canada did not change a great deal, the input mix changed significantly, with capital replacing labor on a fairly constant land base. In Canadian agriculture labor decreased from 49 percent of the total inputs in 1946–50 to 30 percent in 1961–65, while machinery and other capital inputs increased from 32 percent in 1946–50 to 47 percent in 1961–65 (3, p. 17). Labor inputs in U.S. agriculture decreased 56 percent from 18,838 million man-hours in 1946 to 7,976 million man-hours in 1965. Purchased inputs increased from an index (1957–59 = 100) of 79 in 1946 to 113 in 1965 for the United States. Thus agriculture in Canada and the United States is changing from a labor intensive to a capital intensive industry. More machinery, fertilizer, improved livestock, insecticides, pesticides, and improved seeds are combined with less labor on a fairly constant land area to produce a greater output.

Total capital is increasing also in Mexican agriculture, but with emphasis on agricultural plant size adjustment rather than capital-labor substitution.[1] Generally all major components of farm inputs, capital, labor, and land have increased in Mexico. Nonland farm capital increased 43 percent from 1950 to 1960 and, as in the United States and Canada, the composition of farm capital is changing in Mexico. Investments in buildings and other fixed capital declined 7.6 percent from 1940 to 1960, livestock capital remained about the same, machinery approximately doubled, and from 1950 to 1960 the use of fertilizer increased almost 14 times (15, p. 103).

From 1950 to 1960 the Mexican farm labor force increased approximately 1.3 million persons at an annual rate of 2.4 percent (15, p. 93). According to the agricultural census, cropland harvested in Mexico increased at an annual rate of 2.0 percent. The increase and changes in the composition of farm inputs in Mexico were associated with a 5.8 percent annual increase in farm output from 1940 to 1950 and 5.0 percent from 1951 to 1960 compared to a 2.8 percent annual increase from 1927 to 1940 (15, p. 82).

In summary, farm managers in North America saw fit to in-

---

[1] Our data on Mexican agriculture cover only through 1960 and in some cases 1962.

crease greatly the amount of capital committed to farm production from World War II to the present. In the United States and Canada the increase in capital was largely offset by decreases in less productive labor and obsolete capital. But in Mexico capital increases were accompanied by increases in land and labor. Nonland capital per unit of harvested land increased 19 percent in Mexico between 1950 and 1960 (15, p. 100). The increase in capital per person employed in agriculture was 15 percent over the same period. Somewhat comparable data for the United States reflect a 45 percent increase in nonland capital per farm and a 37 percent increase in nonland capital per person in agriculture (19, p. 17).

## MANAGEMENT

Measurements of management are heavily intertwined with individual resource productivity measurements. However, relative investments in general and agricultural education and research are indicative of supplies of management. Labor in Mexican agriculture comprised 94 percent of agricultural worker inputs in 1950 and 85 percent in 1960. Approximately 50 percent of labor is illiterate (27, p. 24). There are about 10,000 farm families per agricultural extension professional in Mexico compared to 540 in the United States. Clearly, education is needed to exploit productivity potential.

The budget for five of ten agricultural research agencies in Mexico in the 1960–65 period was about $4 million per year (27). In the same period, the United States spent about $394 million in public research and $460 million on industry research in agriculture. Key questions in evaluating impacts of the common market are: Where will research dollars or pesos be most productive and where will they be spent?

A rapid input of capital, new technology, and managerial talent in Mexico may be a real possibility. The profit incentive already has led to movement of these resources in a package to Mexico and other countries. In most cases the move was to a region or country in which the managerial talent and technology were readily usable, for example, cotton production and ranching in Australia and Mexico. The direct effects on production are substantial and the indirect effect—education—could be spectacular.

The common result of capital increases in Canadian, U.S., and Mexican agriculture is a tremendous capacity to produce food and fiber. The following paragraphs present some of the important causes and impacts of this change on the productivity and composition of capital in North American agriculture.

## USE OF SPECIFIED CAPITAL INPUTS, 1946–64

Figures 14.1 through 14.5 illustrate the increased use of machinery, fertilizer, livestock, feed, and irrigation water over time. From 1946 to 1964, annual machinery depreciation has increased 284 and 394 percent in Canada and the United States respectively, while tractor horsepower in Mexico increased 174 percent from 1950 to 1962. Over the same period livestock purchases increased 332 and 106 percent in Canada and the United

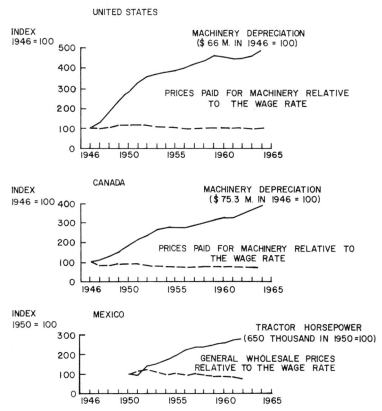

Fig. 14.1—Indexes of machinery inputs and the price of machinery relative to wage rates—United States, Canada, and Mexico, 1946–60.

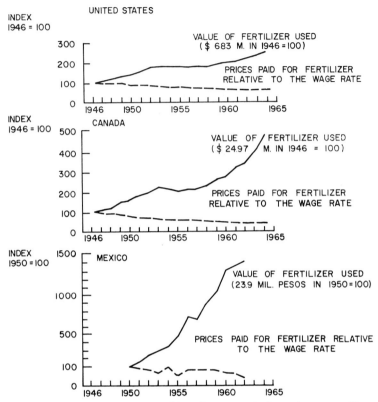

*Fig. 14.2—Indexes of fertilizer inputs and the price of fertilizer relative to wage rates—United States, Canada, and Mexico.*

States respectively, while cattle inventories in Mexico increased 45 percent from 1950 to 1962. Limited availability and rising prices of land, increased irrigation, improved plant varieties, and greater management know-how contributed to 146 and 392 percent increases in fertilizer use in the United States and Canada respectively, while the value of fertilizer nutrients employed in Mexico was 14.4 times larger in 1962 than in 1950. Feed purchases increased 97 percent in Canada and the United States from 1946 to 1964. Irrigation water delivered in Mexico increased 161 percent from 1950 to 1962.

Increased capital use has come about through: (a) generally lower capital prices relative to wage rates, (b) higher productivity of capital relative to labor, (c) substitution of improved technology for older and less productive technology, (d) attempts by

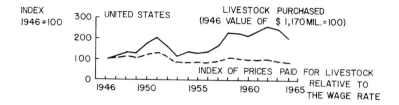

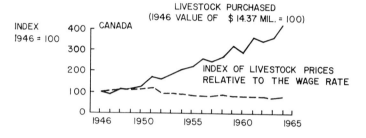

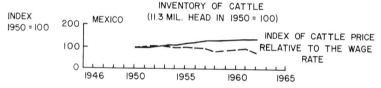

*Fig. 14.3—Indexes of livestock inputs and livestock prices relative to wage rates—United States, Canada, and Mexico.*

individual farmers to increase net income by increasing output, (e) false or short-lived product price expectations, and (f) public and private institutional programs to reallocate resources. All of these forces represent efforts by farm, public, and other institutional managers to obtain optimal allocation of North American resources.

**CAPITAL PRICES**

The impact of generally lower capital prices relative to labor is evident in Figures 14.1 through 14.5.[2] In the United States and Canada, economic growth in the nonfarm sectors has driven nonfarm wages up absolutely and relative to farm wages, resulting in labor migrating from farms to higher paying occupations in the city. As the farm labor supply is decreased, farm wages

---

[2] The nonfarm wage rate was used in determining the relative prices inasmuch as the nonfarm wage more nearly represents the acquisition cost of labor.

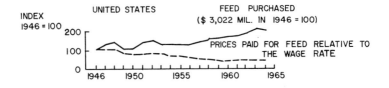

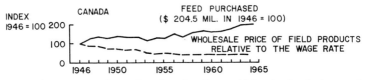

Fig. 14.4—Feed purchased and prices paid for feed relative to the wage rates—United States and Canada, 1946–64.

are forced up and, despite increased prices of capital inputs, the capital-labor price ratio is usually low compared to the relative capital-labor productivity. Thus capital is substituted for labor. But in Mexico nonfarm wages have not greatly exceeded or increased relative to farm wages. Without wage incentives in nonfarm occupations, and with government policies described earlier by Flores, workers have remained in farming and farm labor has remained a more dominant input in Mexican agriculture than in the United States or Canada. With a relatively low cost labor supply, the productivity of capital, although perhaps high, is not high enough compared to its cost relative to labor to induce the capital-labor ratios existing in U.S. and Canadian agriculture.

Data suggest that Mexican agriculture does not have the capital or is not willing to use capital to move out on the production function or shift the MVP curve at the firm level. For example, fertilizer consumption in tons of nutrient elements per 1,000 hectares of arable land in 1960 was 36.2 in the United States and

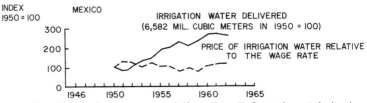

Fig. 14.5—Irrigation water delivered and the price of irrigation water relative to the wage rate—Mexico, 1950–62.

8.6 in Mexico (27, p. 17). Farm studies throughout the United States invariably provide an "optimum plan" calling for increased capital, even though U.S. agriculture is thought to be relatively capital intensive.

## PRODUCTIVITY OF CAPITAL RELATIVE TO LABOR

Despite the continual substitution of capital for labor in the United States and Canada, capital inputs generally remain more productive relative to labor at given price ratios. Quance found this to be the case in studying 28 capital inputs in U.S. agriculture for the 1917–64 period (13, p. 125). For example, during the 1955–64 period, the price of 1,000 hours of labor would purchase the services of three tractors while relative marginal physical products indicated that only .20 tractor services were required to replace 1,000 hours of labor in aggregate farm production with output remaining constant. Thus it has been profitable for farmers to substitute tractors for labor.

## INDIVIDUAL DECISIONS AND MACRO CONSEQUENCES

An individual farm operator sees a perfectly elastic demand for his product and can, at least in the short run, increase his net income by increasing output. With limited land available in a given area, farmers typically increase output by applying more machinery, fertilizer, insecticides, improved livestock, and other capital inputs to a fixed land base. It is only through this type of aggressive innovation that a farmer can maintain a viable enterprise when the macro repercussions of such individual decisions bring about lower farm product prices relative to prices paid for inputs, and bring declining net income per farm relative to nonfarm income.

## FALSE OR SHORT-LIVED PRODUCT PRICE EXPECTATIONS

Farmers must base investment decisions on expected product prices. In estimating ten-, five-, and one-year expected farm product prices in the United States, Lerohl (10, Chap. IV) found that actual product prices have generally been lower than those expected by farmers in periods of declining farm prices. Unrealized price expectations in recent years have undoubtedly caused some overcommitment of farm capital in Canada and Mexico as well as in the United States.

### PUBLIC AND PRIVATE INSTITUTIONS

Public attitudes in North America have long shown a determination to provide low-cost food and fiber for the growing population and to help farmers share in the fruits of economic growth. This attitude is evident in government price support and surplus storage programs, conservation programs, quasi-government agencies such as the Tennessee Valley Authority, laws favoring farm cooperatives, government grades and standards, and Mexico's highway and irrigation projects. These programs, which subsidize the production, processing, and marketing of food and fiber, encourage investment in farm resources.

There is some evidence that private farm capital increases in Mexico are insufficient to exploit potential productivity of public investments, particularly in irrigation (15, p. 94). In general, students of Mexican agriculture conclude that savings and capital accumulation within farms are almost nonexistent (27, p. 20). Internal capital, along with a variety of credit institutions serving agriculture, is well established in the other countries of the proposed common market. Development of comparable credit channels in Mexico is a key step to gaining increases in agricultural production.

From the above summary of capital development in North American agriculture, it appears that farm managers behave as would the "economic man"—changing the input mix in response to generally lower capital prices relative to wage rates. But due to uncertainty and a constantly changing environment, it is not likely that managerial response is the instantaneous, perfect, and final adjustment to a fixed profit-maximizing equilibrium dictated by static economic theory of the firm. In the following section econometric procedures are employed to measure managerial response to the changing environment in North American agriculture and to estimate potential adjustments in the use of capital inputs in a North American Common Market approach to meeting world food needs. We shall examine (a) adjustment behavior of input users and the resulting capital earnings, (b) a measure of managerial performance, and (c) the potential for increasing farm output in North America through increased use of specified capital inputs.

## UTILIZATION, PRODUCTIVITY, SUPPLY, AND POTENTIAL USE OF FARM CAPITAL

Economic theory and the historical behavior of capital input series suggest that Nerlove-type adjustment models[3] are a useful modification of the static economic theory of the firm in estimating production function parameters. One method of obtaining estimates of relative resource earnings is to examine individual farm or enterprise studies. However, we feel that aggregate estimates are more comparable.

Estimates presented here are laden with the usual limitations of aggregation, not least of which are shortcomings in the variety and quality of available data[4] and the estimating techniques employed. The economic theory employed is basically that of the firm and there is no assurance that the net behavior of the industry is representative of individual firms operating under different circumstances. But some of us have a bent for aggregation —perhaps if for no other reason but that a macro approach is best suited to the kind of questions we are asked. And if we view our results as grosser than their detailed appearance implies, useful conclusions may result.

### PRODUCTION ADJUSTMENTS

The elasticity of production $\eta$ is given by:

$$\eta = \frac{\partial Y}{\partial X} \cdot \frac{X}{Y} \tag{1}$$

And in equilibrium,

---

[3] Marc Nerlove (12) is an excellent reference on distributed lag models. Fred H. Tyner and Luther G. Tweeten advocate using adjustment models in estimating agricultural production parameters in (24). And Quance (13) used a modification of the Tyner and Tweeten approach in studying capital adjustments in the U.S. farm sector from 1917 to 1964.

[4] Data for the United States are from published USDA sources. Canadian data are from Canadian government publications. The authors acknowledge the assistance of Ludwig Auer of the Economic Council of Canada and Gordon H. Lloyd, Assistant Agricultural Attaché, U.S. Embassy, Ottawa, in obtaining data on Canadian agriculture. Reed Hertford, of the Economic Development Branch, ERS, USDA, provided the unpublished data on Mexican agriculture used in this chapter. Other data for Mexico are from publications listed in the bibliography. Edmundo Flores assisted in obtaining these publications. Sources of specific variables are delineated in Appendix Table 14.1 at the end of this chapter.

$$MPP_x = \frac{P_x}{P_y}$$

or similarly,

$$\frac{\partial Y}{\partial X} = \frac{P_x}{P_y}$$

Substituting

$\dfrac{P_x}{P_y}$ for $\dfrac{\partial Y}{\partial X}$ in equation (1):

$$\eta = \frac{P_x X}{P_y Y} \qquad (2)$$

which by definition is the factor share of X in producing Y.

This relationship, combined with an adjustment equation, permits the use of an equilibrium factor share technique in estimating production parameters.

The adjustment function:

$$F^t - F^{t-1} = g(F^{t*} - F^{t-1}) \qquad (3)$$

is used where $g$ is the proportion of the desired adjustment $(F^{t*} - F^{t-1})$ in the factor share of X accomplished in year $t$ by the actual adjustment $(F^t - F^{t-1})$. Further: $F^{t*}$ is the function:

$$F^{t*} = a_0 + a_1 I^{t-1} + a_2 P^{t-1} + a_3 K^{t-1} + a_4 T \qquad (4)$$

where

$F^{t*}$ is the equilibrium factor share of input X in year $t$;

$I^{t-1}$ is realized net income per farm in year $t-1$;[5]

$P^{t-1}$ is the acquisition cost of input X relative to prices received by farmers for the product Y in year $t-1$;

$K^{t-1}$ is the acquisition cost of an important substitute input relative to the acquisition cost of the input X in year $t-1$; and $T$ is a time variable.

Now the right hand side of equation (4) is substituted into equation (3) for $F^{t*}$ and the result solved for $F^t$ yielding the equation to be estimated:

$$F^t = g\,a_0 + g\,a_1 I^{t-1} + g\,a_2 P^{t-1} + g\,a_3 K^{t-1} + g\,a_4 T + (1-g)F^{t-1}. \qquad (5)$$

Estimates of adjustment coefficients $g$ are obtained by subtracting the estimate of the coefficient $(1 - g)$ of the lagged factor

---

[5] This variable was not available for inclusion in equations for Mexican inputs.

share $F^{t-1}$ from one. Then substituting the estimated adjustment coefficients into equation (3) and solving for $F^{t*}$ yields production elasticity estimates.

A problem encountered in fitting equation (5) in logarithm form is that large percentage changes in the factor shares from year $t - 1$ to year $t$ sometimes result in unreasonably large annual fluctuations in estimated production elasticities. This problem is alleviated by using moving averages of factor shares in the computations.

Production adjustment equations estimated for selected capital inputs in U.S., Canadian, and Mexican agriculture are tabulated in Appendix Table 14.2 at the end of this chapter. Resulting adjustment coefficients and elasticities of production are summarized in Table 14.2.

Previous work by Quance at Michigan State (13) indicated that expendables are adjusted toward profit-maximizing levels more rapidly than durables, farm-produced durables more rapidly than nonfarm-produced durables, nonfarm-produced expendables more rapidly than farm-produced expendables, and inputs which are unspecialized to the farm sector more rapidly than are

TABLE 14.2

PRODUCTION ADJUSTMENT COEFFICIENTS, AVERAGE ELASTICITIES OF PRODUCTION, SUMS OF ELASTICITIES OF PRODUCTION, AND ANNUAL PERCENTAGE CHANGES IN ELASTICITIES OF PRODUCTION AND IN SUMS OF ELASTICITIES, SPECIFIED INPUTS, UNITED STATES, CANADA, AND MEXICO

| Country and Input | Production Adjustment Coefficient | Annual Average* | |
|---|---|---|---|
| | | Elasticity of production or sum of elasticities | Percent change in elasticity or in the sum of elasticities |
| United States (Sum) | | .3150 | 1.2 |
| Machinery | .1563 | .0999 | —.3 |
| Fertilizer | .4130 | .0342 | 2.7 |
| Livestock | .7293 | .0590 | 3.0 |
| Feed | .6060 | .1212 | 2.1 |
| Canada (Sum) | | .2201 | 2.2 |
| Machinery | .2715 | .0805 | 3.6 |
| Fertilizer | .2745 | .0228 | 5.9 |
| Livestock | .7712 | .0114 | 6.3 |
| Feed | .1997 | .0997 | .3 |
| Mexico (Sum) | | .1256 | 2.8 |
| Tractor H.P. | .4326 | .0352 | .6 |
| Fertilizer | .7531 | .0170 | 16.4 |
| Cattle | .1755 | .0704 | 2.7 |
| Irrigation Water | 1.2400 | .0030 | 7.7 |

* The time period for which production elasticities were estimated was 1949–64 for United States and Canada and 1951–62 for Mexico.

specialized inputs. Obviously such a detailed input classification was not possible in this chapter but, as far as comparison is possible, adjustment coefficients for the capital inputs in United States, Canada, and Mexico substantiate this conclusion.

The production coefficients in Table 14.2 generally indicate that farm managers in United States, Canada, and Mexico adjust quite rapidly to changing economic conditions. And, except for cattle, Mexican farmers appear to adjust available capital inputs more rapidly than do their U.S. or Canadian counterparts.

But resulting elasticities of production indicate that less response to capital inputs is obtained in Mexican agriculture than in either the United States or Canada. For example, the elasticity of production with respect to fertilizer, which is the most comparable of the inputs studied, averaged .0170 in Mexico from 1951 to 1962 while it averaged .0342 and .0228 in the United States and Canada respectively for the 1949–64 period.

Mexican agriculture is less capital intensive than U.S. or Canadian agriculture and, other things equal, we would expect greater response to fertilizer or other capital in Mexico than in the United States or Canada. This is because Mexico would not be as far into stage two of production with respect to capital. But evidently, in the United States and Canada, technological advance in the form of new or improved capital inputs or improvements in managerial capacity has been rapid enough to more than offset the decrease in the elasticity of production caused by the increased use of capital. At any rate, the sum of elasticities for the inputs specified in Table 14.3 has increased 1.2 percent per year in the United States and 2.2 percent per year in Canada. In Mexico, where the substitution of capital for labor has been relatively small, technological advance has resulted in a 2.8 percent annual increase in returns to size with respect to tractor horsepower, fertilizer, cattle, and irrigation water. Note the large annual increase, 16.4 percent and 7.7 percent, in the elasticity of production with respect to fertilizer and irrigation water in Mexico. However, the absolute levels of production elasticities in Mexico are low. Apparently, as T. W. Schultz maintains (14), productivity levels in underdeveloped agriculture comparable to those in developed countries are dependent upon new inputs being introduced which are profitable substitutes for conventional inputs. Of course Mexico is not an underdeveloped country but a developing country.[6] Increases in productivity

---

[6] Actually there appear to be two agricultural sectors in Mexico—one developed and one underdeveloped. Hertford makes this point quite lucidly in (6).

TABLE 14.3

MARGINAL VALUE PRODUCTS AND A MANAGERIAL EFFICIENCY INDEX, SELECTED
CAPITAL INPUTS, UNITED STATES, CANADA, AND MEXICO, AVERAGES FOR SPECIFIED
PERIODS, 1949–64

| Years and Country | Marginal Value Product of a Dollar Invested in | | | | | Managerial Efficiency Index |
|---|---|---|---|---|---|---|
| | Ma-chinery* | Ferti-lizer | Live-stock† | Feed | Irri-gation water | |
| 1949–50 | | | (dollars) | | | |
| United States | 1.34 | 1.01 | .96 | 1.00 | . . . | 88.4 |
| Canada | .94 | 1.28 | .93 | .93 | . . . | 89.9 |
| 1951–54 | | | | | | |
| United States | 1.48 | 1.03 | 1.00 | .99 | . . . | 84.6 |
| Canada | 1.19 | 1.13 | .94 | .98 | . . . | 88.9 |
| Mexico | 1.06 | 1.09 | 1.01 | . . . | .98 | 93.6 |
| 1955–59 | | | | | | |
| United States | 1.40 | 1.00 | 1.01 | .99 | . . . | 87.4 |
| Canada | 1.06 | 1.10 | .97 | 1.05 | . . . | 91.0 |
| Mexico | .96 | 1.05 | 1.07 | . . . | 1.00 | 90.8 |
| 1960–62 | | | | | | |
| United States | .97 | 1.00 | 1.01 | .99 | . . . | 96.1 |
| Canada | 1.01 | 1.16 | 1.00 | 1.02 | . . . | 94.4 |
| Mexico | .95 | 1.04 | 1.01 | . . . | .97 | 89.0 |
| 1963–64 | | | | | | |
| United States | .98 | 1.00 | .99 | .99 | . . . | 97.4 |
| Canada | 1.00 | 1.13 | .98 | .95 | . . . | 94.4 |

\* Tractor horsepower in Mexico.
† Cattle in Mexcio.

presented in Table 14.3, as well as numerous and more elaborate studies presented here and elsewhere, attest to Mexico's agricultural development. But new sources of productivity gains are required if Mexican agriculture is to continue its rapid development. The production adjustment coefficient of 1.24 for irrigation water in Mexico, for example, indicates that this excellent means of development in Mexican agriculture may be overworked. As mentioned earlier, private investment in irrigation has not been great enough to allow irrigation productivity to rise at a capacity ratio.

## CAPITAL EARNINGS AND MANAGERIAL EFFICIENCY

Underlying production functions are assumed of the form:

$$Y = b_o X_1^{b_1} X_2^{b_2} \ldots X_n^{b_n} \tag{6}$$

where $Y$ is the value of output in each country and inputs $X_1$, $X_2$, . . ., $X_n$ are annual expenditures on the specific inputs. It then follows that the marginal value product of one dollar invested in an input $X_i$ is:

$$MVP_{xi} = \frac{b_i Y}{X_i} \tag{7}$$

Marginal value products of a dollar invested in each of the studied inputs were calculated for the years 1949–64 for the United States and Canada and 1951–62 for Mexico. Averages estimates for specified periods are presented in Table 14.3.

Our estimates indicate that generally North American farmers adjust capital investments quite rapidly to changing profit-maximizing rates of use. Machinery investments apparently were quite profitable in the United States and Canada in the early 1950's but by the 1960–62 period machinery MVP's declined to $1.01 per dollar invested in Canada and to less than $1.00 in the United States and Mexico. Despite large increases in fertilizer use in North America, the MVP of a dollar invested in principal plant nutrients averaged $1.16 and $1.04 in Canada and Mexico respectively but averaged $1.00 in the United States for the 1960–62 period. Livestock investments resulted in MVP's 1 percent above acquisition costs in 1960–62 but decreased to 99 and 98 percent of acquisition costs in the United States and Canada in 1963–64. The marginal value product of a dollar invested in feed averaged 99 and 95 cents in the United States and Canada for the 1963–64 period. MVP's of irrigation water investments in Mexico decreased from an average $1.00 in 1955–59 to 97 cents in 1960–62.

Although North American farms are apparently successful at adjusting the rate of use of capital inputs toward profit-maximizing levels, much of the stock of farm capital consists of durables. By adjusting the rate of use of these durables and complementary expendables, managers avoid some potential negative rents. But often, in the long run, the excess capacity of durables becomes obsolete and is salvaged, having earned insufficient returns over its productive life to cover its acquisition cost less salary value. Quance reached this conclusion in previous research (13) and it is substantiated by our estimates of MVP's which in many years were insufficient to cover the original dollar invested.

Using averages for the 1960–62 period for comparison, present investment opportunities appear to be the greatest for fertilizer in Canada and Mexico, feed in Canada, and livestock in the United States. But the 1963–64 estimates indicate that the profit incentive for livestock investments in the United States has vanished. Least attractive are tractor investments in Mexico which our estimates indicate earned 95 cents on the dollar for the 1960–62 period.

Glenn Johnson (9) advocates treating management as a separate enterprise devoted to defining and solving problems, implementing solutions, and bearing responsibilities for decisions and consequent actions. Johnson's view of management is consistent with the divergence between static economic theory of the firm and reality. In a static environment, there would be no need or opportunity for management. If resources were out of equilibrium, the manager would have perfect knowledge of the disequilibrium and would reallocate resources with absolute certainty. His first decision would be his last. So the need for management arises from imperfect knowledge and a dynamic environment.

If we assume managers are motivated by profit maximization, a measure of managerial efficiency is evident in deviations from profit maximizations. For purposes of this discussion, the management index $M_t$, for year $t$, is one minus the input quantity weighted average of the absolute value of deviations of MVP's of studied inputs from profit maximizing levels.

$$M_t = 1 - \sum_{i=1}^{n} W_i \left( \left| 1 - MVP_i \right| \right) \tag{8}$$

where $W_i$ is the value of input $i$ relative to the value of all inputs studied for a particular country and $n$ is the number of inputs studied for a particular country. On this index scale, 100 is maximum managerial efficiency. Resource earnings are equated with resource costs and there are no economic rents. Both overcommitment and undercommitment of resources are weighted equally and result in an index of less than 100.

MVP's greater than acquisition costs result from capital rationing, and resource owners receive positive economic rents on the input units employed, but additional profits greater than the rent could be obtained by expanding use of the input. When MVP's are less than acquisition costs, resources are overcommitted and owners receive negative rents.

In a sense we can view management as a parasite living off the residual earnings of controlled resources. A manager's marginal value product in terms of the production process is zero. Therefore a management index of 100, reflecting no positive or negative rents, would reflect peak efficiency. This index does not measure management in a quantity sense but measures managerial success in allocating resources for maximum profit.

Estimated managerial indexes are averaged over specified periods in Table 14.3. Using the 1960–62 period for comparison, U.S. farmers were 96.1 percent efficient with machinery and feed overcommitted, and livestock undercommitted. Canadian farmers were second to U.S. farmers in efficiency with an average managerial index of 94.4. Canadian farmers were apparently undercommitted with respect to machinery, fertilizer, and feed. Mexican farmers overcommitted tractor horsepower and irrigation water but undercommitted fertilizer and cattle with an average 89 managerial efficiency index for the 1960–62 period.

Over time, managerial efficiency has increased in the United States and Canada as capital rationing in machinery and fertilizer has decreased. Managerial efficiency in Mexico has apparently decreased over time as tractor investments have changed from an undercommitment situation in the 1951–54 period to overcommitment in the 1960–62 period. Mexican farmers have consistently undercommitted fertilizer investments.

### POTENTIAL ADJUSTMENTS IN CAPITAL USE

Our estimates indicate that farm managers in North America adjust quickly to a changing economic environment and in some cases have overcommitted resources to farm production, resulting in resource earnings insufficient to cover acquisition costs. Estimated MVP's indicate that, given present conditions, only fertilizer in Canada and Mexico and possibly feed in Canada offer lucrative investment opportunities. Potential increases in North American farm output from a profit incentive viewpoint are largely dependent upon continuing technological advance shifting the production function up over time with respect to capital inputs, thereby increasing marginal value products of capital investments and encouraging further investments. But, given the inelastic demand for farm products and increasing input prices, economic incentives of this type will surely be dampened by lower farm prices relative to prices paid by farmers.

Some capital inputs such as machinery in the United States

and irrigation water in Mexico are likely to become so costly that their productivity must increase much more rapidly if their rate of increased use is to continue its historic precedent. But other inputs such as fertilizer in Canada and Mexico and feed in the United States may be produced under such economies of size that their acquisition cost to farmers may decrease as their use increases.

With increased prices almost a certainty for nonfarm-produced durables such as farm machinery, and a continuing price-cost squeeze confronting farmers of North America, increased emphasis will likely be on increasing output with farm- and nonfarm-produced expendables—higher fertilizer applications on improved plant varieties and additional feed-fed animals more efficient at converting feed to produce. Of course these developments have been under way for many years. Witness the 24 percent decrease in the number of milk cows on U.S. farms from their World War II level while corn fed to dairy cattle increased 35 percent during the same period (13).

From a technical viewpoint, opportunities for increasing farm output in the United States, Canada, and Mexico are evident in Table 14.4. To increase farm output 10 percent, investments in machinery, fertilizer, livestock, and feed require increases of 31.7 percent in the United States and 45.4 percent in Canada, with other inputs held constant. In Mexico a 10 percent increase in farm output would require a 79.6 percent increase in tractor horsepower, fertilizer, cattle, and irrigation water with other inputs held constant. Of course increases in output will come about by not increasing all these specific capital items by the same percent. Rather, farm managers will expand along their appropriate expansion paths. United States and

TABLE 14.4

SUMS OF ELASTICITIES OF PRODUCTION WITH RESPECT TO SELECTED CAPITAL INPUTS AND THE PERCENTAGE INCREASE IN SPECIFIED INPUTS REQUIRED FOR 10 PERCENT INCREASE IN FARM OUTPUT, UNITED STATES, CANADA, AND MEXICO

| Country | Elasticities of Production With Respect to Selected Capital Inputs | Percentage Increase in Specified Inputs Required for a 10 Percent Increase in Farm Input |
|---|---|---|
| United States | .3150 | 31.7 |
| Canada | .2201 | 45.4 |
| Mexico | .1256 | 79.6 |

Canadian farmers will probably continue to substitute capital for labor on a relatively fixed quantity of land. In Mexico the expansion path evidently calls for a gradual increase in all inputs as the production functions shift up slowly over time. But if economic development in Mexico follows a path similar to that in the United States and Canada, eventually nonfarm employment opportunities and modern capital inputs will bring about a stronger capital-for-labor-substitution effect.

A very important source of productivity in North American agriculture not measured in our estimates is the idle capacity of durables in farm production. One can scarcely imagine the quantity of farm products the United States could produce if all its available land were placed in production. This could be done with only modest increases in farm machinery and complementary expendables. For example, an 80–90 horsepower tractor is used approximately 800 hours per year on a northwestern Oklahoma wheat farm. That is an average of four hours use per day in a 200-day work season from a $7,200 investment that will likely become obsolete in eight to ten years. The same farm has a complete set of complementary machines with a total new cost of approximately $9,410 (28). Typical wheat farms in the southern plains have approximately 616 acres of cropland of which over 200 acres are either idle or are used only to produce soil-conserving crops.

### INTERNATIONAL MOVEMENT OF RESOURCES

Given present production functions of North America and according to our production elasticity estimates, the United States has the greatest potential for increasing farm output, then Canada, and then Mexico. In the short run, the way to increase farm output in North America with the least amount of resources is to employ more machinery, fertilizer, livestock, and feed in the U.S. farm sector. The response could be tremendous, especially if land resources were used to capacity.

If a North American Common Market permitted resources to flow unrestricted from country to country, higher wage rates in the United States and Canada would attract labor from Mexico. A reduced labor supply in Mexican agriculture and increased labor supply in U.S. and Canadian agriculture would increase the marginal value products of labor-saving capital inputs in Mexico and reduce farm capital MVP's in the United States and Canada. Theoretically this would retard capital use in the

United States and Canada and bring about increased capitalization of Mexican agriculture. All of North America would probably then have both the productivity and problems of agriculture in developed countries. Making farm production more "free" in North America would likely increase the magnitude of problems already existing.

## POTENTIAL CHANGES IN CONSUMER WELFARE, FOOD PRODUCTION, AND RESOURCE RETURNS

An issue raised earlier in this chapter serves as a basis for summarizing. Would potential impacts of a North American Common Market on consumers, resource owners, and resource users be acceptable to society in the three countries? The hypothesis is difficult to discard that conditions for increased trade exist, in terms of inequality or disequilibrium in factor supplies and present and potential marginal value products, after transportation costs are considered. It is difficult in view of resource flows between states and regions which long have been taken for granted. We are aware also of inefficiencies that have arisen within countries as a result of acreage restrictions and other impediments to resource mobility. These inefficiencies are similar to those one would expect to result from barriers between countries.

Disparity of resource MVP's and supplies in the three countries assure profitable output, increasing adjustments if causes for a disparity are eliminated by institutional change. Estimates of MVP's presented here do not indicate that removal of barriers would immediately create an incentive to shift resource use. Rather, complete packages of technology and management are necessary in some areas and countries to create a profit incentive. Thus the first phases of a common market would be almost identical to current efforts designed to stimulate agricultural economic development. Hopefully the magnitude of efforts could be greater because owners of private capital could anticipate gains in the intermediate run. For example, such anticipations could be based on observed returns to capital in developed countries.

Under given technology, profit maximization choice rules leading to resource movement assure production increases, if the total amount of resources employed in agriculture does not decline. Two generally recognized phenomena in the agricultural industry, inelastic demand for food (both with respect to income and price) and "resource fixity," would probably cause increased food production at lower prices.[7] Thus benefits to domestic and, under some conditions, international consumers are relatively sure. Unless drastic changes in international food markets occur, residual returns to land and labor in more developed countries could be expected to decline. On the other hand, owners of mobile capital, labor in developing countries, and managers willing to move could receive greater returns to their resources. Admittedly, effects would be neither uniform nor sure.

The extent of contributions to world consumers is questioned by comments such as the following by Heady, "The main impacts [of U.S. food aid] are short run and make little contribution to long-run solutions of food and population problems." (7). General acceptance of this conclusion would indicate an expectation that in the longer run food can be exported through commercial channels to developing nations throughout the world. That expectation is necessary to encourage development of a common market for meeting world food needs.

Other reasons could exist for interest in a common market. For example, the common market could assist development of agriculture in one or more of the three countries involved. Very long-run food needs of North America eventually may require the step. The common market also might be designed to assure a minimax level of food for the market countries. That is, it could be regarded as a strategy for risk and uncertainty, somewhat independent of static efficiency considerations. Decision makers in the North American countries should examine these goals, along with other basic goals and policies proposed elsewhere (7, pp. 186–214 and 224–42).

## REFERENCES

(1) Canada Department of Agriculture, Economics Branch, *Canadian Farm Econ.* 2(2), Ottawa, June 1967.

(2) Dominion Bureau of Statistics, Agriculture Division, Farm Finance Section, *Handbook of Agricultural Statistics, Part II, Farm Income—1926–65,* Ottawa, June 1967. Also mimeographed table.

(3) Furniss, I. F., "Trends in Agricultural Productivity," *Canadian Farm Econ.* 2(1):15–21, April 1967.

(4) Hathaway, Dale E., *Government and Agriculture,* New York: The Macmillan Co., 1963.

(5) Heady, Earl O., *et al., Roots of the Farm Problem,* Ames: Iowa State Univ. Press, 1965.

(6) Hertford, Reed, "The Development of Mexican Agriculture— A Skeleton Specification." Paper presented at the annual meeting of

---

[7] A recent study of divergence between ex ante and ex post returns to agricultural capital (the resource fixity problem) is reported in (13).

the American Farm Economics Association and Canadian Agricultural Economics Society, Guelph Univ., Ontario, Canada, Aug. 14–16, 1967.

(7) Iowa State University Center for Agricultural and Economic Development, *Alternatives for Balancing World Food Production Needs,* Ames: Iowa State Univ. Press, 1967.

(8) Johnson, Glenn L., *et al., A Study of Managerial Processes of Midwestern Farmers,* Ames: Iowa State Univ. Press, 1961.

(9) Johnson, Glenn L., "Methodology for Handling the Managerial Input," unpublished paper, Michigan State Univ., East Lansing.

(10) Lerohl, Milburn L., "Expected Prices for United States Agricultural Commodities, 1917–62," unpublished Ph.D. dissertation, Dept. Agr. Econ., Michigan State Univ., 1965.

(11) National Advisory Commission on Food and Fiber, *Food and Fiber for the Future,* Washington, D.C.: GPO, July 1967.

(12) Nerlove, Marc, *Distributed Lags and Demand Analysis for Agricultural and Other Commodities,* AMS, USDA, Agr. Handbook 141, June 1958.

(13) Quance, C. Leroy, "Farm Capital: Use, MVPs, and Capital Gains or Losses, United States, 1917–1964," unpublished Ph.D. dissertation, Dept. Agr. Econ., Michigan State Univ., 1967.

(14) Schultz, T. W., *Economic Crisis in World Agriculture,* Ann Arbor: Univ. of Michigan Press, 1965.

(15) Secretaría de Agricultura y Ganadería, Secretaría de Hacienda y Crédito Publico, Banco de México, S. A. *Projections of Supply of and Demand for Agricultural Products in Mexico to 1965, 1970, and 1975.*

(16) Tyner, Fred H., and Luther G. Tweeten, "A Methodology for Estimating Production Parameters," Jour. Farm Econ. 47(5):1462–67, Dec. 1965.

(17) U.S. Department of Agriculture, *Agr. Fin. Rev.* XXV, Dec. Supplement, 1964.

(18) ———, *Agricultural Statistics,* 1962, 1965.

(19) ———, *Balance Sheet of Agriculture,* 1966.

(20) ———, ERS, *Changes in Farm Production and Efficiency—A Summary Report,* Stat. Bull. 233, 1963 and later revisions.

(21) ———, ERS, Foreign Development and Trade Division, Economic Development Branch, Mexico, unpublished data provided by Reed Hertford.

(22) ———, *Farm Income Situation,* No. 203, July 1966.

(23) ———, *Livestock and Meat Statistics,* 1957, Stat. Bull. 230, and 1964 Supplement.

(24) ———, Stat. Bull. 319.

(25) U.S. Department of Commerce, *Statistical Abstract of the United States, 1966.*

(26) U.S. Department of Labor, *Employment and Earnings,* Dec. 1964.

(27) Venzian, Eduardo, and William K. Gamble, *A Review of Mexican Agricultural Development, 1950–1965.* Cornell Internatl. Dev. Mimeo. 16, Office of Internatl. Dev., New York State College of Agriculture, Ithaca.

(28) Connor, Larry J., *et al.,* "Alternative Crop Enterprises on Loam and Sandy Soils of Northwest Oklahoma. . . . Resource Requirements, Costs and Returns," Processed Series P-552, Oklahoma State Univ. Exp. Sta., Stillwater, Nov. 1966.

# Chapter 14 Appendix

VARIABLE IDENTIFICATION AND SOURCES OF INFORMATION ON SPECIFIED FARM
CAPITAL INPUTS, UNITED STATES, CANADA, AND MEXICO, 1946–64

| Variable Number | Description | Source* |
|---|---|---|
| | United States | |
| 1 | Realized gross farm income (million dollars) | (18) 1965, Table 686; 1962, Table 687 |
| 2 | Prices received by farmers, all farm products (1910–14=100) | (18) 1965, Table 684; 1962, Table 683 |
| 3 | Farm wage rate (dollars per hour) | (18) 1965, Table 651; 1962, Table 652 |
| 4 | Realized net income per farm, purchasing power of (dollars) | (22) Table 9H |
| 5 | Hourly earnings of workers in manufacturing (dollars per hour) | (26) Table C–1 |
| 6 | Prices paid by farmers for machinery (1910–14=100) | (18) 1965, Table 684; 1962, Table 685 |
| 7 | Machinery depreciation (million dollars) | (22) Table 19H |
| 8 | Current value of fertilizer used on farms (million dollars) | (18) 1965, Table 691; 1962, Table 695 |
| 9 | Prices paid by farmers for fertilizer (1910–14=100) | (18) 1965, Table 684; 1962, Table 685 |
| 10 | Average value of real estate (dollars per acre) | (17) Table 35 |
| 11 | Livestock purchases (million dollars) | (22) Table 14H |
| 12 | Prices paid by farmers for livestock (1910–14=100) | (18) 1965, Table 685; 1962, Table 681 |
| 13 | Prices received by farmers for livestock (1910–14=100) | (18) 1965, Table 683; 1962, Table 684 |
| 14 | Prices paid by farmers for feed (1910–14=100) | (18) 1965, Table 684; 1965, Table 685 |
| 15 | Current value of feed purchased (million dollars) | (18) 1965, Table 691; 1962, Table 695 |
| | Canada | |
| 16 | Machinery depreciation (million dollars) | (2) Table 7 |
| 17 | Realized gross income from farming (million dollars) | (2) Table 1 |
| 18 | Prices paid by farmers for machinery (1935–39=100) | (1) |
| 19 | Prices received by farmers, all commodities (1935–39=100) | (1) |
| 20 | Farm wage rate (1935–39=100) | (1) |
| 21 | Realized net income per farm operator (dollars) | (2) mimeographed table |
| 22 | Value of plant nutrients used on farms | (2) Table 7 |
| 23 | Livestock purchases (million dollars) | (2) Table 7 |
| 24 | Livestock prices, wholesale (1935–39=100) | (1) |
| 25 | Current value of feed purchased through commercial channels (million dollars) | (2) Table 7 |
| 26 | Wholesale price index of Canadian farm field products (1935–39=100) | (1) |
| 27 | Nonfarm wage rate (average weekly wages in manufacturing) | (2) |

* Numbers in brackets refer to bibliography listing.

| Variable Number | Description | Source* |
|---|---|---|
| | Mexico | |
| 28 | Gross farm output (million pesos) | (21) |
| 29 | Prices received by farmers (1960=100) | (21) |
| 30 | Farm wage rate (1960=100) | (21) |
| 31 | Nonfarm wage rate (1960=100) | (21) |
| 32 | Fertilizer, current value of (mil. pesos) (Hertford's quantity series was weighted by his fertilizer price index multiplied by the value of a ton of plant nutrients in the U.S. in 1960 converted to pesos) | (21) |
| 33 | Fertilizer prices (1960=100) | (21) |
| 34 | Value of tractor horsepower (mil. pesos) (Hertford's quantity series was weighted by his index of prices received for livestock multiplied by the value per head of cattle in 1960) | (21) |
| 35 | Wholesale prices (1960=100) | (21) |
| 36 | Value of cattle inventories (mil. pesos) (Hertford's quantity series was weighed by his index of prices received for livestock multiplied by the value per head of cattle in 1960) | (21) |
| 37 | Prices received for livestock (1960=100) | (21) |
| 38 | Value of irrigation water delivered (mil. pesos) (Hertford's quantity series was multiplied by his prices paid for irrigation water series) | (21) |
| 39 | Price of irrigation water (pesos per million cubic meters) | (21) |

# APPENDIX TABLE 14.2

Production Adjustment Equations for Specified Farm Inputs, United States, Canada, and Mexico*

## UNITED STATES

Machinery:

$$\ln\left[\frac{1}{7}\right]^{t} = 1.4623 - .2376\ln\left[4\right]^{t-1} + .3126\ln\left[\frac{6}{2}\right]^{t-1} - .1110\ln\left[\frac{3}{6}\right]^{t-1}$$
$$\phantom{\ln\left[\frac{1}{7}\right]^{t} = 1.4623} (.3347) \qquad\quad (.5612) \qquad\qquad (.5273)$$

$$+ .8437\ln\left[\frac{7}{1}\right]^{t-1} - .6628\ln^{[\text{Time}]}; \quad \hat{g} = .1563; \quad R^2 = .9756$$
$$\phantom{+} (.1707) \qquad\qquad (1.7473)$$

Fertilizer:

$$\ln\left[\frac{8}{1}\right]^{t} = -10.8454 + .0588\ln\left[4\right]^{t-1} - .0089\ln\left[\frac{9}{2}\right]^{t-1} - .6811\ln\left[\frac{10}{9}\right]^{t-1}$$
$$\phantom{\ln\left[\frac{8}{1}\right]^{t} = -10.8454} (.1913) \qquad\quad (.3160) \qquad\qquad (.3959)$$

$$+ .5870\ln\left[\frac{8}{1}\right]^{t-1} + 2.1390\ln^{[\text{Time}]}; \quad \hat{g} = .4130; \quad R^2 = .9599$$
$$\phantom{+} (.2275) \qquad\qquad (1.4747)$$

Livestock:

$$\ln\left[\frac{11}{1}\right]^{t} = -1.1242 - .1866\ln\left[4\right]^{t-1} - .1474\ln\left[\frac{12}{2}\right]^{t-1} + .0224\ln\left[\frac{14}{12}\right]^{t-1}$$
$$\phantom{\ln\left[\frac{11}{1}\right]^{t} = -1.1242} (.0436) \qquad\quad (.1015) \qquad\qquad (.0730)$$

$$+ .2707\ln\left[\frac{11}{1}\right]^{t-1} + .0910\ln^{[\text{Time}]}; \quad \hat{g} = .7293; \quad R^2 = .8857$$
$$\phantom{+} (.0923) \qquad\qquad (.0641)$$

* Numbers in brackets correspond to variables identified in Appendix Table 14.1. Equations for the United States and Canada cover the 1947–64 period while equations for Mexico cover the 1951–62 period. (Numbers in parentheses below coefficients are estimates of standard errors.) Time was entered in each equation as the last two digits of the calendar year.

# APPENDIX TABLE 14.2 (continued)

## UNITED STATES (continued)

### Feed

$$ln\left[\frac{15}{1}\right]^t = -5.1959 + \underset{(.0664)}{.1718}\ ln\left[4\right]^{t-1} - \underset{(.1581)}{.0868}\ ln\left[\frac{13}{2}\right]^{t-1} - .0686\ ln\left[\frac{12}{13}\right]^{t-1}$$

$$+ \underset{(.2291)}{.3940}\ ln\left[\frac{15}{1}\right]^{t-1} + \underset{(.2116)}{.6329}\ ln^{[\text{Time}]};\ \hat{g} = .6060;\ R^2 = .9759$$

## CANADA

### Machinery

$$ln\left[\frac{16}{17}\right]^t = 2.1834 - \underset{(.0704)}{.0327}\ ln\left[21\right]^{t-1} + \underset{(.1583)}{.14846}\ ln\left[\frac{18}{19}\right]^{t-1} - \underset{(.3129)}{.8783}\ ln\left[\frac{20}{18}\right]^{t-1}$$

$$+ \underset{(.1319)}{.7285}\ ln\left[\frac{16}{17}\right]^{t-1} - \underset{(.3595)}{.4648}\ ln^{[\text{Time}]};\ \hat{g} = .2715;\ R^2 = .9815$$

### Fertilizer

$$ln\left[\frac{22}{17}\right]^t = -7.0023 + \underset{(.1230)}{.0256}\ ln\left[21\right]^{t-1} - \underset{(.2564)}{.2443}\ ln\left[\frac{9}{19}\right]^{t-1} - \underset{(.3588)}{.2487}\ ln\left[\frac{10}{0}\right]^{t-1}$$

$$+ \underset{(.2524)}{.7255}\ ln\left[\frac{22}{17}\right]^{t-1} + \underset{(1.2985)}{1.3616}\ ln^{[\text{Time}]};\ \hat{g} = .2745;\ R^2 = .9612$$

## CANADA (continued)

### Livestock

$$ln\left[\frac{23}{17}\right]^{t} = -15.0727 - .2211\ ln\left[21\right]^{t-1} + 1.4488\ ln\left[\frac{24}{19}\right]^{t-1} + .6157\ ln\left[\frac{26}{24}\right]^{t-1}$$
$$(.1153) \qquad (.4952) \qquad (.2320)$$
$$+ .2288\ ln\left[\frac{23}{17}\right]^{t-1} + 3.3187\ ln\left[\text{Time}\right];\ \hat{g} = .7712;\ R^2 = .9836$$
$$(.2538) \qquad (1.1238)$$

### Feed

$$ln\left[\frac{25}{17}\right]^{t} = -.2562 - .1996\ ln\left[21\right]^{t-1} - 1.3839\ ln\left[\frac{26}{19}\right]^{t-1} - .7666\ ln\left[\frac{24}{26}\right]^{t-1}$$
$$(.0598) \qquad (.7486) \qquad (.4132)$$
$$+ .8003\ ln\left[\frac{25}{17}\right]^{t-1} + .3005\ ln\left[\text{Time}\right];\ \hat{g} = .1997;\ R^2 = .8092$$
$$(.1374) \qquad (.1217)$$

## MEXICO

### Tractor Horsepower

$$ln\left[\frac{34}{28}\right]^{t} = -23.6416 + 5.3408\ ln\left[\frac{6}{29}\right]^{t-1} - 3.5267\ ln\left[\frac{30}{6}\right]^{t-1}$$
$$(4.7392) \qquad (1.4778)$$
$$+ .5674\ ln\left[\frac{34}{28}\right]^{t-1} + 5.3940\ ln\left[\text{Time}\right];\ \hat{g} = .4326;\ R^2 = .5789$$
$$(.3536) \qquad (2.7742)$$

313

APPENDIX TABLE 14.2 (continued)

## MEXICO (continued)

### Fertilizer

$$ln\left[\frac{32}{28}\right]^t = -31.6422 - .2309 \; ln\left[\frac{33}{29}\right]^{t-1} + .1847 \; ln\left[\frac{30}{33}\right]^{t-1}$$
$$(.6628) \qquad\qquad (.7274)$$

$$+ .2469 \; ln\left[\frac{32}{28}\right]^{t-1} + 7.0584 \; ln[\text{Time}]; \; \hat{g} = .7531; \; R^2 = .9811$$
$$(.3560) \qquad\qquad (3.4506)$$

### Irrigation Water

$$ln\left[\frac{38}{28}\right]^t = -21.6203 + 1.7159 \; ln\left[\frac{39}{29}\right]^{t-1} + 1.2072 \; ln\left[\frac{30}{39}\right]^{t-1}$$
$$(1.6928) \qquad\qquad (1.2198)$$

$$- .2404 \; ln\left[\frac{38}{28}\right]^{t-1} + 3.6166 \; ln[\text{Time}]; \; \hat{g} = 1.244; \; R^2 = .8237$$
$$(.8541) \qquad\qquad (2.4937)$$

### Cattle

$$ln\left[\frac{36}{28}\right]^t = -5.3269 - .9257 \; ln\left[\frac{37}{29}\right]^{t-1} - .2945 \; ln\left[\frac{30}{37}\right]^{t-1}$$
$$(.8419) \qquad\qquad (.4394)$$

$$+ .8245 \; ln\left[\frac{36}{28}\right]^{t-1} + 1.1829 \; ln[\text{Time}]; \; \hat{g} = .1755; \; R^2 = .5383$$
$$(.6399) \qquad\qquad (.6016)$$

# PART FIVE

# Obstacles in Achievement

# CHAPTER FIFTEEN

# Current National Agricultural Policies: Inventory and Analysis

## JERRY G. WEST

Decisions with respect to public policy vary from those involving major changes to those of only minor significance. Furthermore, the degree of knowledge or level of understanding as to the consequences may be high or low. With the exception of administrative decisions, or those decisions made during times of major crises, most of our public policy decisions are made with incomplete knowledge and involve small changes. The term "incremental politics" has been used to describe these types of decisions.[1] The associated analytical method is labeled "disjointed incrementalism" because it consists of a restricted set of policy alternatives, consideration of only a limited number of consequences for any given policy, adjustment of objectives to policies, serial and remedial analysis and evaluation, and social fragmentation of analysis and evaluation.

Agricultural policy decisions would appear to be of this type. The number of alternatives considered is usually limited; the number of consequences considered is of necessity incomplete; there is a continuing analysis and evaluation; and the viewpoints of various segments of society are presented. If this is

JERRY G. WEST, North Carolina State University, on leave from the Department of Agricultural Economics, University of Missouri.

[1] David Braybrooke and Charles Lindblom, *A Strategy of Decision, Policy Evaluation as a Social Process*, The Free Press of Glencoe, New York, 1963.

an accurate description of the usual procedure, it becomes important to consider our present situation as we think about moving toward a North American Common Market. Specifically we need to look at our current national agricultural policies as we examine some of the obstacles in achievement of potential capacity in North American agricultural production.

It is impossible to provide a complete inventory and analysis of all the relevant current national agricultural policies. Rather, an attempt will be made to describe briefly some of the more important types of programs, indicate effects on kind and quantity of food produced, examine the kinds of impacts on resource allocation and efficiency, and finally speculate as to likely effects of removing production restrictions. No claim is made for originality of ideas but rather the material is a combination of ideas and results from research related to the topic. Emphasis will be given to the agricultural policies of the United States and to a lesser degree those of Canada and only brief attention will be given to Mexico.

National agricultural policies in all of the North American countries date back to the nineteenth century. The types of policies in effect and the degree of government involvement in the agricultural economies have varied over time and as the situation has changed, so have the policies. To some extent the policies are related to the stage of development of the nations' economies as well as the political, social, and economic situation existing at various times for the relevant commodities and types of farming in existence in the three nations.

## TYPES OF PROGRAMS

The national agricultural policies in North America might well be divided into four types. These would include programs affecting availability and cost of inputs, programs affecting prices of products, programs imposing restrictions on production, and those designed to change demand for agricultural products.

All of the North American countries have had programs which were designed to make certain inputs more readily available or available at lower cost. These would include programs designed to make agricultural land available for cultivation under such varied programs as the homestead acts in the United States, the land reclamation programs in Canada and the United States, and the land reform program of Mexico. There have also been programs designed to increase the productivity of the land through conservation measures, irrigation, and application of lime and fertilizer.

Similarly, all of the countries have developed credit programs to increase the capital input in agriculture. In some instances the programs were designed to make credit available where it was otherwise unavailable, while in others the programs were primarily designed to lower the cost of credit to the farmer.

National policies have also encouraged improvement of conditions in the agricultural economies through research and education. These have been many and varied and have improved the management input, developed new or improved methods or machines and materials to be used in production, and in other instances have led to new or improved products.

Programs designed to stabilize or support the prices of products farmers sell have also been an important aspect of national agricultural policies in recent decades. Techniques used have included loans, purchases, deficiency payments, marketing boards, marketing orders, and import duties or restrictions. Objectives of the programs have varied from one of merely attempting to stabilize price to that of increasing domestic prices and incomes. In some instances prices were supported in order to promote self-sufficiency in the production of specific products.

Canada has used marketing boards, offers-to-purchase, and deficiency payments to stabilize agricultural prices. Mexico has relied primarily on import restrictions and price guarantees effected through government purchases to support prices and thereby attempt to achieve agricultural self-sufficiency. The United States has used practically all of the techniques mentioned in its attempt to both stabilize and increase farm income.

Efforts to increase domestic demand for agricultural products have been relatively important in the United States but of only minor significance in Canada and Mexico. The United States has conducted a food distribution program, school lunch and school milk program, and during the 1960's has developed a sizable food stamp program for needy families. Mexico has at various times distributed food to low-income families and has used ceiling prices on certain food items.

Programs to increase export demand have been prevalent in all three countries. All have some type of program to provide credit to potential importers. These vary from government-insured loans to outright government loans to the importing country. Loans insured or made by Canada and Mexico have been primarily short-term loans of one to three years, while those in the United States have ranged up to 40 years under Title IV of P.L. 480.[2] Canada's only other export assistance program of any significance is its policy of freight rate subsidies on products moving to export locations. Mexico has had a compensatory foreign exchange system for certain products such as coffee and cotton in which it grants import permits subject to the exportation of an equal value of commodities it wishes to export.[3] Because of its policy of supporting prices of certain products above world prices, the United States has been forced to make sizable export payments to commercial exporters or export government stocks at prices considerably below cost to the government. Acceptance of foreign currencies under P.L. 480 has been another major aspect of U.S. efforts to export agricultural products.

Programs designed to reduce agricultural production have been limited primarily to the United States. These include such widely publicized efforts as marketing quotas, acreage allotments, the Soil Bank, and acreage diversion programs. Products included have been tobacco, cotton, rice, peanuts, wheat, and feed grains. Canada does not have direct output controls but its Wheat Board does have a system of delivery quotas which may encourage some producers to shift to other products. Three marketing boards in Canada have also instituted controls involving Ontario flue-cured tobacco, Ontario broilers, and British Columbia broilers.[4]

## EFFECT OF PROGRAMS ON KIND AND QUANTITY OF FOOD PRODUCED

Programs to reduce the cost and increase the availability of inputs have led to expansion in total agricultural production. The increases in agricultural production during the late 1800's and early part of this century were in the main a result of the policies to make land readily available at low cost. Credit programs were also developed to facilitate the purchase of land and other inputs. Programs such as the reclamation projects in all three countries have also brought additional resources into production through drainage and irrigation.

---

[2] Under the New P.L. 480 legislation of November 1966, Titles I and IV were combined into Title I.

[3] USDA, *Agricultural Policies of Foreign Governments Including Trade Policies Affecting Agriculture,* Agr. Handbook No. 132, Washington, D.C., 1964, p. 17.

[4] D. R. Campbell, "Overcoming the Canadian Farm Problem—Theory and Practice," *Canadian Jour. Agr. Econ.,* Vol. 14, No. 2, 1966.

Much of the increase in agricultural productivity during recent years may be traced to policies encouraging research and education. Granted private firms have also been engaged in such activities, but much of the work has been the direct result of national policies and programs providing the necessary financial support. Griliches' research on the agricultural production function quantifies the effectiveness of research and education expenditures as a means of increasing agricultural output.[5] Likewise, Heady and Auer found that much of the increase in yields of various crops may be attributed to variety improvement or application of fertilizer.[6] Certainly research and education were major forces behind the development and use of these technologies. The rapid increase in output during recent years with only a very slight increase in total inputs emphasizes the importance of changes in the input mix and the productivity of the new technologies.

These programs to increase the availability of inputs or reduce their cost to the agricultural sector have not usually been selective in their impact. It is true that cultivation of new lands often resulted in expansion of selected crops, but this was not involved in the objectives of such programs. In a similar way, research and education have sometimes been more productive in terms of new technologies for certain products, but such was not necessarily intended. In general, the impact of these types of programs was one of an increase in production of most agricultural products.

Programs designed to stabilize or support the prices of agricultural products have definitely affected the kinds and quantities of food produced. In this instance the programs have probably affected the kinds of products more than the total quantity of food. The impact has varied, depending on the level of support relative to world prices and prices of alternative products.

All of the three countries have supported the prices of certain products as a means of becoming more self-sufficient in the production of such products. Examples would include dairy products in Canada, wool and sugar in the United States, and corn and eggs in Mexico. The higher returns from products included in such programs result in somewhat greater production

---

[5] Zvi Griliches, "Research Expenditures, Education and the Aggregate Agricultural Production Function," *Amer. Econ. Rev.*, Vol. 54, No. 6, Dec. 1964.

[6] Earl O. Heady and Ludwig Auer, "Imputation of Production to Technologies," *Jour. Farm Econ.*, Vol. 48, No. 2, May 1966.

but the effect on the total product mix depends on the extent to which resources are attracted away from the production of other agricultural products.

Perhaps of much greater significance have been those programs supporting the prices of commodities which were not in deficit. Such programs in the United States resulted in production considerably above normal domestic and export needs. Stocks of wheat, feed grains, rice, and cotton built up rapidly during the 1950's. Experience during this period indicated an excess capacity which combined with price supports would result in production much larger than utilization in the absence of controls on production.

Efforts to control production have affected both the type and quantity of agricultural production in the United States during the period since the Korean War. Imposition of acreage allotments and marketing quotas for wheat and cotton resulted in shifts of land from these crops to feed grains and soybeans.[7] The Soil Bank program of the 1950's and the acreage diversion programs of the 1960's have reduced the production of wheat, feed grains, and cotton. Indirect effects of these programs have been such as to result in some reduction in beef, pork, and dairy production and likewise in total agricultural production.

How would U.S. agricultural production have differed in the absence of both price support incentives and efforts to restrict production? Since 1959, a number of studies have been made in an attempt to answer this question.[8] Some of these have estimated effects of past programs while others have estimated future production on the basis of "free market" conditions. In general, the results have indicated somewhat higher production and lower farm prices and incomes had the free market prevailed. The studies indicate a slightly larger increase in livestock production than in crops, which suggests that the programs have not only had a direct effect on production of the products involved but have also indirectly affected the quantity of other products.

Domestic demand expansion programs have had only a very limited impact on agricultural production. Evaluations of the Food Stamp Program indicate increased consumption of meat products and fresh fruits and vegetables, but the participation

---

[7] USDA, *Farm Production—Trends, Prospects, and Programs,* Agr. Inf. Bull. 239, Washington, D.C., 1961.

[8] For an example of such studies and a review of previous efforts, see Luther Tweeten *et al., Farm Program Alternatives,* Center for Agricultural and Economic Development, CAED Report 18, Iowa State Univ., Ames, 1963.

in this program has not been great enough for this increase to have much effect on total demand or subsequent production. The Direct Distribution Program and related Section 32 purchases of agricultural commodities have emphasized products in temporary surplus and have attempted to reduce the magnitude of annual or cyclical price fluctuations rather than provide permanent demand effects.

Efforts to expand export demand have usually been related to domestic price support programs. This was particularly true of the P.L. 480 program in the United States during the late 1950's and early 1960's. In the absence of such export programs, pressure would no doubt have developed for sharply lower price supports or greater efforts to restrict production. This would suggest that such programs have at least had an indirect effect on the kinds and quantities of agricultural commodities produced in the United States.

## IMPACT OF PROGRAMS
## ON ALLOCATION OF RESOURCES

The systems of price support, restrictions on production, and efforts to protect domestic production from imports have definitely influenced the allocation of resources in agricultural production. Such programs have resulted in relative price levels within and among countries somewhat different from those which would have existed otherwise. This has meant some departure from the production of commodities with the greatest comparative advantage. In addition to affecting relative price levels, the price support programs have often led to export subsidies and import quotas which influence world trade patterns.

Programs in the United States provide considerable evidence of distortions in resource allocation. For example, many of the programs have been tied to land which has influenced the input mix and also affected the location of production within the country. Likewise, the objective of reestablishing historic price relationships has resulted in qualities and quantities of products unwanted by consumers. The recent Commission on Food and Fiber cites cotton and butter as prime examples in which high price supports have stimulated the production and sale of man-made substitutes.[9] Recognition of such difficulties has led to a reduction in price supports for some commodities to a level

---

[9] National Advisory Commission on Food and Fiber, *Food and Fiber for the Future,* Washington, D.C., 1967, pp. 63–64.

near world market prices and the use of other techniques to support farm income.

The use of import quotas and other devices to protect domestic producers has resulted in separate national markets for several agricultural products. This would include selected dairy and poultry products, tobacco, and sugar. The production pattern for these items would likely be somewhat different if the products were free to move throughout North America.

Programs limiting the land input have often encouraged greater use of other inputs. In addition to freezing production patterns geographically, they have also tended to remove some high quality land from use while maintaining some marginal land in production. Acreage allotments which are not transferable and mandatory diversion programs tend to increase total production and distribution costs.[10]

National agricultural programs have had some detrimental effects on resource allocation, but there are also beneficial aspects which must be recognized. The contribution of programs such as the Canadian Wheat Board, U.S. price support loans and purchases, and the program of price guarantees to Mexican farmers has been obvious in terms of greater price stability for the products involved. The greater certainty associated with price stability is becoming more important as the proportion of costs increases, which are in the form of purchased inputs. But if the benefits from this increased price stability are to be realized, the frequency and magnitude of change in programs must be minimized to avoid introducing another type of uncertainty which will impinge on the efficient allocation of resources.

An examination of data on changes in the productivity of agriculture in North America indicates very rapid progress during recent years even though some national policies may have had detrimental effects. In fact, both Canada and the United States experienced increases in productivity while operating under quite different types of programs.[11] Canadian agriculture made its adjustments with minimal price protection and no direct output controls while U.S. agriculture was subject to a substantial scheme of price supports and output restrictions. Mackensie's data for the period 1947–51 to 1958–62 indicated a rise in productivity in the United States of 39 percent, compared with

---

[10] Norman K. Whittlesey, "Cost and Efficiency of Alternative Land-Retirement Programs," *Jour. Farm Econ.*, Vol. 49, No. 2, May 1967.

[11] William Mackensie, "Resources and Productivity," *Jour. Farm Econ.*, Vol. 47, No. 5, Dec. 1965.

an increase of 63 percent in Canada, but MacFarlane argues that Canada's comparative advantage relative to the United States has declined in recent years as evidenced by data on agricultural trade between the two countries.[12]

Changes in resources used in North American agriculture have also been in the desired direction in recent decades. All of the countries have experienced a decline in labor used, accompanied by an increase in the use of capital inputs. Price support programs may have actually increased the rate of change in some instances by contributing to greater price certainty which in turn stimulated adoption of new labor-saving technology. Factors such as nonfarm unemployment, age of farmers, and lack of training for nonfarm occupations have retarded shifts of labor out of agriculture much more than the effects of agricultural policies.

Although government agricultural programs may not have had major impacts on efficiency, they have influenced distribution of income considerably. Instead of all gains in productivity being passed on to consumers in the form of lower food prices, some have been capitalized into higher land prices. A large share of the realized capital gains has therefore gone to the non-farm sector in the form of inheritances.[13] The result has been higher fixed costs and lower net income for the new owners of agricultural resources. Income distribution within agriculture has also been influenced by the programs as some regions have benefited more than others and large farms have benefited more than small farms.[14]

## LIKELY EFFECTS OF REMOVING PRODUCTION RESTRICTIONS

Since the United States is the only country with direct output controls, the direct production consequences would be of importance mainly in this country. However, there would also be spillover effects in Canada, Mexico, and other countries importing or exporting the products involved. Markets for wheat, feed-grains, and cotton would experience the greatest impact but the

---

[12] David MacFarlane, Paper presented at the Annual Meeting of the American Farm Economics Association, Guelph, Ontario, Aug. 1967.

[13] Vernon W. Ruttan, "Agricultural Policy in an Affluent Society," *Jour. Farm Econ.*, Vol. 48, No. 5, Dec. 1966.

[14] James B. Herendeen, "Farm Programs and Income Distribution in Agriculture by Economic Class of Farm and by Area," *Income Distribution Analysis*, API Series 23, North Carolina State Univ., Raleigh, Dec. 1966.

poultry and livestock industry would be affected indirectly through lower prices for feed grains.

In 1967 approximately 25 million acres were diverted from production in the United States under the cotton, feed grains, and wheat programs. Another 10 to 12 million acres were re- tired under the Conservation Reserve Program and the Cropland Adjustment Program. Recent USDA estimates indicate that in the absence of production adjustment programs and commodity loans total crop output during 1968–70 would be at least 15 per- cent greater than 1966.[15] Livestock output would average 10 percent larger if there were no rebuilding of grain stocks. Prices of crops would decline an estimated 20 percent and livestock nearly 10 percent. Another indication of the magnitude of pres- ent efforts to restrict production is the estimate that some 10 to 15 percent of grain-producing capacity is being held out of production.[16]

Differences exist among economists as to the exact magni- tude of production increases which would occur if production restrictions were removed. Results of analyses differ depending on assumptions as to price elasticities of supply and demand, other programs in effect, trends in yields and feed conversion rates, and export possibilities. However, there is fairly general agreement that output would increase, prices would be somewhat lower, and net farm income would decline in the short run.

The results of the 1966–67 wheat program in the United States are indicative of the ramifications of relaxation of pro- duction restrictions. Production allotments were increased ap- proximately 32 percent and the result was a record wheat crop of approximately 1.5 billion bushels. Wheat prices dropped sharply from year earlier levels and pressure developed for reduc- tions in allotments. The effects of the increase in wheat pro- duction combined with changes in price support loan levels have been felt in the world wheat market. During the period 1956–64 when U.S. price support loan levels were considerably above world market prices, Canada was the world price leader in wheat with the International Wheat Agreement price as a minimum and the U.S. support price as a maximum.[17] Changes in U.S.

[15] USDA, *Farm Program Needs 1968–70,* March 1967.

[16] Walter W. Wilcox, "Implications of Recent Changes in U.S. Farm Support Price Policies," Paper presented at the Annual Meeting of the Amer- ican Farm Economics Association, Guelph, Ontario, Aug. 1967.

[17] Alex F. McCalla, "Implications for Canada of U.S. Farm Policies," Paper presented at the Annual Meeting of the American Farm Economics Association, Guelph, Ontario, Aug. 1967.

policy have resulted in somewhat lower world market prices and the United States is a much greater competitive factor in wheat pricing.

## POLICIES AS OBSTACLES

To what extent then are national agricultural policies obstacles in the achievement of potential capacity in North American agricultural production? Many of the policies in existence are not obstacles at all but rather contribute toward the achievement of that goal. This would be especially true of those programs designed to increase the availability and reduce the cost of inputs. Rather, these policies actually enhance the potential capacity of agriculture. It is also difficult to see how programs designed to increase demand could be considered obstacles.

Programs designed to stabilize prices of agricultural products may or may not be obstacles, depending on the level at which prices are stabilized and the technique used. Greater price stability will actually encourage better resource allocation but if normal price patterns are distorted then resources will not be allocated in such a way as to achieve the potential capacity. Likewise, import quotas, tariffs, and other measures to protect domestic producers will prohibit resources being used in the production of commodities with the greatest comparative advantage. Furthermore these policies are probably the more serious obstacles to the formulation of a common agricultural market.

Efforts to restrict production are intended to be obstacles. These programs were developed when the concern was with excess capacity rather than achieving potential capacity. Justification is on the basis of the need to maintain a healthy agricultural economy by avoiding price-depressing surpluses. The role to be played by such an approach would of necessity diminish with increases in domestic and export demand for agricultural products.

## IMPLICATIONS FOR FUTURE POLICIES

Incremental politics is evident in recent changes in national agricultural policies, especially in the United States. For example, the Food and Agriculture Act of 1965 moved in the direction of reducing price support rates to levels more in line with world market prices. The recommendations of the recent National

Advisory Commission on Food and Fiber include suggestions for further moves in this direction. Such changes are necessary if some of the obstacles to the achievement of potential capacity are to be removed. This would permit the removal of restrictions on imports such as those carried out in the United States under Section 22 authority in which import quotas were imposed on raw cotton, wheat, wheat products, various dairy products, and peanuts.

In addition to policies resulting in import restrictions and export subsidies, there are other policies which would need to be considered in moving toward a North American Common Market achieving its potential capacity. Greater care would need to be exercised in setting price support levels so as to avoid distorting normal price patterns. Efforts to restrict production would need to be carried out in such a way as to avoid forcing inefficient combinations of inputs and operation of farm units at sizes which would not achieve the potential economies of scale. Policies would no doubt need to be developed to facilitate the adjustments which would be required as regional and national shifts in production take place.

It is unlikely that individual countries in a common market would find it feasible to restrict production of those products which could be readily produced in two or more of the countries involved. To do so would only serve to provide a greater market for the producers in other countries at the expense of domestic production. However, with the formation of a common market, producer interests in North America might be encouraged to jointly take action to reduce production. This might be particularly feasible for commodities such as wheat and tobacco where Canada and the United States export a large percentage of the total moving into world trade.

The national agricultural policies of the nations of North America do not appear to be unmovable obstacles. They are continually changing and can be modified gradually in the direction of a common market if this be the will of nations involved.

# CHAPTER SIXTEEN

# Restrictions on
# Intra-North American Trade:
# Inventory and Analysis

## RICHARD S. MAGLEBY

FACTORS which inhibit trade include geographical hindrances, insufficient supply or demand, lack of information, and man-made devices. This chapter discusses the man-made devices, both tariff and nontariff, which restrict agricultural trade among the United States, Canada, and Mexico.

Trade restrictions reflect a given country's production and trade policies and trade and payment balances. Because of this, I want to first review briefly some aspects of the trade policies and state of trade relations among the three countries.

### TRADE POLICIES AND RELATIONS

In the United States, Canada, and Mexico, trade policies are closely correlated with policies of stabilization of farm prices and incomes. Of particular influence are direct price-support programs. Canada currently maintains mandatory support prices of nine commodities: cattle, hogs, sheep, butter, cheese, eggs, wheat, barley, and oats.[1] Mexico supports partially or fully the prices of wheat, corn, rice, and beans. Products under U.S. price

RICHARD S. MAGLEBY, Western Hemisphere Branch, Foreign Regional Analysis Division, United States Department of Agriculture.
[1] Wheat, barley, and oats grown outside the jurisdiction of the Canadian Wheat Board.

support or subsidy programs are butter, cheese, dry milk, wheat, tobacco, cotton, and peanuts.

Mexico's import policies, in particular, also reflect its policies of stimulating industrial growth and domestic self-sufficiency in most agricultural products. The use of valuable foreign exchange earnings is usually restricted to products which do not substitute for products produced or capable of being produced domestically.

### U.S.-CANADIAN TRADE RELATIONS

The trade balance between the United States and Canada is favorable to the United States in both total and agricultural trade (Table 16.1). The U.S. position in agricultural trade results primarily from large net exports to Canada of cotton, fruits, and vegetables. Movement of capital from the United States to Canada is an offsetting factor to the total trade balance, but occasionally causes alarm among some Canadians.

Formal trade negotiations and discussions between Canada and the United States are centered in the General Agreement on Tariffs and Trade (GATT). Both countries participated fully in the recent Kennedy Round, granting as well as receiving concessions on each others' products. However, Canada, with permission of the United States and other GATT members, participated as a "special trade structure country."[2] Although required to reciprocate benefits received from other countries, Canada was not required to offer a linear cut in its tariff. The results of the negotiations for Canada and the United States are discussed in the commodity sections and summary.

In addition to GATT, representatives of Canada and the United States discuss trade issues regularly at meetings of the United States-Canada Joint Committee on Trade and Economic Affairs. Also, it is not uncommon for trade groups in the two countries to get together and discuss problems. No bilateral agreements which affect agricultural trade presently exist between Canada and the United States.

### U.S.-MEXICAN TRADE RELATIONS

The agricultural trade balance between the United States and Mexico is favorable to Mexico, while the total trade balance is in the United States' favor (Table 16.1). Here again capital move-

---

[2] This status was granted because of Canada's dependence upon export of primary products for which tariffs are generally low or nonexistent.

ment from the United States into Mexico, both in high tourist and investment expenditures, has been an offsetting factor to Mexico's negative total trade position.

The trade balances enter into trade discussions between the two countries. The United States uses its negative balance in agricultural trade with Mexico as an argument for reduced Mexican restrictions on imports of U.S. agricultural products. Mexico, in turn, points to its negative total trade balance with the United States and to its scarce foreign exchange position in defense of its import policies and as an argument for lower U.S. import restrictions on Mexican products.

No formal organization exists at present for trade negotiations between Mexico and the United States. On Mexico's initiative and by mutual consent the Mexico-United States Trade Agreement of 1942 was terminated in 1950. Since Mexico is not a member of GATT, this left the two countries with no contractual agreement under which to discuss trade problems. However, in 1965 a joint Mexico-United States Trade Committee was established for informal discussions between the two countries. Two annual meetings have since been held.

The question of GATT increasingly enters into U.S.-Mexican trade talks. Current U.S. policy is to negotiate tariff reductions only within the multilateral context of the GATT rather than with any particular country, such as Mexico. Although Mexico has considered joining GATT, it so far has been content to enjoy some of the tariff concessions made by the United States and other countries (but extended to Mexico as a most-favored nation) without having to make reciprocal concessions on imports. Mexico's problem as a nonmember of GATT, however, is not being able to directly request concessions on imports for which it is a major supplier.

### CANADIAN-MEXICAN TRADE RELATIONS

Trade between Canada and Mexico is minor for both countries, making up less than 2 percent of imports and exports. Agricultural trade is mostly one way—Mexico to Canada (Table 16.1). However, Canada's exports of nonagricultural goods to Mexico have usually been large enough to place Canada in a positive total trade position with Mexico.

The geographical separation of Mexico and Canada by the United States is a major factor in the low level of trade compared to that between the respective countries and the United States.

TABLE 16.1

INTRA-NORTH AMERICAN TRADE IN 1965, SELECTED ITEMS AND TOTALS*

| Commodity | Canada With U.S. | | Canada With Mexico | | U.S. With Mexico | | Total Intra-regional† |
|---|---|---|---|---|---|---|---|
| | Exports | Imports | Exports | Imports | Exports | Imports | |
| | | | *(million $US)* | | | | |
| Total Trade by Country | 4,670.1 | 5,594.3 | 49.3 | 25.2 | 1,055.7 | 637.9 | 12,082.5 |
| Agricultural Trade | | | | | | | |
| Fruits & vegetables | | | | | | | |
| Fruits | 9.5 | 117.4 | 0.2 | 4.2 | 4.6 | 28.0 | 163.9 |
| Vegetables | 15.1 | 68.0 | ... | 6.2 | 3.9 | 41.7 | 134.9 |
| Live animals | 64.9 | 7.2 | 0.8 | ... | 8.8 | 36.5 | 118.2 |
| Beverages | 106.6 | 3.6 | ... | ... | 0.3 | 1.5 | 112.0 |
| Oilseeds & products | | | | | | | |
| Oilseeds | 2.0 | 52.1 | ... | 1.2 | 1.3 | 0.2 | 56.8 |
| Vegetable oil | 0.3 | 18.6 | ... | ... | 7.7 | 1.4 | 28.0 |
| Oilseed cake and meal | 0.1 | 19.5 | ... | ... | 2.6 | 1.5 | 23.7 |
| Tropical products | | | | | | | |
| Coffee | 0.2 | 11.0 | ... | 3.0 | ... | 65.3 | 79.5 |
| Cocoa-chocolate | 3.9 | 2.1 | ... | ... | 0.2 | 2.6 | 8.8 |
| Other‡ | 3.0 | 0.9 | ... | ... | 0.3 | 5.4 | 9.6 |
| Meat & preparations | 54.5 | 19.6 | ... | ... | 2.9 | 17.7 | 94.7 |
| Cereals & preparations | 26.0 | 43.5 | ... | ... | 16.9 | 0.1 | 86.5 |
| Sugar-syrup | 6.4 | 5.5 | ... | 0.1 | 1.8 | 61.2 | 75.0 |
| Fibers | | | | | | | |
| Wool | 3.6 | 2.7 | ... | ... | 0.9 | 0.4 | 7.6 |
| Cotton | 0.3 | 49.4 | ... | 4.1 | 0.5 | 3.3 | 57.6 |
| Hard fibers | 0.2 | 0.3 | ... | 0.9 | ... | 4.4 | 5.8 |

TABLE 16.1 (continued)

| Commodity | Canada With U.S. | | Canada With Mexico | | U.S. With Mexico | | Total Intra-regional† |
|---|---|---|---|---|---|---|---|
| | Exports | Imports | Exports | Imports | Exports | Imports | |
| Crude materials | | | | | | | |
| Animal§ | 9.2 | 2.7 | ... | ... | 0.3 | 0.3 | 12.5 |
| Vegetable‖ | 14.8 | 14.7 | ... | 0.2 | 4.3 | 5.9 | 39.9 |
| Hides & skins | 22.4 | 17.4 | ... | ... | 9.4 | 0.6 | 49.8 |
| Animal feed¶ | 15.4 | 4.6 | ... | ... | 3.1 | 1.0 | 24.1 |
| Dairy products & eggs | | | | | | | |
| Dairy products | 0.8 | 2.8 | ... | ... | 6.9 | ... | 10.5 |
| Eggs | 0.6 | 3.7 | ... | ... | 0.2 | ... | 4.5 |
| Miscellaneous foods** | 0.4 | 10.0 | ... | ... | 2.6 | 0.1 | 13.1 |
| Tobacco (nonmanufactured) | 0.5 | 4.8 | ... | ... | 3.9 | 1.4 | 10.6 |
| Animal fats and oils | ... | 5.2 | ... | ... | 2.6 | ... | 7.8 |
| Total Agricultural | 360.7 | 487.3 | 1.0 | 19.9 | 86.0 | 280.5 | 1,235.4 |
| Percent Agricultural | (7.7) | (8.7) | (2.0) | (79.0) | (8.1) | (44.0) | (10.3) |

Sources: U.N., *Commodity Trade Statistics—1965*; and U.S. Dept. of Commerce, *U.S. Exports*, FT 420, and *U.S. Imports*, FT 125.
* Caution should be used in making strict comparisons since trade data vary depending upon the side from which they are viewed and the extent to which transshipments are excluded. Dots indicate only that trade was under $100,000.
† The figures in this column should be considered as only rough estimates because of the problem of data comparability noted in footnote*.
‡ Includes tea and maté, spices, and crude rubber (excluding reexports).
§ SITC 291. Includes bones, bristles, casings, etc.
‖ SITC 292. Includes gums and chicle, seeds for planting, cut flowers, etc.
¶ Excludes oilseed cake and meal, and fishmeal.
** SITC 099. Includes extracts, mustard, sauces, soups, yeast, vinegar, etc. Excluded are prepared fats such as lard, margarine, etc.

A further factor limiting Mexican exports to Canada is Canada's tariff preferences to British Commonwealth countries on many products which Mexico produces. These preferences are pointed out in the commodity sections of this chapter.

Canada and Mexico grant each other most-favored nation treatment as the result of a trade treaty signed in 1946.

## GENERAL TARIFF RESTRICTIONS

The total duty assessed to any given product depends upon the category classification; the rate including any preferences; and if the rate is ad valorem, the method of valuation. Also involved are any special fees or surcharges.

### CLASSIFICATION

Both Canada and the United States have their own tariff nomenclature, while Mexico follows the Brussels system. All three schedules have "basket" categories which include items not otherwise provided for and upon which duties are usually high. Also it is difficult to have particular items broken out of the basket category and assessed a lower duty. Some examples of how basket categorization restricts imports of agricultural products are cited later.

### TARIFF LEVELS AND PREFERENCES

Canadian import tariffs are imposed at three levels. The preferential or lowest rate is reserved for member countries of the British Commonwealth and is about half the general or highest rate applying to countries with which Canada has no treaty or trade agreement. Imports from both the United States and Mexico are accorded most-favored nation or middle rates.

The United States has a two-column tariff. The lower or most-favored nation rate applies to imports from Canada, Mexico, and other free-world countries whether or not members of GATT. However, the United States does grant tariff preferences below the MFN rates to some imports from the Philippines. These preferences are being phased out and will be eliminated entirely in 1974. Philippine agricultural products with current preferences include tobacco, copra, shredded coconut, coconut oil, canned pineapple and pineapple juice, sugar, and oil cake and meal.

Mexico grants tariff concessions on specified products only to member countries of the Latin American Free Trade Association (LAFTA). To date these tariff reductions have not greatly affected agricultural imports from Canada and the United States. However, this may change as more products are added to the concession lists or as the now proposed programmed tariff reductions take place within LAFTA.

The agricultural concessions granted in the Kennedy Round will reduce tariff restrictions on trade between the United States and Canada. Canada made concessions on about 52 percent of its imports from the United States (1964 value), while the United States made concessions on about 75 percent of its imports from Canada.[3] Tariff cuts by Canada will average a little over 50 percent while those by the United States will average 65 percent. Because of the border trade between the two countries, the concessions focused on equalizing duties on both sides, including the mutual elimination of tariffs on a number of similar items.

After full implementation of the Kennedy Round concessions, the U.S. tariff on dutiable Canadian agricultural products will average about 6 percent.[4] Dutiable U.S. agricultural exports to Canada will face an average tariff of about 9 percent. Mexico will benefit from some of the Kennedy Round tariff cuts even though a nonparticipant. To my knowledge, no overall evaluation exists of what Mexico may gain. Benefits in particular commodity areas are mentioned later.

**DUTY ASSESSMENT**

Tariffs on dutiable agricultural products entering Canada and the United States are usually either ad valorem or specific, but some are compound. When ad valorem, assessment is based upon (in general terms) the normal wholesale price in the country of export.

Seasonally variable rates on many fresh fruits and vegetables are characteristic of both the U.S. and Canadian tariff schedules. Such rates maximize tariff protection during the domestic marketing season. Also found in the U.S. tariff schedule are differentially higher rates which come into effect when imports exceed specified annual quantities (on a global basis) or a specified value per unit.

---

[3] USDA, *Report on the Agricultural Trade Negotiations of the Kennedy Round*, FAS-M-193, Sept. 1967, pp. 90–91.

[4] Canadian Department of Agriculture, "Canadian Agriculture and the Kennedy Round," *Canadian Farm Econ.*, Vol. 2, No. 3, Aug. 1967, p. 33.

Products entering Mexico face both a specific and an ad valorem duty. Usually the specific duty is minor while the ad valorem duty is substantial. The ad valorem duty is assessed upon the higher of invoice values or an "official price," the latter being the normal wholesale price in the principal supplying country unless notably lower than that prevailing on domestically produced goods. If so, and this frequently occurs, then the "official price" is based upon domestic prices, and a higher duty assessment results.

#### DUTY-FREE ENTRY

Many agricultural products enter duty-free into Canada and the United States, either totally or seasonally (Table 16.2). For the United States in 1966, the proportion was 47 percent of the import value.[5]

Additional items in U.S.-Canadian agricultural trade will become duty-free as a result of Kennedy Round concessions (items in parentheses, Table 16.2). The Canadian Department of Agriculture estimates that with full implementation of concessions, 30 percent of Canada's agricultural exports to the United States and 45 percent of U.S. exports to Canada will enter duty-free.[6]

Except for cattle for breeding purposes and goods purchased by official government agencies, Mexico allows no duty-free entry of U.S. or Canadian agricultural products into interior Mexico. However, Mexico has designated certain isolated areas as "free" zones in which specified goods may enter for use within the zone without payment of duty.[7] Even so, the list of eligible products and the quantities permitted frequently change, depending upon the feasibility of moving in domestic supplies.

Mexico eventually hopes to eliminate the free zones. However, restricted local market potential and isolation from interior markets are large obstacles to overcome. A current program subsidizes freight costs up to 60 percent and refunds the mercantile tax as inducements to move domestic goods into these areas.

---

[5] Thomas A. Warden, "Customs Duties on U.S. Agricultural Exports," *U.S. Foreign Agricultural Trade*, USDA, ERS, Sept. 1967.

[6] Canadian Department of Agriculture, "Canadian Agriculture and the Kennedy Round," *Canadian Farm Econ.*, Vol. 2, No. 3, Aug. 1967, p. 33.

[7] Included are Lower California; Northwest Sonora; Nogales; Angus Prieta; and Chetumal, Cozumel, Isla Mujeres, and Xcalak in Quintana Roo.

TABLE 16.2

AGRICULTURAL ITEMS IMPORTED DUTY-FREE IN 1967 OR TO BE IMPORTED DUTY-FREE AS A RESULT OF KENNEDY ROUND CONCESSIONS, SELECTED COMMODITY GROUPS*

| United States | Canada | Mexico, Interior† |
|---|---|---|
| Fruits and Nuts | Fruits and Nuts | Fruits and Nuts |
| Bananas | Seasonally free | None |
| Citrons | Cantaloupes | |
| Plantains | Pears | |
| Tamarinds | Strawberries | |
| (Apples) | (Apricots) | |
| (Apple juice) | (Cherries, sour) | |
| (Coconut & coconut meat) | (Grapes, *Vitus labrusco*) | |
| (Brazil nuts) | (Peaches) | |
| (Cashew nuts) | (Plums) | |
| (Lingonberries) | | |
| (Pear juice) | | |
| (Raspberries—seasonally) | | |
| Free year around | | |
| Almonds | | |
| Citrus fruit | | |
| Figs | | |
| Tropical fruits | | |
| Walnuts | | |
| (Apples) | | |
| (Citrus, prepared or preserved) | | |
| (Coconuts) | | |
| (Dates, n.o.p.) | | |
| (Dried apricots, pears, peaches) | | |
| (Lemon & lime juice) | | |
| (Nectarines) | | |
| (Passion fruit) | | |
| (Pineapple, canned) | | |
| (Berries, n.o.p.) | | |

Sources: Items 2, 4, 5, and 13 of bibliography.
* Items are fresh unless otherwise stated. Items in parentheses are Kennedy Round concessions.
† Excludes items moving into "free zones."

TABLE 16.2 (continued)

| United States | Canada | Mexico, Interior† |
|---|---|---|
| Vegetables | Vegetables | Vegetables |
| "Other" cowpeas | Free year around | None |
| Truffles | Artichokes | |
| (Beets) | Potatoes, dried | |
| (Turnips) | (Sweet potatoes) | |
| | (Dried herbs) | |
| | (Dried lima beans) | |
| | (Sweet potatoes, frozen) | |
| | Okra, sliced & salted) | |
| | (Hops) | |
| | | |
| | Seasonally free | |
| | Beans, green | |
| | Cabbage | |
| | Carrots | |
| | Cauliflower | |
| | Celery | |
| | Lettuce | |
| | Okra | |
| | Peppers | |
| | Spinach | |
| | Tomatoes | |
| | (Brussels sprouts) | |
| | (Corn on cob) | |
| | (Eggplant) | |
| | (Parsley) | |
| | (Parsnips) | |
| | (Peas, green) | |
| | (Radishes) | |
| | (Turnips) | |
| Animals, Live | Animals, Live | Animals, Live |
| Registered animals for breeding | Registered animals for breeding | Registered animals for breeding |
| Game animals | Bees | |
| Horses for slaughter | (Horses) | |
| (Sheep) | (Dairy cows) | |
| | (Animals, n.o.p.) | |
| Beverages | Beverages | Beverages |
| None | Natural mineral water | None |

TABLE 16.2 (continued)

| United States | Canada | Mexico, Interior† |
|---|---|---|
| Oilseeds & Products | Oilseeds & Products | Oilseeds & Products |
| Palm oil | Castor beans | None except when consigned to |
| Rubber seed | Soya beans | National Bank for Foreign |
| Tung nuts and oil | Calabar beans | Commerce |
| Babassu oil | Oil cake or meal | |
| Croton oil | Peanut shells | |
| Almond oil, sweet | Cotton seed | |
| (Castor beans) | Peanuts | |
| (Sesame seed) | Copra | |
| (Kapok seed) | Palm nuts | |
| | Flaxseed | |
| | Rapeseed | |
| | Castor oil | |
| | Cottonseed oil for canning fish | |
| | Vegetable oils for use in manufacturing | |
| | (Tung oil) | |
| | (Rapeseed) | |
| | (Sesame seed) | |
| | (Sunflower seed) | |
| Tropical Products | Tropical Products | Tropical Products |
| Cocoa beans | Arrowroot | None |
| Cocoa bean shells | Curry powder | |
| Coffee beans | Chicory | |
| Tea and maté | (Coffee, green) | |
| Various spices | (Cocoa beans) | |
| (Unsweetened chocolate) | (Cocoa butter) | |
| (Coffee extracts) | (Cocoa shells) | |
| (Cocoa cake, other) | (Maté) | |
| (Coconuts) | (Vanilla beans) | |
| (Coconut meat, fresh) | (Coconut) | |

Footnotes p. 337.

339

TABLE 16.2 (continued)

| United States | Canada | Mexico, Interior† |
|---|---|---|
| Meat | Meat | Meat |
| Horsemeat | Horsemeat | Casings |
| (Raw meat for feed) | Offals | |
| (Deer meat, fresh frozen) | Salt pork in barrels | |
| | Rennet | |
| | Casings | |
| | Animal liver paste | |
| Cereals | Cereals | Cereals |
| Cassava flour | Bread made with yeast | None |
| Tapioca | Corn grits | |
| Bread made with yeast | Rice, unhulled | |
| (Buckwheat) | (Buckwheat) | |
| (Milled buckwheat) | (Buckwheat flour) | |
| (Rice patna for soup) | | |
| Sugar | Sugar | Sugar |
| (Maple sugar) | (Maple sugar) | None |
| (Maple syrup) | (Maple syrup) | |
| Fibers, Raw | Fibers, Raw | Fibers, Raw |
| Cotton linters & waste | Cotton | None |
| Cotton under 1/8″ | Cotton linters & waste | |
| Jute | Flax | |
| Coir | Hemp or jute | |
| Kapok | Coir | |
| Ramie | Other vegetable fibers | |
| Sisal | | |
| Sumn | | |
| (Flax straw) | | |
| Istle straw | | |

Footnotes p. 337.

340

TABLE 16.2 (continued)

| United States | Canada | Mexico, Interior† |
|---|---|---|
| Animal Feed (excluding oilseeds) | Animal Feed (excluding oilseeds) | Animal Feed (excluding oilseeds) |
| Guar seed | Guar seed | None |
| (Bran) | (Straw) | |
| (Brewers grains) | (Hay) | |
| (Beet pulp, dried) | | |
| (Hay and straw) | | |
| (Grain hulls & screenings) | | |
| (Flaxseed screenings) | | |
| (Milling by-products) | | |
| Dairy Products & Eggs | Dairy Products & Eggs | Dairy Products & Eggs |
| Casein | None | None |
| Tobacco | Tobacco | Tobacco |
| Uncut stems | None | None |
| Animal Fats & Oils | Animal Fats & Oils | Animal Fats & Oils |
| None | Animal grease & oils for use in manufacture | None |
| Hides & Skins | Hides & Skins | Hides & Skins |
| Fur skin, raw, except fox | None | None |
| (Buffalo hides) | | |
| (Whole cattle hides over 12 lbs. each) | | |

341

*Section 22 Fees.* Section 22 of the Agricultural Adjustment Act of 1933, as amended, authorizes the President of the United States to restrict the importation of commodities by imposing quotas or fees if such importation tends to render ineffective or materially interfere with programs of the Department of Agriculture. In most cases the quota route has been followed and this is discussed in the next section. However, special fees are currently in effect on some sugar and sugar derivatives and have existed in the past on peanut oil, almonds, flaxseed, and linseed oil.

*Countervailing Duties.* As protection against imports which benefit from a bounty or subsidy, both United States and Canada can assess a countervailing or additional duty equal to the net amount of such subsidization.[8] However, neither country currently assesses any such duties on each others' agricultural products.

*Antidumping Duties.* The United States and Canada both provide for assessing antidumping duties on goods imported at less than determined fair market prices and which directly substitute for domestic goods.[9] Mexico has no need for such contingency because of its "official" price system. Under the U.S. law, an antidumping duty can be assessed only after prior determination of actual or likely injury to a domestic industry. To date the United States has made no such determinations on Canadian or Mexican agricultural goods. In contrast, the present Canadian law has no injury requirement and has been used to restrict entry of U.S. products. In the Kennedy Round, however, Canada agreed to adopt the new international rules on dumping, including a requirement for prior determination of actual or threatened material injury before duty assessment.

*Surcharges.* In addition to the specific and ad valorem duties, Mexico levies a barter surcharge up to 6 percent on most food imports as a means of securing funds for use in export promotion. To top off the tariff package, a customs surtax of 3 percent is assessed on the total amount of duty.

---

[8] Authorizations are found in Section 303 of U.S. Tariff Act of 1930 and Section 6 of Canadian Customs Tariff Act.

[9] U.S. Antidumping Act of 1921 and Section 6 of Canadian Customs Tariff Act.

# NONTARIFF RESTRICTIONS[10]

## CANADIAN RESTRICTIONS

Canadian nontariff restrictions on agricultural imports include prohibitions, import quotas, and restrictive licensing. The outright prohibitions are few, limited to oleomargarine, other substitutes for butter, and renovated butter.

Under the Export and Import Permits Act of 1954, as amended, import permits issued by the Minister of Trade and Commerce are required for commodities directly competitive with those under domestic price support programs. Products currently included are butter, cheddar cheese, skimmed milk powder, butter fat in any form, and animal casein and caseinates. Also, import licenses issued by the Canadian Wheat Board are required for importation of wheat, oats, barley, and certain products derived from these commodities. These latter restrictions date back to the Canadian Wheat Board Act of 1935.

Import licenses are valid from 1 to 6 months, depending on the product. No exchange permits, prior deposits, or prepayment of duties are required.

## MEXICAN RESTRICTIONS

Nontariff restrictions used by Mexico include embargoes or prohibitions, restrictive licensing, special permits, and quotas. Statutory embargoes exist on a few items which are all nonagricultural except for chocolate confections. However, importation of most agricultural products is subject to prior licensing by either or both the Ministry of Industry and Commerce and the Ministry of Agriculture. Import licenses are denied or restrictively granted for products substitutable for domestically produced goods. Special committees, made up of government and business leaders with interest in the particular product, determine whether licenses are issued.

Past complaints about Mexico's licensing system include the following: institution of restrictions without prior notice or presentation of opposing views, insufficient consideration of quality and domestic availability, and long delays in processing license applications or appeals.

No publication of official policy on the granting of licenses

---

[10] Not discussed are sanitary and health regulations.

for agricultural products has been made by the Ministry of Agriculture. The exact situation is thus not known until the Ministry of Agriculture is consulted, a recommended course of action for all importers.

The major exceptions to the import licensing requirement for agricultural products are food commodities imported by the National Food Supply Agency (CONASUPO). It has imported grains, beans, eggs, powdered milk, and other food products under its program in recent years. Also, vegetable oils cannot enter Mexico unless consigned to the National Bank of Foreign Commerce.

In some cases importation of foreign goods is conditional upon either a compensating export of some other domestic goods or a stipulated purchase of similar domestic goods, such as one domestic unit for every two units imported.

No exchange controls exist in Mexico. Foreign currencies may be freely converted into and out of pesos. Also nonexistent are any requirements for prior deposits or prepayment of duties.

## U.S. RESTRICTIONS

Import quotas are the principal nontariff barriers used by the United States. Products currently affected include sugar, wheat and flour, dairy products, cotton, and peanuts.

The sugar quotas as allocated on a country-by-country basis by Congress are authorized under the Sugar Act of 1948, as amended. Quotas on the other products are authorized by Section 22 of the Agricultural Adjustment Act of 1933, as amended, and consist of two types: global, on a first come, first served basis; and specifically assigned. The exact type used for various programs is discussed later. However, quotas under Section 22 may not be less than 50 percent of imports during the base period and, when specifically assigned, are based on the percentage contribution to total U.S. imports during the base period.

The Meat Import Law of 1964 authorizes the establishment of quotas on imports of certain meats, but such quotas have never been proclaimed. Details on this are given later in the chapter.

Some questions have arisen in GATT regarding the justification of import quotas. In 1955 GATT granted the United States a waiver with respect to import restrictions under Section 22. Since then the United States reports each year as to the status of the quotas and the possibilities of removal.

## SPECIFIC RESTRICTIONS ON COMMODITY TRADE

I now want to get more specific in terms of restrictions on trade in some of the more important commodity groups moving among Canada, Mexico, and the United States.[11] These groups are (in order of value of intraregional trade in 1965, Table 16.1) fruits and vegetables, live animals, beverages, oilseeds and products, tropical products (mostly coffee and cocoa), meat, cereals, sugar, and fibers. I also briefly look at several commodities of lesser trade importance which are noteworthy because of trade restrictions: dairy products and eggs, tobacco, and animal fats and oils.

### FRUITS AND VEGETABLES

United States-Canadian trade in fruits and vegetables is heavily in favor of the United States. Similar trade between the United States and Mexico is substantially and increasingly in Mexico's favor. Fruits and vegetables are also Canada's largest category of imports from Mexico, but little moves in the opposite direction.

There are so few problems in trading most fresh or frozen fruits and vegetables between the United States and Canada that growers in each country consider the other country as part of their normal market. The varieties, grades, packages, and plant quarantine regulations are similar and mutually respected. Tariff duties are minimal on most items although higher seasonal duties are characteristic of both tariff schedules. Canada does not always apply the seasonal duties for the length of time or geographical extent possible. United States citrus enters Canada duty-free.

Concessions in the Kennedy Round will add many new items to the duty-free lists of Canada and the United States and reduce the tariff on others. Canada will eliminate the duty on fresh apples, canned pineapples, some citrus juices, and some fresh vegetables. Duty cuts include a greater than 50 percent reduction on many fresh vegetables, a 50 percent reduction on raisins, and lesser reductions on citrus juices and dried vegetables.[12] No concessions were made on fresh pears and sweet cherries, most canned fruits, and canned and frozen vegetables. Canada also made one nontariff concession: removal of its

---

[11] See Tables 16.2 and 16.3.
[12] USDA, *Report on the Agricultural Trade Negotiations of the Kennedy Round,* FAS-M-193, Sept. 1967, pp. 90–91.

## TABLE 16.3
### CANADIAN, MEXICAN, AND U.S. RESTRICTIONS ON IMPORTS OF SELECTED AGRICULTURAL PRODUCTS, 1967*

| Items | Canadian Restrictions† | | Mexican Restrictions‡ | | U.S. Restrictions |
| --- | --- | --- | --- | --- | --- |
| | MFN | Common-wealth | General | LAFTA | MFN§ |
| | *(specified duties in $Canadian)* | | | | *(specified duties in $US)* |
| **Fresh Fruits** | | | | | |
| Apples | 0.25¢ lb. (free) | free | L, 85% | | 0.25¢ lb. (free) |
| Citrus | free–15% (free) | free | L, 50–100% | | SR on grapefruit, 0.9–1.5¢ (concessions) |
| Grapes | SR, free–10% or (free–1¢) | free | L, 75% | | SR (free) up to 12.5 (6)¢ lb. |
| Peaches & pears | SR, free to 1.5¢ or 10% | free | L, 50–85% | | SR, 0.25–0.5¢ lb. (concessions) |
| **Tropical** | | | | | |
| Bananas | 50¢ cwt. | free | not relevant | | free |
| Mangos | free | free | not relevant | | 3.75¢ lb. |
| Papaya | 15% (free) | free | not relevant | | 17.5 (8.5)% |
| Pineapples | free | | not relevant | | about 1.2¢ each |
| Melons | free | | L, 85–110% | | around 1–1.5¢, SR on cantaloupes |
| **Dried Fruits** | 1–3¢(1.5) or 10% | free | L, 60–110% | | 1–2¢ (concessions on some items) (free) |
| **Canned Fruits** | | | | | |
| Juice | 7.5(5)% | free–5% | L, 40–50% | | apple, 0.5¢/gal.; citrus 20–35¢ gal. (concessions) |
| Peaches | 2.25¢ lb. | 1.75¢ lb. | L, 60–110% | 9% | 20 (10)% |
| **Fresh Vegetables** | | | | | |
| Potatoes | 37.5¢ cwt. | | L, 20% | | TQ, 37.5 or 75¢ cwt. |
| Most others | SR, free to 2¢ lb. or 10% (many concessions) | | L, 20% | | SR, under 1¢ up to 2–3¢ lb. (many concessions) |
| **Canned Tomatoes** | 1.5–2.0¢ lb. | free | L, 70% | | 17 (13.6)–21 (14.7)% |

Footnotes p. 349.

346

**TABLE 16.3 (continued)**

| Items | Canadian Restrictions† | | Mexican Restrictions‡ | | U.S. Restrictions |
| | MFN | Commonwealth | General | LAFTA | MFN§ |
| | *(specified duties in $Canadian)* | | | | *(specified duties in $US)* |
| **Live Animals** | | | | | |
| Breeding | permit, free | | permit, free | | permit, free |
| Other | | | | | |
| Cattle | 1.5¢ lb. (free on dairy cows) | free | E, 20% | | TQ, 1.5–2.5¢ lb. (.7¢ on dairy cows) |
| Sheep, lambs | $2.00 head | free | E, 30% | | 75¢ head (free) |
| Swine | 1 (0.5)¢ lb. | free | E, 23% | | 1 (0.5)¢ lb. |
| Baby chicks | 2¢ each | free | L, 10% | | 2¢ each |
| Hens and turkeys | 2¢ lb. | free | L, 5% | | 2¢ lb. |
| **Oilseeds** | | | | | |
| Soybeans | free | | L, 40% | | 2 (1)¢ lb. |
| Cottonseed | free | | L, 20% | | 0.3¢ lb. |
| Copra | 0.95¢ lb. | free | not relevant | | 1.25¢ lb. except Philippine is free |
| Peanuts | free | | L, 50% | | Q, 4.5–7¢ lb. |
| Sesame | 7.5% (free) | 5% (free) | L, 40% | | 0.59¢ lb. (free) |
| Flaxseed | 10¢ bu. | free | L, 40% | | 1¢ lb. |
| **Vegetable Oils** | | | | | |
| Soybean oil | free–20 (17)% | 15 (10)% | L, 5% | | 45 (22)% |
| Cottonseed oil | 10% | free | L, 5% | | 3¢ lb. |
| Coconut oil | 10% | free | L, 40% | | 3¢ lb., except Philippine |
| Linseed oil | $1.55 cwt. (10)% | | L, 40% | | TQ, free or 1¢ lb. |
| Peanut oil | 10% | free | L, 40% | | 4.5¢ lb. |
| Sesame oil | 20% | free | L, 40% | | 4¢ lb. 1.5 (0.7)¢ lb. |
| **Oilseed Cake and Meal** | free | | L, 10% | | mostly 0.3¢ lb. |
| **Tropical Products** | | | | | |
| Coffee, toasted | 4 (2)¢ lb. | 3 (2)¢ lb. | L, 45% | | free |
| Coffee, extract | 7¢ lb. | 5¢ lb. | L, 45% | | free–3¢ lb. (free) |

Footnotes p. 349.

347

TABLE 16.3 (continued)

| | Canadian Restrictions† | | Mexican Restrictions‡ | | U.S. Restrictions | |
|---|---|---|---|---|---|---|
| Items | MFN | Common-wealth | General | LAFTA | MFN§ | |
| | *(specified duties in $Canadian)* | | | | *(specified duties in $US)* | |
| Cocoa, beans | $1.00 cwt. (free) | free | L, 35% | | free | |
| Cocoa, powder | 22.5 (15)% | | L, 100% | | 0.75 (.37)¢ lb. | |
| Cocoa, butter | 2.2¢ lb. (free) | free | L, 45% | | 6.2 (3)% | |
| Chocolate (not swt.) | 3–4 (1–2)¢ lb. | | L, 110% | | 0.625¢ lb. (free) | |
| Tea | free | | not relevant | | free | |
| Spices | 5–15% (concessions) | (mostly free) | L, 20–60% | | free–7.5¢ lb. (mostly free) | |
| **Fresh or Frozen Meat** | | | | | | |
| Beef | 3¢ lb. | | L, 13% | | 3¢ lb. | |
| Mutton | 6¢ lb. | | L, 13% | | 2.5–3.5 (1.7)¢ lb. | |
| Pork | 1.25 (.5)¢ lb. | | L, 23% | | 1.25 (.5)¢ lb. | |
| Poultry | 12.5% | | L, 20–23% | | chickens: 3–5¢ lb. | |
| Offals | 1 (.5)¢ lb. | | L, free | | VR, 1 (.5) or 5 (2.5)% | |
| **Meat Preparations** | | | | | | |
| Sausages, pork | 2¢ lb. | free | L, 50–60% | | 1.6–3.2 (1.6)¢ lb. | |
| Canned pork | 20–25% | 15% | L, 50–60% | | 2–3¢ lb. | |
| Canned beef | 30 (20)% | 15% | L, 50–60% | | 15 (7.5)% | |
| **Cereals** | | | | | | |
| Wheat | L, 12¢ bu. | L, free | L, 20% | | Q, 21¢ bu. of 60 lbs. | |
| Rice, brown | free | | L, 15% | | 1.25–1.5¢ lb. | |
| Rice, clean | 70 (50)¢ cwt. | 50¢ cwt. | L, 15% | | 2.5¢ lb. | |
| Barley | L, 7.5¢ bu. | L, free | L, 15% | 10% | 7.5¢ bu. of 48 lbs. | |
| Corn | 8¢ bu. | free | L, 1% | | 25¢ bu. of 56 lbs. | |
| Rye | 6¢ bu. | free | L, 15% | | 6¢ bu. | |
| Oats | L, 4¢ bu. | L, free | L, 15% | 10% | 4¢ bu. of 32 lbs. | |
| Sorghum | 7.5% (8¢ bu.) | 5% (8¢ bu.) | L, 5% | | 0.4¢ lb. | |
| Wheat flour or meal | L, 50¢ bu. | L, free | L, 45% | | Q, 52¢ cwt. | |
| Cornmeal | 50 (40)¢ | free | L, 1% | | 50¢ cwt. | |

| Items | Canadian Restrictions† | | Mexican Restrictions† | | U.S. Restrictions |
|---|---|---|---|---|---|
| | MFN | Common-wealth- | LAFTA | General | MFN§ |
| | (specified duties in $Canadian) | | | | (specified duties in $US) |
| **Cereal Preparations** | | | | | |
| Breakfast cereals | 15–20 (12.5–17.5)% | 15–20% | | L, 45% | 5 (2.5)% |
| Macaroni, etc. | 1.25 (.6)¢ cwt, | free | | L, 40% | 1–1.5¢ lb. (0.5–0.7)¢ lb. |
| Bakery products | 17.5–25% | free–20% | | L, 110% | 6.5 (3)% |
| **Sugar** | | | | | |
| Raw sugar | $1.50 cwt. | $0.36 cwt. | | L, 60% | Q, 0.66¢ lb. |
| Molasses for feed | 1¢ gal. | free | | L, 60% | 0.01¢ lb. |
| **Fibers** | | | | | |
| Cotton, under 1⅛″ | free | | | L, 35% | Mexico's Q = 18.5 thou. bales, free |
| Cotton 1⅛″ & over | free | | free, Q | Q, L, 6% | Q, 1.75–3.5¢ lb. |
| Linters & waste | free | | free | L, 35% | free |
| Hard fibers | free | | not relevant | | mostly free |
| **Dairy Products** | | | | | |
| Evaporated & condensed milk | 3¢ lb. | 2.5¢ lb. | | L, 35% | 1–1.7¢ lb. |
| Dry milk & cream | L, 4 (3.5)¢ lb. | L, 2.5¢ lb. | 6–9% | L, 15–30% | skim: 1.5¢ lb. milk: TQ, 2–6.5¢ gal. cream: TQ, E, 15–56¢ gal. |
| Fresh milk & cream | 20 (17.5)% | 15% | | L, 35% | |
| Butter | L, 12¢ lb. | L, 8¢ lb. | free | L, 40% | TQ, Q, L, 7 or 14¢ lb. |
| Cheese | L, 3.5¢ lb. | L, 3¢ lb. | free | L, 110% | Q, L, 12 (6)–25% |
| **Eggs** | | | | | |
| Fresh | 3.5¢ doz. | 2¢ doz. | | L, 40% | 3.5¢ doz. |
| Dried | 25 (20)% | 10% | | L, 25% | 27¢ lb. |

Sources: The U.S., Canadian, and Mexican tariff schedules; Canada Department of Finance, *Canada Tariff Concessions Agreed in the Kennedy Round Negotiations*, June 1967; U.S. Government Printing Office, *Report on United States Negotiations, Vols. I and II*; and USDA, *Report on Agricultural Trade Negotiations of the Kennedy Round*, FAS-M-193, Sept. 1967.

* Figures represent tariff duties; those in parentheses will be the final results of Kennedy Round concessions. Letters refer to restrictions as follows: L means restrictive import licensing; E, embargo or import prohibited; Q refers to quota, TQ to tariff quota, SR to seasonal tariff rates, and VR to value rates.

† The MFN rates are applicable to Mexico and the United States. Where Commonwealth rates are not shown, the rate is the same as that under MFN.

‡ General rate applies to both the United States and Canada. Only the ad valorem duties are shown, since the specific duty usually minimal in comparison. When the LAFTA rate is not shown, it is the same as the General.

§ Applies to both Canada and Mexico.

prohibition on imports of fresh fruits and vegetables in three-quarter bushel baskets.

As concessions to Canada, the United States will eliminate the duty on fresh apples and turnips, and reduce by 50 percent the duty on a number of other fruits and vegetables. No concession was granted on potatoes. The latter item is subject to a tariff rate quota which halves the duty from 75 to 37.5 cents per hundredweight for imports under specified annual quantities.[13] The Canadian duty on U.S. potatoes is a straight 37.5 cents per hundredweight.

The principal growth items in Mexican exports of fruits and vegetables to the United States have been fresh tomatoes, cantaloupes, watermelons, frozen strawberries, fresh oranges, orange juice concentrate, canned pineapples, onions, and peppers. Because of climate and abundant and low-cost labor, Mexico competes well in these and other fruit and vegetable items and is desirous of further increasing exports. United States duties on fresh tomatoes, lettuce, and strawberries vary seasonally and are relatively low. Duties on cantaloupes and watermelons vary seasonally and are higher, 20 to 35 percent ad valorem. Other items on which the Mexicans have complained about U.S. duties being too high include some tropical fruits, frozen strawberries, oranges and tangerines, cabbage, carrots, fresh as well as canned pineapples, and lime juice.

Mexico allows little importation of fruits and vegetables other than minor amounts into the border-free zones. Of concern to U.S. growers are the severe restrictions, embargoes, and high duties on importation of fruits which Mexico produces in minor quantities, such as apples, pears, and peaches. Also, Mexico has only a small canned fruit industry, but places prohibitive ad valorem duties of 50 to 110 percent on most canned fruits and juices. Again the Mexican philosophy is that such products would substitute for other domestically produced fresh products.

### LIVE ANIMALS

Registered cattle, sheep, and swine of accepted breeds move without tariff duty among Canada, Mexico, and the United States. All three countries require that a prior import permit be obtained from the respective Ministry or Department of Agriculture, but this is usually freely given except when a new breed is

---

[13] One hundred fourteen million pounds of seed potatoes and 45 million pounds of table potatoes.

involved. Most U.S. exports of livestock to Canada and Mexico are registered animals for breeding purposes.

Movement of nonregistered cattle is primarily from Mexico and Canada to the United States where they are subject to differential duty rates according to weight and to tariff rate quotas. In 1965 most of the calves and mature cattle (700 pounds and over) were below the tariff rate quotas and so entered at the lower rate of 1.5 cents per pound instead of 2.5 cents. Imports of feeders (200–699 pounds), which make up the majority of cattle imports in terms of value, are assessed at a straight 2.5 cents per pound regardless of quantity. In 1963 this worked out to about 13 percent ad valorem.[14]

Movement of nonregistered livestock into Mexico for eventual slaughter is currently prohibited by Mexico, but when not prohibited, ad valorem duties range from 20 to 30 percent. Movement of such livestock into Canada is subject to duties of 1.5 cents per pound for cattle, $2.00 per head for sheep, and 1.25 cents per pound for swine.

Canadian tariffs are at or below the U.S. level on cattle, substantially above on sheep, and the same on swine. Concessions in the Kennedy Round will reduce by 50 percent the U.S. duty on dairy cows and both the U.S. and Canadian duties on swine, and eliminate the U.S. duty on sheep.

Tariff duties on baby chicks and live poultry appear minor. Movement into Mexico is allowed only under prior license and, in the case of baby chicks, has dropped substantially from that of 1956–60.

## BEVERAGES

Much controversy exists as to whether beverages should be considered an agricultural commodity. The decision is not difficult for farm-produced wines but is considerably so for distilled beverages. In the case of intra-North American trade in beverages, nearly all is alcoholic and most of this is Canadian exports of whisky to the United States. Mexico also has a favorable balance in beverage trade with the United States, but the volume is minor compared to Canada's.

Mexico's ad valorem duties on most beverages are a restrictive 100 to 110 percent. Tariff duties in Canada and the United States are lower than those of Mexico and, on many

---

[14] United States Tariff Commission, *Beef and Beef Products*, TC Publication 128, June 1964, p. 128.

items, will be further reduced as a result of the Kennedy Round. Alcoholic beverages exported to Canada require a restrictively issued import license from the respective provincial Liquor Boards.

Beverages in small quantities move duty-free across the U.S.-Mexican and U.S.-Canadian borders. More stringent U.S. restrictions on such movements into the United States in recent years have been a particular source of Mexican complaints.

### OILSEEDS AND PRODUCTS

Canada is a major importer of U.S.-produced oilseeds (mostly soybeans, shelled peanuts, and cottonseed), oilseed cake and meal (mostly soybean, but some cottonseed and linseed), and vegetable oils (mostly soybean, cottonseed, and linseed). Most oilseeds and oilseed cake and meal enter Canada duty-free. Vegetable oils are usually assessed a 10 to 20 percent ad valorem duty, but this duty will be reduced on many items as a result of Kennedy Round concessions.

Mexico is attempting to achieve self-sufficiency in oilseeds and products. Imports of oilseeds and oils are restricted by licensing or ad valorem duties of 20 to 50 percent except when consigned to the National Bank of Foreign Commerce. Some soybean cake and meal is imported under license at an ad valorem duty of 10 percent.

Mexico exports peanuts, sesame seed, and occasionally some copra, safflower seed, and sesame oil. United States restrictions vary on entry of these products. A global quota under Section 22 has limited peanut imports since 1953. Copra may enter at a duty of 1.25 cents per pound, but faces competition from Philippine copra entering duty-free. Current U.S. duty on sesame seed will be gradually eliminated as a concession in the Kennedy Round, while the duty on sesame oil will be cut by 50 percent. Very little sesame oil from any source currently enters the United States. Imports of sesame seed are increasing: Mexico supplied about 6 percent in 1966.

### TROPICAL PRODUCTS

Imports into the United States of coffee beans and soluble coffee, cocoa beans, tea, and many spices are free of duty. Nominal U.S. duties exist on cocoa products and other spices. Unsweetened chocolate and most spices not already free will move to the duty-free list as a result of the Kennedy Round.

Canada gives tariff preferences on most tropical products to Commonwealth countries. These preferences undoubtedly have a negative influence on Mexican imports. However, in the Kennedy Round, Canada agreed to cut MFN duties on coffee beans, cocoa powder, unsweetened chocolate, and spices, and to allow duty-free entry of cocoa butter. These cuts will reduce the margin of British Commonwealth preference and benefit Mexico.

### MEAT AND PREPARATIONS

In 1965 Canada exported nearly three times as much meat and meat preparations to the United States as it imported. Mexican trade with the United States in 1965 was six to one in favor of Mexico. Canadian-Mexican trade was nil.

Most Canadian and Mexican exports to as well as imports from the United States are fresh beef and pork. Canadian and U.S. duties are minor and no import controls are exercised. Mexico allows some entry of beef and mutton at a 13 percent ad valorem duty but severely limits imports of pork and poultry by restrictive licensing and a 23 percent duty. Movement of preserved, prepared, and canned meat to Mexico is even more restricted by ad valorem duties up to 85 percent, and in the case of some pork products, prohibited entirely. Canadian duties on canned meats are higher than those of the United States.

As a result of the Kennedy Round, U.S. duties will be reduced on fresh pork and lamb, sausages, and canned beef. The concession on fresh pork was the largest single concession made to Canada. Canadian duties will come down on fresh pork, some preserved meats, and canned beef. None of these reductions by Canada or the United States will especially benefit Mexico.

Under the Meat Import Law of 1964, imports of beef, veal, and mutton into the United States may be made subject to quota by presidential proclamation if yearly imports are forecast to exceed by 10 percent certain target levels. No proclamation has yet been made.

### CEREALS

Trade in grains between the United States and Canada is a small proportion of the total volume produced. Although Canada imports considerable corn from the United States (about one-fourth its total supply), imports are likely below what would exist in the absence of subsidized freight rates on movement of feed grains within Canada. Import licensing by the Canadian

Wheat Board prevents imports of wheat, barley, and oats and most of their milled products. Brown or rough rice is imported freely since domestic production is nonexistent.

Mexico has achieved self-sufficiency in wheat and does not issue import licenses. Production is still fairly high-cost, however. Elimination of support prices and opening the borders would likely result in imports from the United States and Canada. Mexico has permitted some importation of rice and feed grains to supplement domestic supplies. Corn and sorghum face nominal duties.

United States quotas on imports of wheat for human consumption limit imports from Canada to just under 800,000 bushels of wheat and 3.8 million pounds of flour. In absence of this quota, imports of high-quality Canadian wheat into the United States would likely be greater, even at a tariff of 21 cents per bushel. Mexico is limited to imports of 100 bushels of wheat and 1,000 pounds of flour. United States duties on imports of corn are restrictive, 25 cents per bushel, but are relatively minor on other feed grains.

Imports of cereal preparations are restricted by licensing or medium to high duties in Canada and Mexico. Concessions in the Kennedy Round were made by both Canada and the United States on breakfast cereals, macaroni and similar products, and on bakery items. Even so, Canada's duties on breakfast cereals and bakery items will remain above those of the United States.

## SUGAR

Imports of sugar into the United States are subject to absolute quotas under the Sugar Act of 1948, as amended and extended. Mexico, along with the Dominican Republic and Brazil, has the second highest pro rata share, next to that of the Philippines.

Mexican exports of sugar to Canada are severely limited by a British Commonwealth tariff preference of about three-fourths the MFN duty.

Both Canada and the United States import some molasses from Mexico. Canada's MFN duty of one cent per gallon is eliminated to Commonwealth countries, which gives them a slight advantage over Mexico. The U.S. duty is only a fractional cent per gallon on molasses for feeding purposes.

## NATURAL FIBERS

Canada places no restrictions on imports of any natural fiber. The United States restricts importation of raw cotton by quotas on all types except rough or harsh under ¾-inch staple and by duties on long and extra-long staple. The quotas are the principal U.S. restriction and are on a country basis for short staple and global basis for long and extra-long staple. Mexico's share of the quota on the short staple is 18,500 bales, or about 60 percent of the total permitted importation of short staple.

No U.S. quotas or duties exist on importation of cotton linters, raw jute, henequen, or other vegetable fibers which Mexico produces. United States concessions in the Kennedy Round on broom corn and on some other straws and fibrous vegetable substances will benefit Mexico. A concession on flax straw and on "other processed jute" will benefit Canada.

Mexico restricts importation of short staple cotton from the United States by a prohibitive duty. Extra-long staple cotton from the United States faces licensing, an ad valorem duty of 6 percent, and competition from other countries for a global import quota of 4,000 bales. Very little enters Mexico.

### DAIRY PRODUCTS AND EGGS

Intra-North American trade in dairy products and eggs is mostly outward from the United States. The United States exports dry milk, cheese, and eggs to Canada and eggs, dry milk, and canned milk to Mexico. From Canada it receives some eggs, cheese, and butter. Mexican exports to the United States are nil. Trade between Canada and Mexico in dairy products is virtually nonexistent.

Mexico restricts imports of dairy products by licensing and by ad valorem tariffs ranging from 15 percent on dry skim milk to 110 percent on cheese. Allowed imports move mostly into the border-free zones where duties are not in effect. In 1964 severe limitations were placed on free-zone entry of evaporated milk by quotas, refusing licenses, or requiring importers to purchase one can of domestically produced product for every two cans imported. Restrictions have recently been relaxed and U.S. exports have recovered to near normal levels.

Some dry milk is imported into Mexico by CONASUPO, the state trading agency, and thus not subject to duties. Until recently, U.S. suppliers have usually outbid others for this market. However, during the past year or two as U.S. supplies of nonfat dry milk declined, France and other foreign suppliers have moved to supply CONASUPO's requirements.

Imports of dairy products into the United States are subject to both absolute and tariff rate quotas. In July 1967 absolute quotas were extended to several high-volume items not previously covered. The new proclamation limits dairy imports from all sources to around 1 billion pounds of milk equivalent, or about 1 percent of domestic production. Imports in 1966 were nearly three times this in milk equivalent.

Imports of fresh or frozen cream into the United States are prohibited except for some from New Zealand. Quotas on dry milk and especially dry cream, American type cheeses, butter, and products containing concentrations of butterfat limit imports from Canada. United States tariff rate quotas are such that only a small proportion of imports are eligible for the lowest duties. Canada has resented both the absolute and tariff quotas, feeling that its exports to the United States, especially of cheese, could be greatly increased. However, in the recent presidential proclamation, a global quota was established for cheddar cheese aged 9 months or more. Canada has been the principal supplier of this type of cheese and will likely be the major beneficiary.

Mexico has long maintained that a market exists in the United States for Cajeta, a confectionary product made of condensed goat's milk and sugar. To date this product remains classified as a commodity similar to malted milk and subject to a Section 22 quota. Mexico would like it exempted.

The United States made tariff concessions on various non-American types of cheese in the Kennedy Round. Few of these are exported by Canada, however. The United States made no concessions on dairy products subject to Section 22 quotas. As a concession to the United States, Canada will cut the tariff on powdered milk.

Fresh eggs are subject to licensing and high duty in Mexico, except when moving into the free zones. Exchange of eggs between Canada and the United States is substantially in U.S. favor. The U.S. duty on fresh eggs has been slightly higher than Canada's, but will be reduced as a result of the Kennedy Round to the same level, 3.5 cents a dozen. Canada will reduce its tariffs on dried and frozen whole eggs.

## UNMANUFACTURED TOBACCO

All three countries produce and trade in tobacco. Up until 1960 U.S. exports to Mexico were on the increase. Since then Mexico has imposed tobacco licensing requirements on unmanufactured tobacco which have reduced imports from the United States. In 1966 licensing requirements were further extended to include the Lower California free zone and movement from the free zone into interior Mexico of cigarettes containing foreign tobacco. Mexico now feels that her domestic production of various tobaccos is such as to preclude most imports of U.S. tobacco.

United States-Canadian trade in tobacco is heavily in U.S. favor. Import duties in both countries are low and no nontariff barriers exist. Although the United States grants duty-free entry to a portion of tobacco imports from the Philippines and lower than prevailing duties on the remainder, this preference probably has no effect on imports from Mexico more than Canada because of the types of tobacco involved.

## ANIMAL FATS AND OILS

The United States is the world's largest exporter of tallow and greases. Canada is also an exporter. Mexico is an importer, although movement into Mexico dropped off considerably after import licensing was imposed in 1959 to promote domestic production of oilseed. Exporters in the United States maintain that tallow and greases could be used in Mexico's feed industry but such importation has been resisted by Mexico's domestic oil industry.

A fate similar to that of tallow has also befallen U.S. exports of lard to Mexico, now limited by licensing requirements to small quantities mostly into the border zones.

## SUMMARY AND CONCLUSIONS

All three North American countries have numerous restrictions affecting intraregional trade, although most were not instituted solely for this purpose. In general the nontariff restrictions, the quotas and licensing, are greater obstacles than the tariff restrictions.

From the standpoint of present trade restrictions, two commodity areas appear to be the logical beginnings of a free trade or common market arrangement. The first is fresh and processed fruits and vegetables. As previously mentioned, trade in such between the United States and Canada already is relatively unrestricted. Adjustment problems would also be relatively minor. In order to join in, Mexico would have to make substantial changes in policy with regard to imports of horticultural products.

Another market arrangement suggested by present trade and trade restrictions is some type of livestock and meat community, maybe involving feeds as well. Prices of livestock and meat are already closely correlated between Canada and the United States. Also, federal meat inspection is nearly identical in the two countries. Canada would be faced with removal of freight subsidies on feed grains, greater imports of corn, and possibly some relocation of her livestock feeding industry. Mexico would also face difficulties in joining, namely removal of its restrictions on movement of meat and cattle.

## REFERENCES

(1) Canada Department of Agriculture, "Canadian Agriculture and the Kennedy Round," *Canadian Farm Econ.*, 2(3), Aug. 1967.

(2) Canada Department of Finance, *Canada Tariff Concessions Agreed in the Kennedy Round Negotiations Under the General Agreement on Tariffs and Trade*, Ottawa, Canada, June 1967.

(3) Haidar, Walter, *Foreign Trade Regulations of Mexico*, U.S. Department of Commerce, Overseas Bus. Repts. 66-62, Oct. 1966.

(4) Información Aduanera de México, *Nueva Tarifa del Impuesto General de Importación (Restructurada)*, Tercena Edición, 1967.

(5) International Customs Tariffs Bureau, *International Customs Journal—Canada*, Brussels, 1966.

(6) Masson, Francis, and J. B. Whitely, *Barriers to Trade Between the United States and Canada*, Canadian-American Committee, 1960.

(7) Office of the Special Representative for Trade Negotiations, *Report on United States Negotiations at General Agreement on Tariffs and Trade 1964–67 Trade Conference*, Vols. 1 and 2, GPO, 1965.

(8) Shertz, Lyle P., and Kay Neeley, *Barriers to International Grain Trade in Selected Foreign Countries*, USDA, FAER-126, May 1965.

(9) Southworth, Constant, and W. W. Buchanan, *Changes in Trade Restrictions Between Canada and the United States*, Canadian-American Committee, 1960.

(10) U.S. Department of Agriculture, *Agricultural Policies of Foreign Governments Including Trade Policies Affecting Agriculture*, Agr. Handbook 132, Mar. 1964.

(11) ——, *Agricultural Policies in the Western Hemisphere*, ERS, FAER-36, Oct. 1967.

(12) ——, *Agricultural Protection by Non-Tariff Barriers*, ERS-Foreign 60, Sept. 1963.

(13) ——, *Report on the Agricultural Trade Negotiations of the Kennedy Round*, Foreign Agr. Serv. Rept. M-193, Sept. 1967.

(14) U.S. Department of Commerce, *Preparing Shipments to Canada*, World Trade Inf. Serv., Part 2, No. 62-50, 1962.

(15) ——, *Selling in Canada*, Overseas Bus. Repts. 67-52, Aug. 1967.

(16) U.S. Tariff Commission, *Beef and Beef Products*, TC Publication 128, June 1964.

(17) ——, *Tariff Schedule of the United States Annotated (1965)*, TC Publication 163.

(18) Warden, Thomas A., "Customs Duties on U.S. Agricultural Imports," *U.S. Foreign Agricultural Trade*, USDA/ERS, Sept. 1967.

# PART SIX

# Policies and Programs Needed

# CHAPTER SEVENTEEN

# Possible Economic Arrangements

## G. E. BRANDOW

IN ORDER TO KEEP this chapter reasonably brief it has been written in general terms, but a multitude of specific situations must somehow be dealt with if a common agricultural market is ever created in North America. No claim is made that even all major problems have been anticipated.

I have not followed closely the injunction to "assume first that we wish to attain maximum contribution to world food needs." One of the several possible common market arrangements considered in this discussion is based on the assumption that the participating nations stand ready to operate agriculture at forced draft and will clear markets by exporting North American surpluses to poor countries. But this is not the situation most likely to exist. The forced-draft assumption is an important one. If pressure on agricultural production should bid up prices sharply and farmers should become highly prosperous, a common market might be easy to establish. But if surplus capacity should exist and prices drag, the all-too-familiar demands for aid for domestic agriculture would be strong, and agriculture might be the most difficult sector to bring into a common market, as has been the case in the European Economic Community.

G. E. BRANDOW, Department of Agricultural Economics, Pennsylvania State University. The author gratefully acknowledges the helpful comments of Donald J. Epp.

A common market, as the term is used here, would allow complete mobility of agricultural commodities in commerce on the North American continent, and prices for any one commodity would be uniform over the whole area except for quality, location, and similar differentials of the kind ordinarily found in a unified market. Greater mobility of factors than now exists is not assumed. Five possible arrangements for a common agricultural market are discussed:

1. Free market.
2. Free market plus food aid limited only by available supplies.
3. Import and export controls.
4. Direct payments and input subsidies.
5. Price support, production control, and supplementary devices.

## FREE MARKET

One means of making a common market work is to maintain a strictly free market for farm commodities, in the sense of imposing no governmental restrictions on production or marketing, supporting no prices, and providing no subsidies to farmers in the form of direct payments or assistance in acquiring production inputs. There would follow two kinds of results having important implications for income distribution and resource allocation. In the first place, farmers currently protected in some degree from the competition of more efficient producers in their own or other North American countries would receive lower relative incomes, and pressure to shift their labor and other resources to other employment would be strong. In the second place, total farm output in the United States, free from all restraints, would increase enough to lower the level of farm prices appreciably, for efficient and inefficient farmers alike. Thus existing pressure for a general shift of resources from agriculture to other pursuits would be intensified.

Instituting such a common market policy would be wholly rational only if the countries could bring about the indicated resource transfers fairly promptly. Unless resources were shifted, the principal gains in net national product expected from such a policy would not be achieved. Rather, there would be a redistribution of income in favor of nonfarmers and some redistribution of income within agriculture in favor of efficient farmers. Long experience with the mobility of farm labor and land responding to conventional economic stimuli shows that responses are slow, delayed, and imperfect. A logical step accompanying establishment of a common, free market for North American farm products, therefore, would be a program to improve farm resource mobility by providing alternative employment in rural areas, retraining farm workers, and shifting submarginal farm land to other uses. But this is neither a new need nor a new idea. Success along these lines is needed aside from any consideration of a common market, and experience with programs to date has mainly demonstrated the difficulty of being sufficiently effective.

One may question whether a strictly free market for farm products is desirable for efficiency, economic progress, and equity for individuals, but this is an old debate that will not be taken up again here. Clearly, however, objectives of participating nations as expressed in current domestic farm programs, development policies, and international trade controls would need to be drastically revised if a free common market were to be politically acceptable.

## FREE MARKET PLUS FOOD AID
## LIMITED ONLY BY SUPPLIES

A program to provide free or below-cost food to poor countries could be operated by a member country under any common market arrangement if the purpose of aid were entirely to help the recipient countries. Joint action with other common market countries might be desirable but would not be essential. Food would be purchased in the market for shipment abroad, and demand for this purpose would be part of total market demand.

Surplus disposal has been an important reason for U.S. food shipments under P.L. 480 and is likely to be one purpose of any substantial shipment program in the next decade. When this is important, at least part of the cost should be shared by the common market countries according to some measure of farm benefit. Problems of operating a food aid program would then become complicated enough to require a common market agency for administration and to resolve conflicting interests of member countries.

Conceivably the common market countries might decide to export food on concessional terms on whatever scale was needed to clear markets of unrestricted production at prices generally satisfactory to farmers. This would be a means of dealing with demands for agricultural income support in each country. It would require some shift of farm production toward a product mix more heavily weighted by export products. Import barriers would be needed to prevent the inflow of products into the common market for purchase and export as food aid, and subsidies on commercial exports would be necessary to bridge the gap between "prices generally satisfactory to farmers" and prices existing in commercial foreign trade. (Prices at which farm products move in international trade often are below "prices generally satisfactory to farmers" in North America.) The annual money cost of the program probably would be large, and how the cost should be shared among member countries would be a controversial issue.

A program under which food aid was tied exclusively to the availability of food surpluses in North America would be defective on a number of counts from the standpoint of developing adequate food supplies in developing countries. But it is a possible approach, and it would be a more acceptable one if the volume of food called for by aid considerations approximately matched available surpluses. Of the various arrangements considered here, it most closely approaches the assumption of maximum contribution to world food needs. If this purpose were paramount, an indispensable condition would be that the governments stood ready to provide markets at favorable prices for all that farmers produced.

## IMPORT AND EXPORT CONTROLS

The European Economic Community depends heavily on variable import levies and export subsidies to keep Community prices of a number of farm products above the levels at which they move in international trade. This is feasible for an area that is on an import basis or is approximately self-sufficient for leading farm products. Such devices, by themselves, would not be practical for holding North American farm prices at current levels because the area is a large net exporter of wheat, feed grains, soybeans, cotton, tobacco, and several other products. If production were in no way restrained, the volume of some products available for export under subsidy in commercial channels would be so large that the North American Common Market would be engaged in arrant dumping, and retaliatory political and economic measures would defeat the policy.

Thus it would be more difficult to support farm income in

a North American Common Market than in the EEC. Intervention in trade with countries outside the common market might be part of a politically acceptable arrangement, but intervention would be a necessary supplement to other measures rather than the primary means of achieving the market's goals.

## DIRECT PAYMENTS AND INPUT SUBSIDIES

Especially if no market-wide programs were adopted to support farm income, member countries might wish to give some assistance to their producers. Direct payments of the supplementary type are a way of doing this. (I distinguish supplementary payments that merely add to income—e.g., the U.S. wool payments— from compliance payments to induce participation in a production control program—e.g., the U.S. feed grain and wheat payments.) But problems appear: if, for example, the United States gave ordinary supplemental payments to its wheat growers when the North American Common Market was not controlling production, the United States could justly be accused of subsidizing its wheat growers in competition with Canada's and Mexico's.

Thus a common market probably should permit supplemental payments only under certain conditions. Such payments could be allowed when production was small—for example, if the producers did not account for more than 5 percent of the commercial common market supply. Or supplemental payments might be permitted when limited so as to provide no incentive to current or future production. This might involve making payments only on a base amount of production rather than on all of output.[1] Compliance payments would be acceptable and are discussed in another context in a later section.

Input subsidies are another form of producer assistance that individual countries might wish to use. Such aids range all the way from Mexico's water subsidies for development purposes to the U.S. agricultural conservation payments that aggravate chronic surpluses, and no way of drawing a clear line between them seems possible. Subsidies for farm inputs sometimes are part of regional development projects that are not confined to agriculture. Since development and ordinary income subsidy overlap so much here, the question is a particularly sticky one,

---

[1] Possible means of limiting payments are discussed in G. E. Brandow, "Direct Payments With Production Controls," *Economic Policies for Agriculture in the 1960's,* Joint Economic Committee print, 86th Cong., 2d Sess., 1960, pp. 65–74.

and rigid rules do not seem feasible. Input subsidies, credit assistance, and technical aid should be permitted unless in particular cases the effect is materially to alter production and comparative advantage of producers in different member countries.

## PRICE SUPPORT, PRODUCTION CONTROL, AND SUPPLEMENTARY DEVICES

As already suggested, the present national efforts to support farm income probably would have to be replaced by common market policies having roughly similar results if a common agricultural market were to be politically feasible. The sensitive and strategic commodities in this regard are the great field crops—wheat, feed grains, soybeans, cotton, and tobacco. Producers of these crops would suffer the greatest income declines if no programs were available and, except for soybeans, these are the commodities for which programs now are most significant, especially in the United States. Milk is also highly important.

The dominance of U.S. agriculture on the North American continent is especially obtrusive when one considers common market arrangements involving substantial government intervention. For most farm products important to two or more of the three countries, the U.S. output is several times that of either of its neighbors. The principal exceptions are wheat and sugar, for which the United States is less dominant. In some instances where the United States is by far the major producer, existing U.S. price support and supply control programs could be continued after formation of a common market, and the advantages of getting Canada and Mexico to participate might not be worth to any country the trouble of working out suitable arrangements.

Three general guidelines might be laid down to establish the terms under which price supports and production controls could be used in the common agricultural market:

1.  No program could restrict the shipment or exchange of commodities within the market.
2.  A member country that wished to support the price or control its own production of a particular commodity could do so, provided each of the other member countries consented to any restrictions on imports from nonmember countries that proved necessary to make price support effective. The consent requirement would be the major means by which nonparticipating member countries could protect their con-

sumers. Two member countries could join in a single commodity program if the third agreed to necessary import restrictions, and all three member countries could join in a
program for any commodity. No program could be discontinued or materially modified without 12 months prior
notice to other member countries.
3.   Except for programs in effect under (2) above, the only
interventions permitted to governments would be (a) supplemental direct payments as already defined, limited so as
not to encourage output expansion, and (b) input subsidies,
farm credit, and technical assistance, subject to general restrictions discussed earlier.

Under this arrangement, the United States could continue
its feed grain program much as it now is. Since domestic feed
grain prices in the United States are consistent with foreign trade
prices, no formal consent by Mexico or Canada would be required. Feed grain prices throughout the common market would
be brought to the level prevailing under the U.S. program but
would be more stable and, on the average, higher than in the
absence of any program whatever. Canadian grain transport
subsidies probably would have to be dropped as unworkable, as
McCalla has said. The U.S. soybean program could also be
continued.

Probably the United States and Canada would wish to work
out a joint wheat program. The certificates paid for by millers
of wheat for domestic food use under the U.S. program would
have to be dropped in any case because they would force prices
of wheat-derived food, especially flour, in different common market countries to be out of line with each other if wheat prices
were in line. A feed grain type of program, jointly operated and
paid for by the United States and Canada, would be a possible
arrangement for wheat. Probably price supports should be set
somewhat below the International Wheat Agreement minimums
so that North American suppliers would not price themselves out
of international markets, but no export subsidies should be employed. Total returns to U.S. producers would be significantly
reduced unless limited supplemental payments were also paid.

The United States and Mexico probably should agree on a
cotton policy but, in light of the difficulties the United States
encounters when it must agree only with itself, a joint program
would not be easy to develop. Again, a feed grain type of program seems most feasible. The level of price support and the

attractiveness of inducements to participate would be crucial and controversial. Probably concern about program costs would lead to a modest program under which there would be a strong tendency for production to shift to the low-cost areas both within and between countries. Member countries could augment the program with limited, supplemental payments, which would slow down the shift in location of production but probably would not prevent it indefinitely. Canada's consent to import barriers would be necessary.

Since the U.S. tobacco program is really a series of programs for different types, with high price supports and rigid controls for some types and none at all for a few, each common market member country could do about as it wished for its types of tobacco. A common import policy would be necessary, however, and export subsidies would raise so many problems that probably they would not be used. Excise taxes on tobacco products in member countries should be made consistent. Sugar policy would be a real tangle, which is nothing new for this commodity. Probably a workable arrangement would be for the U.S. policy to be extended to the common market, with Mexico and Canada given domestic market allotments based on recent production.

The United States and Canada could jointly operate a price support program for manufactured milk. The program might be designed more to stabilize prices than to provide substantial income support to producers. If any country wished to give more income assistance to its dairymen, it could use limited supplemental payments. Fluid milk programs could be operated on a market-area basis as is now done under the U.S. marketing order program. Similar though not necessarily identical programs could be operated within provinces or other geographic areas of Canada or Mexico, but more attention would have to be paid than at present to potential milk supplies from the United States.

For many other farm products, such as meat animals, poultry products, fruits, and vegetables, essentially a free market on the North American continent would prevail. Specific protection important to some specialized producers but not of major significance in the market as a whole would be lost as internal trade barriers fell. No agreement on a common market is possible unless member nations are willing to accept such consequences in agriculture and industry. Marketing orders and marketing boards dealing with specific products in particular locations could be continued and even much expanded. Domestic food consumption subsidies and purchase programs such as those operated by the U.S. government to ease specific surplus situations would not necessarily be modified. Protection against imports from nonmember countries would be demanded in some cases. Perhaps the best arrangement would be a moderate tariff representing about the same degree of protection to each commodity on the tariff list; the countries would then bargain about whether particular commodities were to be put on the list or admitted free.

Whenever price supports, production controls, and direct payments to farmers are widely used, a program to provide food on concessional terms to poor countries has a dual purpose—to aid recipients and to support domestic farm income. How a food aid program is operated has an important bearing on the burden of price support and production control operations. Thus, under the arrangement discussed in this section, the common market probably should establish a food assistance agency that would make concessional export decisions and coordinate them with supplies and farm programs within the market. The cost might be shared on two bases: one part of the cost, deemed to represent foreign assistance per se, might be shared according to national incomes; another part, representing aid to farmers, might be shared according to the expanded market the program provided for each nation's products.

Stocks of feed grains, wheat, and perhaps some other commodities should be adequate to meet most unforeseen contingencies. Stability of feed grain supplies and prices is necessary, if not always sufficient for stability, in the great meat animal, dairy, and poultry industries. And a program of food assistance to poor countries carries with it an obligation to supply food as needed rather than as growing conditions happen to make it available. Thus the common market might require, as a condition for any price support and supply control program for strategic commodities, that the program carry out also a reserve stock policy laid down by the common market. If no program capable of assuming such a responsibility existed, the common market should undertake a storage program of its own.

## CONCLUDING REMARKS

A discussion of a common agricultural market is likely to veer off into arguments about food costs to consumers and the merits of government intervention. Much of this is irrelevant to a common market, for if citizens of a nation want minimum-cost food and no government intervention in preference to other things, they can scrap farm support programs and eliminate all import barriers on foods and farm supplies.[2] (They would also be well advised to change some practices in the processing and distribution of food.) As already indicated, a common market might be set up to incorporate either no supports and interventions or heavy use of them. This chapter deals with possible common market arrangements rather than with the pros and cons of alternative farm policies in or out of a common market.

If price supports and supply controls were authorized under the guidelines proposed in the last section, the bargaining opportunities open to member countries would be a negotiator's delight. Member countries could not balance gains and losses on each commodity, but concessions on one might be offset by advantages on another. The opportunities for compromise offer one of the best possibilities that a common agricultural market might be made to work.

Consideration of possible programs adaptable to various commodity situations repeatedly focuses attention on voluntary production control of the type used in the United States for feed grains and on limited supplemental payments to producers. The appeal of the feed grain type of program for use in a common market is the same appeal that led to its adoption in the United States—it tackles the essential job of supply control, even if in a clumsy manner, and it coerces no one. Its cost is its greatest handicap, one likely to be more limiting in a common market than in the affluent United States. Supplemental payments would be the means of providing more income support to one nation's producers, when desired, than common market policy made possible. Limitation of payments to avoid incentives to expand production would be essential; even so, payments would tend to hold producers in business longer than they would otherwise stay. Limited, supplemental payments are imperfect from an economic standpoint, but they may be the best way to provide the flexibility required on political grounds. Probably the difficulty of finding workable methods of supporting prices at high levels, cost considerations, and objections from member countries not under pressure to support a particular group of

---

[2] A common market would improve the results of some changes in policy, however. For example, Canada probably would gain more from removing tariff on feed grains if at the same time the United States removed restrictions on imports of livestock products.

farmers would result in a somewhat less ambitious farm support policy for the common market than the United States now has.

Some significant shifts of production toward more efficient use of resources would occur, as suggested for cotton and for commodities for which no specific programs were proposed. Such mal-allocation as exists for other farm products would not be worsened and might be modestly improved. Nevertheless, no great gains in economic efficiency could be promised for any common agricultural market arrangement that was approximately consistent with the policies pursued independently by the member nations, and changes in those policies would not require the formation of a common market. The usual advantages of a common market in permitting economies of size, specialization, and the like are more compelling for industrial than farm products. Thus creation of a common agricultural market probably would be justified mainly on broader economic and political grounds than apply to agriculture alone.

# CHAPTER EIGHTEEN

# Needed Economic Mechanisms and Institutions

DAVID L. MACFARLANE and L. A. FISCHER

THE AUTHORS of this chapter have just completed a monograph on the implications of freer (not free) trade in the North Atlantic Community.[1] Despite the failure of the Kennedy Round discussions on agriculture, we did embrace some optimism with respect to the opportunity for the expansion of trade in agricultural products across the Atlantic. Thus we feel it is commendable that economists are generating research on an issue which may well become relevant to public policy in five, ten, or twenty years—that is, organizing the resources of agriculture for a maximum contribution to meeting world food requirements.

May we point to the fact that the assignment we have been given severely circumscribes our chapter. The task is to suggest or indicate the economic mechanisms and institutions required for the attainment of complete agricultural resource integration on a continental basis. And in the assignment the economic mechanisms and institutions for a common agricultural commodity market are excluded. Specifically then we must address ourselves to the following questions:

DAVID L. MACFARLANE, Department of Agricultural Economics, McGill University; L. A. FISCHER, Department of Agricultural Economics, McGill, University.
[1] *The Prospects for Trade Liberalization in Agriculture*, Montreal, Private Planning Association of Canada. (In press)

1. What kinds of institutional and economic mechanisms would achieve this complete integration?
2. How would educational, governmental, and financial institutions change?
3. Over what time period would such a condition have to become operative?
4. How would current economic and institutional services and structures have to be altered?

While we have noted that the chapter would necessarily be circumscribed you will appreciate that to provide even preliminary answers to these questions would more than tax a short discussion, let alone the ability of the authors.

Within the context of the present chapter, economic mechanism refers to the complex of techniques, institutions, and organizations which serve to advance the implementation of economic policy objectives. It includes the guiding and regulation of production and marketing through the price mechanism and by government policies. It thus includes the influencing of private and public decisions respecting the structure of production and marketing institutions and operations. Here, for instance, the provision of credit by public institutions and the control over the activities of private lenders would be critically important. But our definition carries us further. It includes the provision of training and education for those who work in agriculture and those who migrate from the industry.

Two preliminary questions are suggested immediately to Canadians or Mexicans: First, recognizing that we live under the shadow of an economic giant or colossus, we naturally ask which of our agricultural institutions could and which could not survive a common agricultural commodity market? Would not our Canadian country elevator system for small grains, or our dairy processing plant organization, have to change so extensively as to represent essentially new marketing institutions? The same question might well be asked about some Mexican marketing institutions. The second and more important question is: To what extent would the introduction of a common market permit the retention of characteristic national agricultural institutions and policies in Mexico and Canada? The European Economic Community (EEC) had to face this question and came up with an unequivocal answer: Each country would pursue independently its internal farm policy so far as measures of agricultural rationalization are concerned. And while the

Common Agricultural Policy (CAP) aims at a single commodity market, this does not remove from the six still sovereign states regulatory control over farm production and marketing. For instance, the role of cooperatives will continue to be far more important in some than in other countries. Let us say that the most the CAP does is to insulate its common market against third countries and to subject the markets of each of the six to increased competition from the other five. But even here there are barriers to a single fully competitive common agricultural market.

On a North American level our historical development as well as national pride and sensitivity would likely require a somewhat similar answer. We should hope that such a North American market would not be inward-looking, as is commonly said about the EEC. In fact, let us suggest that because of the historical importance of North American farm exports an outward-looking posture would be necessary. And one of the most important potential opportunities in such a market would be to provide a single or common approach to agricultural exports, both commercial and those involving foreign aid. A common agricultural market giving free rein to the forces of comparative advantage, with an appropriate transition period, we (as economists) could likely face. But, purely on political grounds, no country would likely be prepared to abandon its distinctive policies on agricultural rationalization, on agricultural education, or on the structure of other government institutions dealing with agriculture. But, as suggested, some of these might be severely shaken by the introduction of a common market. Thus we may state that a common agricultural market would require harmonization of national policies respecting agriculture, not the adoption of a single continent-wide farm policy. Putting the same issue in other terms, we must face squarely the issue of supranational powers. These there must be if we are to have complete integration of agriculture. But again these must be limited. The experience of the EEC is instructive in this context. Purely political considerations cannot be buried in the pursuit of farm income, farm efficiency, and welfare targets. Let us suggest that our whole approach to supranational power be limited on the one hand to a minimum necessary to secure a fairly workable arrangement for the integration of our agriculture, and on the other hand limited by the barrier imposed by national political considerations.

## KINDS OF MECHANISMS FOR
## COMPLETE INTEGRATION

Let us turn to the first of the four questions which have been posed: What kinds of economic institutions and mechanisms? Here, a useful point of departure is the experience of the EEC and the Council of Mutual Economic Assistance (COMECON). In both situations the issue of supranationality delayed and greatly circumscribed the progress of these groups. According to Heathcote "a supra-national organization is one which (a) by-passes the nation-state's authority and deals directly with the citizen; which (b) takes over some functions traditionally exer-cised by the nation-state; and (c) is in the position to originate decisions not only on behalf of the State but despite it."[2]

The Rome Treaty created four main authorities in the EEC: (a) the Assembly, (b) Court of Justice, (c) Council of Ministers, and (d) the Commission. The first two function as legal bodies to review proposals of the Commission and to observe the legal re-quirements of the Treaty. The Council of Ministers occupies an important role in the harmonization of the economic and politi-cal goals of the members. Each member state delegates one representative to the Council to study any particular question. Each state has veto power at this level. The Commission con-sists of nine members, two each from France, Germany, and Italy, and one from each Benelux country. In the latter stages of the transitional phase the Commission became very powerful and members were practically irremovable. But, under French pres-sure, an amendment reduced Commission powers, and now it recommends on basic issues to the Council of Ministers and represents the Community in international affairs. The mara-thon discussions on the CAP demonstrated the weakness of the Commission. The following committees serve the Commission: (a) The European Investment Bank; (b) The European Develop-ment Fund; (c) The European Social Fund; (d) The Administra-tive Commission for the Social Security of Migrant Workers; (e) The Budgetary Policy Committee; (f) The Monetary Policy Com-mittee; (g) The Committee of Central Bank Governors; (h) The Short-term Economic Policy Committee; (i) The Medium-term Economic Policy Committee; and (j) The Transport Committee. These are listed to illustrate the types of issues confronted by a

---

[2] Nina Heathcote, "The Crisis of European Supra-nationality," *Jour. Common Market Studies*, Vol. 2, 1966, p. 141.

common market. Each committee has task forces dealing with individual sectors of the economy. Of course agricultural policy turned out to represent the most difficult aspect. But the institutional machinery has been made to work, and the longer it continues in operation, the more difficult it would be to dismantle it. The governments of the Six have complied quite satisfactorily with the regulations of the Community, and thus far have not in matters of importance resorted to the use of the very important escape clauses.

While economic considerations dominate the EEC mechanism, political reasons were responsible for the creation in 1949 of the COMECON. Consequently the lack of unity both in political goals and in economic policies brought on a host of difficulties and resulted in changes both in membership and institutions. Eventually the reorganization of June 1962 brought about the prevailing structure. The system distinguishes between two categories of organizations, the permanent bodies and those constituted as necessity arises. The permanent institutions are: (a) the COMECON Council, (b) the Conference of State Representatives, (c) the Standing Commissions, (d) the Secretariat, (e) the Executive Committee, and (f) the Bureau of Plan Coordination. The highest authority, and on a political level, is the COMECON Council. In close cooperation with the Executive Committee, it makes recommendations to the members. The competence of these two bodies includes the direction of the implementation of plans, harmonization of investment programs, as well as overall direction of research. Duplication and confusion as between the activities of the Commission and the Secretariat have weakened the entire COMECON program. The Conference of State Representatives is composed of one delegate of each member state. Its competence includes all problems which call for the revision by the Council. It is authorized to adopt or reject recommendations prior to their submission to the Council. The Standing Commissions consist of experts delegated by member countries to deal with details of plans accepted by the Council and the Executive Committee. By 1962 there were 19 permanent commissions specializing in three main sectors of the economy: (a) manufacturing industry; (b) other economic sectors, including agriculture; and (c) scientific sector. The Commissions' main concerns are the determination of priorities in allocating outputs of certain key products, formulation of foreign trade agreements, selection of new investment projects, and coordination of production plans.

According to Korbonski, "the highest COMECON authorities have been unable to issue instruction and regulations directly binding on national agencies and individuals in member states. Their decisions must first be ratified by members and then incorporated into the national law of each country. . . . Little is known about the actual decision processes within COMECON. It seems that the lack of an authority to make decisions is the main obstacle (through the COMECON vehicle) to real *economic progress* in the countries involved."[3]

During the first decade of the COMECON, Moscow "provided the blueprint for the bloc's economic policy and was likely to have the final say insofar as the preparation and implementation of national economic policies were concerned."[4] Over the following period this political pressure eased and members have been much freer to pursue almost independent goals. Again this weakens the organization.

In terms of economic mechanisms and institutions, the critically important decisions are in the extent of supranationality. Some supranational organizations are necessary. The choice is between giving the supranational agency (a) power to require national governments to comply with its regulations (as in the EEC); or (b) power to recommend to the legislative bodies of the governments concerned (as in the COMECON). The former arrangement would be more effective, but more difficult to achieve, particularly if the common market included only the agricultural industry. Of course it should be recognized that on some issues the supranational agency might be given authority of the first type, while on others it would be limited to the second. Drawing on the experience of the EEC and COMECON, and simplifying to the greatest possible extent the minimum supranational institutional structures required would be (a) a representative political body and (b) a Secretariat. The latter could be divided into several bodies with varying degrees of autonomy, or each with complete autonomy. These would be responsible for planning, for executive functions, and for developing and administering common services.

Several contributors in this book have referred to the implications for the agriculture of the three countries of common markets and common prices. It has been suggested that, in the case of Canada, some programs and their implementing organiza-

[3] A. Korbonski, "COMECON," *International Conciliation,* Carnegie Endowment for International Peace, Sept. 1964, pp. 14 and 21.

[4] Korbonski, p. 6.

tions might well disappear. The Canadian Livestock Feed Board was suggested as one of these. The Canadian Dairy Commission and its production quota and price support programs might well represent another. Professor McCalla suggested that the United States' wheat certificate program might be preserved in a common market, but we should like to question that. And it would appear that the very comprehensive direction of Mexican agriculture would have to give way to much greater operation of market forces. But with an appropriate transition period such change might be accommodated with advantage. Generalizing at this point, a common market would require fewer programs and institutions interfering with resource and product flows. In fact a common market which would not be price oriented might be of questionable value. And the gain in pursuing comparative advantage, both to farmers and consumers, should allay most fears. This does not mean that there would be no advantage to be gained from some continent-wide farm adjustment programs. Wheat might be an illustration. But even here the existing well-developed institutional structures might be employed. Their objectives or tasks would be redefined.

## HOW WOULD EDUCATIONAL, GOVERNMENTAL, AND FINANCIAL INSTITUTIONS CHANGE?

Some governmental institutions have been considered. What of educational institutions? We in Canada hold in great admiration the U.S. Land-Grant College system embracing as it does teaching, research, and extension, and effecting a close coordination of federal and state activities respecting agriculture. For peculiar constitutional reasons, Canada has been unable to follow the American structure and thus has a fragmented and not well-coordinated approach in these areas. Nor is there prospect for change. Mexico, with a strong central government system, is in a better position on these matters. Extension and research are under control of federal agencies.

Again credit institutions reflect history, cultures, and the peculiar structural characteristics of the agriculture of the three countries. Canadians generally admire American farm credit institutions, particularly those concerned with production credit and credit for cooperatives, which are far more advanced than those of Canada. And Mexico with three government or government-supported farm credit institutions has a basic structure well designed to meet the needs of agriculture within the context of Mexican social and economic objectives. A supranational farm credit agency or coordinating body could effectively assist existing national credit agencies rather than replacing them. As has been noted, a common market credit agency could very well result in pumping into Mexican agriculture the credit resources needed to speed the structural adjustments of the agriculture of that country.

## THE TRANSITION PERIOD

Here one can be brief. Emphasis must be given to the exceedingly important differences within the agriculture of each country, let alone among three distinctly different countries. And, in each of the countries, agricultural policies are a vehicle for pursuing social as well as economic objectives. These considerations point to the desirability of a long transition period which could, as has occurred in the EEC, be shortened by agreement. When we suggest a long transition, we are thinking of periods from 10 to 20 years, but with explicit agreement that provisions of the market arrangement be effected in stages. Thus it is possible to think of positive achievements and results in periods as short as three to five years.

## HOW WOULD PRESENT INSTITUTIONAL SERVICES AND STRUCTURES BE ALTERED?

The answer to this is exceedingly difficult, and must be conjectural. We take the general position that some national institutions or structures would have to disappear in accommodating to a common internal price; others would be modified. We also embrace the view that some distinctively national institutions, for example, education, research, and extension, would in their essence be preserved, but would become more effective through the provision of services originating in the Secretariat of the common market. The same might be said of the national institutions concerned with the rationalization or restructuring of agriculture as required by the existence of a common market.

The extent to which individual countries make favorable institutional adjustments would in part determine the gains which would be secured from adjusting in the direction dictated by comparative advantage. A Canadian study attempted measures of comparative costs and found the cost differences to be very large. The study suggests that large gains could be realized from policies which encourage resource shifts consistent with comparative costs.[5]

We are sure we can safely say that regardless of how far the three countries under study move toward a full common market, the research reported and discussed in this book will make an important contribution toward each country's better understanding of its own farm problem. And this research and these discussions will give to us, to farm leaders, and to governments in the three countries an understanding of the gains to be secured by closer cooperation on this continent.

Whether on a commercial or on an aid basis North American agriculture will have an exceedingly important role to play in meeting world food needs. Any cooperation among the three countries in managing their food resources, including ultimately a common market, would improve greatly the effectiveness with which these world food needs are met.

## REFERENCES

Agoston, Istavan, *Le Marche Commun Communiste,* Librairie Droz, Geneve, 1955.

Baldwin, David A., and Frank Smallwood (eds.), *Canadian-American Relations,* The Public Affairs Center, Dartmouth College, Hanover, N.H., 1967.

Brandenburg, Frank R., *The Making of Modern Mexico,* Englewood Cliffs: Prentice-Hall, 1964.

Canadian Agricultural Economics Society, *Interregional Competition in Canadian Agriculture,* Ninth Annual Workshop of the C.A.E.S., Macdonald College, Quebec, June 17–20, 1964.

——, *Meeting the Needs of Tomorrow's Commercial Farmers,* Eleventh Annual Workshop of the C.A.E.S., United College, Winnipeg, June 22–24, 1966.

Coppock, John O., *Atlantic Agricultural Unity,* New York: McGraw-Hill, 1968.

——, *North Atlantic Policy, The Agricultural Gap,* New York: Twentieth Century Fund, March 1963.

Dawson, John A., *Changes in Agriculture to 1970,* Ottawa: Economic Council of Canada, Staff Study No. 11, 1964.

Economic Council of Canada and Agricultural Economics Research Council of Canada, *Conference on International Trade and Canadian Agriculture,* Ottawa: Queen's Printer, 1966.

*Food and Fiber for the Future,* Report of the National Advisory Commission on Food and Fiber, Washington, D.C., 1967.

Haviland, William E., *International Commodity Agreements,* Canadian Trade Committee, The Private Planning Association of Canada, Montreal, 1963.

---

[5] *Conference on International Trade and Canadian Agriculture,* Ottawa, Queen's Printer, 1966, No. 77–204.

Heady, Earl O., Edwin O. Haroldsen, Leo V. Mayer, Luther G. Tweeten, *Roots of the Farm Problem,* Iowa State Univ. Press, Ames, 1965.

Hillman, J. S., and E. L. Menzie, "Attempts to Expand Agricultural Exports Through United States Government Action," *Canadian Jour. Agr. Econ.* 1:1–16, 1964.

Johnson, D. Gale, "Agriculture and Foreign Policy," *Jour. Farm Econ.,* 1964, pp. 915–29.

Letiche, John M., "European Integration: An American View," *Comparative/International Series,* Univ. of California, 1965, pp. 1–22.

Mansholt, S. L., "Regional Agreements for Agricultural Markets," *Proceedings, 11th International Conference of Agricultural Economists,* 1961, pp. 83–94.

Menzie, Elmer L., "Special United States Restrictions on Imports of Agricultural Products," *Jour. Farm Econ.,* 1963, pp. 1002–6.

Padgett, L. Vincent, *The Mexican Political System,* Boston: Houghton-Mifflin Co., 1966.

Shefrin, F., "Trends in Canada's Agricultural Trade Pattern," Economics Branch, Canada Department of Agriculture, Ottawa, 1965.

Simpson, Eyler N., *The Ejido: Mexico's Way Out,* Chapel Hill: Univ. of North Carolina Press, 1937.

Sinclair, Sol, "EEC's Trade in Agricultural Products With Non-member Countries," *Internatl. Jour. Agrarian Affairs,* 1965, pp. 287 99.

Tuinman, Abe S., "The European Economic Community and Its Agricultural Policy," *Jour. Farm Econ.,* 1963, pp. 974–82.

Uri, Pierre, *Partnership for Progress,* New York: Harper and Row, 1963.

U.S. Department of Agriculture, *Agricultural Policies of Foreign Governments,* FAS, Agr. Handbook 132, 1957.

———, *The World Food Budget,* Foreign Agr. Econ. Rept. 19, 1964.

Vernon, Raymond, *The Dilemma of Mexico's Development,* Cambridge: Harvard Univ. Press, 1963.

# PART SEVEN

# Challenges and Opportunities

# CHAPTER NINETEEN

# Needed Policies

**S. C. SCHMIDT and H. G. HALCROW**

A COMMON MARKET involves complete integration of all important areas of economic activity, from commodity and factor markets to the development of human and natural resources. It allows free trade among member countries and protects them by a common external tariff against outside countries. This requires elimination in the various countries of institutional barriers to the flow of commodities and resources in the common agricultural production and marketing system. It also demands establishment by the involved countries of uniform internal policies and institutions to administer the common customs tariffs and trade policies with the rest of the world. A common market of Canada, Mexico, and the United States—a North American Common Market for Food and Agriculture (NACM)—would thus require that these countries reconcile their differences about national objectives and the hierarchy of their priorities and come to some agreement about the programs to achieve their common objectives. All this accomplished, a North American Common Market for Food and Agriculture could help expand exports and increase general welfare in its member countries by broadening their markets and increasing their efficiency.

Our discussion of the policies needed for effective implemen-

S. C. SCHMIDT, Department of Agricultural Economics, University of Illinois;
H. G. HALCROW, Department of Agricultural Economics, University of Illinois.

tation of a North American Common Market for Food and Agriculture is divided into three parts: (a) those policies concerned with farm commodities, (b) those affecting inputs and factor markets, and (c) those needed for development of human and natural resources. Since this chapter is a summary, it will attempt to draw these policies into an integrated framework without going into detailed discussions of the ramifications of each policy suggested.

## FARM COMMODITIES

The policies needed for farm commodities depend on the degrees to which different agricultural segments are advantaged or disadvantaged by the common market and on the compensations considered appropriate to redress the balance. This appraisal of the major commodity groups attempts to point out the advantages and disadvantages to producers and to indicate other changes that may affect market prices and consumption patterns.

### WHEAT

In the past, quotas, licenses, and other restrictions have virtually prohibited trade in wheat among Canada, the United States, and Mexico. In spite of this, U.S. policies have strongly influenced Canadian prices and sales as the two countries have competed in third country markets, and U.S. and Canadian price policies have affected Mexico's wheat trade in the same way they have affected that of most other exporting countries. Until 1963 world wheat prices were largely determined within the duopolistic market structure created by the export policies of the United States and Canada, as the Canadian Wheat Board sought to maximize sales returns within the price constraints of the Board's initial payments at the lower level and of the U.S. support price at the upper level. Within this context Canada operated as a price leader and the United States as a price follower since the United States was a residual supplier in commercial markets because of its high price supports, acreage restrictions, and export subsidy programs.[1] Mexico's wheat prices were held well above those of the United States, Canada, and the world market, which required Mexico to subsidize wheat exports to maintain domestic prices.

---

[1] For further discussion, see Alex F. McCalla, "Implications for Canada of United States Farm Policies," and H. G. Halcrow, "Discussion," *Jour. Farm Econ.*, Dec. 1967.

Recently however—beginning in 1963–64 and becoming more pronounced in 1964–65—there has been a shift in U.S. wheat policies to lower price support levels, certificate payments, and decreased export subsidies.[2] United States market prices for wheat have moved closer to those of the world market and have come closely in line with those of Canada[3] and Mexico.[4] Free trade and free market pricing between the United States and Canada would result in large shipments of Canadian hard spring wheat to the United States to mix with U.S. winter wheats. United States winter wheat exports would increase to countries outside the NACM. United States exports of winter wheat would increase by more than the increase in imports as total exports from the NACM increased, and the U.S. winter wheat producers would benefit further from smaller sales of Canadian spring wheat in third countries. Thus the greatest adverse effect would be on Mexican producers and on spring wheat growers in the United States as both became subject to increasing competition from intercountry trade.

Major policy decisions needed to implement an NACM for wheat will revolve around the size and duration of compensatory subsidies to wheat producers in the shift to the common market pricing system. The subsidies could, for instance, be continued indefinitely or tapered off. There are other decisions. The current U.S. certificate program is compatible with a free trade area but inconsistent with the general principles of a common market. We will have to determine how long compensation like this should continue and whether production restrictions should be applied to reduce the costs of government programs. Canada has paid a subsidy to its railroads to compensate them for not being permitted to raise rates. This has resulted in producers getting higher prices than would otherwise be the case. Consider, for instance, the effect on prices of the fact that the Canadian

---

[2] The 1966 average wheat price received by producers was $1.63 a bushel. Farmers participating in the wheat program also received certificates that averaged 59 cents a bushel. The estimated price equivalent thus received by cooperators was $2.22 compared with the $2.13 average estimated "blend price" for all producers.

[3] For the 1965–66 marketing year, the final return to Canadian farmers—after transportation, handling, and Canadian Marketing Board costs were deducted—was $1.69 (U.S.) a bushel in Manitoba No. 1, $1.66 in Manitoba No. 2, and $1.58 in Manitoba No. 3.

[4] The Mexican government's 1965–66 support price to farmers was $1.99 (U.S.) a bushel. In 1966–67, this was reduced to $1.74 a bushel in the states of Sonora, Sinaloa, and Baja California, which produce about two-thirds of Mexican wheat crops. It remained at the 1965–66 level in the other states.

rate for wheat from Moose Jaw to Fort William/Port Arthur is 12 cents a bushel compared with the U.S. rate of 47.4 cents a bushel for the comparable distance from Goodland, Kansas, to Chicago.[5] Under the authority of the Temporary Wheat Reserves Act of 1955, Canada also pays interest and storage costs of wheat stocks above 178 million bushels held by the Canadian Wheat Board.[6] It will have to be decided if practices like these are consistent with common market policy.

Another factor that will affect policy for an NACM is the International Wheat Agreement, to which all three countries are signatory. It will require means of allocating quotas among the NACM countries and of accommodating free market pricing within the NACM to the arrangements of the IWA which apply externally. The new World Grains Arrangement is another factor which will require study. In principle, however, such agreements or arrangements need not create a greater problem for the NACM than they do for a single country if the three countries can agree on a common approach. The various export subsidy aid programs carried out by the United States and Mexico and the contract sales made by Canada to the USSR and China could also be continued within the framework of the NACM, although we scarcely need to be reminded of the political problems involved.

Since wheat prices in the three countries of the NACM have closed most of the price gap that previously existed among them, the chief remaining policy questions center on the subsidies and other programs that may be used to move toward a uniform production and marketing system.

## FEED GRAINS

The feed grain markets of the NACM are not institutionalized so governmentally as the wheat market, but they have stronger ties through (a) larger internal trade, (b) integrated livestock markets, and (c) a tradition of relatively free market pricing, both internally and with third countries.

Although the United States, Canada, and Mexico trade more feed grain than wheat, the total amount of this trade has been

---

[5] Lyle P. Schertz and Roy L. Neeley, *Barriers to International Trade in Selected Foreign Countries*, USDA, FAS, Foreign Agr. Report No. 126, May 1965, p. 22.

[6] Carrying charges paid by the government of Canada to the Canadian Wheat Board amounted to $24.3 million for the 1966–67 crop year; Canada Dept. of Agriculture, *Canadian Farm Econ.*, Vol. 2, No. 2, June 1967, p. 26.

small compared with the trade between these countries and the rest of the world. The only feed grain that Canada has imported in significant quantities has been corn from the United States. Although the United States was the sole supplier of Canada's corn import requirements, these shipments accounted for only 3.2 percent of total corn exports in 1965. In 1964 and 1965, imports of U.S. corn into Canada totaled $28.7 million and $26.7 million respectively (Table 19.1). These imports came in over a tariff of 8 cents a bushel. (This compares with tariffs of 4 cents a bushel on oats and $7\frac{1}{2}$ cents a bushel on barley, neither of which was imported and both of which are subject to importation licenses approved by the Canadian Wheat and Feed Boards.)

Canada also imported $25.6 million worth of feeding stuffs from the United States, or 98 percent of its total imports in this category. The bulk of these imports consisted of oilseed cakes and meals and other vegetable residues. The magnitude of these purchases in total U.S. exports was small, amounting to only 9.2 percent of the total.

Reciprocal Canadian exports of feeding stuffs to the United States were valued at $22.6 million in 1965 and supplied close to 38 percent of U.S. total imports. They represented about 37 percent of total Canadian exports.

Canadian coarse grain exports consist of barley, oats, and rye. In 1965 Canada exported $7.7 million worth of barley to the United States, which used most of it for malting purposes. These shipments accounted for 19 percent of total Canadian barley exports and over 97 percent of U.S. barley imports. Canada also exported feed barley to Western Europe, Japan, and Israel. In addition to barley, the United States also purchased substantial volumes of oats and rye from Canada.

Exports of U.S. feed grains to Mexico have been almost negligible because of the tariff system and licensing requirements. In fact, in the last three years Mexico has changed from a net importer to a significant net exporter of both wheat and corn, a most encouraging development for the Mexican economy. By 1965–66 Mexico was exporting 1.3 million tons of corn compared with none two years earlier,[7] although it should be pointed out that this gain has been made by subsidizing exports up to a third of their price.[8] The only grains imported into Mexico from the United States in any significant quantity were rice and barley valued at $2.5 million and $7.4 million respectively

---

[7] UN, FAO, *World Grain Trade Statistics, 1965–1966,* Rome, 1966, p. 59.

[8] Corn price support for the 1965–66 crop in Mexico was $1.83 per bushel.

TABLE 19.1

THE SHARE OF TWO-WAY TRADE BETWEEN CANADA AND THE UNITED STATES IN SELECTED AGRICULTURAL COMMODITIES, 1965

| Commodities | SITC Code | U.S. Exports to Canada | | | Canada's Exports to U.S. | | |
|---|---|---|---|---|---|---|---|
| | | Value | Share in total U.S. exports | Share in total Canadian imports | Value | Share in total Canadian exports | Share in total U.S. imports |
| | | | *(percent)* | | *($ mil.)* | *(percent)* | |
| **Livestock and Products** | | | | | | | |
| Live animals | 001 | 5.9 | 16.6 | 100.0 | 64.8 | 91.2 | 59.6 |
| Meat, fresh | 011 | 11.8 | 8.6 | 43.3 | 45.0 | 79.7 | 18.5 |
| Meat, dried, etc. | 012 | 6.0 | 43.4 | 100.0 | 5.3 | 59.5 | 86.6 |
| Cheese | 024 | 0.9 | 25.7 | 14.4 | 0.2 | 1.8 | ... |
| Eggs | 025 | 3.3 | 28.4 | 94.7 | 0.5 | 55.5 | 71.4 |
| **Fish** | | | | | | | |
| Fish, fresh | 031 | 7.3 | 35.0 | 64.0 | 129.0 | 83.4 | 34.0 |
| Fish, canned | 032 | 4.9 | 17.3 | 38.9 | 3.4 | 11.8 | 9.7 |
| **Grains** | | | | | | | |
| Corn | 044 | 26.7 | 3.2 | 100.0 | 7.7* | 19.0* | 97.4* |
| Cereal preparations | 048 | 3.5 | 7.1 | 53.6 | 8.4 | 52.8 | 45.1 |
| **Fruits and Vegetables** | | | | | | | |
| Fruits, fresh | 051 | 77.3 | 46.3 | 61.8 | 6.5 | 45.7 | 2.2 |
| Fruits, dried | 052 | 5.9 | 11.2 | 41.8 | ... | ... | ... |
| Fruits, preserved | 053 | 38.2 | 31.7 | 61.5 | 2.8 | 39.4 | 4.3 |
| Vegetables, fresh | 054 | 53.6 | 47.6 | 85.0 | 14.4 | 48.3 | 13.3 |
| Vegetables, preserved | 055 | 9.6 | 26.9 | 48.5 | 5.5† | 56.7† | 1.1† |
| **Feeds and Oilseeds** | | | | | | | |
| Feeding stuff | 081 | 25.6 | 9.2 | 98.3 | 22.6 | 36.6 | 37.7 |
| Oilseeds | 221 | 52.1 | 7.4 | 92.2 | 2.0 | 2.2 | 3.1 |
| Tobacco, unmanufactured | 121 | 4.7 | 1.2 | 83.9 | 0.4 | 1.2 | ... |
| Cotton | 263 | 50.8 | 10.0 | 77.8 | 3.5‡ | 83.3‡ | ...‡ |
| Fertilizers, crude | 271 | 12.7 | 18.8 | 98.4 | ... | ... | ... |

TABLE 19.1 (continued)

| Commodities | SITC Code | U.S. Exports to Canada | | | Canada's Exports to U.S. | | |
|---|---|---|---|---|---|---|---|
| | | Value | Share in total U.S. exports | Share in total Canadian imports | Value | Share in total Canadian exports | Share in total U.S. imports |
| | | | *(percent)* | | *($ mil.)* | *(percent)* | |
| Crude Materials | | | | | | | |
| Hides and skins | 211 | 8.6 | 7.8 | 89.7 | 5.2 | 24.6 | 8.3 |
| Fur skins | 212 | 4.9 | 11.8 | 44.5 | 17.1 | 58.9 | 15.9 |
| Forestry Products | | | | | | | |
| Wood and pulpwood | 242 | 24.2 | 19.4 | 99.6 | 28.5 | 56.6 | 66.6 |
| Lumber | 243 | 37.6 | 31.4 | 87.0 | 325.5 | 70.8 | 91.3 |
| Pulp and waste paper | 251 | 14.6 | 6.7 | 88.4 | 348.6 | 75.3 | 90.7 |
| Oils and Fats | | | | | | | |
| Animal oils and fats | 411 | 2.9 | 1.5 | 71.8 | 9.2§ | 63.8§ | 17.4§ |
| Vegetable oils | 412 | 11.2 | 4.5 | 54.1 | 14.7‖ | 66.2‖ | 13.7‖ |

Source: Computed from OECD, *Commodity Trade*, Series B and C, Paris.
* Magnitudes refer to barley (SITC group 043).
† Magnitudes refer to sugar (SITC group 061).
‡ Magnitudes refer to wool and other animal hair (SITC group 262).
§ Magnitudes refer to miscellaneous crude animal materials (SITC group 291).
‖ Magnitudes refer to miscellaneous crude vegetable materials (SITC group 292).
... Insignificant.
Space does not permit the presentation of trade data by subgroups or items (the four- and five-digit code of the SITC). They are given in the source footnote above.

# TABLE 19.2

## The Share of Two-way Trade Between Mexico and the United States in Selected Agricultural Commodities, 1965

| | | U.S. Exports to Mexico | | | | | Mexico's Exports to U.S. | | |
|---|---|---|---|---|---|---|---|---|---|
| Commodities | SITC code | Value | Share in total U.S. exports | Share in total Mexican imports | Commodities | SITC code | Value | Share in total Mexican exports | Share in total U.S. imports |
| | | ($ mil.) | (percent) | (percent) | | | ($ mil.) | (percent) | (percent) |
| Livestock and Products | | | | | Livestock and Products | | | | |
| Live animals | 001 | 6.1 | 17.2 | 84.9 | Live animals | 001 | 24.3 | 100.0 | 31.2 |
| Meat, fresh | 011 | 2.5 | 1.8 | 100.0 | Meat, fresh | 011 | 18.3 | 99.4 | 7.5 |
| Milk and cream | 022 | 6.8 | 4.6 | 98.2 | | | | | |
| Grain | | | | | Fish | | | | |
| Rice | 042 | 2.5 | 1.0 | 95.2 | Fish, fresh | 031 | 47.0 | 99.7 | 11.8 |
| Barley | 043 | 7.4 | 9.6 | 100.0 | Fish, canned | 032 | 2.9 | 96.6 | 5.5 |
| Corn | 044 | 1.5 | .1 | 100.0 | | | | | |
| Cereals, unmilled, other than those above, and wheat | 045 | 3.1 | 1.3 | 92.3 | Grains | | | | |
| | | | | | Corn | 044 | 3.2 | 4.1 | ... |
| Fruits and Vegetables | | | | | Fruits and Vegetables | | | | |
| Fruits, fresh | 051 | 3.2 | 1.9 | 80.9 | Fruits, fresh | 051 | 19.7 | 86.4 | 5.6 |
| Fruits, dried | 052 | .7 | 1.3 | 66.6 | Fruits, preserved | 053 | 16.1 | 87.5 | 19.7 |
| Fruits, preserved | 053 | .6 | .4 | 70.0 | Vegetables, fresh | 054 | 23.3 | 88.5 | 43.4 |
| Vegetables, fresh | 054 | 3.4 | 3.0 | 93.9 | Sugar and Honey | 061 | 71.9 | 92.6 | 12.8 |
| Vegetables, preserved | 055 | .5 | 1.4 | 87.5 | Coffee, Tea, Cocoa, and Spices | | | | |
| Feeds and Oilseeds | | | | | Coffee | 071 | 58.0 | 88.4 | 6.1 |
| Feeding stuff | 081 | 6.4 | 2.1 | 56.2 | Cocoa | 072 | 3.3 | 100.0 | 1.8 |
| Oilseeds | 221 | 1.3 | .1 | 100.0 | Spices | 075 | 1.9 | 76.0 | 4.7 |

TABLE 19.2 (continued)

**U.S. Exports to Mexico**

| Commodities | SITC code | Value ($ mil.) | Share in total U.S. exports (percent) | Share in total Mexican imports (percent) |
|---|---|---|---|---|
| Tobacco, unmanufactured | 121 | 3.9 | 1.0 | 98.4 |
| Fertilizers, crude | 271 | 1.9 | 2.8 | 100.0 |
| Crude Materials | | | | |
| Hides and skins | 211 | 9.2 | 8.4 | 96.9 |
| Crude vegetable materials | 292 | 4.3 | 8.4 | 74.5 |
| Forestry Products | | | | |
| Wood, pulpwood | 242 | 1.7 | 1.3 | 92.8 |
| Lumber | 243 | 2.8 | 2.3 | 100.0 |
| Pulp and waste paper | 251 | 8.3 | 3.7 | 77.8 |
| Textile Fibers | | | | |
| Wool and other animal hair | 262 | .8 | 6.0 | 4.9 |
| Cotton | 263 | .4 | ... | 75.0 |
| Jute | 264 | ... | ... | ... |
| Oils and Fats | | | | |
| Vegetable oils | 412 | 7.0 | 2.8 | 94.7 |

**Mexico's Exports to U.S.**

| SITC code | Value ($ mil.) | Share in total Mexican exports (percent) | Share in total U.S. imports (percent) | Commodities |
|---|---|---|---|---|
| 081 | 4.8 | 90.5 | 4.6 | Feeds and Oilseeds Feeding stuff |
| 112 | 1.2 | 70.5 | ... | Alcoholic Beverages |
| 121 | 1.3 | 39.3 | 1.5 | Tobacco, unmanufactured |
| 251 | 1.4 | 73.6 | ... | Pulp and Waste Paper |
| 221 | .3 | 15.7 | ... | Oilseeds |
| 263 | 48.1 | 30.9 | 13.2 | Cotton |
| 292 | 7.8 | 88.6 | 5.5 | Crude Vegetable Materials |
| 413 | 1.4 | 77.7 | 13.0 | Animal, Vegetable Oils and Fats, processed |
| 271 | .8 | 100.0 | 9.6 | Fertilizers, unmanufactured |

Source: Computed from OECD, *Commodity Trade*, Series B and C, Paris.
... Magnitude insignificant.

(Table 19.2). These purchases covered practically all (95 to 100 percent) of Mexico's import needs. The United States also supplied Mexico with $6.4 million worth of feeding stuff, 56 percent of total Mexican imports in this category. Mexico has had no trade in grains and feeding stuff with Canada.

An NACM would open up considerable opportunity for exports of feed grains from the United States to both Canada and Mexico. Canada would be a large importer of U.S. corn, which would have a significant effect on the Canadian livestock industry, which would benefit from cheaper feed, and on certain grain farmers who, unless they were also livestock feeders, would face additional price competition. Those most affected would be corn and winter wheat growers in Ontario and barley growers in the Western provinces. These corn imports also would provide the corn-processing industry, which uses about half the corn imported from the United States, with cheaper grain for starch and distilling.

Since much of the corn produced in Ontario is used on farms or industries located in the province of Quebec, the removal of the Canadian freight subsidy on feed and the 8 cents a bushel tariff on U.S. imports would increase the competitive position of U.S. corn in both Eastern and Western Canada.[9]

The price elasticity of Canadian demand for corn imported from the United States was found to be quite high (—1.4), suggesting that the lower prices achieved by the removal of existing tariffs would have a more than proportional effect on Canadian imports. It was estimated that the tariff removal would increase imports by as much as 9.5 percent over the 1946–61 average.[10] This great an increase in the supply of corn would lower Canadian feed grain prices, which could not only reduce the feed input costs for livestock producers but also pose an adjustment problem for the grain producers. A decrease in the spread between Canadian wheat and feed grain prices could shift the composition of grain output.[11]

In general, the effects of an NACM in feed grains would be these: Canada would not only produce more livestock but it

[9] A study of the effect of feed freight assistance was made by T. C. Kerr, *An Economic Analysis of the Feed Freight Assistance Policy,* Agr. Econ. Res. Council of Canada, Ottawa, 1966.

[10] Dennis W. Ware, "The Economic Implications of Free Trade in Agricultural Products Between Canada and the United States," Ohio State Univ., unpublished Ph.D. dissertation, 1965, pp. 110–11.

[11] E. E. Weeks, "Maximum Profit Livestock Rations That Include Wheat." *Jour. Farm Econ.* 47:669–80, Aug. 1965.

would also become a larger exporter of livestock and meat products to the United States and Mexico. Mexico would increase its imports of U.S. corn sharply and its livestock production would increase as well. An NACM would also increase U.S. exports to outside countries. There appears to be little basis for producers to fear that other exporting countries would ship significant amounts of grains to the NACM over the long run, although a free market without a common external tariff could encourage considerable imports of Argentine corn, which has domestic prices as much as a third lower than U.S. or Canadian prices. Rather, the chief policy decisions concern the effect of an NACM on feed grain producers in Canada and Mexico. Increased livestock production in these countries will reduce the need for compensatory payments to feed grain producers there; but the fact remains that as Mexican imports of U.S. corn increase sharply and as Mexican corn prices fall by about a third, the Mexican government will be faced with several alternatives, one of which will be to subsidize producers during the transitional period.

### LIVESTOCK AND LIVESTOCK PRODUCTS

In 1965 the United States exported about $25 million worth of livestock and meat to Canada, while Canada exported about $119 million to the United States. The U.S. exports accounted for all of Canada's imports of live animals and dried meats and for 43 percent of the value of its imports of fresh meat (Table 19.1). Canada's exports of fresh beef and veal, pork, and feeder and fed cattle to the United States, on the other hand, accounted for 60 percent of the value of U.S. imports of live animals, 87 percent of its dried meat imports, and 18 percent of its fresh meat imports. The relationship of these particular exports to total U.S. and Canadian exports in these categories gives them a much more important role in the Canadian economy and, although the total amount of this trade is not large, it can amplify or dampen short-term fluctuations in both countries.

Generally, however, Canadian and U.S. livestock prices move in unison. Fed-cattle prices in Canada in 1965 followed the same trend as those in the United States. Pork prices in 1965 also followed parallel courses in the two countries, as lower supplies in both caused prices to rise. (The United States is the chief market for Canada's pork and pork products, most of it hams, backs, and bellies, and Canada in turn imports fresh and frozen U.S. pork, most of it bellies and sides, to cover supply deficits in the Eastern provinces.) Both countries also impose tariffs on fresh meat of 3 cents a pound for beef and 1¼ cents a pound for pork,[12] and their tariffs on cattle and calves are about the same except that Canada does not impose quotas on imports. The direction of the flow of livestock and livestock-product trade between the two countries is thus determined by price and supply rather than by barriers. Whenever the spread between Canadian and U.S. prices exceeds the tariff rates, livestock and meat products move from the lower to the higher priced market.

Eliminating duties and restrictions on U.S.-Canadian trade under a common market may therefore have little effect on the magnitude and pattern of the flow of cattle, beef, and veal between the two countries, although it could somewhat increase trade and narrow the few price gaps that exist. One of its most likely effects would be to increase meat or livestock shipments to the United States as Canadian feeders benefit from lower feed costs and larger markets. Such cattle imports into the United States would, as now, generally supplement and complement domestic production and involve increased use of feed grains and labor. Another likely effect would be to increase competition between the two countries for sales of variety meats, hides and skins, tallow, and breeding cattle in foreign markets. For although U.S. beef exports—including some pickled and cured beef and somewhat less canned beef—are relatively minor compared to its imports, most of their value is accounted for by packinghouse products, variety meats, and especially tallow, hides, and skins, exported mainly to Western Europe.

The major U.S. and Canadian adjustments for a common market would be to coordinate existing legislation (a) on interprovincial and international trade in agricultural products, particularly that now administered under the Canadian Agricultural Products Standards Act, (b) on livestock and livestock-product marketing, and (c) on provincial and federal support of livestock prices, like that authorized by the Agricultural Stabilization Act of 1958.

The necessary adjustments in Mexico would be somewhat

---

[12] In the Kennedy Round, their tariffs were reciprocally reduced from 1¼ to ½ cent a pound on fresh pork and from 1 to ½ cent a pound on live hogs. No reciprocal concessions were made on fresh, chilled, or frozen beef, veal, or live cattle. USDA, *Foreign Agriculture Including Foreign Crops and Markets*, Vol. 5, No. 41, Oct. 9, 1967, pp. 3–4.

different. Between 1961 and 1966, the United States has imported an annual average of $57.6 million worth of Mexican livestock and meat products, about two-thirds of it live cattle of 200 to 700 pounds, brought in mainly for feeding, and the other third boneless beef. The average annual U.S. exports to Mexico were $13.6 million.[13] During this same period, beef consumption has risen by more than production, which has resulted in a decline in total exports.[14] Per capita consumption of beef and all meats can be expected to continue to rise, commensurate with rising incomes. If lower feed prices under an NACM were to encourage more cattle feeding in Mexico, that country could probably further increase its domestic meat consumption, raise the level of its feed imports, particularly U.S. corn, and decrease its live cattle exports, even as it increased production so much that it could boost its meat exports.

Livestock is a major part of Mexico's agricultural exports and an important source of dollars. Compared with the United States and Canada, however, the Mexican livestock economy is characterized by frequently defective business handling, organization, and management, by low technical and economic efficiency in marketing, and by protective tariff structures and trade policies.[15] Entirely apart from any question of a common market, these problems demand high priority in government policy. Productivity, for instance, could be increased by programs for controlled breeding, pasture rotation, improved feeding, and more efficient health and disease controls. The marketing system could be improved by programs to establish organized markets, official and enforced grading standards, modern slaughterhouses, and more meat-packing plants. Producers could be greatly aided by price control and easier livestock credit.[16] Finally, trade in a common market will require reducing the specific and—particularly high—ad valorem duties which burden the trade of all livestock and livestock products except breeding animals and fresh milk. In view of the weak competitive position of the Mexican livestock industry, however, the removal of the protectionist tariff structure and concomitant transi-

[13] John E. Riesz, *Livestock and Meat Industry of Mexico,* USDA, FAS, FAS-M-185, March 1967, pp. 4–5.

[14] Robert H. Wuhrman, *World Beef Trends,* USDA, FAS, FAS-M-173, June 1966, pp. 11–12.

[15] UN, FAO, *Livestock in Latin America: Status, Problems and Prospects: I. Colombia, Mexico, Uruguay and Venezuela,* New York, 1962, pp. 40–46.

[16] In 1962 the stock farmer's share of the retail price in Mexico was 25 percent compared with over 50 percent in the United States.

tion to a common market must be accomplished in stages and by the concurrent adoption of the development policies suggested above.

A last comment on the overall effect that a common market would have on U.S. livestock producers may be in order. A study made by Menzie, Hillman, and Waelti[17] has shown that Brandow's[18] retail price flexibility estimate of —1.15 would put the range of possible reduction in U.S. farm prices, due to increased beef imports from all countries, between 2.4 percent in 1955 and 12.8 percent in 1962. Considering, however, that these imports have tended to change directly with U.S. domestic prices, they have had a generally stabilizing effect on the livestock economy in the United States. Another study by Ware[19] estimated that removing U.S. duties and quotas on Canadian cattle would increase by 27 percent the number of cattle 700 pounds and over exported into the United States. Even with this increase, however, these cattle would be only a small proportion of the total U.S. slaughter of cattle over 700 pounds and would have limited influence on the U.S. livestock economy. Nor, Ware estimated, would eliminating the 1½ cent a pound tariff on dairy cattle have much effect on their prices in the United States, although it would increase the flow of Canadian dairy cattle to the United States.[20] On the whole, then, eliminating tariffs would benefit U.S. consumers and dairymen and would have little effect on the livestock industry.

#### DAIRY PRODUCTS

The dairy industry is one of the most highly protected segments of agriculture in both Canada and the United States. For example, Canada levies an ad valorem 20 percent tariff on each gallon of whole milk or cream imported, collects 12 cents a pound on butter imports, and requires import permits on butter, cheddar cheese, and dried skim milk. The dairy industry in Canada—like the poultry industry there—is disadvantaged by a

---

[17] E. L. Menzie, J. S. Hillman, and J. Waelti, *The Relevance of Livestock and Meat Imports to the United States,* Univ. of Arizona Tech. Bull. 164, July 1964, pp. 23–24.

[18] G. E. Brandow, *Interrelationships Among Demand for Farm Products and Implications for Control of Market Supply,* Pennsylvania State Univ. Bull. 680, Aug. 1961, pp. 38–43.

[19] Ware, p. 135.

[20] Ware, pp. 128–29. Under the Kennedy Round, it should be added, the United States cut this duty by 50 percent in exchange for reciprocal concessions from Canada.

22½ percent ad valorem import duty on equipment and by an 8 cents a bushel duty on corn. The United States has graduated duties on milk, cream, butter, and most cheese, and it reinforces these by quotas which effectively limit the importation of dairy products. Imports of Canadian cheddar cheese, that country's main dairy export, are limited to 614,120 pounds per year. Most other trade in dairy products between the United States and Canada is practically nonexistent.

A common market would improve the competitive position of Canada's dairy industry and could enhance its importance in world markets, but a common market would also adversely affect the U.S. dairy industry, particularly in the north central and northeastern regions and acutely in New England and the adjacent territory. Compensatory programs for dairymen in these areas would probably be necessary, at least during a transition period. However, the purchases of Canadian dairy cattle also made possible by the common market would provide a complementary source of supply in the eastern and midwestern United States for dairymen who found it advantageous to buy rather than to raise their replacement stock.[21]

The dairy industry in Mexico is also highly protected, although perhaps less so than in the United States and Canada. Ad valorem duties on some products are especially high, ranging from 15 percent on milk powder to 50 percent on cheese.[22] Although fresh milk is exempted from burdensome specific and ad valorem duties, Mexico's trade in dairy products with the United States and Canada is practically nil, except for the small quantities of powdered milk it imports from Canada. Mexican dairying is further hampered by having no milk marketing and processing system comparable to the United States and Canada. Its marketing and processing are carried on by producers, independent processing plants, cooperatives, or middlemen. The industry is highly inefficient and could be integrated into a common market only after its overall performance was enough improved to be in line with that of the other member countries.

The immediate objectives of dairy policy for a common agricultural market of Canada, Mexico, and the United States would be two in number. First, the U.S. Federal Milk Marketing Order program and the Canadian Dairy Support program

[21] In the Kennedy Round the United States reduced its tariff on dairy cattle over 700 pounds from 1½ cents a pound to 0.7 cents a pound. Canada, in turn, granted tariff-free entry to dairy cows imported for breeding purposes. The preceding discussion on livestock is pertinent.

[22] UN, FAO, *Livestock in Latin America:* . . . p. 44.

would have to be coordinated, with particular reference to the levels and methods of price supports and to the disposal of surplus stocks in home and foreign markets. Second, intergovernmental assistance programs would have to be initiated to aid producers' structural adjustments.

### POULTRY PRODUCTS

Trade in poultry products among Canada, the United States, and Mexico is very small compared with production. The little trade that does exist between the United States and Canada is restricted by Canadian import tariffs of 5 cents a pound on broilers, 5 to 10 cents a pound on turkeys, $12\frac{1}{2}$ cents on chickens, and $3\frac{1}{2}$ cents a dozen on eggs, and by U.S. import tariffs of 2 cents a pound on live poultry, 3 cents a pound on chicken meat, and $8\frac{1}{2}$ cents a pound on turkeys. In recent years, most of the trade has been in hatching eggs and breeding stock shipped from Canada to the United States. Canada is a net importer of poultry meat, live poultry, and shell eggs.

An NACM would provide cheaper feed to the Canadian poultry industry and consequently contribute to the expansion of its production. The United States would, however, still retain considerable comparative advantage in poultry and egg production. Consequently U.S. exports of eggs and poultry (including turkey) to Canada would increase. The Canadian poultry industry is highly institutionalized; poultry sales are handled by marketing boards that assign producers' quotas, and egg prices are supported by deficiency payments. An NACM will thus require policies and programs to facilitate adjustments in the Canadian poultry industry and to expose its producers to market forces.

### FRUITS AND VEGETABLES

Fruits and vegetables present a more heterogeneous pattern of trade among the three countries of the proposed NACM because more individual commodities are involved. Most of Canada's imports of fruits (citrus, fresh and dried fruits, and fruit juices) and vegetables come from the United States. Indeed, these imports represent the principal commodity groups in Canada's total imports from the United States. Their value was $185 million in 1965, $77.3 million of it for fresh fruits and about $54 million for fresh vegetables. These purchases covered approximately 62 percent of Canada's fresh fruit and 85 percent of its fresh vegetable import requirements. As corollary, the share of these commodities in total U.S. exports amounted to 46 and 48 percent respectively (Table 19.1). Canadian tariff concessions made at the Kennedy Round may even further stimulate U.S. exports: tariffs on fresh and frozen apples, limes, nectarines, and blueberries, on dried peaches, pears, and apricots, and on lime and lemon juices were entirely eliminated. Tariffs on cranberries and raisins were cut in half; and the tariff-free periods for a number of vegetables including brussels sprouts, corn on the cob, green onions, radishes, and broccoli were lengthened.[23]

The effect of a common market on Canadian imports of U.S. fruits and vegetables—much like the effect of these Kennedy Round concessions—would be concentrated on specialized fruit- and vegetable-growing regions in the provinces of Nova Scotia, Ontario, Alberta, and British Columbia. Canadian potato growers under a common market, however, would also face increasing competition from their American counterparts: Western Canadians from Americans in Washington and Idaho, and Canadians in the Maritime provinces from their neighbors in Maine.

On the other hand, neither U.S. reciprocal tariff concessions in the Kennedy Round[24] nor the formation of a common market would greatly affect Canadian exports. Canada exports very few fruits and vegetables to the United States, except for seasonal shipments of special products. Most Canadian exports, in fact, are of apples, carrots, turnips, blueberries, and canned or frozen vegetables to Western Europe and of potatoes to the United States and South America. The exception might be that the expanding production of Canadian peas and beans processed as frozen products would benefit from a wider common market.

In the main, the United States imports only those fruits and vegetables that are not produced commercially or that supplement domestic production on a seasonal basis. Mexico supplied about 31 percent of all U.S. fruit and vegetable requirements in 1965, and about 40 percent in 1966. Among the principal fruits the United States imported, 97 percent of the strawberries, 84

---

[23] USDA, *Foreign Agriculture Including Foreign Crops and Markets,* Vol. 5, No. 38, Sept. 18, 1967, pp. 3–5.

[24] The U.S. concessions provided free entry for fresh apples, raspberries, maple sugar and syrup, and turnips, and reduced tariffs on blueberries, currants, berry jams and jellies, grapes, and carrots by 50 percent. USDA, *Foreign Agriculture Including Foreign Crops and Markets,* Vol. 5, No. 38, Sept. 18, 1967, pp. 3–5.

percent of the melons, and most of the limes, mangoes, oranges, pineapples, and tangerines came from Mexico.[25] Similarly, 80 percent of the U.S. imports of fresh vegetables came from Mexico, which was the sole source for U.S. imports of tomatoes and the leading source for asparagus, string beans, brussels sprouts, cabbage, carrots, cucumbers, eggplant, onions, garlic, peas, peppers, and squash imports. The United States granted no concessions on the major Mexican vegetable and fruit exports during the Kennedy Round.

Transition to a common market would require policies to facilitate regional specialization in production, to compensate producers hurt by price changes after the removal of trade restrictions, to provide credit or aid to producers who want to raise their productivity or shift to other crops, and to coordinate the U.S. state and federal marketing orders with the Canadian marketing board arrangements.

**FOREST PRODUCTS**

Canada is the world's leading exporter of forest products and was by far the major supplier of 1965 U.S. imports of rough-sawed wood and pulpwood (67 percent), of lumber (91 percent), and of pulp and waste paper (91 percent). These imports totaled more than $700 million and constituted over 70 percent of all Canada's forestry exports (Table 19.1). Softwood lumber (mainly spruce and Douglas fir) and wood pulp imports predominated; imports of pulpwood and hardwood lumber were of comparatively small importance. The latter, in fact, constituted less than 10 percent of total U.S. lumber imports. United States forestry exports to Canada, on the other hand, were only worth $76 million in 1965, but they accounted for 90 percent of Canada's imports. They consisted largely of sawlogs and sawed lumber, both softwood and hardwood.

The tariffs and other obstacles to trade between the two countries vary from generally low or nil on unprocessed products to high on various processed products. The U.S. ad valorem import duties on softwood lumber amount to only 0.6 percent to 1.6 percent,[26] and pulpwood, wood pulp, and miscellaneous products such as logs, poles, staves, railroad ties, and lathes enter duty-free. On the whole, in fact, close to four-fifths of the

---

[25] Richard B. Schroeter, *U.S. Imports of Horticultural Products*, USDA, FAS, FAS-M-191, Aug. 1967, pp. 3–6.

[26] Duties on hardwood lumber are, on the average, about 50 percent above those for softwood lumber.

Canadian forest products imported into the United States enter duty-free. Similarly, except for dressed lumber, Canada imposes no import duties on comparable forest products purchased from the United States. A common market would have small effect on the magnitude of U.S.-Canadian trade in these unprocessed products. Actually, Canada and the United States agreed during the Kennedy Round to establish free trade in softwood lumber products.

Manufactured products, however, are another issue. Both countries maintain very high tariffs—up to 60 percent ad valorem —on these. Newsprint is both the sole exception and the most important single item in this category, and it enters the United States duty-free. On all the other items, however, a common market in manufactured forest products would have an appreciable effect on trade.

The value of two-way trade in major wood manufactures in 1965 was as follows:

| | SITC code | United States' exports to Canada | Canada's exports to U.S. |
|---|---|---|---|
| | | (million dollars) | |
| Veneers, plywood, etc. | 631 | 8.9 | 34.4 |
| Wood manufactures | 632 | 8.1 | 31.5 |
| Paper and paper board | 641 | 50.6 | 707.1 |
| Articles made of paper board | 642 | 15.3 | 1.5 |
| Furniture | 821 | 16.6 | 4.9 |
| Printed matter | 892 | 121.1 | 9.4 |
| Total | | 220.6 | 788.8 |

Neither the United States nor Canada has a very large export market for forest products in Mexico. That country is generally self-sufficient in forest products and confines its imports to a few items like pulp, waste paper, paper, and paper board. A common market would have little effect here.

In sum, then, the major policy decisions for an NACM in forest products will have to take place in Canada and the United States. The United States is the world's largest importer of forest and wood products and has a large net import balance with Canada, the world's leading exporter. Canada has a comparative advantage in forest products requiring little processing, such as lumber and newsprint, while the United States has a comparative advantage in forest-product manufactures. Thus an NACM would produce shifts in the utilization of forest resources, and in the specialization of production and processing, as exports of lumber and newsprint products from Canada to the United States and exports of various wood manufactures from the United States to Canada both increased. The decisions for the two countries will be whether, how, and to what extent they subsidize their lumber or wood-manufacturing industries during the transition to a common market.

## TOBACCO

United States tobacco exports—mainly cigar leaf—to Canada were valued at $4.7 million in 1965, which far exceeds the half million dollars' worth of Canadian tobacco that the United States imported that year. These U.S. exports accounted for 84 percent of Canada's tobacco import requirements, but in terms of total transactions with third countries, the amount of trade was small in absolute value. In fact, U.S. and Canadian tobacco sales to each other constituted only 1.2 percent of their respective total exports.

Reduction of Canadian tobacco tariffs under an NACM could bring that country's domestic tobacco prices down 20 to 30 cents a pound, with severe repercussions on tobacco production, particularly in the provinces of Ontario and Quebec. In the same vein, removal of U.S. tariffs like the 50 cents a pound on stemmed tobacco would expose U.S. producers to Canadian competition.

Considering the different marketing and price support systems of both countries and the high degrees of concentration in the processing and manufacturing industries, transition to a common market could be made only gradually. The policy decisions to be made here center on (a) the extent to which production should be encouraged to develop in areas with greatest comparative advantages, (b) the extent and form of compensation to be given to producers who need to shift to alternative crops, and (3) the coordination of excise tax policies.

## HIDES AND SKINS, FUR SKINS

The United States is a major supplier (90 percent) of hides and skins imported into Canada. This $8.6 million trade, however, was a minor part (8 percent) of total U.S. export in this category. Canada's exports of hides and skins to the United States totaled $5.2 million, 25 percent of Canada's total exports but only 8 percent of all U.S. imports. Because such imports into Canada were duty free, and because such imports into the United States had a tariff of only 4 percent ad valorem, a common market on hides and skins would have little effect on trade or domestic prices.

Canada's exports of fur skins to the United States amounted to $17.1 million in 1965 and accounted for 60 percent of total Canadian exports. The corresponding U.S. exports to Canada that year amounted to $4.9 million, about 12 percent of total U.S. exports. Because the U.S. tariff on fur skins is from 5.5 to 37.5 percent, a common market would expand markets for Canadian fur traders. The effect on U.S. consumer prices would be somewhat tempered by the fact that Canadian imports in 1965 were only 16 percent of U.S. total imports of fur skins.

### COTTON

Canada provided a market for about $51 million worth of U.S. cotton in 1965. This was 10 percent of total U.S. cotton exports and about 78 percent of total Canadian cotton imports. Since this is already on a free trade basis, the NACM would have little effect.

The situation is different with respect to Mexico, a net exporter of cotton. Thus it would be necessary to devise policies that (a) are consistent with prevailing U.S. domestic acreage allotment and price support programs, (b) do not discourage Mexican production, and (c) facilitate coordination of export sales programs.

## INPUTS AND FACTOR MARKETS

The major inputs to agriculture that would be affected by development of a common market are: (a) the farm labor force, (b) the terms and availability of credit, and (c) the supplies and prices of the many inputs purchased for agricultural production. The major decision will be on the extent to which free trade and resource mobility are to be encouraged in the factor markets and on policies each NACM country follows to encourage and develop the major factor inputs.

### FARM LABOR

Continued decline in the number of farms and increased mechanization reduce farm labor requirements and give impetus to emigration or the acceptance of underemployment. Other and related features of the farm labor market are: (a) the fact that farm wages are lower than industrial wages, (b) the seasonality of farm employment, (c) the inadequate education and training, and (d) the poor housing and health facilities of many farm workers. All of us are well aware of the nature and causes of these phenomena, and we all know the programs that have been developed in the past to cope with these problems in the United States.[27] The establishment of a common market may add a new dimension to existing problems and create new ones associated with the geographical and occupational mobility of labor.

In the broadest perspective, free trade in labor inputs would result in a flow of labor from Mexico to the United States, an occurrence particularly important to the U.S. fruit and vegetable industries. Until its termination on December 31, 1964, it was P.L. 78 that regulated the would-be flow of Mexican labor seeking employment in U.S. agriculture. Under this "bracero" program, as many as 400,000 Mexican nationals took farm jobs at wages generally below those accepted by U.S. workers. The Mexican nationals were largely unskilled and semi-skilled laborers who were hired to work in sugar beet, fruit and vegetable, and similar operations requiring large amounts of hand labor. Largely because of pressures from labor unions, who argued that importing labor under the "bracero" program reduced employment opportunities for U.S. workers and depressed their wages, Congress did not extend P.L. 78. The Immigration and Nationality Act (P.L. 414) now regulates the terms and conditions under which foreign labor may seek employment in the United States. It restricts the entry of foreign labor for temporary employment to cases when U.S. workers are not available. Underlying this congressional action were the technological and structural changes in U.S. agriculture that have diminished prospects for labor transfer from Mexico to the United States in the last few years.

Canada, like the United States, has a shortage of agricultural labor compared with Mexico, and there is an indication that Canada is experiencing a greater shortage than the United States. It may be that the prospects for labor mobility between Mexico and Canada under the common market are greater than they are between Mexico and the United States. There is, however, a relatively small and localized market for seasonal labor

---

[27] USDA, ERS, *Rural People in the American Economy,* Agricultural Economic Report 101, Oct. 1966. G. Edward Schuh, "Structural Changes in the Farm Labor Market," *Implications of Changes on Farm Management and Marketing Research,* CAED Report 29, Iowa State Univ. Press, Ames, 1967, pp. 22–50.

in Canada of the type traditionally supplied by Mexican nationals.

The basic question for policy concerns whether the common market should allow a free flow of agricultural labor among the participating countries. We cannot answer this question here since it is part of the overall manpower policies of each of the three countries and its answer must depend on these. Perhaps the best that can be asked for agriculture is that it be freely competitive within its own national setting and that its policies be consistent with the nonagricultural sector. Indeed if labor were completely mobile across national boundaries, the effect would be to reduce the absolute and comparative costs of production for high-labor intensive crops. With lower labor costs, the United States' comparative advantage on these crops would increase.

Corollary policy questions are whether the common market countries should place labor in a special category and regulate its flow or take special measures to protect the wage rates in the United States and Canada against such pressures. In view of the wide disparities in living conditions and wages in the various regions of member countries, and in view of the continuing trend toward more capital-intensive agriculture, intramarket migration can be expected to increase. The attendant adjustment problems may require consideration of a common employment policy covering minimum wage legislation,[28] coordinated social security and public welfare systems, and extended unemployment insurance to farm workers. The adjustment problems could also require discussion of unionization of seasonal and nonseasonal workers[29] and establishment of collective bargaining, or suggest widening the scope of "Poverty Programs" supported under the authority of the Economic Opportunity Act (Title III B).

Success of the common market for food and agriculture depends only to a minor degree on obtaining a freer flow of labor among the three countries. The labor-intensive sectors of agriculture in the United States and Canada have mechanized rapidly in the recent past.[30] This has happened later in Mexico but

---

[28] Minimum wage coverage to farm workers was extended by the 1966 amendments to the Fair Labor Standards Act that became effective Feb. 1, 1967. Accordingly, the minimum rate was set at $1.00 an hour, to be raised to $1.15 a year later and to $1.30 on Feb. 1, 1969. However, this legislation has quite a limited coverage; it applies only to the largest farms that average seven workers per farm.

[29] Charles T. Schmidt, "Farm Labor Unionization," *Farm Policy Forum,* Vol. 19, No. 3, 1966–67, pp. 22–28.

[30] *Conference International Trade and Canadian Agriculture,* sponsored by Economic Council of Canada and Agricultural Economics Research Council of Canada, Banff, Jan. 10–12, 1966, pp. 163–75.

the trend is expected to continue.[31] Recent studies for the United
States suggest that by the 1980's labor will represent only about
10 percent of total inputs used by agriculture.[32] The conditions
under which agriculture uses labor and the skills that the labor
provides are important to policy, but the magnitude of aggregate labor supply will become less and less important as a
factor cost in the common-market countries as time goes on.

### AGRICULTURAL CREDIT

The NACM would have little if any effect on credit terms offered
to agriculture in the United States; it would have more effect
in Canada as capital markets became more highly integrated;
and its relatively greatest effect would occur in Mexico where
additional sources of credit, if developed, would provide an
important stimulus to modernization of agriculture and to output increases. The main policy needed to implement the NACM
would be to do in Mexico, with due allowance for differences in
conditions, some of the things that have proved effective in the
United States and Canada. The United States, for instance, has
supplemented its banking system with a comprehensive government-sponsored cooperative credit program. Canada has recently
moved into government-supplied long-term credit and into
government-guaranteed intermediate and short-term credit.

### PURCHASED INPUTS

Purchased agricultural inputs that demand consideration in
plans for an NACM include farm machinery, fertilizer and other
farm chemicals, tractor fuel and other petroleum products, and
building materials.

*Machinery.* The main flow of trade in farm machinery has
been from the United States to Canada and Mexico. In 1965
U.S. exports of farm machinery to Canada were $273.0 million,
which accounted for 92.7 percent of Canada's imports and 43.0
percent of U.S. exports (Table 19.3). In the same year U.S. exports of farm machinery to Mexico were $32.1 million, of which
$19.9 million was for farm tractors, $6.5 million for harvesting
equipment, and $4.3 million for cultivating machinery. This

---

[31] Banco de Mexico, *Projections of Supply and of Demand for Agricultural Products in Mexico to 1965, 1970, and 1975,* Aug. 1966, pp. 91–105.

[32] Earl O. Heady, *U.S. Agriculture in 1980,* CAED Report 27, Iowa State
Univ. Press, Ames, 1966, pp. 4–5.

TABLE 19.3

The Share of Two-way Trade Between Canada and the United States in Selected Primary and Industrial Commodities, 1965

| Commodities | SITC code | U.S. Exports to Canada | | | Canada's Exports to U.S. | | |
| --- | --- | --- | --- | --- | --- | --- | --- |
| | | Value | Share in total U.S. exports | Share in total Canadian imports | Value | Share in total Canadian exports | Share in total U.S. imports |
| | | *($ mil.)* | *(percent)* | | *($ mil.)* | *(percent)* | |
| Petroleum, crude | 331 | * | † | † | 258.9 | 100.0 | 22.8 |
| Petroleum products | 332 | 56.2 | 13.6 | 30.6 | 8.8 | 86.2 | .8 |
| Fertilizers, crude | 271 | 12.7 | 18.8 | 98.4 | * | † | † |
| Fertilizers, manufactured | 561 | 13.2 | 8.6 | 87.4 | 88.3 | 85.3 | 72.8 |
| Chemical materials, NES | 599 | 144.6 | 18.9 | 88.3 | 14.6 | 37.0 | 11.7 |
| Agricultural machinery and implements | 712 | 273.0 | 43.0 | 92.7 | 131.0 | 88.8 | 32.1 |

Source: Computed from OECD, *Commodity Trade*, Series B and C, Paris.
\* No trade.
† Not relevant.

was 68.3 percent of Mexico's imports but only 5 percent of total U.S. exports (Table 19.4). There has also been significant trade in farm machinery from Canada to the United States: U.S. purchases amounted to $131.0 million in 1965, 88.8 percent of Canada's exports and 32.1 percent of U.S. imports. There is hardly any trade in farm machinery from Mexico to the United States, and practically none either way between Canada and Mexico.

The common market would have little direct effect on trade in farm machinery between the United States and Canada since there are no farm machinery tariffs now except on imports of dairy and poultry equipment into Canada. The market would provide considerable scope for expanding this trade, however, as a consequence of more complete integration of the two economies. The NACM could also affect imports into Mexico of some types of machinery that have not thus far been important in trade. Although Mexico had no tariffs on imports of tractors, cultivators, and combines in 1966, there were tariffs from 8 percent to 25 percent, plus a 3 percent customs fee, on such items as corn-shelling and harvesting equipment, produce graders, and some dairy equipment.[33]

The three NACM countries are so close to free trade in farm machinery now that it would require little further change in policies to make this a complete free trade area. The NACM would have little effect on machinery prices between the United States and Canada except for lower prices on dairy and poultry equipment and various electric motors and equipment in Canada.

However there still remains a considerable array of farm inputs, including building materials, plumbing fixtures, pipes, tubes, wire fencing, tools, and bags and sacks of all kinds, that are burdened by import duties.[34] Removing these duties could lower prices and hence contribute to lower factor costs. Trade liberalization also could result in lower prices for a few types of equipment in Mexico.

The broader and more important policy questions concern actions that governments could take internally to bring down the costs of machinery to farmers. These steps could include reduction or elimination of sales taxes on farm machinery, development of more adequate credit for machinery purchases, vocational training in machinery use and repair, and encourage-

---

[33] ALALC, *Lista Nacional de México, 1966,* pp. 89–99.
[34] Canada Dept. of Agriculture, *Canadian Farm Econ.,* Vol. 2, No. 3, Aug. 1967, p. 37.

## TABLE 19.4

### The Share of Two-way Trade Between the United States and Mexico in Selected Primary and Industrial Commodities, 1965

| Commodities | SITC code | U.S. Exports to Mexico | | | Mexico's Exports to U.S. | | |
|---|---|---|---|---|---|---|---|
| | | Value ($ mil.) | Share in total U.S. exports (percent) | Share in total Mexican imports | Value ($ mil.) | Share in total Mexican exports (percent) | Share in total U.S. imports |
| Petroleum, crude | 331 | 1.4 | 28.5 | 100.0 | 13.9 | 100.0 | 3.3 |
| Petroleum products | 332 | 15.3 | 3.7 | 97.1 | 15.9 | 92.4 | 3.9 |
| Fertilizers, crude | 271 | 1.9 | 2.8 | 100.0 | .8 | 100.0 | 9.6 |
| Fertilizers, manufactured | 561 | 8.5 | 5.5 | 72.8 | * | † | † |
| Chemical materials and products, NES | 599 | 25.4 | 3.3 | 37.8 | 2.8 | 30.4 | ... |
| Agricultural machinery and implements | 712 | 32.1 | 5.0 | 68.3 | .4 | ... | .2 |
| Cultivating machinery | 712.1 | 4.3 | ... | 87.7 | * | † | † |
| Harvesting machinery | 712.2 | 6.5 | 4.8 | 79.7 | * | † | † |
| Dairy farm machinery and equipment | 712.3 | .2 | ... | 50.0 | * | † | † |
| Tractors | 712.5 | 19.9 | 4.7 | 61.8 | ** | † | † |
| Agricultural machinery, NES | 712.9 | 1.4 | ... | 93.3 | * | † | † |

Source: Computed from OECD, *Commodity Trade*, Series B and C, Paris.
* No trade.
† Not relevant.
... Magnitude insignificant.

ment of cooperatives (where feasible) to share machines among groups of farmers. The attractiveness of such policies depends on the emphasis attached to the goals of increasing output or decreasing cost for domestic and export purposes.

*Fertilizers and Other Chemicals.* The fertilizer and chemical production of the NACM countries has changed rapidly in recent years. In each country, output has increased rapidly, and in some cases it has doubled in a matter of two or three years.[35] Prices have remained remarkably steady[36] while they have fallen in relation to costs of most other farm inputs.

Canada is a net exporter of manufactured fertilizers to the United States and a larger net importer of chemical materials such as insecticides, fungicides, and weed sprays. In 1965 Canada exported $88.3 million worth of fertilizer to the United States and imported $25.9 million. During the same year Canada imported $144.6 million of U.S. insecticides, weed sprays, and other chemical materials and exported about one-tenth as much.

United States exports of fertilizer to Mexico were much smaller: $10.4 million in 1965. Mexico, like Canada, imported a much larger amount of U.S. chemical materials, totaling $25.4 million in 1965.

Because both Canada and Mexico use as yet relatively small quantities of fertilizers, insecticides, and other chemicals per acre, the prime objective of a common policy is to stimulate the intensity of their application.

*Petroleum and Petroleum Products.* Trade in petroleum and its products runs heavily in Canada's favor (Table 19.3). In 1965 all of Canada's crude petroleum exports, valued at $258.9 million, went to the United States, plus $8.8 million of petroleum products. United States exports to Canada consisted entirely of petroleum products amounting to $56.3 million. The tariff on crude petroleum imported into the United States was 4 percent ad valorem in 1965. The Canadian tariff on motor fuel was as high as 20 percent ad valorem.

Canadian crude oil has its largest markets in the Midwest (Minnesota, Wisconsin, and Michigan) and in the Pacific Coast states (especially Washington and Oregon) where it has a competitive price advantage over other oils. This advantage arises from two circumstances: first, that oil is moving by pipelines into the U.S. markets which reduces handling and transporta-

---

[35] FAO, *Fertilizers, An Annual Review of World Production, Consumption, and Trade, 1965,* Rome, 1966, pp. 58–63.
[36] *Ibid.,* pp. 181 ff.

tion costs and, second, the exemption of Canada and Mexico from mandatory import quotas.[37]

The NACM would, it appears, greatly increase the flow of trade between the United States and Canada in petroleum and petroleum products. The major effect would be to reduce the price of gasoline and some other products in Canada. It would also make the United States a more attractive market for Canadian crude oil, and prices in both countries would decline if all other conditions remained the same. This would lower factor costs to agriculture and lead to expanded output.

Common policies would be needed with respect to (a) the allocation of quotas to third country suppliers, especially Venezuela and the Middle Eastern countries; (b) conservation practices, extraction rates, and depreciation allowances; and (c) taxes on sales to consumers.

## HUMAN AND NATURAL RESOURCE DEVELOPMENT

The NACM, by itself, presents no unique need for human and natural resource development programs that does not already exist in each of the individual countries. If, however, the NACM is designed to greatly expand exports and, at the same time, to provide abundance for home markets, then a vast array of new policies may be needed. These will range over a wide spectrum including rural area development programs, further aid to education and manpower training programs, subsidies to industries supplying other inputs to agriculture, changes in tax laws, credit, and other things.

## CONCLUSION

Major policy questions for an NACM center on determining compensation to be given to industries affected by changes in the terms of trade and on defining export goals. It appears that some economists feel that the overriding goal for the common market is meeting world food needs. Since resources for an exportable food surplus from North America are limited, we must finally ask whether the NACM resources should be reallocated

---

[37] Effective June 1, 1959, import quotas on crude oil, unfinished oils, refined products, and liquid petroleum products were removed on shipments entering the United States by pipeline, motor carrier, or rail from the country of production.

to expand this exportable surplus or whether equivalent resources should be allocated to nonagricultural endeavors, especially to the production of farm inputs for export or to the export of other—not necessarily agricultural—technological and
human resources. Although this question was not assigned to
us, it is crucial for policy.

We suggest that a common market should have rather limited export objectives based on economic and political realities.
It could be misleading to suggest that North America will or
even should meet the food needs of the rest of the world or that
an NACM is the best way to do it. The primary effect of an
NACM would be to increase trading efficiency with countries
which are currently major commercial markets. These are
mainly the developed nations: Japan, West Germany, Netherlands, United Kingdom, Italy, etc. We can increase food exports
without a common market policy. The NACM can, however,
contribute to the goal.

We end, therefore, with a question rather than a conclusion. How much emphasis is best given in the NACM to this
goal versus other possible action? Perhaps the NACM is best
viewed as a means for generally enhancing efficiency rather than
as a primary means for meeting the food shortages of the developing countries.

# CHAPTER TWENTY

# The World Food Situation: Challenges and Opportunities Facing North America

## GLENN L. JOHNSON and VERNON L. SORENSON

THE CHAPTERS in this book stress certain notes of caution which we share. First, the welfare implications of the concept of a common market have been recognized repeatedly. A common market by definition implies a degree of economic isolation from the rest of the world by the member countries. Without some isolation through barriers to the flow of goods and services, it is meaningless to conceive of a customs union with unified but differentiated policies, each of which is in some degree required to have a "common market." This means that a common market is contrary to both the political and economic principles that have guided U.S. international commercial policy in modern times. Since the reciprocal trade agreements program began in 1934, the dominant economic objective in American policy has been to achieve greater freedom in trade on a multilateral basis. Operationally this has led to principles for policy that call for a reduction in trade barriers with reciprocity and the most favored nation or nondiscrimination concept. We have, of course, deviated from these principles in major ways, but usually the reasons, in terms of other values, are apparent. The United States accepted the concept of a common market in Europe and in other areas,

GLENN L. JOHNSON, Department of Agricultural Economics, Michigan State University; VERNON L. SORENSON, Department of Agricultural Economics, Michigan State University.

with rather clear-cut objectives related to security and promoting economic growth and development. The United States supports prices and manipulates trade of farm commodities, but again for rather understandable domestic political reasons. Despite these and other exceptions, the free trade principle has remained intact in U.S. policy.

The basis for this position is a somewhat restrictive and obsolete interpretation of nineteenth century classical and neoclassical economic theory. If we question this interpretation—and the formation of a North American Common Market does—the question that arises is where do we go from here. The escape is found in a less restrictive interpretation of classical and neoclassical theory. For international policy this theory, as interpreted by modern welfare theorists, argues that when we are considering institutional changes which violate the Pareto conditions of optimality, both within countries and among countries, completely unrestricted international commercial trade (including factor movements) cannot be either defended (as the best) or attacked (as less than the best) on welfare grounds; similarly, neither can restrictive actions imposed by trading countries to seek specific ends.[1] Such changes, rather than a policy of avoiding such changes, can be at least defended by going beyond Pareto-better welfare economics. We feel it is imperative that we go beyond Pareto-better welfare economics to consider adjustments which may hurt some persons and groups in order to contribute to the solution of the world food problem.

Second, we have questioned the meaning of the world food gap. At the 13th meeting of the International Conference of Agricultural Economists held in Sydney in August 1967, there was little agreement on the nature of the world food gap. Thorkil Kristensen stressed the excess of prospective food needs (not effective demand) over production possibilities in view of population prospects.[2] W. D. Borrie, a noted Australian demographer substantiated Kristensen's population estimates though not without dissent from Colin Clark and one or two others.[3] On the supply side, however, the dissent was more pronounced. P.

---

[1] For an analysis of the application of welfare concepts to trade policy see: J. E. Meade, *Trade and Welfare: The Theory of International Economic Policy*, Oxford Univ. Press, New York. Discussion of policies in this context has focused largely on tariff protection and has led to considerable theoretical development; see, for example, Harry G. Johnson, *International Trade and Economic Growth*, Harvard Univ. Press, 1965, Chap. II.

[2] Thorkil Kristensen, "The Approaches and Findings of Economists," International Conference of Agricultural Economists, 13th Meeting, Sydney, Australia, 1967.

[3] W. D. Borrie, "Population Growth—Demographic and Sociological View-

Kaarlehto of Finland took Kristensen to task for failing to note that small errors in growth rate projections would permit food supplies and demand (even needs) to balance. T. W. Schultz, Odvar Aresvick, and others pointed to the impacts of changed technologies and policies in countries such as India and Pakistan as likely to cause Kristensen to underestimate supplies.[4] Personal observation by one of the authors of this chapter in West and East Africa, India, Nepal, Pakistan, Japan, Okinawa, Taiwan, and the Philippines supports these criticisms of Kristensen's viewpoint. New rice varieties, fertilizer, water controls, tube wells, plant protection, better terms of exchange for agriculture, all promise very substantial increases in production in the Indian subcontinent and Southeast Asia. Here, the new varieties of rice and wheat produced at Los Banos and in Mexico are of crucial importance, even though not reflected in the trend data for recent years which Kristensen extrapolated into the future. In Africa, with its much more favorable man/land ratios, improvements in the terms of exchange for agriculture (which can be made by the countries involved) plus genetic work on grain sorghums, millet, and corn promise similar expansions. In fact in Africa it appears that production is constrained more by restrictions on the demand than on the supply side, even with traditional technologies. In this book, chapters by Christensen, Tontz, Mackie, Heady *et al.*, and Smith have stressed the capacity of North American agriculture to outstrip effective world demand for food and to produce more, perhaps, than the continent could afford to give away as food aid. Substantial references have also been made to the Abel-Rojko papers[5] which more or less reverse last year's USDA stand on the food gap and argue with our preliminary thoughts and those presented here.

Thus, viewed from North America, it is not enough to assume that the world's nutritional needs will be automatically translated into enough effective demand to absorb all that can be produced in North America plus the production that should be stimulated in the less developed world. Care must be exercised lest we let our concern about the world food gap cause us to

---

points," International Conference of Agricultural Economists, 13th Meeting, Sydney, Australia, 1967.

[4] T. W. Schultz, "World Agriculture in Relation to Population, Science, Economics, Disequilibrium and Income Equality: Reflections and Unsettled Questions," International Conference of Agricultural Economists, 13th Meeting, Sydney, Australia, 1967.

[5] Martin E. Abel and Anthony S. Rojko, *The World Food Situation, Prospects for World Grain Production, Consumption and Trade*, FAER-35, USDA, 1967.

produce and dump food abroad to the detriment of the agricultural economies of the developing countries.

## FOUR QUESTIONS

We have been and are skeptical about a North American Common Market. One thing seems clear: the primary reason for forming a common market is not the problem of maximizing the ability of North America to contribute to the solution of the world food problem, relevant as that objective may be. The challenges and opportunities for making this contribution exist, however, and it is to these challenges and opportunities that we now address ourselves, with or without a common market.

Rational policies for North America or North American countries to follow in seeking an optimum contribution to the world food problem would need to deal with at least four kinds of questions. These are as follows:

1. What kinds of overall economic policies and trading relationships should be sought by North American countries to provide an optimum contribution by North American and other advanced countries to the solution of the world food problem?
2. What kinds of trade-aid and international income transfers from advanced to less developed countries would most effectively promote expansion of agricultural production in developing countries?
3. What kinds of restructuring are needed in the agricultures of North American and underdeveloped countries in order to best tackle the world food problem, including the use of food aid?
4. What kinds of technical assistance and resource transfers through intergovernmental or multilateral aid would most effectively contribute to improving food production in less developed countries?

## OVERALL ECONOMIC POLICIES AND TRADING RELATIONSHIPS

During the past quarter of a century a number of significant trends have affected international commercial relations. Stimulated by the early arguments of Keynes that positive government action is needed to direct economic activity, the environment for development of both national and international policy in agriculture has changed.[6] All industrial countries have adopted national economic policies to insure business expansion and stability and increasingly are adopting comprehensive national economic planning. This of course has its consequence in the general international environment. International commerce has been conducted within a framework of national monetary and fiscal policies, aimed at full employment, and supplemented where necessary by restrictions on currency convertibility and other measures that influence international commerce through the price system—such as import duties, export subsidies, currency depreciation, and the like—as well as more direct measures including quotas, exchange controls, and bilateral trading arrangements. Steady postwar progress has been made in improving convertibility among industrial countries (the most recent being full liberalization by France on January 31, 1967) and reducing quantitative trade restrictions. Major progress was made in the Kennedy Round for tariff reduction on nonagricultural products. But these gains have been achieved during a time when all major industrial countries have enjoyed a long period of generally full employment. Commenting on the continuation of this progress toward currency transferability and trade liberalization, Triffin characterizes these as:

. . . fair weather objectives which can only be pressed forward in an environment of high economic activity and employment. . . . In times of depression, each nation will almost inevitably resort again to trade restrictions and currency inconvertibility in an effort to insulate its own economy from external deflationary pressures. These policies cannot be successful in the end, as each country's actions tend to aggravate the difficulties of others, widening and deepening the contractionist tendencies at will. National anti-depression policies of this character have always proved in the past one of the main factors in the spread of aggravation of international recessions. This spiral can be broken only by collective arrangements giving operational meaning to the interdependence of the various countries' policies.[7]

If we accept this skepticism by Triffin—and we probably should—it leads to two generalizations concerning policy for North American countries which we feel have not been stressed adequately. First, because of its sheer weight in the total of

---

[6] For an excellent brief account of the early Keynsian influence see: J. B. Condliffe, *The Commerce of Nations*, W. W. Norton, Inc., pp. 603–12.

[7] G. Myrdal, *An International Economy: Problems and Prospects*, Harper and Brothers, New York, p. 81.

world economic activity, a prime responsibility exists in the United States in particular, and in Canada as well, to maintain full employment with minimal interference to international adjustment. Second, we feel that we should accept leadership in formulating collective arrangements with other countries and regional groupings in laying the foundations for improved international cooperation to maintain business stability, to improve international liquidity, and in general to achieve a reduction in the autarchy of national economic policies. While we cannot in this chapter discuss the full range of challenges and opportunities involved at this level of policy, we must assume that solutions to these problems will be achieved; otherwise, the discussion of the challenges and opportunities related specifically to agriculture will be an intellectual exercise with little prospect of implementation.

Turning now to agriculture and North America's role in the world food problem, there has been general agreement here that a great technical potential exists for expansion in North American output both in the short run and over time. The evaluations of capacity presented here, however, shed some but inadequate light on the relevant issues. As stated in several chapters, the real challenges and opportunities involve economic and political questions concerning: (a) what changes will occur in total effective farm-level demand for food produced in North America, (b) how should North American agricultural output be adjusted, (c) and what methods should be used to achieve an appropriate international balance in agricultural production.

Overall requirements for food production in North America will depend on growth in domestic and commercial export demand, and on political decisions on quantities of food aid. We accept the opinion expressed by Heady and others, and now current in academic and governmental circles, that food aid should be viewed as of limited value in solving the world food problem. Nevertheless we recognize, along with Christensen and others, that there will be a continued need for food aid shipments over an extended future period. Policies on output adjustment thus must recognize this need along with expanded domestic and international commercial requirements.

In the short run, management of existing excess capacity to maintain reasonable stocks and meet annual fluctuations in requirements is the major production policy issue.[8] In a longer

---

[8] As recently suggested, "Additional production capacity can be obtained at relatively low cost as long as we have idle crop acreage and underutiliza-

run perspective, the problems of achieving an appropriate production policy become more complex. The challenge is to develop internal policies on resource use as changes occur in prices, productivity, and needs beyond effective demand. Stated otherwise, the challenge is to develop a production policy that (a) counters the tendency toward an overcommitment of resources noted by Heady, Quance, and others, (b) promotes efficiency and cost reduction, and (c) encourages output in line with changes in composition as well as level of total requirements. Achieving changes in agriculture that serve over time to adjust output in line with demand, and fulfill objectives related to efficiency and other ends, involves the entire complex of policies related to price level, investment in land, capital, and technology, as well as improvement in quality and adjustment in the quantity of human resources employed. Some techniques for bringing about these kinds of adjustments will be dealt with later in this chapter. The major points that should be made at this time are: (a) realism must be used in assessing prospective requirements, and (b) the political basis needs to be established for achieving appropriate distribution of output within North America and consistent production policies.

This, as others have stressed, suggests that an international dimension needs to be added to all agricultural policy decisions. The international policy challenge that faces North American countries, however, is much more pervasive than this. Throughout the postwar period and particularly in the Kennedy Round, the United States has sought multilateral reductions in trade barriers. These efforts have been aimed largely at reducing protection in higher cost countries on the assumption that markets for American farm products could be expanded. Efforts should be continued to achieve multilateral reductions in trade barriers and shifts in production toward areas with comparative advantage. It needs to be recognized, however, that both economic and political restraints affect the extent to which these kinds of shifts are feasible.

One of these restraints is imposed by the need for food production in excess of that required to fulfill effective or commer-

---

tion of other resources in agriculture." Easily obtainable expansion to add upwards of 60 million tons of grain could be achieved even with existing levels of technology and resource productivity. M. L. Upchurch, "The Capacity of the United States to Supply Food for Developing Countries," Iowa State University Center for Agricultural and Economic Development, *Alternatives for Balancing Future World Food Production and Needs,* Iowa State Univ. Press, Ames, 1967.

cial demand. When we measure world food requirements partially in terms of needs rather than in terms of effective demand, the calculus of supply and demand explicit in comparative advantage theory, though still applicable, no longer applies in the usual sense. If food transfers are needed on a concessional basis (despite the absence of effective demand), then competitive adjustment in world commercial agricultural markets does not lead to regional surpluses that can be transferred to deficit or need areas. Thus if carried to the extreme, the search for gains through adjustment to comparative advantage as indicated by effective demand is not compatible with solution of the world food problem as we have defined it.

Second, we need to recognize the imperatives of politics, namely that farm incomes will be protected in all advanced countries, and that a high level of agricultural output relative to effective demand seems to be desired in all countries. Up to this time, high cost countries, including the United States on such products as dairy and sugar, have stopped short of trade liberalization that would place a major burden of direct income support on governments or that would have a major dislocating effect on domestic agriculture. This leads directly to the point made here and many times by agricultural economists in recent years: in order to achieve progress in trade policy, domestic and international policies must be dealt with jointly in the bargaining process. The objective and the process, however, may be quite different if this bargaining is in the light of world food needs rather than in the light of competitive interrelationships and expanded trade largely within the community of advanced countries.

Trade bargaining in this context should be based on long-term considerations that allow time to change the structure of agriculture and improve the competitive position of high cost countries. A better structured agriculture with larger farms would reduce general cost levels and, at the same time, expand total capacity. Given the potential world demand for food, adjustment to comparative cost advantage, which exists largely because of differences in organization of agriculture, would not appear wise and in any event is not politically feasible. Simultaneous adjustment to comparative advantage through reorganization in high cost areas, along with locational adjustment dictated by natural resource availability, can serve the dual ends of increasing production capacity and minimizing cost. At the same time, policies should be instituted that encourage an adequate but not an overcommitment of resources in developed countries relative to effective demand and to well thought-out decisions concerning magnitudes of food aid. Part of the challenge is to produce to meet well thought-out targets for food aid rather than to use food aid as a means for the disposal of surpluses produced by malfunctioning, poorly controlled, agricultural economies.

It is apparent that action by North American countries alone cannot achieve these goals. North America in its own right, no matter how well organized and how complete the adjustment within the continent, can achieve only limited marginal gains from improved distribution of production and changes in agricultural resource-use patterns without cooperation of other advanced countries. Further, North America should not be the only source of flexibility in the total level of resources committed to agriculture. Another opportunity, then, is that of providing leadership to achieve long-run multilateral cooperation in a more broadly oriented approach to agricultural production and trade problems.

## TRADE-AID AND INTERNATIONAL INCOME TRANSFERS

The second major set of challenges and opportunities involves the creation and implementation of policies which will improve the ability of less developed countries to earn income through international markets and, in turn, to contribute to their own general economic development, including agriculture. We feel that this area, with a few minor exceptions, has been neglected. The export problems facing developing countries are numerous. The rate of demand expansion for most products in developing countries is relatively low. For many agricultural raw materials, the inroads of technology through development of synthetic substitutes have been extremely important. These two factors have prevented rapid long-term expansion in the demand for the principal export commodities of many countries and in some cases these markets have shrunk through time. In addition, price elasticities of demand are low and production fluctuates on a cyclical or weather-induced basis, both of which lead to considerable price instability. These characteristics, along with trade barriers that discriminate against processed or semiprocessed products and in some cases raw materials, particularly in Europe, create obstacles that have led to the underdeveloped countries' dissatisfaction with their position in international markets. In addition, some developing countries, through their own levies and taxes, isolate their domestic producers of export commodities from world demand. Thai and Burmese rice, Nigerian palm oil, and Nigerian cocoa are three cases in point. These considerations, along with rapidly expanding demand for imports for development purposes, have caused balance of payments positions to deteriorate. In many cases an important share of the export earnings of developing countries is required merely to service foreign debt.

Policy proposals to improve the transfer of income from developed to developing countries have taken two forms: (a) to provide expanded credit and financial facilities to finance both long-term and short-term deficits by developing countries, and (b) to establish international commodity arrangements that provide preferential treatment for developing countries in commodity markets. It is clear that these are critical issues and can be solved only through agreement among the world's major financial powers.

Several commodity agreements have been brought into operation during the recent past, but these have not been particularly successful. As recently stated by E. M. Ojala:

The experience with international commodity agreements since the war has not been without its successes. But, the record falls far short of the goals reflected in the Havana Charter. An enormous buildup of world stocks of wheat, a general state of surplus or near surplus for most agricultural commodities in world trade (except beef and oil seeds), severe shortages of food commodities in many parts of the world, harmful price fluctuations, and a long decline in the terms of trade of the agricultural exports of developing countries have not been prevented. In terms of world commodity problems, the results of postwar efforts, useful though they may have been in many instances, can only be described as meager.[9]

The common market proposed world agreements for cereals, livestock, and dairy products in the Kennedy Round that would create overall international management of prices and quantities of traded products. The need for commodity agreements was also emphasized at the first UNCTAD conference.

Negotiations on the EEC proposals have concluded with a limited agreement on wheat. There is little prospect that further

---

[9] Dr. E. M. Ojala, "Some Current Issues in International Commodity Policy," *Jour. Agr. Econ.*, Vol. 18, No. 1.

negotiation will take place in the near future. The UNCTAD position is that commodity policy, in addition to serving an over-all stabilization role can serve a special role in stimulating economic development. The conference suggested that:

> . . . a basic objective of international commodity arrangements is, in general, to stimulate a dynamic and steady growth and insure reasonable predictability in the real export earnings of developing countries, so as to provide them with expanding resources for their economic and social development, while taking into account the interests of consumers in importing countries.[10]

To achieve this, the conference recommended a number of specific objectives for international commodity arrangements which include: (a) fixing of equitable and stable prices for primary commodities, especially those exported by developing countries; (b) increasing the consumption and imports of primary commodities, including those in semiprocess and processed forms from developing countries; (c) assuring access to markets; and (d) achieving coordinated commodity production and marketing policies among countries.

The recommendation is made that developed countries forego virtually all the import restrictions important to commodities exported by developing countries, and that they eliminate all export subsidies and other actions that unnecessarily reduce world commodity prices. It is apparent that important restrictions exist in developed countries against exports from developing countries and that export subsidies of developed countries reduce world prices on some products. Thus important gains probably could be achieved if all advanced countries cooperated in eliminating subsidies and trade barriers that affect export products important to developing countries. Little is heard in UNCTAD discussions about the deleterious effects of export taxing by developing countries on the demand for their own exports. Still further, even less is heard about how such taxing by producing countries reduces effective demand within such countries for both export and domestically consumed products. Important gains could be made by eliminating such taxing. The challenges and opportunities involved in making such gains are discussed later in this chapter.

Whether further improvement of the position of developing

---

[10] FAO, Commodity Policy Studies, *Agricultural Commodity Trade Prospects, Problems and Policies, Special Studies Program*, No. 2, Section VI.

countries can be achieved through price fixing or access arrangements is less clear. Increased income transfers could be achieved through agreements that limit the tendency toward self-sufficiency in industrial countries on products that are competitive with exports from developing areas. Beyond this, the complexities involved in progress increase greatly. If price elasticity of demand is low, then higher prices can be used to increase income transfers. An important disadvantage could be that higher prices could bring forth excess or substitute production in the less developed countries and require a worldwide quota system and/or production controls. With this degree of control, major administrative problems and problems of achieving an equitable balance among countries would inevitably arise. On the other hand, the advantage would exist in that aid would be transferred "through the market," much as is the case of domestic price support, and not through direct grants.

Certainly there is an ample challenge here for the leadership of North American economists and statesmen to provide some assurance of security as to size of export earnings of developing countries.

Coordination of internal and external policies by both advanced and developing countries will be necessary to achieve any substantial progress. Thus cooperation among all important trading groups will be required but, most important, will involve agreement among the advanced countries on the approaches that can and should be taken in providing trade assurances for developing nations.

## NEEDED STRUCTURAL CHANGES IN THE AGRICULTURAL ECONOMIES OF BOTH DEVELOPED AND UNDERDEVELOPED COUNTRIES

Another set of challenges and opportunities are found in policies to improve agricultural structures. Several chapters have stressed that, to maximize the North American contributions to the solution of the world food problem, restructuring would be required in the agricultural economies of North American countries. Restructuring will be required also in the less developed countries. The required restructuring is more basic than the integration of internal domestic (or internal common market) policies with international policies. It also goes beyond the Pareto-better economic adjustments which would optimize output in a free enterprise economy. It is necessary to recognize that neither microeconomic restructuring by farm management men nor macro-economic restructuring by economic planners is sufficient to handle the world food problem; instead, technological, educational, and institutional restructuring are also needed. The institutional restructuring which is required involves the development of nonexistent control mechanisms for eliminating over-commitment of resources in both North American agriculture and in the agricultural economics of the less developed world. The challenge involved in creating these control mechanisms is tremendous and has not been handled well by either domestic or technical assistance workers.

Among the developed countries which make non-Pareto-better contributions to the world food problem are the United States and, to a much lesser extent, Canada, both in the potential North American Common Market. In these two countries, in European countries, and in Oceania, adjustments should be sought that move toward a lowest cost basis for producing the food needed. It is apparent that, in the present situation among advanced countries, further short-run gains can be achieved by shifting production to areas of comparative advantage. Many of these gains are being attained and will be attained through competitive adjustments to rising wage rates, advances in transportation technology, introduction of land- and labor-saving technologies in agriculture, and the like. Other changes, however, are being prevented by price support measures that protect high cost production, particularly in some countries.

The damages to be imposed by more liberal trade policy would fall on persons in both the developed and undeveloped world, for both worlds are characterized by barriers to trade and production expansion in which persons have vested interests. In the developed world, the vested interests are mainly among producers and the civil servants and politicians who serve producers. In the undeveloped world, the vested interests are found among civil servants, politicians, and economic planners who impose tax barriers and adverse pricing policies on agriculture in order to attain various ends, including aggrandizement of personal positions. In addition, in the underdeveloped countries the group of persons with such vested interests tends to be augmented by consumers if the consumers have organized political power. The interest of consumers in low food prices is often pursued by them and by politicians without regard to production consequences or in the mistaken belief that producers in the developing countries are unresponsive to either low or high prices.

Thus, with few exceptions, the underdeveloped countries maintain adverse terms of exchange for their agricultural producers. This is done in those underdeveloped countries which export by imposing taxes on exports, thereby lowering internal prices for both domestic consumption and export. Thai rice and Nigerian palm produce are cases in point. For those underdeveloped countries which import, concessional sales (P.L. 480, for example) provide the means of lowering internal prices and shifting the internal terms of exchange against agriculture. In both the food exporting and importing underdeveloped countries, pressure is also put on the terms of exchange for agriculture by import duties, taxes, and by inefficient government production of the factors of production such as fertilizer, irrigation water, improved seeds, improved breeding stock, and the like.

The developed economies of the western world are characterized by the overcommitment of resources to agricultural production.[11] Empirical evidence of this overcommitment includes: (a) low MVP's of labor in agriculture relative to off-farm wage rates, (b) low MVP's for capital relative to acquisition or replacement costs, (c) low MVP's of land relative to land prices, and (d) chapters in this book by Christensen, Heady *et al.,* Mackie, Smith, and Quance. Other evidence is the production of larger quantities of produce than can be sold at prices which will simultaneously cover off-farm wage rates, acquisition costs for capital, and interest on land prices. As a result, political pressures build up for price supports, domestic disposal programs, and programs to extend food aid abroad. In fact, one has the uneasy feeling that part of the interest in the conference on a North American Common Market, when it was formulated, grew out of a desire to find ways to dispose of larger quantities of agricultural output than can be sold at prices which cover the costs listed above. Such overcommitment of resources to agriculture in a developing country wastes the resources of that country and leads in turn to surplus disposal programs which provide the means whereby underdeveloped importing countries unwisely maintain adverse terms of exchange for their producers.

At this juncture, another point needs to be made. It is our observation that in many of the underdeveloped economies with free enterprise agriculture, resources are overcommitted to agri-

[11] Glenn L. Johnson, "Overcommitment of Resources in the Production of Farm Products," *Implications of Changes (structural and market) on Farm Management and Marketing Research,* Center for Agricultural and Economic Development and Farm Foundation, and NCR4, Chicago, Apr. 24–26, 1967.

culture relative to the prices the entrepreneurs actually receive and pay.[12] We go beyond T. W. Schultz to argue that the agricultural economies in underdeveloped countries have exceeded his stagnant equilibrium at which low MVP's equal marginal factor costs; instead, they are operating so that the low MVP's are below marginal factor costs based on acquisition prices and above marginal factor costs based on salvage values. In those underdeveloped countries which maintain artificially adverse terms of exchange for agriculture, the wastage is different than in the developed countries. On private account, in both kinds of countries, resources are overcommitted, returns are low, and capital losses are incurred. On public or national account, however, the difference is that the undeveloped countries undercommit, underproduce, tax or depress prices with concessional sales commodities, and neglect profitable production opportunities, while the developed countries overproduce, subsidize, and dispose of surpluses abroad which they produce with resources having better alternative uses at home.

It is not hard to see that major opportunities for adjusting food production and improving resource use are to be found in simultaneous changes in both the macroagricultural and microagricultural structures of both the developed and less developed countries. The challenge is to create new institutional controls on resource use which will:

1. Prevent the waste of resources overcommitted to agricultural production in the developed countries.
2. Utilize more effectively resources in agricultural production in the underdeveloped countries by:
   a. changing the taxing policies of the underdeveloped exporting countries while
   b. insisting that concessional imports not be used so as to retard production expansion in those developing countries which import.

Exploiting these opportunities and meeting this challenge require a greater understanding of the operation of the present agricultural structures of both the developed and underdeveloped countries than stated in the chapters of this book.

There is not space here to present the detailed theory and

---

[12] This general conclusion is based on studies and observations of one of the authors, Glenn Johnson, over a period of several years in Thailand, Nigeria, Colombia, Pakistan, and India.

data on the performance of agricultural economies controlled largely by the free choices of large numbers of entrepreneurs, whether peasants or commercial farmers. Ordinary neoclassical theory used under explicitly, but rarely stated, relevant assumptions leads to most of the important conclusions.[13] The relevant assumptions are that (a) acquisition costs exceed salvage values for important inputs used by the farm firm, (b) entrepreneurs are imperfectly informed about significant continuing changes in technology, institutions, and/or the human agent, and (c) entrepreneurs, as a result of their imperfect knowledge, make a continuing series of mistakes in acquiring productive resources through time. Under these assumptions, in both the developed and less developed worlds, attempts of entrepreneurs to minimize losses from successive errors in levels and combination of resource use result in:

1. The production of more than can be sold at prices (to the firm) which will cover acquisition costs (to the firm) of the resources used.
2. MVP's for resources which will not cover their acquisition cost but exceed their salvage value if the firm disposes of them, which is to say of course, that such fixed resources are priced internally according to the opportunity-cost principle.
3. Ex post, non-Pareto-better capital losses relative to acquisition costs.
4. The determination of firm size by past mistakes in organization which fix important resources in firms, thereby activating the law of diminishing returns as successive quantities of the remaining variable resources are used in conjunction with the fixed resources.

---

[13] Glenn L. Johnson and Lowell Hardin, *The Economics of Forage Evaluation*, Purdue Agr. Exp. Sta. Bull. 623, 1955; Clark Edwards, "Resource Fixity and Farm Organization," *Jour. Farm Econ.*, Nov., 1959; Glenn L. Johnson, "Supply Functions—Some Facts and Notions," *Agricultural Adjustment Problems in a Growing Economy*, Iowa State Univ. Press, 1956; Glenn L. Johnson, "The State of Agricultural Supply Analysis," *Jour. Farm Econ.*, May, 1960, pp. 441–42; Glenn L. Johnson, "Implications of the IMS for Study of Responses to Price," *A Study of Managerial Processes of Midwestern Farmers*, edited by Johnson et al., Iowa State Univ. Press, 1961. Recent examples of policy and farm business applications of this theory include Dale Hathaway, *Government in Agriculture*, the Macmillan Co., 1963, and the Phase II Model of the NC54 study of feed grain and livestock production in the Midwest. Other applications are by Theordor Heidhues, "A Recursive Programming Model of Farm Growth in Northern Germany," in *Jour. Farm Econ.*, Aug. 1966, and Robert Young, *An Economic Study of the Eastern Beet Sugar Industry*, Michigan State Univ. Agr. Exp. Sta. Bull. 9, 1965.

Of these four theoretical consequences, the first three are in rather obvious accord with the performance of free enterprise agricultural economies. The fourth, though less obvious, explains the atomistic organization of family farms around fixed supplies of family laborers, earning less on the farm from age 30 to 65 than they would have earned had they left agriculture at age 20, but still earning more than they would if they were to leave at, say, age 40, 45, etc. This unsatisfactory basis for determining firm size involves ex post non-Pareto-better losses. Such losses, in turn, theoretically free both us and agricultural development planners, more generally, from felt constraints to preserve competitive adjustments in the name of Pareto-better welfare economics. These losses also explain both the (a) dissatisfaction of the underdeveloped economies with small-holder agriculture and (b) the rather unsuccessful quest to date of the developed countries for new public controls and new forms of business organizations (contract farming, corporation farming, vertical integration, etc.)

At this time, we see no reason to expect abatement of the tendency of free enterprise agricultural economies to overinvest. Instead, the recent near disappearance of U.S. surpluses after stringent surplus disposal actions has been followed by pressures to expand output which cause us to expect that U.S. production will soon be overexpanded again relative to effective demand.

The task of overcoming these tendencies involves (a) non-Pareto-better changes (which is not so questionable because, as argued, so does the operation of the free market under the relevant assumptions listed above), (b) competitive adjustments, and (c) structural changes. These changes are required with respect to (a) firms producing raw materials, (b) firms producing marketing services, (c) macropolicies and programs affecting commodities, and (d) domestic trade and international activities including the formation, adoption, and operation of common markets. Until these changes are accomplished, there will be a danger that the creation of a North American Common Market will merely provide a more coordinated mechanism than the present Canadian and U.S. governments for disposing of surplus agricultural production abroad.

In order to avoid these difficulties, the following appear to be challenging lines to follow in restructuring North American agriculture to prevent resource overcommitment:

1. Refrain from using such slogans and catchy phrases as "the population explosion," the "world food gap," "war on hun-

ger," and "conquest of hunger" to justify overexpansion of food production in North America.

2. Expand agricultural economic research along lines suggested by McCalla, King, Capel, and Craddock to improve our economic intelligence with respect to:
   a. the effects on production of investments in new technologies, institutional changes, income demand elasticities, education, etc.
   b. changes in effective demand, both domestic and foreign.
   c. the decision being made by public officials and farmers.
3. Make extension work more specific with respect to the macroconsequences and microconsequences for investment decisions of the research recommended in (2) above.
4. Give special attention to research and education which will make decisions for young men considering farming:
   a. independent of whether or not they were born on farms.
   b. dependent on the best obtainable knowledge about prospective earning on their expenditures, investments, and labor over their lifetime.
5. Consider enabling legislation:
   a. to give associations of producers more control over rates of investment in and rates of entry into the production of different agricultural products.
   b. while establishing governmental checks on the monopolistic practice in which such associations would likely be tempted to engage.
6. Refrain from abandoning present governmental arrangements for controlling production until (if ever) items (1) to (5) above remove the need for such controls.
7. Include deliberate production beyond effective world demand and the maintenance of adequate reserve stocks of food only for well thought-out reasons while avoiding the need for "crash programs" to dispose of unwanted surpluses unintentionally generated as in the past.

In the undeveloped world, it is important that policies and programs be changed to eliminate public underinvestment in the face of private overinvestment in agricultural production. North American countries can bring pressures to bear along these lines as preconditions for the receipt of both food aid and technical assistance to insure that:

1. Food aid is not used to depress prices to domestic producers in the developing countries below profitable levels.

2.  Technical assistance is not given to help expand agricultural systems where productivity is depressed by destructive domestic taxing programs and pricing policies.

## OBJECTIVES AND POLICIES FOR TECHNICAL ASSISTANCE

Presently the United States is the main provider of food-aid assistance from the proposed North American Common Market. In the past the effectiveness of food-aid assistance has been reduced when used as a means of surplus disposal. In the last section, we argued that the problem of controlling the tendency toward surplus production would not be solved by the formation of common markets but that it required restructuring of the mechanisms for controlling the commitment of resources to agricultural production. We also outlined the broad characteristics of a method for creating such a control mechanism.

If we assume that the domestic problem of creating such controls has been solved, then the task of rendering technical assistance is made much easier to handle.

The problem of technical as contrasted to food-aid assistance involves (a) the creation and transplantation of technology, and (b) assistance in bringing about the restructuring of the agricultural economies of the recipient countries.

Of these two, we will discuss assistance in restructuring first, as the structures which are adopted determine both the advisability of giving technical assistance and the kind of assistance which should be given.

The experiences of one of the authors, since 1961, in observing and studying a wide range of underdeveloped agricultural economies leads to the following generalizations:

1.  With few exceptions most undeveloped countries maintain adverse terms of exchange for their farmers either through the use of cheap concessional imports, if they are importers, or through export taxes, if they are exporters.
2.  Most underdeveloped economies organized on a free-enterprise basis tend to overcommit labor and traditional forms of capital to farm production while overpricing land.
3.  In most underdeveloped countries, the combination of (1) and (2) results in:
    a.  overproduction on private account.
    b.  underproduction on public account.

These generalizations strongly suggest a great challenge and opportunity for North American agriculturalists in the technical assistance programs for the less developed countries. These countries need to strengthen their agricultural economics research and investigations particularly in the fields of:

1. Price, taxation, and trade policy as these policies affect:
   a. production and supply.
   b. demand.
2. Farm management and marketing work with particular attention to new ways of organizing the basic units of production for commodities and marketing services in response to changes resulting from:
   a. technical research and technological transfer.
   b. institutional changes resulting especially from changes in the policies and programs of both the developed and less developed countries.
   c. educational advances.
   d. economic growth with its concomitant changes in wage rates, prices, capital availability, per capita incomes, savings, etc.

A high proportion of the world's agricultural economists are concentrated in the proposed North American Common Market area. This suggests that such a common market should provide for the organized use of these resources as part of its contribution to the world food problem.

The creation and transplantation of agricultural technology is the second aspect of technical assistance to be discussed here. The lessons of the past few years indicate that:

1. Only a small fraction of the agricultural technology of the advanced temperate zone is directly transferable to the underdeveloped countries of the tropics.
2. That expanded use of the readily available technologies of the underdeveloped countries which are known to farmers and extension workers is deterred more by adverse national policies of the underdeveloped countries themselves than by the lack of:
   a. extension resources.
   b. administrative shortcomings of the developing countries.
3. That basic research is capable of producing needed technology for the underdeveloped tropics. By basic, we mean the

type of research done at the International Rice Research In-
stitute, at the International Maize and Wheat Improvement
Center, and at the Nigerian (formerly West African and
British supported) Institute for Oil Palm Research.

The British government and the American foundations have
been more successful than either the U.S. or Canadian governments in supporting basic research in the less developed countries. The U.S. government has unwisely put major emphasis on
extension-like activities to transplant U.S. technology and speed
up the use of indigenous technology, neither of which have had
high payoffs. The Canadian government has not, to our knowledge, made a substantial overseas effort relative to its available
skills and resources in either agricultural research or extension.
In the field of university-level agricultural education, USAID's
success probably compares favorably with that of the U.S. foundations and with that of any other country. A major shortcoming
of the overall U.S. aid effort here has been its underemphasis on
research and agricultural policy and its fight in losing battles to
place extension in faculties of agriculture, as part of its overall
premature emphasis on extension. Another shortcoming involves
the sometimes unproductive rivalries among U.S. governmental
agencies other than AID, AID itself, American universities,
American Foundations, and UN agencies. This suggests that a
North American Common Market organization could do much
to mobilize Canadian resources, to reorganize U.S. resources and
to exploit the example of the maize and wheat improvement center in Mexico to improve technical assistance to the undeveloped
agricultural economies.

Birth control technology also presents a third challenge and
opportunity for North American countries to assist food deficit
countries. Lay and some professional thinking on the population
explosion and the world food gap tends to treat population
growth as the sole shifter of demand. There is a real difference
between change in need through population growth and growth
in effective demand. The barriers to growth in food supplies
are to be found both on the side of demand (effective) and on
the side of supply. Growth in effective demand (even in the face
of population growth) is required to stimulate the production
of foodstuffs in the underdeveloped countries. If the divergence
between need and effective demand, and hence between needs
and supplies, is to be closed, it will be necessary for per capita
real incomes to increase in the developing countries. In the de-

veloping world, increases in per capita real income will be smaller unless success is achieved in restricting population growth. Thus population control technology is an important kind of technical assistance needed by the underdeveloped countries of the world.

The argument for tying acceptance of birth control to food aid would be strengthened by first taking steps to promote an expansion in the developing countries of effective domestic demand and, hence, production by (a) refraining from dumping North American food in such countries, (b) giving foreign producers in the underdeveloped countries better access to advanced country markets, and (c) encouraging developing countries not to tax their agricultural economies on a destructive basis. Such actions successfully pursued would partially justify U.S. and Canadian insistence that food donations to meet needs not covered by effective demand be tied to the acceptance of birth control measures to reduce the gap between effective demand and needs. Such a strategy would make birth control technology and advice integral components of technical and food assistance programs.

# Index

437